The Men Who Knew Too Much

The Men Who Knew Too Much

HENRY JAMES AND ALFRED HITCHCOCK

Edited by Susan M. Griffin and Alan Nadel

Oxford University Press, Inc., publishes works that further
Oxford University's objective of excellence
in research, scholarship, and education.

Oxford New York
Auckland Cape Town Dar es Salaam Hong Kong Karachi
Kuala Lumpur Madrid Melbourne Mexico City Nairobi
New Delhi Shanghai Taipei Toronto

With offices in
Argentina Austria Brazil Chile Czech Republic France Greece
Guatemala Hungary Italy Japan Poland Portugal Singapore
South Korea Switzerland Thailand Turkey Ukraine Vietnam

Published by Oxford University Press, Inc.
198 Madison Avenue, New York, New York 10016

www.oup.com

Library of Congress Cataloging-in-Publication Data
The men who knew too much : Henry James and Alfred Hitchcock / edited
by Susan Griffin and Alan Nadel.
p. cm.
Includes bibliographical references and index.
ISBN 978-0-19-976442-6 (hardcover : alk. paper) — ISBN 978-0-19-976443-3 (pbk. : alk. paper)
1. James, Henry, 1843–1916—Criticism and interpretation. 2. Hitchcock, Alfred,
1899–1980—Criticism and interpretation. 3. Motion pictures and literature—United States.
I. Griffin, Susan M., 1953– II. Nadel, Alan, 1947–
PS2124.M46 2011
813'.4—dc22 2011007077

1 3 5 7 9 8 6 4 2

Printed in the United States of America

CONTENTS

PREFACE

Hossein Amini, screenwriter for the 1997 film *The Wings of the Dove*, argues that "film as a medium is so well suited to subtext" that Henry James is its perfect prose partner. "You're able to tell two different stories at the same time, which I think is the essence of James's kind of work," Amini explains. "There are three or four ideas going on at the same time, which makes a film so tempting to try, to capture some sense of that. But I still think it's almost impossible to capture what he does with his prose." Alfred Hitchcock's response would be, "Why try?" While most of Hitchcock's films were adaptations (46 of the 56 features he directed), he told Truffaut, "What I do is to read a story only once, and if I like the basic idea, I just forget all about the book and start to create cinema." He considered filming "literary masterpieces" a fool's game, insisting that "I'll have no part of that!" It is no accident that there is no Alfred Hitchcock film "based on a novel by Henry James." But reading James with Hitchcock is another matter.

A matter of wit and a matter of serendipity, as a matter of fact. We came together, a small group of us, for a weekend symposium on James and Hitchcock, organized at Dartmouth by Donald Pease. We ate well, read papers, shared thoughts, exchanged comments, and occasionally imbibed, all with a liveliness and wit that might have delighted Lambert Strether or daunted Roger Tornhill or amused David Lodge. From these spirited, sometimes surprising, conversations emerged a panel for the 2008 James conference in Newport, Rhode Island, where enthusiastic response further titillated our imagination. What if we invited the smartest people we knew—James scholars with work on film, film scholars with acute literary sensibilities—to pair a work by James with one by Hitchcock and make of it what they would. Given the prolific output by each master, we realized immediately the folly of looking for selections based the idea of "coverage." Nor were contributors assigned either particular fiction–film pairings or specific topics. Instead, we looked to be surprised, sometimes by the pairings, more often by the fecund range of implications found by our contributors, implications not only for the works they were discussing but also for broader issues of representation and narrative, of language and culture, of perception and interpretation suggested by the imagination that they brought to the project. To them all we are grateful, as much for the stimulating dialogues that emerged in the process of coediting, as for the relish with which they accepted the challenge of this unique intellectual adventure.

We also appreciate the support of our editor, Shannon McLachlan, and the astute and generous comments from the group of readers to whom she sent the prospectus and the manuscript. Amanda Konkle was a wonderfully deft, diligent, and reliable research assistant; Cindy Britt and Nick Wood worked meticulously and thoughtfully, often long distance. Funds from the University of Kentucky's Bryan Chair, and the University of Louisville's Justus Bier Professorship and the University Committee on Academic Publication, helped support the project. Our spouses, Douglas Sharps and Sharon Kopyc, proved once more they understood the ways in which our lives as academics divide time unequally between domestic prudence and unruly manuscripts.

For, despite the neatness of using paired sets, *The Men Who Knew Too Much* is a particularly unruly manuscript, in some small way therefore comparable to the always astonishing variety and range of James's prose and Hitchcock's films. That is one of the reasons we chose not to align the essays chronologically, and that some films and fictions appear in more than one essay. Freed from questions of adaptation, fidelity, and interpretation, our canny critics chose to bring James and Hitchcock together as fans and scholars of both men might have wished possible.

—SMG & AMN

The Men Who Knew Too Much

Reading James with Hitchcock, Seeing Hitchcock through James

Susan M. Griffin and Alan Nadel

At the turn of the nineteenth century, Henry James sought to establish the novel as a legitimate art form, even while struggling to reach a wide audience, just as, over the course of the twentieth century, Alfred Hitchcock endeavored to create popular films that were intellectually rewarding and formally complex. Famously meticulous, they both fostered and, at times, frustrated their own successes with demands for total artistic control, plotting their creations in extensive detail. Employing a distinctive style—there is no mistaking a James sentence or a Hitchcock scene—to engage concerns at once deeply psychological and broadly social, they depicted complex characters entrammeled by manners, custom, and law. It is almost impossible to imagine how Hitchcock could, without ever looking though the camera, direct a film to render shots and sequences as rich, demanding, and nuanced as the periodic sentences James was able to shape in verbal dictation. Like their fellow genius of modernity, Pablo Picasso, both Hitchcock and James manifested a relentless reflexivity, forged out of the need to create ever more difficult intellectual and aesthetic problems, so as to push their own imaginations to their most fecund limits.

James, born to a prosperous New York family in 1843, spent much of his childhood and adolescence moving from place to place—America to Europe, school to school—as his eccentric and impractical father, Henry, Sr., attempted to give his children the broadest and best possible education. These travels gave the James children an early cosmopolitanism but also contributed to the psychological unease that pervaded the family. Henry, of whom his brother William once said "he's really . . . a native of the James family, and has no other country," himself described that familial nation as "a company of characters . . . withal so fused and united and interlocked" (Perry 1974, 412; James 1983, 4). As young adults, the James siblings competed for parental love and financial support even as they struggled for independence. It is hardly surprising that family dynamics and the often disconcerting connections between love and power become central to James's fiction. And, although it would be a mistake to draw a direct biographical connection—Henry was, after all, his mother's favorite, the "Angel" of the family—the plight of children abandoned and abused by parents figures prominently in fictions like "The Pupil" (1891), *What Maisie Knew* (1897), and, most famously, "The Turn of the Screw" (1898).

In contrast, if Hitchcock was precocious, he was improbably so. Born in 1899, he was out of school at age fourteen, owing to the untimely death of his father, a petit bourgeois food merchant. In need of a trade, Hitchcock acquired skills as a technical clerk and a draftsman, which at his own initiative he put to use designing titles for silent movies. Able to parley this skill into a full-time job in the struggling post–World War I British film industry, he quickly learned the craft of production by volunteering for every task available. Before he was twenty-six years old, Hitchcock was given directorial responsibilities for *The Pleasure Garden* (produced in 1925, released in 1927). With that film he commenced a project that lasted half a century: inventing and refining the forms of cinematic representation. "From the days of the silent movies right up to the present time [1976]," he explained, "I have never had any interest in motion pictures that I call 'photographs of people talking.' These have nothing to do with cinema whatsoever" (Spoto 2008, 317).

While Hitchcock's styles and themes have been extensively examined, his personal life, despite numerous biographies, remains more elusive because his moviemaking activities anchor all those biographies. Hitchcock anecdotes—of which there are many—overwhelmingly involve contracts or film productions or the consequences of those productions. He met his wife, Alma Reville, in the British film industry during his predirectorial days, and they continued to work, usually together, throughout an unusually long engagement period. From the outset, the relatively innocent and sexually naïve Hitchcock found himself in a world of philandering, promiscuity, and fast living. Despite this, and despite his interest in cultivating his own celebrity, he avoided sexual contacts, and his emotional involvement by all accounts never exceeded a naughtiness more characteristic of an adolescent Catholic schoolboy than a film director shooting and socializing in England, France, and Germany, during the Jazz Age. "It is true," Hitchcock biographer Patrick McGilligan (2004) believes, "to say of Alfred Hitchcock what biographer Leon Edel wrote of Henry James: . . . all his life he harbored 'within the house of the [artist's] inner world the spirit of a young adult female, worldly-wise and curious, possessing a treasure of unassailable virginity and innocence. For this was the androgynous nature of the creator and the drama of his [art]: innocence and worldliness'" (228).

These traits, as they were reflected in James's writing, led some Americanist critics to regard his work as foreign. They characterized James as an overly refined, elitist, and sexless artist who held himself apart from the rough and tumble democracy of Real America. Part of the basis for this (mis)judgment is the fact that the "action" of James's narratives often exists in the detailed representation of intricate psychological processes, in the nuanced exchanges that constitute self and society. In "The Art of Fiction" (1884), he declared that "It is an incident for a woman to stand up with her hand resting on a table and look out at you in a certain way; or if it be not an incident, I think it will be hard to say what it is" (1884, 1986: 174).

James's style, in fact, was less a foreign mannerism than an overt expansion of the artistic potential of his medium. Consistently making high-reaching claims for writing, "The Art of Fiction" has proved to be James's most influential work of criticism, an essay that argues that fiction is, precisely, an art. Widely read in and deeply influenced by his literary predecessors—especially Nathaniel Hawthorne, George Eliot, and Honoré de Balzac—James sought to surpass them, not by writing better versions of Victorian novels but by changing the novel form. His 1873 prediction is at once disingenuous and ambitious "To produce some little exemplary works of art is my narrow and lowly dream. They are to have less 'brain' than *Middlemarch*; but (I boldly proclaim it) they are to have more *form*" (James 2009, 104). Serious writers of fiction must free themselves of the tyranny of the happy ending and the easy read. "The 'ending' of a novel is," James complained, "for many persons, like that of a good dinner, a course of dessert and ices, and the artist in fiction is regarded as a sort of meddlesome doctor who forbids agreeable after-tastes" (James 1884, 1986: 169). Instead, James insisted, writers and readers alike should share the pleasures of the difficult: "The enjoyment of a work of art, the acceptance of an irresistible illusion, constituting, to my sense, our highest experience of 'luxury,' the luxury is not greatest, by my consequent measure, when the work asks for as little attention as possible" (James 1909, 1986b: 358).

Exactly the same impetus to convert film from pastime to art form obsessed Hitchcock. In *The Lodger* (1927), for example, shooting upward through a specially made glass floor, he created shots of a man pacing so as to produce in a silent film the visual equivalent of the sound of footsteps, a form of synesthesia that he would emulate eight years later in *The 39 Steps* (1935), when he provided an audio equivalent to the experience of discovering a stabbed corpse by conjoining the shrill blast of a train whistle with the horrified close-up of a cleaning woman's face. Ever conscious that cinema was not a means to record a narrative, but a discrete medium for producing one, Hitchcock within a decade developed an inventive and nuanced cinematic language, independently augmented in *Blackmail* (1929) (England's first "talkie") by a complex audio stylistics.

Understandably, both men shared the keen modernist interest in point of view, as that term conjoined cognitive perception and psychological understanding. James had been, from the start, an avid and sensitive perceiver of his surroundings, and his early exposure to changing places and manners had provided a fund of vivid visual memories and a habit of observation that continued throughout his life and permeated his writing. Not only did rich visual imagery come to serve as a medium for depicting thought, but the "restless analyst," as James referred to himself upon his return visit to America at the beginning of the twentieth century, is an epithet that accurately characterizes both his narrators and his central characters. From Winterbourne spying on Daisy Miller as she strolls in the Roman Colosseum to Isabel Archer in *The Portrait of a Lady* (1881) glimpsing her husband seated in the presence of another woman to Maggie Verver in *The Golden Bowl* (1904) pacing up and down before the smoking room windows, observing how her family and friend have arranged themselves, James's characters gain knowledge, make sense, and wield power through seeing. Increasingly, what fascinated James as subject and as structure was the problem of point of view, of making what he called "centers of consciousness" the architecture for his fictions.

Similarly, Hitchcock, who began his film career creating visuals, explored with particular interest cinema's potential for representing unconventional points of view: "characters in the world of make-believe drawn into bizarre real-life dramas; voyeurism; the camera observing an observer; the rapid transition from watcher to watched; the dizzying staircase—and mischievous humor" (Spoto 2008, 9). Having integrated the technical accomplishments of early American directors, including Griffith, Keaton, and Chaplin, with the breakthroughs of the Russian montagists and the German Expressionists, Hitchcock created a fast-paced and plot-driven style that also reflected the tension between the objective and the subjective, the psychological and the social. By the mid-1930s, in other words, he had invented a cinematic equivalent to free indirect discourse.

Critical and commercial resistance to James's continuing experiments with form grew over the course of his career but surfaced as early as 1876, when he was fired as a travel correspondent to the *New York Tribune*. Told that his letters were not short and "newsy" enough, James replied: "If my letters have been 'too good' I am honestly afraid that they are the poorest I can do, especially for the money!" (James 1975, 63). Indeed, the refusal (or failure) to constrain his prose becomes a near-constant refrain in James's *Notebooks* and correspondence. Then, too, writing largely for American and British readers, Henry James faced traditional Anglo-American suspicion of "immoral" novels. The implicit censorship exercised by circulating libraries like Mudie's, known for selecting only fiction that could be read safely in the middle-class family circle, remained a factor until 1894. In fact, *Daisy Miller* (1878), *Washington Square* (1881), and *Portrait of a Lady* (1881) were all purchased and distributed by Mudie's.[1] In "The Art of Fiction," James protested against the infantilizing of fiction: "For many people art means rose-coloured window- panes, and selection means picking a bouquet for Mrs. Grundy. They will tell you glibly that artistic considerations have nothing to do with the disagreeable, with the ugly; they will rattle off shallow commonplaces about the province of art and the limits of art till you are moved to some wonder in return as to the province and the limits of ignorance" (James 1884, 1986: 177). For James, in contrast, "the province of art is all life, all feeling, all observation, all vision" (177). To establish a level of freedom commensurate with the scope of his vision in his very commercial medium, Hitchcock also had to struggle with those who would edit, alter, or censor his conception. Hitchcock's perceived antagonists included method actors who privileged motivation over affect, stage actors who exploited the space around them instead of hitting their marks, censors who threatened to hack scripts and delimit distribution, and, particularly, producers and studio heads who interfered with casting, publicity, and story structure. It was the promise of greater artistic control, therefore, that drew Hitchcock, at the end of the 1930s, from England to Hollywood, where, it turned out, the contractual freedom David O. Selznick offered in order to lure him was persistently undermined by the pervasive interference that anyone under Selznick's micromanaging was forced to endure. By 1947, it was impossible to negotiate a new contract with Selznick because Hitchcock understood that to develop his cinematic prowess in a way that would complicate his work, control of the films had to take priority over financial obsessions.

One might thus view the way Hitchcock created a public persona—crafting his celebrity into a brand—as a device to leverage artistic control. James, too, was not "above" the desire for popularity. While "Daisy" and especially *The Portrait of a Lady*, his first masterpiece, sold well, throughout his career James increasingly attempted—and failed—to gain a popular audience for his fiction. Indeed, short fictions like "Greville Fane" (1892) and "The Private Life" (1892) explicitly depict what seemed to him his own bifurcated aims: the determination to write fiction with form and complexity and the desire to reach a popular audience. The same tension informed James's lifelong—and failed—attempts to work in the theater, with the debacle of his 1895 *Guy Domville*. Biographers, following James's own lead in the *Prefaces to the New York Edition*, have seen James's playwriting failures as shaping his fictional style, helping him to move toward "scenic" form. Formative, too, was the fact that, beginning with *What Maisie Knew*, James, crippled by writer's cramp, began dictating his work to a typewriter (the contemporary term for a typist). This change in writing technologies is inseparable from James's shift into what we have come to call the late style: syntactically intricate, "supersubtle," intensely interior.

If Hitchcock was more successful in his pursuit of celebrity, the scope of reputation he sought and the independence that accrued to it only materialized after a period in the late 1940s and early 1950s of interesting, if sometimes problematic experiments—*Strangers on a Train* (1951), *I Confess* (1953), *Stage Fright* (1950), (which contains a "lying" flashback), *Rope* (1948), and *Under Capricorn* (1949) (both shot in excruciatingly long takes), and *Dial M for Murder* (1954) (a 3-D film shot in a one-room set). In the mid-1950s, Hitchcock achieved the blend of mastery and the contractual independence that produced some of the richest and most widely written about films in American cinema: *Rear Window* (1954), *The Man Who Knew Too Much* (1956), *Vertigo* (1958), *North by Northwest* (1959), *Psycho* (1960), and *The Birds* (1963).

But most significantly, his television show, *Alfred Hitchcock Presents*, increased exponentially his international celebrity, his authority, and his wealth. Premiering in 1955, the enormously successful show ran for a decade in prime time, enjoyed broad global distribution, and had a huge afterlife in syndication. Although Hitchcock only directed 17 of the 270 episodes, he introduced all of them, and these introductions as a group constitute a quintessential Hitchcock opus. Hitchcock had personally drawn the trademark profile caricature that filled the screen at the outset of each episode, and his head provided the shadow that filled that caricature. Each episode started, in other words, when Alfred Hitchcock presented anew the shadow of Hitchcock filling the image of Hitchcock that Hitchcock had created.

Accompanying this spectacle of self-reflexivity (and self-promotion) was music from Gounod's "Funeral March of the Marionettes," suggested by Bernard Herrmann, who scored Hitchcock's films during the same period. In combination, the piece's title, its melodic oscillation, and its playful syncopation suggest the tension between pleasure and terror. Thus, Hitchcock's task each week was to make his audience ignore the music's cautionary note about the danger inherent in anthropomorphizing manipulated images, in many ways a preoccupation throughout Hitchcock's career and, arguably, a requirement central to the enterprise of narrative cinema. Hitchcock undertook this task by addressing the audience directly with a succinct blend of arch, macabre, and droll comments that succeeded in, as McGilligan (2004) put it, "ameliorating [the show's] subversive excesses" (526). Hitchcock also shot different introductions for different audiences. In America, he poked fun at the sponsors—reflecting his longstanding complaint about commercial interference—and abroad he made jokes at the expense of Americans. Hitchcock eventually broadened the show's (and his own) appeal even further by recording for foreign audiences introductions in French and German.

The cosmopolitan reception of this very American television series highlights the ambiguity Hitchcock shared with James regarding national identity. Although James had been writing reviews, fiction, and travel accounts professionally since 1864, Henry's first—controversial—success was *Daisy Miller*: what was seen as its attack on the American Girl was applauded in England and deplored in the United States. This reaction to "Daisy" set the pattern for a strain of American criticism that lasts well into the 1960s: the argument that Henry James was, fundamentally, not an American writer. The fact that James came to make his home abroad and, at the end of his life, became a British subject, seemed proof positive of his national apostasy. There is no question that James, who took up various residences in France, Italy, and England before finally settling in the latter, came to feel at home in Europe. But Americans remained the subjects of his work, and his lifelong, complex, critical engagement with American culture, politics, and people bespeaks James's deep personal identification with the United States.

The work of both men is marked by abundant retrospective analysis and reevaluation. The precipitous decline in the quality of Hitchcock's work in the 1960s and 1970s in part reflects a bifurcation in the film industry. Younger, chiefly European, filmmakers, rejecting wholesale the tenets of the Classical Hollywood Style, were finding in "art house" audiences a niche that situated them as the antithesis of superficial successes such as *The Sound of Music* (1965). While this new generation more astutely and explicitly recognized Hitchcock's artistry than Hollywood ever had, they were radically altering cinematic style in ways irreconcilable with the parameters within which Hitchcock had worked. After seeing Antonioni's *Blow-Up* (1966), Hitchcock exclaimed, "These Italian directors are a century ahead of me in terms of technique! What have I been doing all this time?" (quoted in McGilligan 2004, 681).

Equally, Hitchcock's personal life, or at least the psychology of it, has become the topic of speculation. His own conservative lifestyle notwithstanding, he was notoriously risqué in his interpersonal exchanges, often to the discomfort of some of his more reserved leading ladies (although he more than met his match in Carole Lombard). Despite allegations that late in his career he made a few unsuccessful overtures to actresses—most infamously Tippi Hedren—Robin Wood has speculated, based on Hitchcock's marriage to Alma followed by a sudden weight gain, on the pattern of homophobia in his films, and on his treatment of women, that Hitchcock was a repressed homosexual. Consistent with his instructions that people call him "Hitch . . . I have no cock," Donald Spoto (2008) believes on the other hand that he was fixated on specific women but suffered from impotence and may have actually had sexual intercourse only once in his life (57). His films, writes McGilligan (2004), "evince more than a passing curiosity in all manner of sexuality—straight, homosexual, and anything in between. . . . The Jesuit in him was attracted by taboos and fascinated by sin—and sex ranked high in the Catholic pantheon of sins" (65). His obsession with transgressive behavior, especially as it worried the limits of bourgeois respectability, was not reflected in his behavior but rather channeled into his art. As Hitchcock biographer John Russell Taylor (1978) explains, he "may have been all his life the perfect bourgeois, product of his class and background, but he has never given any indication of complacency, the characteristic bourgeois vice, about the nature of the human condition, or about the possibility of simply separating and recognizing good and evil, right and wrong" (62).

So, too, Henry James's work and life have been viewed as alternately conservative and subversive. Almost immediately after his death in 1916, James was taken up by critics as the first modernist, even as some modernist writers relegated his works to the loose, baggy, realist monsters that James himself had grown to disdain. James was, of course, himself a Victorian novelist and a Victorian, a man who met and socialized with Dickens and Eliot. But he was also the contemporary and acquaintance of Joseph Conrad and Ford Madox Ford. He lived through the American Civil War and saw the beginnings of World War I. His supposed rules of writing were systematized by Percy Lubbock in *The Craft of Fiction* (1921). His experiments with point of view were seen as paving the way for the more radical innovations of Virginia Woolf and James Joyce. At the same time, the critical tradition that patronized James as prissy and verbose continued. As fiction's boundaries were stretched by gritty naturalism, explicit sexuality, and an insistence on democratic and demotic inclusiveness, "Henry James" became shorthand for the artist of the Ivory Tower.

Shorthand, too, for "repressed homosexual." James's bachelor existence, his deep identification with female protagonists, and his elaborate style were all read as marks of a failed heterosexuality or, with the development of women's and gay studies, of a hidden homosexuality. Over the past two decades, however, new historical and archival work on James has yielded a different picture. Access to materials that had largely been controlled by some members of the James family and by Leon Edel, James's first and still most important biographer, has given us a more substantial James, a highly social man with a large circle of affectionate friendships, astute in managing his career, and capable of deep homoerotic attachments. Debate about the exact nature of Henry James's sexual experiences continues, of course, and the multiple, intricate, queer (to use a favorite term of James's) desires, intimacies, and identities in his texts remain open to perhaps infinite interpretation. And here, as so often, readers have a sense of engaging with a Henry James who has anticipated and delights in the reader's part. In the final Preface to the New York Edition of his fiction, James describes the process of rereading his work as a shared act of "revision": "What has the affair been at the worst, I am most moved to ask, but an earnest invitation to the reader to dream again in my company and in the interest of his own larger absorption of my sense" (James 1909, 1986a: 389).

Hitchcock's work also engages a sense of active revisioning, not just in his explicit (*The Man Who Knew Too Much,* 1934 and 1956) or his implicit remakes (*The 39 Steps*, *Saboteur* [1942], and *North by Northwest*), but also through an extensively rich array of allusions, a characteristic that has proven particularly influential for later filmmakers. His last four films tend to look back—often quoting his earlier works—in the same way that American directors such as Brian de Palma, who were starting their careers when Hitchcock was culminating his, would conflate citation and influence. The pervasive references to Hitchcock's work, starting in Europe and spreading to the United States in the late 1960s and thereafter, reflect a change not just in the production of films but more significantly in the production of filmmakers.

In the same way, arguably, that the creation of the Modern Language Association in 1883 may have been instrumental in the canonization of James, the academic institutionalizing of Film Studies programs and Film Poduction programs made Hitchcock an academic subject, one richly mined from a wealth of perspectives. For auteur, psychoanalytic, cognitive, feminist, and narratological approaches, his opus provided equally abundant exempla. Pop and art filmmakers alike appropriated his techniques—or tried to. In 1998 Gus Van Sant even remade *Psycho* (1960) by duplicating the film shot-by-shot. Born at almost exactly the same moment as exhibition cinema, Hitchcock made it an articulate medium before it acquired sound and then taught it to speak the unconscious images of the modern age. The limits of his influence are immeasurable: it is unlikely that Hitchcock, despite his fluency in French, ever read Lacan's writing, but it is highly likely that Lacan saw Hitchcock's films. So did film scholars of every critical approach and filmmakers of every school and nationality.

What does watching Hitchcock tell us about reading James? Looking closely at the works of the two Masters side by side, we discover resonances and gain specific insights about subjectivity, especially female subjectivity; the workings of the gaze and the psychoanalytic; the secret and the unsayable; the intertwined trajectories of desire and power. As Jonathan Freedman (Chapter 9) points out, we can well imagine the two artists in shrewd, amusing, wide-ranging conversation. For, as these essays make abundantly clear, reading James with Hitchcock is highly engaging and deeply pleasurable. Their coupling returns us to what customary or cursory encounters can inure us to: the often uneasy delights of the two Masters' intricate, amusing, awful work.

"Awful," because, as Philip Horne, echoing Michael Moon,[2] points out, the works of Henry James and Alfred Hitchcock are strange: unorthodox in their eras, sui generis, larger and odder than the critical, ethical, and political schema we apply to them. Surely this is a lesson that we should have learned from the fictions and films themselves, works in which fixing, naming, and defining proves a deadly assertion of power ("The Turn of the Screw," *Vertigo*), in which solving the mystery is either impossible (*The Sacred Fount* [1901], *Suspicion* [1941]) or irrelevant ("The Figure in the Carpet" [1896], *The Wrong Man* [1956]), or in which we never discover what we want to know (hence those golden bowls and Macguffins). The truth does not set us free (*The Portrait of a Lady*, *Marnie* [1964]). Not that we inevitably finish with the truth.

James and Hitchcock refuse their audiences complete enlightenment, while habitually depicting individuals whose drive for knowledge propels narrative action, even though those characters may, themselves, be ambivalent about knowing. Attention to Hitchcock's detectives, agents, and counteragents makes us newly aware of their counterparts in James's stories. For example, Brenda Austin-Smith (Chapter 2) demonstrates how *The 39 Steps* positions *The Ambassadors* (1903) as a tale of spies and lies. But knowledge is resisted as well, especially in James: unlike Richard Hannay, Strether tries very hard to suppose "nothing." When deferral and resistance do occur in Hitchcock's films, their patterns can illuminate James's narratives. Following the looping spirals of *Vertigo*, Eric Savoy (Chapter 10) illustrates how these forms describe the actions of Jamesian characters while visibly delineating the structures of Jamesian rhetoric, indeed Jamesian writing. But James's writing, viewed through the heuristic of Hitchcock's films, reveals patterns that exceed geometric symmetry and genre convention, such that they break, more than confirm, the strict "rules" that Percy Lubbock's *The Craft of Fiction* (1921) extracted from James's criticism. We can see the tensions caused by this stubborn individuality in Hitchcock's struggles with Selznick, James's with William Dean Howells, and both men's with the marketplace. Pressed to make their works conform to conventional morality, James and Hitchcock nominally cooperate. The male star cannot be a murderer, so Max De Winter's guilt in *Rebecca* (1940) is modified. The female protagonist cannot be an adulteress, so *Portrait of a Lady*'s Isabel Archer flees from her lover to her husband. Yet, these "corrections"—partial and ambiguous—complicate rather than clarify. The two artists evade definitive closure—especially moral closure—with open-ended "conclusions." And when we attempt to line up Hitchcock's works with James's, we realize how often the parts of their narratives simply do not fit, how much remains unexplained: Why do the birds attack? What was "the figure in the carpet"?

These Hitchcockian oddities are part of why we call James "modern," and they underscore why his celebrated innovations are, like Hitchcock's, inextricable from their eccentricities. Each man, moreover, redefined the medium in which he worked.

Mark Goble (Chapter 14) directs us to James's and Hitchcock's awkward ages: periods when each confronts new audiences and technological innovations as symptomatic of an unease that never fully disappears from either's career. If James was famously poised between two eras in the history of the novel—perhaps the last great nineteenth-century novelist, perhaps a protomodernist—reading James with Hitchcock reveals how uneasily James fits our periodizations. Aviva Briefel (Chapter 11) shows us how Hitchcock's more obvious distance from the Victorian past, which he used to such great effect in films like *Psycho*, helps reveal James's own careful construction of a closer Victorian era against which he could fashion his modernity. *Psycho* highlights the fact that the anachronistic setting, character, plot, and genre of "Turn of the Screw" display, not a separate, frightening past, but its eerie imbrication with the present.

James is odd, too, in his female protagonists and their narratives. American feminists in particular have exempted James's fiction from what Nina Baym called "melodramas of beset manhood." The misogyny that first-generation feminists uncovered in writers like Cooper and Hemingway was, if not absent, at least drawn into question in James's work, and subsequent criticism has explored in detail the complexities of James's sympathetic depictions of, and identifications with, the female. While Hitchcock has rarely been regarded as the champion of his female stars, Tania Modleski has allowed us to recognize Hitchcock's complex ambivalence in matters of gender. And, turning from the dangerous, often abject, situations of Hitchcock's women to James does not provide the expected relief. Instead, thinking about James's heroines with Hitchcock's makes vivid what, lost in the subtleties of James's prose, we sometimes lose sight of: the truly ugly situations of those awkward young girls, Nanda Brookenham and Maisie Farange; the telegraphist "in the cage" and the governess at Bly; Catherine Sloper and Kate Croy.

Reading with Hitchcock reminds us also of the malevolence, brutality, violation, and crime that haunt James's prose both figuratively and literally. Mary Ann O'Farrell (Chapter 5) shows vividly how "both the novelist and the director render the experience of knowing and the nature of knowledge as sudden, violent, material, and concussive." We all know, of course, that bad things happen in James stories (he hated the Mrs. Grundy tyranny of the happy ending), but so much is implicit that those who dislike him complain that "nothing ever happens." Nonetheless, for O'Farrell, James's "articulation of the impression strongly received . . . takes on a literal and physical dimension, and the Jamesian concussion, if it is not actually a blow to the head, may still be a physical event effecting the transfer of knowledge—a blow to the brain, as it were." And then there is the fact that Miles is dead at the end of "The Turn of the Screw"; Lord Mark's blackmail creates disaster in *The Wings of the Dove*; Maisie is abandoned; Kate sells sex; Madame de Bellegarde poisons her husband in *The American*. Fathers despise daughters (*Washington Square*), and mothers ruin them (*Maisie*, *The Awkward Age*); husbands loathe wives (*Portrait of a Lady*), and women marry for money (*The Golden Bowl*).

Although in turning from Hitchcock's films to James's fictions, one would expect a diminishment of physicality, the shift can, in effect, render Jamesian bodies more vividly present. Believing that readers of his prose required no supplement, James deeply resented illustration: "the author of any text putting forward illustrative claims (that is producing an effect of illustration) by its own intrinsic virtue and so finding itself elbowed, on that ground, by another and a competitive process" (James 1909, 1986a: 379). Picturing should take place in the reader's encounter with the text itself, not before it in a frontispiece nor next to it in an illustration. Paying attention to Hitchcock's mise en scène, we notice where James's bodies are situated. Perhaps not accidentally, it was a film theorist, Kaja Silverman, who brilliantly plotted the positionality of desire and sexuality in James. Following the dizzying spirals of *Vertigo*, Savoy here traces their counterparts in *Wings* and *Ambassadors*. Freedman reads gesture, not as a formal, representational sign for inner emotion (as in early–nineteenth century actors' manuals), but as, precisely, movement of the body. Focusing on an important Hitchcock motif, he directs our attention to how hands, and the way things are touched, mean and function in James, to physical encounters between self and other, to action in the world. In contrast to the distancing necessary to vision, the tactile demands a sensory and sensuous proximity, and, with it an altered epistemology. Alfred Hitchcock's filmic cameos, overt instances of an artist's self-created public profile, alert us to how thoroughly "Henry James" corresponds to a set of visible images. Further, we are reminded that these artists are corporeal creatures whose "sensuous education," to use James's term, informs, often obliquely and queerly, their work. The bodies stranded on Hitchcock's *Lifeboat* (1944) lie in multiple relations to his own expatriated, and changing, frame. In *The Ivory Tower*, James locates a possible artistic and national identity in the substantial bulk of Rosanna Gaw.

Directing the physical movements of actors and characters, the artist is also attempting to direct the emotions of audiences. Hitchcock and James are well aware that their styles demand not a passive but an active audience. "Watching a well-made film, we don't sit by as spectators; we participate," Hitchcock insists. "I believe the audience should work" (Gottlieb 1995, 146, 109). James hopes for readers who share his fascination with the difficult: "The enjoyment of the work of art, the acceptance of an irresistible illusion, constituting, to my sense, our highest experience of 'luxury,' the luxury is not greatest, by my consequent measure, when the work asks for as little attention as possible. It is greatest, it is delightfully, divinely great, when we feel the surface, like the thick ice of the skater's pond, bear without cracking the strongest pressure we throw on it" (James 1909, 1986b: 358). These demands are not surprising coming as they do from the master of the film thriller and a writer known for intricate novels of psychological realism. What is perhaps less expected is the frequency with which James, à la Hitchcock, acknowledges—at times gleefully—how much he entices, bullies, scares, and tricks audiences into doing their part. "I know how to prepare them," Hitchcock admits, "how to give them a laugh at the right moment, and I know how to make them react by clutching their seats with fear, almost screaming . . ." (Gottlieb 1995, 150). "You see, I am a great believer in making the audience suffer" (272). James, perhaps more subtly, nevertheless suggests that "reflexion and criticism" in readers must be "skillfully and successfully drugged" by the writer. He pushes both metaphor and technique: "There are drugs enough, clearly—it is all a question of applying them with tact (James 1907, 1986: 281). Elsewhere he boasts that "The Turn of the Screw" is "a piece of ingenuity pure and simple, of cold artistic calculation, an *amusette* to catch those not easily caught (the 'fun' of the capture of the merely witless being ever but small), the jaded, the disillusioned, the fastidious" (James 1908, 1986: 340). Judith Roof's essay (Chapter 8) suggests who that select audience might be: critics of "The Figure in the Carpet" and *Marnie*, she shows, are trapped into reproducing "the economy of desiring desire that haunts the texts themselves."

Caught, suffering, drugged, screaming, we find ourselves again and again happily at the mercy of Henry James and Alfred Hitchcock. The essays in this volume vividly enact the enjoyments of, not only Hitchcock's films and James's fictions, but also of thinking through those experiences together. Once one starts, it is hard to stop: What of *Rebecca* with *Portrait of a Lady*, *The Sacred Fount* and *Rear Window*, *The American* and *The Man Who Knew Too Much*?

And so it works in reverse as well. James has a lot to tell us about cinema in general and about Hitchcock in particular because, as this collection gives evidence, James's sensibility was in many ways cinematic. He was profoundly concerned with control of the gaze, with its powers and implications, long before there emerged a technology of animation to which the gaze would be central or a narrative medium based on that technology. He interrogated cinematic conventions for the most part before the medium of film existed and certainly before its traits and themes became conventional. Working, in other words, in a pure abstract laboratory of what might be called a cinematic imagination, James engaged formal problems, without interference from concrete exempla, in much the way that, near the end of his life, he wrestled with the American scene by engaging its tangible traits with increasingly abstract language.

Envisioning a technology whose immanence, on the heels the railroad, the photograph, the telegraph, the typewriter, and the telephone, promised an intensity that would lay claim to reality, James's cinematic imagination helped focus the attractions and discomforts of modernity. For Patrick O'Donnell (Chapter 6), James's late novella, *In the Cage*, about a telegraph operator vicariously engaged in an affair that her transmissions facilitate, focuses the impact of modernity, reflecting, as John Carlos Rowe (Chapter 12) notes, James's awareness that "whoever controls the system of communication also controls social and economic power." In such a power network, O'Donnell, following Slavoj Žižek, explains, "identity [is] fundamentally voyeuristic: filling in the blanks, as it were, by perversely observing the holy and unholy acts of others." Thus, when we ask, as Goble does, why the young women in *The Awkward Age* and *The Lady Vanishes* (1938) are both "vulnerable to wayward information," the specter of modern technology that informs James's concern with conditions of expression and of legibility haunts as well Hitchcock's conversion from silent film to sound, and later from Great Britain to Hollywood. As much of James's later work does, the opening sequence of Hitchcock's *Blackmail* (1929, the UK's first talkie) looks back to an earlier form of artistic representation, the close-ups of spinning wheels suggesting the advent of modernity. *Blackmail* stages, for Donatella Izzo (Chapter 7), "a confrontation between two historical and social worlds, one ostensibly prevailing over the other technologically." But that technological superiority, read through James, is the vacant hub around which cinema's illusion of a desirable alterity is animated. The act of circling and the language of circumlocution that Savoy identifies in James guarantee an excess that circumvents the emptiness of the Real. Such is the effect, O'Donnell explains, of the excess of meaning that Hitchcock's birds signify by making the film:

> Allegorically, about nothing in particular, that is, an allegory of particularity . . . per se: the real, in James's metaphor of the carpet, only comprehensible as a series of holes or gaps to be filled in; a thousand gulls and black birds [as] sheer contingency writ large . . .

The trauma of an emptiness in cinematic representation, seen through James's vertiginous prose, is the touch of the reel—the confrontation with the two-dimensional play of light that, by virtue of spinning, emulates reality. Consider, for example, the moments when a malfunction locks on one frame until the image melts into oblivion under the bulb's heat. The fear that haunts cinematic representation, in other words, is that the frames will cease to circulate around the reel, that the image of desire will lose, ultimately, any symbolic power at all.

This fear is medium specific: in fiction we do not see objects but words; so too, do taste, sound, and smell "appear" only *through* language, while in cinema, sight and sound are (ostensibly) unmediated. Film produces a rupture between direct perception and inferential, highlighting what Freedman identifies as "the conundrum at the center of touch—its simultaneous establishment and undoing of a firm line of difference and class markers of distinction between body and world, [that] become the basis for James's interrogation of intimacy." James indicates what cinema will confirm: while we can watch with a safety not threatened by extreme close-ups, nudity, graphic violence, or gore, we cannot touch the objects of our fascination, cannot caress the silver screen. To do so would mark the lunacy of trying to situate ourselves on the same tactile plane as the one created by our auditory and visual perceptions. This is the division between drive and desire crucial for O'Donnell to understanding the subject of modernity whom James places in the cage. Such a barrier—the bane and fortification of the characters in *The Golden Bowl*—stands as the margin of frustration in Hitchcock, something betrayed, as Freedman shows, by Hitchcock's prolific attention to hands, those organs most associated with exactly that which is beyond the reach of cinema.

Similarly, the extensive talk in *The Wings of the Dove,* Izzo demonstrates, is ultimately overwhelmed by the power of silence: "James seems to be simultaneously investigating the operation of language as a tool of manipulation and a token of social exchange, and straining beyond words towards an unprecedented form of verbal narrative." If, as Izzo suggests, we envision *The Wings of the Dove* as a silent movie, perhaps it is because all movies privilege gaze over speech. This would make film the plenitude for which James's prose was in constant search, such that the fulfillment of his cinematic imagination is the site where the parameters of the gaze can be honed within 1/24th of a second and still animate limitless desire for a world whose boundaries cannot completely be reeled in.

James thus anticipates the way in which cinema will employ the reel to avoid the trauma of the Real. Read through what Savoy identifies as the vertiginous in James, *Vertigo* reveals a cluster of representations that exceed reduction into the realm of symbolic substitution. That cluster of spectral experience may also typify in general the cinematic, because cinema is a process linking a spinning set of images to the pleasure of their cognitive and thematic reassembly into moving pictures. Near the end of *The American Scene* (1907), for example, James's ride in a Pullman train evokes a cinematic perspective: "when the question arises of giving some account of these [impressions] a small sharp anguish attends the act of selection and the necessity of omission" (311). This is exactly the problem of cinema, which creates an imaginary elsewhere through systems of metonymic substitution. For James, the animation of perspective is also the animation of the perceived, space acquiring its dimension through the instability of the window that frames it. Perpetually postponed, like "some massive monument covered still," the figure of the nation in *The American Scene* is, Brian Edwards (Chapter 3) explains, ever deferred.

That deferral constitutes a structural necessity of cinematic representation. After all, in cinema, Roof asks, how do we foreclose the space of cinematic narrative, a space comprised by absences? In this regard, *The American Scene* becomes a template for what Roof calls "the cinematic economy": not knowledge but the idea of knowing. That economy, in "The Figure in the Carpet," lures us into the quest of the protagonist, even though in the end, as Roof underscores, we will only confront the absence of an answer as it becomes the presence of our desire, *qua* desire. As O'Donnell notes, Hitchcock, sharing James's awe at the "magnitude of reality," produces narratives that "never add up to anything," providing, instead, "a succession of loosely associated images . . . an endless procession of contingencies, images, objects, events, persons."

James, while harking back to the conventions of nineteenth-century Gothicism, also points us forward to the world of Hitchcockian cinema, in which the infamous McGuffin—Hitchcock's name for the unseen and undefined excuse that motivates the spectator's curiosity—dissolves into the pleasure of desiring it. The dissolve, so often in cinema signifying a conclusion, is an apt a way to end narrative in a world that had appeared out of nowhere, constructed on a scaffold of absence. "Whatever foundational ambiguity persists," Roof explains, "in ['The Figure in the

Carpet' and *Marnie*], narratives animated by ambiguity, that foundation does not precede or catalyze the narratives; it is not originary. Instead ambiguity emerges out of the condition of desiring knowledge itself . . . Telling is generated to generate tellings."

In making us aware of how the train window anticipates the cinematic apparatus, moreover, James suggests the connection between cinematic space and national space, a recurrent motif in Hitchcock's work. If from the earliest decades of the twentieth century, cinema has been viewed as a proliferator of national narratives, it was also regarded from the beginning of the twentieth century as a potential danger to mental and physical health. Hence the Hayes Office in 1922, the Motion Picture Production Code in 1930, the appointment in 1934 of Joseph Breen to enforce the Code, the Congressional hearings in 1937, 1942, 1947, and 1952, and the Office of War Information during WWII, all to control in the name of national interests the image of the nation and the imaginary of its values. Popular cinema, even when in private hands, was always a national product, in every sense of that phrase. It was the haberdasher that suited the body politic, as well as the elaborate costume that body wore to its most audacious masquerades. The movies were endemic to the birth of a nation, or so Lenin believed, as did D. W. Griffith.

In this regard, Lenin and Griffith had an exemplary antecedent in James, struggling with his national identity just prior to World War I. If James wrestled with the abstract idea of nation, it is important to remember that he had a mind in which the abstract was adamant, crystallized in much the way that vision was concretized by cinema. Consider how James gives, in *The American Scene,* not what the title promises, but rather its homophonic (American) cousin, himself, the American, seen, seen after decades of expatriation, donning the mantle worn by Emerson's representative men, to make visible the network of felt conditions and conditional visions that located his sensibility.

James's attempt, not long after writing *The American Scene,* to forge an Anglo-American alliance in support of World War I anticipates, as Susan Griffin shows (Chapter 1), Hitchcock's similar confrontation with his own national orientation. In the alignment of bodies and deployment of body parts in *Lifeboat,* Griffin makes clear, Hitchcock was enacting a Jamesian struggle with the relationship between a type and its representation. If that relationship was an informing principle of Hollywood casting departments, Hitchcock, viewed through James, was surely casting the national identities of a nation at sea, a nation comprising its own allies and enemies as types and countertypes. In his concern over the fallibility of representation, the reality that art appropriates and eludes, James also underscores the implications of what, in the age of Hitchcock, could be called a cinematic sense of identity.

James helps us understand that in the modern world national identity might always be an issue of casting and shows, as well, how impossible it is to do that task successfully. *What Maisie Knew* can be read as glossing the issues of casting that Hitchcock foregrounded in *Lifeboat.* Maisie—herself, like James and Hitchcock, a transnational figure—casts her family members, auditioning a series of candidates for the principals. Employing a chain of cinematic substitutions that betray not only the thematic but also the financial considerations of cinematic production, James exposes the aporia functioning in a structural relationship to knowledge, even when it entails relationships that are supposed to be "natural," such as the familial. Should parentage participate in the same chain of substitution as do the meanings and their detectives in "The Figure in the Carpet?" Can't familial relations exist beyond the shadow of a doubt? If, for James, the answer is no, for Hitchcock it is even more frighteningly so, because, as Thomas Byers (Chapter 13) argues, "Hollywood films, much more than the realist novel, may be a likely site for anxieties about metonymic substitution based on modernity because . . . Hollywood films are constructed by substitution in very specific technological and stylistic ways and the project of Hollywood style is to . . . disavow that fact."

The heuristic of Maisie—what she could know, how she constructs her perspective and subject position from the knowledge made available to her—if that problem frames James's experiment in fiction, it also frames conceptually a whole realm of film theory focused on the subject position of the spectator. *The Ambassadors,* as Austin-Smith explains, helps us understand the complicity of those "recruited by circumstance." Lambert Strether is the quintessential moviegoer, as is Hannay, who in *The 39 Steps*, Austin-Smith notes, "simply appears on screen in the act of buying his ticket." Hannay's subsequent train ticket becomes an extension of his theater ticket, so that in his ride he is surrogate for the viewer, a point emphasized by viewing Hannay in conjunction with that "ideal spectator," Strether. As Austin-Smith makes clear, Strether is "the prototype of the person for whom cinema was intended," constructed by James as "a modern sensibility prone to seduction by visual impression."

Helping us see what is mysterious and suspenseful about ethical dilemmas, why ethics can never be separated from perception, cognition, and, for lack of a better term, mise-en-scène, Strether allows us to recognize the site where, in Hitchcock, cinematic suspense intersects with ethical failures. For Strether, as for Hannay and all the interested parties for whom they are surrogates, negotiating detachment, Austin-Smith points out, is strenuous and precarious. Like them, the cinematic audience always engages in set of power relations, represented by tacit acceptance of or tacit resistance to conventions. Because *In the Cage* can be read as examining the empowerment of women in the work force at the end of the nineteenth century, James allows us to see that, while Hitchcock seems to be constructing spectral relations of the sort described in Laura Mulvey's influential essay (1975) on visual pleasure in narrative cinema, he is also creating the context wherein women, as Rowe puts it, struggle "dramatically to replace their commodified bodies with their own abilities to act and choose." Such women, rather than be circumscribed by "the systematic logics of patriarchy . . . talk back [and thereby] help expose the process of patriarchal voyeurism."

James's writing also limns Hitchcock's concerns about the Victorianism of the world into which Hitchcock was born and its vestiges in the repressive Production

Code. The self-consciousness with which James invokes, in *The Turn of the Screw*, the conventions of Victorian respectability, turns those conventions, Briefel demonstrates, into terrifying ghosts of the Victorian age. James's ghost story helps us see how the specter of Victorian conventions, through the agency of the Production Code, haunted directors working from the 1930s to the 1960s. During that time, sexual activity, homosexuality, sacrilege, profanity, disrespect for authority, or critique of capitalism were horrors Joseph Breen sought to censor. Although the Code (denoting standards) sought to impose respectability, it instead created a second code (meaning encryption) that mirrored everything the Code tried to repress. This second code produced ghosts of respectability that haunted with growing visibility Hitchcock's canon. In *Psycho*, Hitchcock confronts them directly, as directly and, we could argue, as violently as James does in *The Turn of the Screw*.

Finally, James indicates, in a way that anticipates postcolonial criticism, that the cinematic audience is as much a victim of its conventions as a participant in them. In *Washington Square*, by including several all-too-conventional audiences, James demonstrates their complicity in the power relations implicit in their expectations. Even more, he demonstrates the suppression and potential violence in the audience's tacit complicity with its own victimization. Doesn't cinema construct a courtship narrative with an unlikely audience, one ill suited for its suitor, one based on expectations and motives that are utterly transparent? Aren't spectators always, to some extent, Catherine Slopers, wishing to be seduced and wary of what they lose in the process? This seems to be what Hitchcock especially knew as he toyed relentlessly with convention—with the authority it wielded and the violence behind that authority. Like his duped heroes and heroines, his audience was continually drawn toward the implicit assurances with which he presents absurd situations matched only by the absurdity of our ceding our imagination to them. But spectators also assume the role of Catherine's well-intentioned yet brutally cruel father, Dr. Sloper, who must, as Alan Nadel shows (Chapter 4), purchase his complacency by turning Catherine into the equivalent of a colonial subject, bereft of the capacity for having her intentions recognized, her meanings heard.

> The deepest quality of a work of art will always be the quality of the mind of the producer. . . . No good novel will ever proceed from a superficial mind.
>
> —Henry James.

> Film directors live with their pictures while they are being made. They are their babies just as much as an author's novel is the offspring of his imagination.
>
> —Alfred Hitchcock

James famously reflected on these practices and problems in a body of literary criticism, most significantly in the Prefaces to the New York Edition of his work. While Hitchcock was often more circumspect about his purposes, he also could be surprisingly forthcoming. And James, despite the prolific metacommentary in his essays and letters, could still retain a hint that something had been crucially unsaid, that a subtle misdirection had been carefully inserted. James, in both his fiction and nonfiction, at times seems to be playing a Hitchcockian joke, just as Hitchcock often appears as a self-mystifying Jamesian Master. This shared double play of artistic explication and complication makes a dual study[3] of their work all the more valuable: in combination, they foreground their metacritical plenitude.

When juxtaposed each becomes a little more transparent in the objectives and machinations of his craft. To the extent that they gloss one another, therefore, they reveal implicit theories of criticism. As "theorists" in this sense, and as artists, they both privilege the importance of misdirection. James is profoundly aware of the imperatives of an absence that is often masked by the implicit presence of the omniscient narrator who, most conventionally, dominates the realistic psychological novel. By the same token, because the conventions of mainstream cinematic editing rely on the play of absence as much as they do on creating a window on reality, Hitchcock's exploitation of vacant spaces, false trails, and unseen evidence helps us comprehend James's critique of omniscience. Entailed in such a critique is the construction of the gaze, a device of equal prominence for both James and Hitchcock. In this sense, among many others, both Hitchcock and James are students of epistemology, each astutely aware of the factors that contribute to the threshold of cognition and, equally, to the threshold of deception.

Hitchcock's and James's interest in propriety, moreover, seems so obvious that it verges—like authorial presence in the realistic novel and in mainstream cinema—on being overlooked by virtue of its ubiquity. Yet when we consider the emphasis both artists place on respectability, as a set of necessary conventions and as a device that can be manipulated, we better understand the structural role of conventions and the conventionality of narrative structure. The "too much" that James and Hitchcock may have known, therefore, is not a matter of abstract theories that hobble their art. Rather, they knew too much to settle for the happy ending, the easy answer, the simple motivation, the linear narrative, the single point of view, the final word. Masters of their media, they transformed what we mean by "fiction" and "film"; deeply political, psychological, and social, their work resists dogma and certitude. In sum, *The Men Who Knew Too Much* constructs a heuristic, grounded in a solid and broad set of parallels, that has produced, we believe, a collection of innovative, theoretically savvy, provocative, and widely useful criticism.

1

National Bodies

Susan M. Griffin

Both Alfred Hitchcock and Henry James famously crossed the Atlantic for their art. James's long-time residence abroad culminated in his becoming a British subject in 1915; Hitchcock never took on American citizenship, but he lived and worked in the United States for forty years. Although these divided or, more, accurately, multiple allegiances brought criticism in the artists' lifetimes, recently such complex national identities have come to be regarded less in terms of loyalty and disloyalty and more as instances of what we have come to call "rooted cosmopolitanism."[1] As experiences, their expatriations were perhaps most difficult at the onsets of World War I, in James's case, and World War II, in Hitchcock's. For the elderly James, the war in Europe revived memories of his earlier failure to serve in the Civil War, even as it seemed to signal a final rupture with the past: "The first sense of it all to me after the first shock and horror was that of a sudden leap back into the violence with which the American Civil War broke upon us" (1914–15, 1968: 11). In 1914, he engaged in war efforts indirectly but ardently: fund-raising, visiting wounded soldiers, joining committees, and sending letters and supplies to his houseman, Burgess Noakes, who was serving in the Army. Hitchcock, who was already resented in England for having "gone Hollywood," was much criticized for not returning to his homeland during the early years of World War II. His 1944 film *Lifeboat,* perhaps in answer, explicitly promotes Allied unity,[2] as did two propaganda films that he directed, *Bon Voyage* and *Aventure Malgache*, for the British Ministry of Information in 1944.

We can learn much from how, during these wartime periods, James and Hitchcock negotiate their own complex national and gender identities through images of bodies. Both artists confront and imaginatively participate in their respective world wars, in part, through the picturing of nationalized bodies, including their own. James, sitting out World War I, describes self and situation to Edith Wharton on August 1914 in distinctly corporeal terms:

> I feel on my side an immense community here, where the tension is proportionate to the degree to which we feel engaged—in other words up to the chin,

> up to the eyes, if necessary. . .. I *go* to sleep, as if I were dog-tired with action—yet feel like the chilled *vieillards* in the old epics, infirm and helpless at home with the women, while the plains are ringing with battle. (Edel 1984, 715)

Although he remains "home with the women," James describes himself in terms that locate him deep in the trenches: "up to the chin, up to the eyes . . . dog-tired with action." The War was, James complained bitterly, conspicuously absent from American newspapers; James intended to make it visibly present even if that meant appearing in public himself (Lockwood 1915, 144). He reidentifies himself, becoming the chairman of the American Volunteer Ambulance Corps, whose work he publicized in American newspapers with a series of pieces meant both to raise funds and to urge the United States to join its allies in fighting Germany. Bravely presenting himself for a photograph and an interview—public exposures of the personal that he normally shunned—James declared, "I can't put . . . my devotion and sympathy for the cause of our corps more strongly than in permitting it thus to overcome my dread of the assault of the interviewer" (Walker 2004, 138–39). Allied with the ambulance drivers, he opens himself to assault—an analogy that, however ironic, James makes without irony.

Hitchcock, too, explicitly understood his art during this period as war efforts figured corporeally. Explaining why he directed two propaganda films for the British Ministry of Information, he said: "I felt the need to make a little contribution to the war effort, and I was both overweight and overage for military service. I knew that if I did nothing I'd regret it for the rest of my life; it was important for me to do something and also to get right into the atmosphere of war" (Truffaut 1967, 159). He went into these propaganda projects having just completed *Lifeboat,* a work that he called "a microcosm of the war" (155) and one that gathers and displays a range of bodies. Hitchcock's patriotism is demonstrated in his depiction of a cross-section of American and British men and women—merchant marines from both sides of the Atlantic, military nurse and shell-shock victim, millionaire and former thief—who are united by the war.

Both Hitchcock and James understand patriotism, not as mindless assent, but as critical engagement. The general public, however, tended to interpret these discriminating analyses differently. In *Lifeboat*, the healthy physiognomy of a German soldier is displayed in pointed contrast to the suffering bodies of American and British men and women. Bosley Crowther (1944) of the *New York Times*, who at first praised *Lifeboat*, almost immediately rethought his opinion, condemning what he saw as its positive—and hence unpatriotic—depiction of the German captain. His criticism was quickly picked up by others, who called this character a poster boy for the Nazis.[3] Political columnist Dorothy Thompson gave the movie "ten days to get out of town" (Truffaut 1967, 156).

James was similarly misunderstood: it was *as an American* that he became a British subject. That is, his audience for the act was clearly the citizens of his native land, whom he hoped to spur into entering the war.[4] Instead, his behavior seemed to prove he had been un-American all along. As the *New York Times* (1915) sniped, "The contrast of the raw, as he finds it, with the finished, of the American with the European, of the simple with the complex or the decorative, has been his main business or pleasure, and after all his subtleties and ironies, 'Daisy Miller,' once so famous, is still the dominant note of Jamesism. [He is] essentially critical and not creative. . . ." ("Mr. James"). James's citizenship, concluded the *Times*, had been "long lightly held," so his defection was not much of a loss: "after all, the United States wants no citizens by compulsion."

These public perceptions of the two artists' idiosyncratic sophistication—their complicated ambiguities—overlaid what were already well-established public personae. The "supersubtle" minds of James and Hitchcock were known to their audiences, not in the abstract but very much in the flesh. With their immediately recognizable, portly profiles, both James and Hitchcock offered, often deliberately, selves vividly represented in cartoons, caricatures, and photographs. Alfred Hitchcock's body marks his art most literally through the cameo appearances he included, starting with *The Lodger* in 1926. But those filmic appearances were only a part of deliberately crafted public images: for example, in casual California, Hitchcock insisted on a uniform of white dress shirt, dark suit, and tie.[5] And he came to use his bulky outline as a kind of "branding." Hitchcock sketched a simple profile that served to identify "Alfred Hitchcock" on record albums, board games, postage stamps, and, of course, television shows.

While the figure of the literary Master was nowhere near as commercially successful, James, too, was conscious of how his visual appearance inflected his readers' and critics' reactions. The public images of "Henry James" are not, of course, always entities of his own making. A series of sketches by F. Opper, including Figure 1.1, depict a distinctly stout James whose clumsy body—and prose—continually trip him up during his 1904–1905 return visit to America (see Edel 1978b, "Five Caricatures"). Max Beerbohm's caricatures consistently identify James by his bulk. Then there is H. G. Wells's famous characterization of James's prose (and James himself) as "a magnificent but painful hippopotamus resolved at any cost, even at the cost of its dignity, upon picking up a pea that has got into a corner of its den" (Edel 1984, 110).

That Hitchcock's and James's material public images are part of the presentation of their art is made explicit in an uncannily Jamesian speech that Hitchcock gave when honored by the Screen Producers Guild in 1965, an experience that he likened to that of a drowning man:

> I think I shall avail myself of the time given me to acquaint you with the person to whom you have given this award. Who is this man? Who is the real Alfred Hitchcock? I shall begin by correcting several misconceptions about myself which have grown up over the years. It is high time I set the record straight.

FIGURE 1.1 Getting it backwards. "Just as one tumbles back into the street in appalled reaction from them."

First of all, there seems to be a widespread impression that I am stout. I can see you share my amusement at this obvious distortion of the truth. Of course I may loom a little large just now, but you must remember, this is before taxes.

I am certain that you are wondering how such a story got started. It began nearly 40 years ago. As you know, I make a brief appearance in each of my pictures. One of the earliest of these was *The Lodger*, the story of Jack the Ripper. My appearance called for me to walk up the stairs of the rooming house. Since my walk-ons in subsequent pictures would be equally strenuous—boarding buses, playing chess, etc.—I asked for a stunt man. Casting, with an unusual lack of perception, hired this fat man! The rest is history. HE became the public image of Hitchcock. Changing the image was impossible. Therefore I had to conform to the image. It was not easy. But proof of my success is that no one has ever noticed the difference.

Our cherubic friend had a tragic ending. It was during the 1940s while he was trying desperately to make an appearance in a picture. Unfortunately Tallulah Bankhead wouldn't allow him to climb into the lifeboat. She was afraid he'd sink it. It was rather sad watching him go down. Of course, we could have saved him, but it would have meant ruining the take. He did receive an appropriate funeral. We recovered the body, and after it had dried out, we had him buried at sea.

> You may be sure that in securing an actor for my next picture I was more careful. I gave casting an accurate and detailed description of my true self. Casting did an expert job. The result: Cary Grant in *Notorious.*
>
> As you know, I still remain a prisoner of the old image. They say that inside every fat man is a thin man trying desperately to get out. Now you know that the thin man is the real Alfred Hitchcock (Hitchcock 1965, 1995: 55–56).[6]

This witty exegesis on the art of representation recalls Henry James's many explorations of the topic. In James's "The Real Thing" (1892), for example, an illustrator finds that a "real" lady and gentleman fail miserably as models for his depiction of the gentry; it's the Cockney model who serves best as the basis for his art.[7] James further complicates matters by raising the possibility that the miserable failure lies not in the "real" or "pretend" models' shortcomings but in the artist's flawed perception and skill. After all, in response to a friend's comment that Milly Theale in *The Wings of the Dove* (1902) was an authentic portrait of James's cousin, Minnie Temple, James insisted, "Poor Minny[8] was essentially incomplete and I have attempted to make my young woman more rounded, more finished. In truth, everyone, in life, is incomplete, and it is [in] the work of art that in reproducing them one feels the desire to fill them out, to justify them, as it were" (Edel 1975, 324).

In his after-dinner speech, Hitchcock repeatedly raises, but never definitively answers, the question of which images accurately represent the "true" Alfred Hitchcock: those on the screen—the stair climber, the bus boarder, the chess player? The actor who played these cameo roles? The self described in the speech? The movie star "Cary Grant" (whom even Cary Grant said he wanted to be)? The films as a whole? As he uncovers and conceals himself, Hitchcock invokes the contrivances that create the cinematic "real."

"Reduco"

Hitchcock's speech proffers *Lifeboat* as an exemplum of signifying bodies, a suggestion that the film certainly bears out. The lifeboat of the title, launched after a transatlantic ship's fatal encounter with a German U-boat, gradually takes on a diverse group of American and British survivors: male and female, rich and poor, black and white. Hitchcock's own body enters the film, as usual, through one of his cameos. As he remarked to Francois Truffaut, this appearance is one of his most clever. In fact, two versions of Hitchcock appear in a newspaper advertisement for "Reduco," an imaginary weight-loss product.[9] The director explains: "At the time I was on a strenuous diet, painfully working my way from three hundred to two hundred pounds. So I decided to immortalize my loss and get my bit part by posing for 'before' and 'after' pictures" (Truffaut 1967, 158). Of course, *Lifeboat*'s audience was not to know this in advance, and the first body that is actually seen in the film, that of a bulky man floating face down in the water with "Deutsches Reich/U 78"

FIGURE 1.2 Hitchcock's two bodies.

written across his back, tantalizes with the possibility that it might be Hitchcock's own. The director did, in fact, consider this choice for his cameo: "I must admit that I had an awful time thinking it up. Usually I play a passer-by, but you can't have a passer-by out on the ocean. I thought of being a dead body floating past the lifeboat, but I was afraid I'd sink" (Truffaut 158). So Hitchcock substituted the enemy form for his, a substitution made even more interesting by the fact that the German body that later climbs out of the water and into the lifeboat (that of a rescued sailor "Willy" [Walter Slezak], who is, in fact, the U-Boat captain) is nearly identical in shape. This masculine bulk, sustained by the well-prepared German's secret supplies, represents health, strength, and superior intelligence.

Tallulah Bankhead's body was supposed to be *Lifeboat*'s main attraction, as the publicity materials and posters show (Hitchcock repeatedly said that the movie revolved around her). Predictably, there is an early lingering shot that shows her examining a run in her stocking, directing our gaze to her "gams."[10] Nonetheless, the leg that matters most in the film is male and phallic. It belongs to Gus (William Bendix), the regular fellow from Brooklyn, dumb but honest, naïve, strong, and true. Gus's sexual worth is situated, blatantly, in his legs: he is desperately (and, we learn, rightly) worried that, without a leg, and thus unable to jitterbug, he will lose his girl. While Gus's German origins are made manifest in the way his robust body visually echoes Willy's, German aggression has, he complains, separated him from his Old World family, changed his name (from Schmidt to Smith), and truncated—we might say

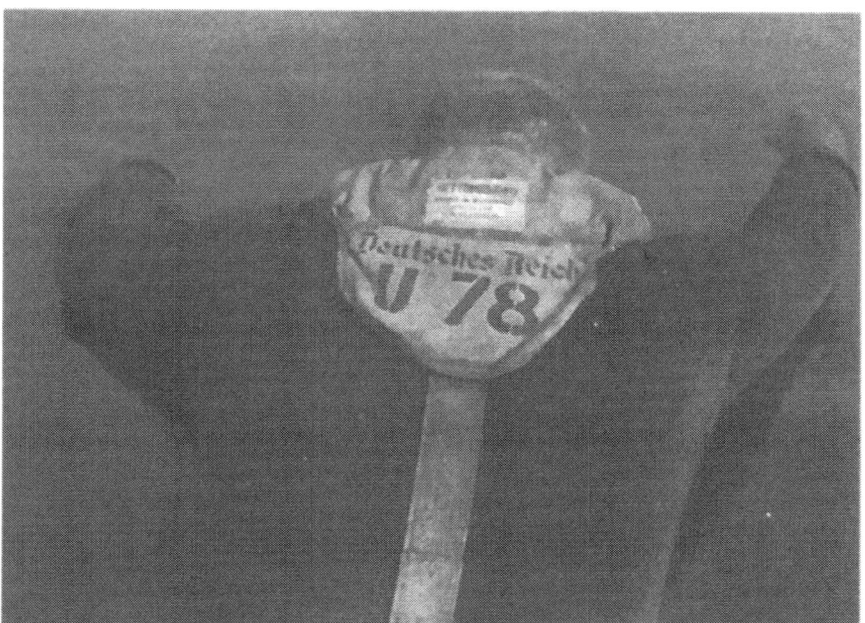

FIGURE 1.3 A third Hitchcock?

performed an amputation on—his identity: he can no longer be German-American; he must be solely American. Once in the war, Gus experiences this aggression directly: he is wounded in the leg by the U-boat attack, the leg is then amputated by the submarine commander, who claims to be a surgeon. Gus is reduced by the Germans to what their Superman calls "a poor cripple dying of hunger and thirst."

The darkness of Hitchcock's comic sensibility makes it almost inevitable, then, that our first glimpse of the director himself is at Gus's hands—indeed, the marine holds a newspaper well up so we can see clearly a "Reduco" advertisement with side-by-side bodily profiles of Hitchcocks fat and thin. What would normally be perceived as Hitchcock's healthy weight reduction becomes ironic in time of war and especially on the lifeboat, where the bodily reductions are drastic and life-threatening. As the ill-prepared and ill-supplied survivors of the Allied ship shrink and weaken, even Kovac (John Hodiak), the male sex symbol in the film, becomes associated with "Reduco," insofar as he spends a great deal of time reading that tattered newspaper, falling asleep with Hitchcock's two bodies spread across his torso. *Lifeboat* raises the possibility that war has cut American and British males down to size, subtracted from their potency, left them helpless and adrift: "little men," as Connie (Tallulah Bankhead's character) calls them. After all, it is the maimed Gus—maimed by two kinds of German expertise, military and surgical—who prompts the commander's blunt articulation of German eugenics: "[B]etter to let him die. What are you going to do with people like that?"

Like a Gypsy, like a Jew, Gus has become less than human. The strong and healthy are better off without him.

But (and) "people like that" are also, in the microcosm of the lifeboat, the Americans and the British, none of whom can measure up to the German's full-bodied strength, resources, and expertise. Weak, sick, and inept, the only way the Allies can overcome the German is by combining into a single body and acting as one. This is, in fact, a vivid illustration of Hitchcock's stated intention:

> We wanted to show that at that moment there were two world forces confronting each other, the democracies and the Nazis, and while the democracies were completely disorganized, all of the Germans were clearly headed in the same direction. So here was a statement telling the democracies to put their differences aside temporarily and to gather their forces to concentrate on the common enemy, whose strength was precisely derived from a spirit of unity and of determination. (Truffaut 1967, 155)

Yet *Lifeboat*'s critics were at least partially right in seeing the movie as—if not pro-German—ambiguous, perhaps even ambivalent, regarding the Allies' joint actions. On the one hand, *Lifeboat* critiques individualism: both of the "elite" characters, Constance "Connie" Porter (Bankhead) and Rittenhouse (Henry Hull), must learn to become part of an equalized community.[11] To function successfully as a group, the individual identities of each member must be submerged; class, race, and sexual differences must be erased. Just so, the Allies need, in Hitchcock's analysis, to stop thinking and acting separately. Yet what Hitchcock calls above "a spirit of unity and of determination" is, also, quite simply, a mob mentality (see Figure 1.4). We watch as the British and Americans swarm together and collectively force Willy into the ocean and to his death. Their faces disappear; we see only the backs of their bodies shoving together into one mass. What finally motivates successful, united Allied action is loss: Willy's grasp is fatally loosened by Gus's boot, which is used to beat the German commander's hands. The empty boot is the trace and sign of the missing: Gus's amputated leg, the disappearance of his body, and the corpses of all those lost in the ocean. It cannot restore wholeness, creating, only and instead, another (albeit enemy) loss.

Scenes where the hands of someone hanging onto an edge are assaulted recur in Hitchcock's work (perhaps most famously in *North by Northwest* [1959] and in *Saboteur* [1942], in both cases with figures hanging from national monuments) and in cinema generally.[12] But, importantly, such attacks are typically the acts of the villains who take advantage of the hanging character's position of weakness. The fact that the bad guy plays dirty—using his feet to stamp on the other's fingers—reinforces our perception that this is not a fair fight. In contrast, good characters inevitably risk their own lives to pull others up to safety. In *Lifeboat,* the Allies—anomalously, unconventionally, frighteningly—alternately use their position of strength for good and for evil. They repeatedly pull survivors up and into the boat, whether those bodies are male or female, black or white, rich or poor, American or British. Or even

FIGURE 1.4 Americans and British united "like a pack of dogs."

German—and even twice. There can be no doubt of their rectitude. Yet this same group viciously swarms the desperately clutching Willy. When Truffaut questioned him about this shot, calling it repulsive, Hitchcock replied, "Yes, they're like a pack of dogs" (1967, 156).

The narrative arc of *Lifeboat* leads its characters and, presumably, its audience to the realization that the preservation of Britain and the United States as independent nations depends, somewhat paradoxically, on the recognition of and identification with others who are different. But what Hitchcock shows—and, I would suggest, fears—is that union may mean the *elimination* of difference and the loss of individuality. Who wants a nice, tame Tallulah Bankhead? Who wants an American Hitchcock? Or an English one? Our pleasure is in his performances of "The Englishman in America." Who wants a "Reduco" of the twisted, ironic, multiplying Hitchcockian self?

"My Appearance Attracts General Attention"

For Henry James, facing an earlier world war, a united effort by the United States and Britain seems wholly desirable. What complicates the matter is the aging James's own situation. His urgent desire for unity among nations coincides with his increasing return to the problem of his own heterogeneous national identity. Of course, what has been called "the international theme" stretches across James's career. Only in his late writings, however, do narratives of return become a preoccupation, plots in which characters confront and choose—or find they have chosen—nationalized forms of self. James's writings around 1914 (especially his unorthodox introduction of a fat American Girl, Rosanna Gaw,[13] in *The Ivory Tower* [1917])—and his descriptions of his own physical failings and dislocation—figure power as well as vulnerability, limning his shifting historical and national identities as aging artist.

During the summer of 1914, James took up work on *The Ivory Tower.* He was, at the time, acutely, painfully aware of his seventy-year-old body: suffering attacks of shingles, episodes of heart trouble, the extraction of nearly all of his teeth ("the wounds, the inconvenience, the humiliations" [Edel 1978a, 509]), and the return of the digestive problems that plagued him nearly all of his life. It is at this moment that James locates a version of himself in an insistently fleshly American Girl: Rosanna Gaw, the only daughter of the self-made multimillionaire, Abel Gaw. Like so many of James's other late fictions ("The Jolly Corner" [1908], *The Sense of the Past* [1917]), *The Ivory Tower* plays out possible permutations for native-born Americans. What sort of person would the experience of living in America create? What would mark the differences if that person had lived abroad? Rosanna Gaw, with comic dignity, illustrates what might have become of Henry James.

Critics have long recognized, of course, how often James's female characters represent aspects of the author. But Rosanna Gaw and her predecessor, Catherine Sloper of *Washington Square* (1881), are anomalous in their size.[14] When, in the late seventies and early eighties, James was privately distancing himself from his family and publicly constructing himself as a cosmopolitan author, he wrote the story of Catherine, a heroine whose stoutness figures self-nourishment, self-sufficiency—and self-protection.[15] His careful letters home during this period tell a similar story, one that bought James time in Europe without parental interference but with parental financial support. And in these early representations, created for his first public—the James family—we can see how James, like Hitchcock, ironically deploys bodily images of the self. In 1880, he assures his mother: "I wish you could see me in the flesh. I think a glance would set your mind at rest. . . . I am in superb health and so fat that my flesh hangs over my waistband in huge bags. My appearance attracts general attention" (Edel 1975, 343). Similarly, after the winter of 1879, when, famously, he dined out 140 times, Henry describes himself to his brother William, "I am as broad as I am long, as fat as a butter-tub and as red as a British *materfamilias"* (Edel 1975, 343).

If these seem odd assertions, perhaps an earlier (1874) letter *from* James's mother, Mary, can help explain: "I feel so often that I want to throw around you the mantle of family affection, and fold you in my own tenderest embrace. It seems to me darling Harry that your life must need this succulent fattening element more than you know yourself" (quoted in Feinstein 2000, 42–43). The family dynamic played out in the James family letters is, to say the least, complex: the languages of money and health become the medium of competition, and deft mixtures of aggression and affection are presented as humor.[16] For my purposes here, suffice it to say that, for Henry, breaking away from his family meant nourishing himself, rather than feeding off the maternal embrace, fattening on dinners out, and earning enough to buy his own bread. At this moment he creates his first fat American heroine, Catherine Sloper, who, like her creator, defies and separates from her parent.

The two roundly feminized Jamesian figures of Henry and Catherine also appear at a time when James's nationality is a matter of public debate. Reactions to James's writings between 1878 and 1880 make him acutely conscious that he is writing about his native land while residing in Europe. He composes a critical biography of Hawthorne for the *English Men of Letters Series* (1879), in which he pointedly distinguishes himself from his literary forbears; depicts an American girl in "Daisy Miller" (1878) only to be criticized in the United States and celebrated abroad; portrays English gentlemen visiting America in "An International Episode" (1879) and is reprimanded in Britain. James's transatlantic situation and self do not make their ways into his female, fictional counterpart, who is wholly and simply American: a trip to Europe is wasted on Catherine, who is rooted in Washington Square, occupying the parental home to the last. If Catherine, in part, acts out James's physical and parental drama, her thorough and unthinking Americanness is an identity James leaves behind, along with his own childhood home in the Square (a fact that James underscores by the pointed omission of *Washington Square* from the New York Edition of his work).

Like Catherine Sloper, Rosanna Gaw's appearance complicates her part in a conventional marriage plot. But, unlike Catherine, who becomes strong only with age, Rosanna is a figure of power from her youth, one who is able to serenely reject the man (Horton Vint) who is interested in her money. Rosanna's size is repeatedly commented upon: she is "a truly massive young person" (1), "the large loose ponderous girl" (1), "his big plain quiet daughter" (8), "she represented quantity and mass" (9), and "there was a great deal of her, so that she would have pressed down even a balance appointed to weigh bullion" (this last is her multimillionaire father's image) (9). Rosanna herself says that at sixteen, "I was huge and hideous" (33). James emphasizes that the young woman wears no corsets, dressing in loose wrappers that reveal, rather than conceal, her flesh. But these comic descriptions are not dismissive. Rosanna garners respect both from *The Ivory Tower*'s other characters and American readers. A 1918 review in *The Nation* called her "a big sensible American girl with an enormous fortune left to her by that weazened captain of industry" ("Henry James in the Ivory Tower" 237).

What the *Nation*'s description of Rosanna highlights is that, as Alan Hollinghurst (2004) has recently pointed out, *The Ivory Tower* is about bequests: a story of contemporary America that raises the question of how a younger generation, born into leisure, will use their forbears' brutally earned fortunes (vii). The daughter of a man who is completely consumed by financial rivalry (the shock of finding out that his ex-partner may not be dying sends Abel Gaw to his grave), Rosanna Gaw is perhaps the character in the novel with the greatest distaste for vulgarity, whose tact and sensitivity separate her from most of her fellow Americans. James offers her as an unexpected protagonist for the times: exceptional, perhaps, but completely American nonetheless. She represents the hope that some few of the new generation will transform the wealth crudely "grabbed" by their coarse, ruthless fathers (business being, in the lexicon of the novel, "the awful game of grab").

But, in the fragment of the novel that we have, Rosanna can only achieve this transmutation (purifying money's sordid origins within an ivory tower)[17] vicariously. Like Ralph Touchett (*The Portrait of a Lady* [1881]) before her—another character whose body distances him from the novel's action—Rosanna envisages and helps create a life for someone else. She populates the nation's future not by marrying and bearing new citizens but by imagining another's story. She is not a mother but a fairy godmother[18]—not an actor, but an artist. And it is in this artistry that, perhaps predictably, I read Rosanna Gaw as a figure for Henry James. When we first see Rosanna, she is shaded by "a vast pale-green parasol, a portable pavilion from which there fluttered fringes, frills and ribbons that made it resemble the roof of some Burmese palanquin or perhaps even pagoda" (1), an image that looks forward to the intricately crafted ivory tower and back to Maggie Verver's (*The Golden Bowl*) elaborate pagoda—Jamesian figures for art, arrangement, and knowledge.

Graham Fielder is the nephew of Abel Gaw's former business partner, Frank Betterman, and a close companion during Rosanna's youth. Rosanna twice shapes the narrative arc of Graham's life. When he was fourteen and she, sixteen, she "began to enjoy the advantage—if advantage it was—of its seeming so ridiculous to treat the monster I had grown as negligible that I *had* to be treated as important" (33). There is an echo here of James's description of the artist as "that queer monster . . . an obstinate finality, an inexhaustible sensibility "(Edel 1984, 706). Rosanna's literal size is perhaps emblematic of James's now substantial written corpus.[19] Certainly her "quantity and mass" represent—and seem to create—her generative force, enabling her to imagine and arrange the remarriage of Graham's mother. This remarriage means that Graham will mature in Europe, not America, and thus remain free from his American uncle's sordid business. The European education in refinement that creates the adult Graham Fielder is a tale plotted by Rosanna Gaw, a story whose forward arc she shapes again when she dictates the terms of Mr. Betterman's will, making sure that Graham will inherit his millions. With Rosanna, James playfully tries out one way to be an American artist and, by giving his stand-in a truly fat body, makes her peculiarly Jamesian: a powerful artificer, removed from the scene of action.

We do not know how this story ends. The war in Europe interrupts, and James's attention switches away from Newport views to the threatened horizons of

England, England as an island, situated, as James repeatedly visualizes it, "within the rim." His final essays and letters return again and again to this image of an enclosed, but potentially penetrable, space, one reinforced by James's constant awareness of events across the Channel in France and Belgium.[20] And reinforced as well by the accelerating break-down of James's body. Even food and medicine seem to threaten his physical integrity: we find him worrying both about the dangers of stimulants (will drinking cocoa have negative effects?) and taking what he refers to as "dynamite" (nitroglycerin).

Faced with the fragility of both identity and island, finding that he can only visit his home in Rye as an "Alien Under Police Protection," James makes a last attempt to firmly locate, to make himself whole, by becoming a British subject: "I feel that if I take this step I shall simply rectify a position that has become inconveniently and uncomfortably false, making my civil status merely agree not only with my moral, but with my material as well, in every kind of way" (Edel 1984, 760).

James asserts that he is already British by virtue of his long residence in England. Proving his patriotism, Hitchcock shows the American and British peoples as one, a unity about which, I have suggested, he was ambivalent. For James, that loyalty means finally choosing between the two, a choice he presents as simply arranging for his legal identity to match his British "moral" and "material" self. Yet this emphatic statement is undermined by later letters. He closes a note to John Singer Sargent with "It would really have been *so* easy for the U.S. to have 'kept' (if they had cared to!) yours all faithfully" (Edel 1984, 774) and, in another letter, insists that Woodrow Wilson could have stopped him "with one wiggle of his little finger."[21] James implies *not* that he is no longer American but that Americans have failed to recognize him *as* American. Indeed, James's despairing break with the United States is precisely the sort of purifying excision of complex identifications—the stark break with the past—that both Hitchcock and James sought to avoid.

The Jamesian body has been the focus of much recent biography and criticism, fostered, in part, by the growing availability of many letters in which James elaborates on his physical state.[22] But critical interest in Henry James's physical self dates back at least to Edel (1956), who argues that the writer's "obscure hurt"—his "war injury"—was both indicative and formative of his masculinity, his self-definition, and his authorship. So, too, Truffaut (1967) maintains that Hitchcock's body helped create and position him as a man and as a director; he describes Hitchcock as "a singular man, not only by virtue of his physique, but also by virtue of his spirit, his morality, and his obsessions. . . . When, as an adolescent, he realized that his physique isolated him from others, Hitchcock withdrew from the world to view it with tremendous severity" (346). Looking at the two artists' later depictions of bodies suggests how flesh continues as a medium for complex and multiple self-representations. "Henry James" and "Alfred Hitchcock" are visibly performed, marketed, and played out across a range of embodied characters. In particular, their wartime forms prove useful vehicles for the analysis of each man's cumulative history of political identifications. Their national loyalties, isolations and alliances, and strengths and vulnerabilities are visibly traceable in the physical contours of these formidable presences.

2

Secrets, Lies, and "Virtuous Attachments"

THE AMBASSADORS AND *THE 39 STEPS*

Brenda Austin-Smith

Henry James and Alfred Hitchcock do not at first blush lend themselves to extended comparison. The explicit violence of Hitchcock's murder mysteries could not, it would seem, be more removed from the repressed, high-toned melodrama of James's fiction. But the work of both artists importantly shaped the histories of their particular media. In their exploration of the tensions between character and plot, James and Hitchcock take up the nature of identity, the ravaging effects of knowledge on the self, and the survival of trust and connection in the wake of deception and betrayal. Paula Marantz Cohen (2008) remarks that James "makes for a particularly felicitous comparison" with Hitch, "since he and Hitchcock marked a sort of terminus for their respective forms—James, for the Victorian novel; Hitchcock, for classical narrative film. Both also pointed forward—one to modernism, the other to independent film and postmodernism."

These similarities are strikingly evident in two works that occupy contrasting positions in the careers of each figure: James's Major Phase triumph *The Ambassadors* (1903), written twenty-seven years after James committed himself to a home in England, and Hitchcock's early masterpiece *The 39 Steps* (1935), released four years before Hitchcock's move from London to Hollywood. *The Ambassadors* was, famously, James's favorite—"frankly, quite the best, 'all round,' of all my productions"—while Hitchcock is said to have been particularly fond of *The 39 Steps* (Harris and Lasky 2000, 51). As mutual foils, these artifacts engage and refract each other, their juxtaposed elements offering echoes and anticipations that enlarge the prospects of both the moral decisions and actions of their characters. The exchanges that I limn between the worlds of Lewis Lambert Strether and Richard Hannay (Robert Donat) operate a bit like intertextual Hitchcockian cameos: qualities and situations in one work appear in the other, though modified by medium as well as by plot demands. James and Hitchcock come together in the form of traces and suggestions, rather than in the stout personages of their respective authors.

FIGURE 2.1 The open window in *The 39 Steps* opens on to the other, Jamesian text.

Lambert Strether's discovery late in *The Ambassadors* that Chad Newsome and Marie de Vionnet are indeed intimate, and that their intimacy is "like lying" (1903, 1994: 315), confirms one of the many correspondences between James's novel and Hitchcock's film. In both fictional realms, the forms taken by deceit, betrayal, and dishonesty invite investigation, often by reluctant sleuths recruited by circumstance to the practices of discernment and unmasking. The reading of *The 39 Steps* and *The Ambassadors* proposed here explores the similarities between spies and ambassadors, between acts of legitimate and illegitimate surveillance, and between sexual and political intrigue. These two texts depict international engagements as occasions for erotic and national betrayal, while also suggesting that "foreign relations" provide opportunities for personal transformation. Certainly Richard Hannay, the Canadian hero of *The 39 Steps*, takes Strether's exhortation to "Live all you can" to heart as he makes his desperate way from London to Scotland, recasting Strether's enlightening European sojourn as flight from murderous pursuers. The deep richness of conversation between these two works, though, lies in the connection of the protagonists to their surroundings, and in the relationships contemplated, formed, and rejected by these men who fail at their tasks of rescue, and who end their tales in ambiguously chosen exile from the easeful lives they once inhabited.

Hannay's predicament in *The 39 Steps* is the familiar Hitchcockian one of the Wrong Man, though as an apparent innocent abroad, he also presents a version of James's International Theme. Examining Robert Donat's performance as Hannay,

William Rothman (1984) describes it as one that exemplifies "grace," as well as one that assumes its creation's right to privacy. Donat's animation of Hannay is so confident and individual that Rothman considers Hannay not actually to *be* a character in the typical sense, but to strike viewers instead as "our full equal" (116), as much a person to us as we are to ourselves. This view of Hannay qualifies his vulnerability to the kinds of cultured predations visited upon naïve or brash American characters by many of James's Europeans. The tendency of James's innocents to give themselves away in conversation, to offer all of their thoughts and self-protections to others, or to act in accordance with their own self-absorption, gives social opponents a purchase on the character, an opening into the self, that often results in profound emotional exploitation. Hannay's belief in himself, in the rightness of his being where he is and how he is, provides him with immunity from the psychological dangers that beset the Jamesian naïf, no matter what challenging physical circumstances he encounters. As Rothman stresses, Hannay has no dark secrets to hide or to share. He neither asserts nor withholds himself but, rather, stands in disinterested and good-natured appreciation of what is around him. Watching him move and react to people and situations with definition, intelligence, and flair, we are certain he must be an excellent dancer.

Attending a music hall entertainment one evening in London, Hannay is accosted after a disturbance in the theater by a strange woman, who gives her name as Annabella Smith (Lucie Mannheim). She asks him to take her home and, once there, claims to be a secret agent. Later that night she is murdered in his apartment. Staggering into the room in which he is sleeping, a knife protruding from her back, she presses a map of Scotland into his hands and urges her mission on him before dying. Believing now in her story of spies and military secrets, Hannay dons a series of disguises and assumes various identities as he eludes both the authorities, who take him for the mysterious woman's murderer, and the shadowy figures who now pursue him as they did Annabella, intent on killing him as well. Traveling by train to Scotland with Annabella's map as his guide, Hannay rushes for protection into the compartment of a woman named Pamela (Madeleine Carroll), pretending to know her, but she turns him over to the police. He escapes capture by climbing out of the train and makes his way to a village where a jealous farmer (John Laurie) with a young wife, Margaret (Peggy Ashcroft), agrees to give him shelter. The suspicions are heightened by the interactions between Hannay and Margaret over dinner. Margaret, realizing both Hannay's predicament and her husband's untrustworthiness, helps Hannay escape. Hannay arrives at the house of Professor Jordan (Godfrey Tearle), the man he believes Annabella Smith was trying to reach, and tells the Professor everything he knows about the spy plot to smuggle secrets out of the country. Holding up his own hand, the Professor reveals the partial digit that marks him as the ring-leader of the spies. The Professor shoots Hannay, who falls to the floor of the study. After the Professor departs, Hannay, unhurt, recovers consciousness and reports what has happened to the disbelieving police, who arrest him. After escaping their clutches, being mistaken for a political candidate, and being turned over once again by Pamela, he ends up handcuffed to her in the back of a car driven by the Professor's henchmen. Hannay and Pamela, attached to each other, leap out of the car, scramble over the moors, and take refuge in an inn, posing as newlyweds. Pamela is finally convinced of Hannay's innocence, and together they return to London in time to foil the Professor's plot, though Mr. Memory (Wylie Watson), the conduit for the state secrets, dies. In the last shot of the film, Hannay and Pamela clasp hands, finally choosing their connection to each other.

Though younger by decades than Lambert Strether, Hannay shares with him the Jamesian condition of the fine mind subject to bewilderment, searching the landscape for clues, for readable and reliable signs of alliance and opposition. As he travels by train, car, and then foot, from the urban south to the rural north of Scotland, the increasing emptiness and desolation of the countryside becomes the physical approximation of his isolated state in which nothing and no one can really be trusted, even though Hannay proceeds to place his trust in just about everyone he encounters, as does Strether. So steadfast is his faith in appearances that he takes Pamela as the kind of woman who would join in his amorous pretense in order to save him from wrongful arrest; believes John, the Scottish farmer, will not turn him in if paid not to; and assumes that Professor Jordan could not possibly be the evil mastermind Annabella has warned him against. That he is wrong on all counts does not disturb his sense of self or fundamentally affect his relationship to those around him. Adjusting rapidly to his changing circumstances, he leaps from trains and windows and police cars, all nimbleness and quick thinking, without undergoing any of the questioning and self-doubt that might be expected of someone confronting such an unreliable world. Thomas M. Leitch (1991), describing the comedic spirit of the group of Hitchcock films to which *The 39 Steps* belongs, writes that in such films "it is fun to be in love; it is fun to be mystified and perplexed; it is fun to risk danger and possible death" (87). Though he is framed, chased, betrayed, shot, and forcibly confined over the course of the film, Hannay remains psychologically intact, his confident core untouched by his experiences, at least, perhaps, until the very end.

Rothman sees the music hall opening of *The 39 Steps* as an essential setting for the events that follow. It reflexively suggests the film of which it is a part and also directs us to Hannay's transformation from spectator to actor as he confronts each trap he finds himself in "by discovering a role and performing it" (1984: 119). Hannay, says Rothman, is an improvisational actor who responds to the situation in which he finds himself by reacting to it "on the spot" (119). Several of these provisional identities, in fact, return later in the film to define him more concretely, as Lesley Brill notes (1988). Not only does he flee, in Scotland, the jealous husband he had conjured up in desperate fantasy when trying to escape from his own flat, but at the end of the film he has also become in real life the lover he pretended to be on the train leaving London when he forced a kiss on Pamela. The suggestion of the film is not only that identity for Hannay is a temporary, forced choice, brought about in some form or other by the approach of the authorities, but also that the array of possible ways for him to "be" is limited, and that some of them are likely to come round again, in slightly varied form. His options are not infinite.

Lambert Strether, too, has an experience of the "sharp rupture of an identity," but it is in relation to young Chadwick Newsome's transformation rather than his own. "You could deal with a man as himself—you couldn't deal with him as some-one else" he muses (1903, 1994: 90).[1] It is an observation we can imagine someone making of Hannay, who in several respects might well remind us of Chad Newsome, a man similarly self-assured and "marked out by women" (98). And yet Strether does deal with Chad for most of the novel as if Chad weren't really "after all, only Chad," but an improved and youthful version of Strether himself. Strether is both amazed and unsettled by the man that Chad has become in Paris. He sees in this new Chad the hand of a creative presence, as yet unnamed, who has obliterated all traces of the youth's "New England female parent" (92) and set in their place the confident face and graceful disposition of "a man of the world . . . a man to whom things had happened and were variously known" (97). Like Hannay, Chad simply appears, fully formed and in command of the social landscape, which in this instance, as in *The 39 Steps*, is the theater, activating in this text, too, the theme of performance. The question of Chad's alteration, his international makeover—he seems more than a collection of domestic raw materials that has received a high, foreign finish—is the crucial one for Strether. Chad's transformation affects Strether because it appeals to his romantic view of what he might have made of himself had he kept his promises to himself some quarter of a century earlier, and at the same time is the occasion for Strether's refusal to acknowledge the sexual nature of the "things" that have happened to Chad, that the "irreducible young Pagan" with his "massive manhood" (92) "variously" knows. Strether's recognition of the change in Chad is also the first application of his own expanded sense of apprehension, awakened in him by this return to the splendid city.

"Is it then a conspiracy?" asks Strether of Maria Gostrey in Book Third of *The Ambassadors*. Strether's own mission, to return the wayward Chad Newsome to the bosom of Woollett's privileged small-mindedness, has met its first frustration in the pleasure Strether has rediscovered in "the corruption . . . of Europe" (83). He has just returned from a visit with Chad's friend, Little Bilham, the young man he watched smoking on the balcony of Chad's fashionable apartment. Standing in broad daylight on the street below, unlike the thugs who lurk under the streetlight outside Hannay's rooms, Strether is an inept shadow man, open to invitations to join those he has vowed to "approach . . . wait for . . . deal with . . . [and] master" (79) for breakfast. Plenitude, rather than Hannay's physical privations, is the enemy of Stether's commitment to the task of surveillance, pursuit, and rescue. Enjoying the company of his newfound friends, he nevertheless wonders "if the occasion weren't in its essence the most baited, the most gilded of traps" (76), and if perhaps Little Bilham acts primarily as an agent for Chad, to compromise Strether, to draw information from him that would aid Chad in his project of sophisticated evasion. "What's he up to, what's he up to?" Strether thinks to himself of Little Bilham, all the while noting the "wise savour" of the food, the distraction of young, bohemian companionship working on him like a glass of excellent, but drugged, wine. Strether's suspicions are shared by Maria Gostrey, who is certain that Chad and Little Bilham have arranged "[e]very move in the game" (88), Chad having acted, in Mark Goble's words, "by remote control" (2007, 420).[2] And in its own way, the substitution of Chad for Little Bilham as the expected guest in the theater box, the unveiling of the man behind the putative plot to subvert Strether's mission—"They were in the presence of Chad himself," says the narrator, rather melodramatically (1903, 1994: 89)—has an air not unlike Hannay's sudden realization that the man to whom he has told his secrets is the man with the missing finger tip, the leader of the foreign spy ring (Figure 2.2).

It is difficult to imagine two protagonists who contrast more sharply in their relations to the settings in which they find themselves than Strether and Hannay. Hannay's environments are all temporary backdrops for his thrilling improvisations. As a man on the run, he has no real chance to "take in" the scenery he moves through once he flees from London, but this note is actually struck early on in the film. Hannay simply appears onscreen in the act of buying his ticket, as if he were purchasing a spot in the film. We remember, too, that even the furniture in the apartment to which he brings Annabella Smith is covered in sheets, a sign of his recent arrival, perhaps, but also that he does not fully engage with or surrender to his living spaces. Strether is also a man away from familiar surroundings but, despite himself, cannot resist the many "impressions" he receives from the city he hasn't seen for several decades. If, as Rothman writes, Hannay models the actor who masters several roles, then Strether might be seen as the ideal spectator, the prototype

FIGURE 2.2 Hannay's realization that he has told his secrets to the man with the missing finger tip, the leader of the foreign spy ring.

of the person for whom cinema is intended. The possessor of a modern sensibility prone to seduction by visual impressions, Strether responds with the perfect blend of emotions to what he sees, moving through curiosity, desire, envy, regret, and, finally, detachment as he encounters the scenes and people before him. Though not as urgently in motion as is Hannay, Strether nevertheless makes "restlessness . . . his temporary law," wandering through the Parisian streets to the Luxembourg Gardens, where he feels "the cup of his impressions truly to overflow" (1903, 1994: 58–59). It is here, too, that his own sense of pursuit is delicately rendered, as, watching the "terraces, alleys, vistas, fountains, little trees in green tubs, little women in white caps and shrill little girls at play," he wonders "what he was doing with such an extraordinary sense of escape," as if Mrs. Newsome, in the form of her letters, "had followed on his heels" (59).

In his intense absorption of Paris, Strether experiences a sense of dislocation similar to Hannay's, though its occasion is his immersion in his surroundings rather than in his passing through them, leaping from rock to rock across a Scottish stream as Hannay does. Strether's disorientation is at once aesthetic, emotional, and moral, and occurs as a phenomenological experience of complex simultaneity, rather than as the sequence of confusions that is Hannay's lot. The city appears to him as "a huge iridescent object, a jewel brilliant and hard, in which parts were not to be discriminated nor differences comfortably marked" (64). Strether cannot possibly sort through his impressions of his environment; he has instead to recognize that "wherever one paused in Paris the imagination reacted before one could stop it. This reaction put a price, if one would, on pauses; but it piled up consequences till there was scarce room to pick one's steps among them" (69). The image of a wreck that arises from this description of processing multiple impressions suggests the ultimate effect of Strether's visit on his Woollett-based moral verities, as much as it anticipates the figurative train that Strether mourns having missed in his epiphanic speech to Little Bilham in Book Fifth.

The role of misunderstanding and implication in these two stories of personal and international intrigue is another source of rich and provocative alignments between the works. Tony Williams (2007), writing on Hitchcock's adaptation of John Buchan's novel, claims that Hitch's version focuses on "the fragility of civilized values," concentrating as it does on the "odyssey" of Richard and Pamela and their "antagonistic relationship" to their own society as they make their way, handcuffed together, across the moors at night. While not as starkly dramatized, and certainly not as physically dangerous, the relationships between Strether and Maria Gostrey, Strether and Marie de Vionnet, and between Chad and Marie de Vionnet, pose similar questions about the resilience of social conventions and personal commitments in the face of accidental misreadings and deliberate misdirection. Certainly Hannay would have fared better had he been aware that the "Professor" of whom Annabella spoke was the one person that he should avoid at all costs, rather than the person whom he should be determined to seek out in Scotland. This is mere bad luck. It is another thing altogether when Strether, the ambassador for

Mrs. Newsome, abandons his mission to become instead the emissary of Marie de Vionnet, as Julie Rivkin has put it (1986, 823).

The nature of these misreadings and misdirections is often erotic, or at least involves the possibility of romantic and sexual entanglements, as well as affective treachery. Though Chad Newsome's putatively "virtuous attachment" to Marie de Vionnet is the most infamous, there are other connections in *The Ambassadors* that suggest possibilities at least one of the participants is aware of and uses for political or personal advantage in the diplomatic maneuvering that characterizes the novel. Neither Chad nor Marie de Vionnet is in a hurry to dispel Strether's initial supposition that it is Jeanne who is the reason for Chad's lingering in Paris. And Strether himself is content to stay silent when Marie de Vionnet remarks on her old school chum Maria's "happiness." The implication, he understands "was that *he* was Maria Gostrey's happiness" (1903, 1994: 162). Of course, it is just this sort of misdirection that plunges Hannay into the international espionage plot of *The 39 Steps* in the first place. Annabella chooses him, apparently randomly, from the departing theater crowd and asks him to take her home with him. Agreeing, he shrugs and says prophetically, "It's your funeral." When Hannay, realizing that his building is under surveillance by the men responsible for Annabella's murder, escapes his apartment, he does so by engaging the arriving milkman in a story of adulterous intrigue. Unconvinced initially by Hannay's tale of espionage, the milkman responds immediately when Hannay changes tack, instead presenting himself as a man sneaking away from a tryst with a married woman neighbor. "Why didn't you tell me before, old fellow?" says the milkman, surrendering his white uniform to Hannay in brotherly sympathy, "I was just wanting to be told." Hannay's train flight from London in *The 39 Steps* provides the occasion for a second erotic feint, when, avoiding pursuit, he ducks into a compartment and forcefully embraces Pamela, faking an intimacy that results in a passionate kiss. Later, Hannay will also convince the innkeeper's wife that he and Pamela, chained at the wrist, are actually an eloping couple so much in love that they cannot bear being apart from each other.

The milkman's offer of protection for Hannay in exchange for a sexual secret is a perfect inversion of the protection held out by Strether to Chad in *The Ambassadors*, when Strether offers Chad immunity from his family's accusations based on the older man's acceptance of the liaison with Marie de Vionnet as one above reproach. An important difference between the two situations, though, is that unlike the characters in Hitchcock's thriller, who are driven by the plot to seek out secrets, Strether, despite his commission, seems intent on avoiding the knowledge that all but stares him in the face. As Little Bilham remarks to Strether on the topic of his chosen obtuseness, "you're not a person to whom it's easy to tell things you don't want to know" (1903, 1994: 123). Conscious as he is of keeping watch over Chad, Strether wishes to discriminate between the kind of close observation he undertakes on behalf of Mrs. Newsome, and his own "straight" social interaction. The narrator tells us, for example, "It hadn't at any rate been in the least his idea to spy on Chad's proper freedom" (128). Rather than demonstrate the consummate ability of the personal tactician to nourish his suspicions, or plan his moves ahead of time, Strether presents himself as the opposite sort of character to Maria Gostrey: "I never think a step further than I'm obligated to" (326).

Though Hannay's impersonations are not of the same order as Chad Newsome's personal transformation—we cannot say they have made Hannay better than he was before, though they have certainly brought his resourceful capacities to the fore—they have allowed him to escape enemies and situations he still does not completely comprehend. Like Strether, he moves through "a maze of mystic closed allusions" (165). And his disguises do not expose someone else to serious or lasting harm, until he reaches the isolated farm and meets the young and wistful crofter's wife, Margaret. In these scenes, Hannay pretends to be a mechanic looking for work. Margaret soon realizes who he really is, and her silent communication with Hannay over dinner is witnessed by her husband, John. On a pretext, John leaves the house, only to stand outside and spy on the couple through the window. They are engaged in a passionate conversation, leaning over the table toward each other, which he interprets as a lovers' exchange. After returning to the house, John agrees to hide Hannay from the approaching police, but Margaret doesn't trust him and, in a private moment, urges Hannay to flee. As she helps Hannay escape, handing him her husband's best coat, he asks her name, and kisses her good-bye while promising never to forget her. Margaret's own awakened longing for something other than the oppressive coupling that defines her life is apparent in the way she shuts the door, and in her beautiful sorrow-filled face that lingers in the frame as the shot fades. She has reassured Hannay that she will not be in danger for what she has done, that John will do no more than pray over her. But in a later scene of offscreen confrontation between them, the slap we hear but do not see, followed by Margaret's cry of pain, announces the start of an even harsher marital regime. Or perhaps, as Rothman suggests, Margaret has suffered this violence throughout her marriage and has lied to Hannay to protect him from full knowledge of her situation.

If there is something of Chad in Hannay, then there is certainly something of Marie de Vionnet in Margaret. Margaret's appeal, to Hannay and to the viewer, is as poignant as that of Marie de Vionnet to Lambert Strether, who, learning of her wretched marriage to a "brute," an "impertinent reprobate," responds to her sadness, "her beautiful suppliant eyes" (1903, 1994: 147). Marie instantly becomes for Strether "the poor lady" because "clearly she had some trouble" (148). He notes that somehow, "she made their encounter a relation," and concludes that "her trouble was deep" (148). At the end of this interview, Strether vows to "save" Marie de Vionnet if he can, unaware at the time that what menaces her is not the disapproval of Woollett but Chad's reversion to type. Strether indeed keeps his promise, which is more than Hannay, noticing the kind but not the degree of Margaret's distress, and preoccupied by his own predicament, offers her. Chad, declares Strether in *The Ambassadors*, would be a "brute . . . a criminal of the deepest dye" if he left Marie de Vionnet after all she has done for him, and Hannay's departure after all Margaret has done for him is in some sense a moral failure not unlike

Chad's own. Writing of this scene in his book on Hitchcock, Brill contends that it "underlines a theme that runs throughout the film from the death of the woman spy in the opening movement to the kicking chorus line of the last shot: the equivocal status of many women and their intermittent brutalization by men" (39). The corrosive effect of this theme, Brill continues, is to present the outlines of a world "in which love and forgiveness between men and women do not exist" (39), a world that we can recognize as that of *The Ambassadors*.

The shot of the jealous crofter spying on what he mistakenly believes to be the germination of infidelity calls to mind the climactic scene in *The Ambassadors* in which Strether finds himself an unintentional witness to a situation in which adultery is confirmed. In each case, communication between the internal pair—the ones in the boat drifting down the river, and the ones in the isolated farm kitchen—is instant and deep. Hannay and Margaret have just met, but their sympathetic responses to each other are immediate and genuine. Unlike Pamela, Margaret trusts Hannay; her belief in him transcends her knowledge of his criminal guilt or innocence, making it beside the point of their connection. We could imagine her saying to Hannay, as Marie de Vionnet says to Strether, as he readies himself to take leave of her in the antechamber of her "noble old apartment," "*You* would have been a friend" (1903, 1994: 238–39). As he watches Chad and Mme de Vionnet on the river, before he even recognizes them, Strether understands that they are "expert, familiar, frequent—that this wouldn't at all events be the first time" (309). An instant later he identifies them and realizes that they are "intensely debating . . . the risk of betrayal" (310). Surely this is also what the crofter believes he is seeing as he watches Margaret and Hannay through the window.

Such examples illustrate the kinds of harm that attend interactions in these two fictional worlds, one of outright spies and the other of those who work, as Marie de Vionnet puts it, *en dessous*. In Hitchcock the dangers usually manifest themselves in physical damage rather than in the less traceable injuries to psyche and spirit that James's people endure. Personal relations are in each text fraught with tension as characters try to decipher incomplete communications and witness ambiguous exchanges, deciding as they watch and listen who is safe, who is not, and whose side they are on. Above all, they dread exposure. Though James's characters are not visibly armed, their diplomatic intercourse partakes of sharp encounters, registered internally as the narrator reports the current of their unspoken thoughts and feelings. These are filled with alarms and warnings, the fear of being "given up" and handed over, of hearing one's doom sounded, of being "pulled down" by a word or a gesture from someone hitherto relied on as safe. Strether, walking into Sarah Pocock's hotel room, can thus sense his ruin in Marie de Vionnet's tone of voice and in a few moments feel himself climbing, as he thinks, into the small rocking boat of her "situation," thereby surrendering to Sarah's suspicion of him as having gone over to the other side (see Figure 2.3). In the treacherous landscapes of espionage and diplomacy, securing the trust and belief of others is essential to survival. In films like *The 39 Steps*, this theme expresses itself through the relationship between

FIGURE 2.3 In the treacherous landscapes of espionage and diplomacy, securing the trust of others is essential to survival.

the central couple of the film and what Brill describes as the dependence of Hitchcock's heroes "upon the heroines' belief in their innocence" (63). For Hannay, the challenge is to convince Pamela that he is telling the truth about the spy ring. When he first happens upon Pamela in the train compartment and enlists her in his deception, he is incensed that she does not take him at face value, as it were, as if his kiss alone, and its power to loosen her grip on her glasses, should vouch for his honesty. Strether's position is more complicated. Marie de Vionnet must convince him to believe in her "sublimity" so that the question of her and Chad's sexual innocence will not count with him against them. Strether in his turn attempts to convince Mrs. Newsome, the Pococks, and Waymarsh to believe in the new magnificence of Chad and in the trustworthiness of the woman responsible for it. For all his efforts, he ends up himself a subject of surveillance, "unjustly suspected in Woollett" (305). These persuasive tasks enlist characters in the observation of others and in the representations of motives and actions in ways consonant with their joining the "chain of ambassadors" (Rivkin 1986: 820). Remembering the jealous farm husband at the window, Pamela overhearing the conversation that changes her view of Hannay, Waymarsh claiming to know nothing of Mrs. Newsome's cables, and Strether realizing that Sarah Pocock has been sent out, not to fetch Chad, but to observe *him*, we can see as well the proliferation of a chain of spies. The differences between the two roles—one emphasizing the cloaked observation of putative truth and the other stressing the public representation of politically advantageous "truth"—collapse.

"A man in trouble must be possessed somehow of a woman" says Marie de Vionnet to Strether in Book Seventh, "if she doesn't come in one way she comes in another" (1903, 1994: 179). Strether and Hannay, both men in trouble, are possessed of their share of women, and it is through the variety of these connections that each comes to realize of what he is capable. Both men face women who are, in more or less literal senses, afraid for their lives, and both honor the commitments they have made to see things through to the end. But neither could be said to have succeeded in their attempts at rescue. Hannay exposes the spymaster and brings a halt to the plot to export military secrets, but he is helpless to protect Annabella or to forestall the murder of poor Mr. Memory. Neither does he rescue Pamela. He escapes the clutches of the criminals and of necessity takes Pamela with him, but is she who works her own way out of the handcuffs. Strether, for all his efforts, fails in his first mission and, having adopted a new one, cannot save Marie de Vionnet from Chad.

Variations of homelessness and attachment shade the conclusions of both works. Early in the novel, Strether refers to "the general safety of being anchored by a strong chain," referring to the security Woollett represents for Chad's future. He is at first unaware of how completely he himself is bound by the same invisible links, but in time dispossession becomes his practice. At the novel's conclusion, he faces the fullness of his "break" as he considers Maria Gostrey's question "To what do you go home?" (346), which echoes Marie de Vionnet's earlier "Where *is* your home?" (323). Strether will return to Woollett, but not in the same way, and not as the same man he was when he left it. As he himself puts it, he now *sees* what he did not before; he is a man who knows too much.

The image of Richard and Pamela handcuffed together and stumbling across the moors of Scotland asserts itself again here. Made complicit by proximity, they are the emblem of an irritated though genuinely "virtuous attachment" that eventually leads to reconciliation, and, perhaps, even to love, though as with Strether, Hannay and Pamela are "independent of any home at all" (Leitch 1991, 121). The final shots of Hitchcock's film are striking. We watch from the side of the stage that we have faced up to now. Mr. Memory slowly collapses, reciting his final secret, and Hannay and Pamela move to stand in front of us, backs to the camera so that we watch them covertly, from behind. The handcuff dangles from Hannay's wrist as he moves surreptitiously to take possession of the woman, to get, unlike Strether, something out of the affair for himself. He is, after all, only Hannay. But in the final shot of Hannay reaching out to grasp Pamela's hand behind the backs of the authorities bending over the dead body of Mr. Memory, a garish line of chorus girls kicking their way across the stage to the right, there is enough Jamesian ambiguity to suggest that having done its work in solving a particular mystery, this connection will no more outlast its moment than does the one between Strether and Maria Gostrey. The damage done to trust by the arts of diplomacy and espionage threatens the integrity of all intimacies, an insight accepted by Strether, but resisted by Hannay, in their respective final gestures.

Hannay's insistent clutch at Pamela's hand in the closing moments of the film seems, despite the appearance of romantic certitude, an imitation of real choice.

There is an air of mere propinquity about their clasped hands. Hannay seems drawn to Pamela because of their shared ordeal, rather than because of some more heartfelt connection, such as the one he forged so quickly with Margaret, the crofter's wife. And, in what looks like the mistake of confusing his feelings for Pamela with the intensity of their experience together, he is poised to make the kind of emotional error so common to James's youthful protagonists, who bond, like Isabel Archer, with bearers of experience or like Christopher Newman, with figures of romantic circumstance. It is also a moment in which we see Hannay in quite a different light. Instead of the good-natured puzzlement and physical confidence that has attended him to this point in the film, there is real need as he reaches for Pamela. He seems to require steadying. The various identities he has claimed and then cast aside as contingencies required sat more lightly on him than does his last appearance here as a vulnerable man seized by something he wants to believe is love, but which may be only desperation.

Not so Lambert Strether. Having botched his ambassadorial mission and misread the gleaming surface of Chad Newsome for something more substantial, Strether has traveled in the opposite direction from Hannay. Strether started out accepting the imposed verities of Woollett but concludes by choosing a life without certainty, free of his damaging dependency on the moral order of the Newsomes. And though the chance of a life with Maria Gostrey offers him one last possibility to surrender to what seems like narrative inevitability, Strether quietly loosens the grip of the romantic plot upon him, ending the novel in possession—for perhaps the first in a very long time—of himself.

3

Henry James and Alfred Hitchcock after the American Century

CIRCULATION AND NONRETURN IN *THE AMERICAN SCENE* AND *STRANGERS ON A TRAIN*

Brian T. Edwards

In a 1915 essay "The Founding of *The Nation*," published on the magazine's fiftieth anniversary, Henry James focuses briefly on the difficulty of recall. James, writing at the age of seventy-two, associates this challenge, not with his advanced age, but rather with a change in historical episteme: "My difficulty comes from the sense that to turn from our distracted world of today to the world of the questions surrounding, even with their then so great bustle of responsibility, the cradle of the most promising scion of the newspaper stock as that stock had rooted itself in American soil, is to sink into a social lap of such soft, sweet material as to suggest comparatively a general beatific state" (1915, 1956: 284). The observation echoes a strand that appears too in the Preface to *The American Scene* (1907), and elsewhere in his late fiction, wherein James derives a "freshness of eye" from the changes to the United States in his absence (1907, 1994: 3).

The 1915 essay, not much read these days, is the concluding gesture in Leon Edel's 1956 *The American Essays of Henry James*, bringing it to a greater readership at the moment of American Studies' consolidation. For Edel, one of the key figures in that process, the connections between these essays and James's fiction are "not difficult to relate." Further:

> The work of Henry James is a record of innocence either wholly untouched by Europe or corrupted by it. Otherwise expressed, it becomes the tragedy of un[a]wareness. It expresses to the full the novelist's brooding sense of what it meant to be an American, creator of a New World that in the fullness of time would have to meet and face the Old. It is this understanding of the destiny of America, its future role as a nation among nations, which gives Henry James's writings about his own country and its people a singular relevance today. . . . [T] his mind, and the pen it guided, were ever concerned with the American consciousness and the American character. (xvi–xvii)

This is a familiar account of James's work. But James is revealing precisely the opposite of what Edel claims him to be arguing, instead sloughing off an American consciousness. Edel's characterization of this as an "American essay"—with the concomitant definition of America as marked by "innocence"—is of course part of the edifice that the early Cold War establishment of American Studies constructed to delimit and frame what I call a vernacular canon. The disruption of the vernacular tradition of American Studies—its organization of the canon and its influential method of reading—is an imperative if we are finally to move beyond the exceptionalism that has limited the field. It seems then all the more important to attend anew to James's point in this occasional essay.

James reflects on what his own residence outside "the nation" means for his writing for *The Nation:*

> Though I suppose I should have liked regularly to correspond from London, nothing came of that but three or four pious efforts which broke down under the appearance that people liked most to hear of what I could least, of what in fact nothing would have induced me to, write about. What I could write about they seemed, on the other hand, to view askance; on any complete lapse of which tendency in them I must not now, however, too much presume. (James 1915, 1956: 288)

This *multilateral consciousness* of the late James is precisely what Edel is working so hard to reincorporate in his critical introduction. It appears again in *The American Scene*'s Preface, where James's "great advantage" of perception is the commingling of the "freshness of eye"—"almost as 'fresh' as an inquiring stranger"—with the acuteness of "an initiated native" (1907, 1994: 3). This James of *nonreturn* is what my essay will attempt to identify.

After the American Century

Recently, Dilip Gaonkar and I (2010) have argued for a reading strategy—for works that emerge from or intersect with the United States—disencumbered of American Studies' practices that developed with the "American Century."[1] We argue that the dominant strand of American Studies emerged as a "vernacular" tradition, within which the pre-World War II conception of American "unity in diversity" (the argument of Vernon Parrington's foundational *Main Currents in American Thought* [1927]) was reified as a method and an archive. This vernacular tradition would in turn yield significant insight into the interplay of United States cultural production and material histories, but also pervasive blindness to multilateral strands present in many and manifold "American" works. American Studies has tended to reincorporate precisely those modes of reading that would profoundly challenge its own imperative to find unity in diversity, such as, most recently, diaspora studies and accounts of the sociocultural experience of globalization. What is needed is a reading strategy that is not beholden to the "American Century," one that does not see the United States as anchor but rather as node in a variety of intersecting circulatory matrices. So doing means considering the "specter" of America as it finds its way via its fragments in multiple locations and with unexpected meanings, disaggregated from the powerful pull of exceptionalism.

Turning to hypercanonical figures such as Henry James and Alfred Hitchcock might seem surprising. There remains, however, much work to be done in rereading those figures who emerged powerfully within Americanist practice—especially at its vernacular center. To be sure, James and Hitchcock have long seemed to sit particularly uneasily within American Studies, not only because both lived apart from their homelands and changed or renounced their nationalities (provoking critical anxiety and machinations), but also, and more importantly, because both in their later work were increasingly interested in fragments and in the question of perspective, particularly as regards the subject of the nation itself.

In the late short story "Crapy Cornelia" (1909), the disjuncture at the center of the fiction—that of the unbridgeable distance between the "old" New York recalled by James's alterego White-Mason, back in New York after two decades abroad, and that of the nouveau riche widow Mrs. Worthingham—is figured by a black hat. More than the "crapy" self-denial of old Cornelia's clothing against the brilliance of the stylish widow, it is the figure of the occlusion of sight. James notably alludes to a new technology for looking in order to describe the fracturing of perspective itself evoked by Cornelia's almost anachronistic clothing. The hat is "an ornament . . . that grew and grew, that came nearer and nearer, while it met his eyes, after the manner of images in the cinematograph. It had presently loomed so large that he saw nothing else" (James 1909, 1972: 199–200).[2] That the lack of continuity between Cornelia and Mrs. Worthingham, and the generations and consciousnesses they stand for, is imagined as a visual blockage—here the close-up that occludes all vision and elsewhere in the story "the passage from a shelter to a blinding light" without "goggles—alerts us to the shards associated with James's discovery of the nonreturn of the diasporic American (White-Mason, here, but James himself in *The American Scene* and "The Founding of *The Nation*").

The cinematic analogy in James's description of Cornelia's black hat is itself suggestive.[3] One of the promises of juxtaposing James and Hitchcock is that a Jamesian Hitchcock might emerge, loosened from the interpretive problem of nationality, and new strands of meaning could in turn be located in Hitchcock's most elusive film texts.

Hitchcock's films of the 1950s and early 1960s are often read in their Cold War "context," as complex formulations of the problems of binaries, of a (de) colonized consciousness, and as somehow reflective of the filmmaker's movement from the United Kingdom to the United States coincident with the shift of geopolitical power from the former British Empire to the post-World War II United States. A *Jamesian* Hitchcock suggests that James's own late obsession with abstracted images, objects or "things" in circulation, and the author's anguish at the impossibility of locating fixity beneath the occluding shroud of noise and public spectacle seem to prefigure or be *taken up* in Hitchcock. Indeed, *Strangers on a Train* (1951), *Dial "M" for Murder* (1954), *Rear Window* (1954), *The Man Who Knew Too Much* (1956), *North by Northwest* (1959), and *The Birds* (1963) are in various ways obsessed with that which signifies multiply even in its silence or occlusion. The mystery of "the massing" of the birds in *The Birds,* or the multiple meanings of "Ambrose Chap(p)el(l)" and "Arab talk" in *The Man Who Knew Too Much,*[4] or the true identity of the false George Kaplan in *North by Northwest*—in all cases, repetition or multiplication leads to non-sense as well as a superfluity of sense, as if the two were the same or interrelated. This seems a recurring paradigm, too, within *The American Scene*—Hitchcock's James—a key text for engaging a James "after the American century." Furthermore, James's abstraction of perspective—the turning of the object such that the thing itself recedes and the turning emerges—is in this light the harbinger not quite of postmodernism, but of cultures of circulation.

America as "Node": Cultures of Circulation

The late James of "The Founding of *The Nation*," *The American Scene,* and stories such as "The Jolly Corner" (1908) and "Crapy Cornelia" and the Hitchcock of the 1950s and early 60s are opened up by attention to what Benjamin Lee and Edward LiPuma (2002) have termed "cultures of circulation."[5] Lee and LiPuma argue that scholarship tends to see "meaning and interpretation" as "key problems for social and cultural analysis." But now, the "category of *culture*" is trying to catch up to the economic processes that have changed so quickly with the advent of circulation-based capitalism: "[C]irculation is a cultural process with its own forms of abstraction, evaluation, and constraint, which are created by the interactions between specific types of circulating forms and the interpretive communities built around them" (192).

I suggest that the *movement* at the center of *The American Scene* and *Strangers on a Train* is a key overlooked aspect of the texts' *meaning*. It is notable that the Pullman car is central to *The American Scene* and *Strangers on a Train*. The Pullman car is the instrument, venue, and perspectival point from which these authors' thinking about circulation emanates. James locates many such figures—Cornelia's hat, the blocked "aperture" of the closed door at the emptied ancestral home in "The Jolly Corner"—frequently choosing metaphors that allude to modern technologies of looking (the train window, the cinema, the photographic aperture). For James, "the total image" is deferred in the concluding chapter to *The American Scene* by the rapid movement of the Pullman car carrying James to Florida. This is not an essay about the train or the aperture, per se, but rather the anguish about the fixity—"some massive monument covered still"—that reveals itself to James as deferred once movement becomes the figure itself.

"Some Massive Monument Covered Still": James's *The American Scene*

In "The Jolly Corner," the specter of nonreturn becomes briefly visible. The "idea of a return" haunts Spencer Brydon, thirty-three years absent from New York. Its impossibility is figured by "his opening a door behind which he would have made sure of finding nothing, a door into a room shuttered and void" (James 1908, 1945: 612, 608). The void behind that door, the nothing that can be found once one has "kept it up, so, 'over there,' from that day to this" (613), transmogrifies into a haunting "*alter ego*" (614), an "opposed projection" (627) of himself that will confront Brydon as the "prodigy of a personal presence" (633). To confront this terror becomes the very reason for the return to New York at the age of fifty-six:

> He had come back, yes—come back from further away than any man but himself had ever traveled; but it was strange how with this sense what he had come back *to* seemed really the great thing, and as if his prodigious journey had been all for the sake of it. Slowly but surely his consciousness grew, his vision of his state thus completing itself: he had been miraculously *carried* back—lifted and carefully borne as from where he had been picked up, the uttermost end of an interminable grey passage. Even with this he was suffered to rest, and what had now brought him to knowledge was the break in the long mild motion. (636)

This consciousness, however, is not after all a return, but rather, as the story's concluding line suggests, a final wrenching apart of the two Spencer Brydons. "'And he isn't—no, he isn't—you!'" (641). Alice Staverton says to Brydon, releasing him from the possibility of return itself. If the Spencer Brydon who remained in New York is not the Spencer Brydon who flirts with the "idea of a return," the psychic irresolution of the ghost story only makes sense by considering the specter of nonreturn as its outcome.

Similarly, in "Crapy Cornelia" an apparent return to New York by a long absent New Yorker leads to a disconnection of the before and the after. Here, White-Mason encounters Cornelia Rasch and her obscuring black hat just as he is on the verge of suturing the old White-Mason of the left-behind New York with the new "things" of Mrs. Worthingham, associated with the modern New York of fifty-story skyscrapers. But Cornelia's presence at Mrs. Worthingham's apartments disrupts this possibility and diverts the movement of the story. "'It must have been to help me you've come back,'" White-Mason suggests to Cornelia (1909, 1972: 219). While Cornelia offers to help White-Mason by encouraging him to make his affections for Mrs. Worthingham known, she ultimately helps him *not* to bridge that gap, not to conjoin the before and the after. And like Alice Staverton in "The Jolly Corner," Cornelia in the story that bears her name allows for the multilateral consciousness of the diasporic Jamesian character to remain unsutured. Again this gap is figured through a visual technology—two photographs of the same forgotten individual (White-Mason's former lover, from the "old" days): two variants that in their subtle differences suggest the prism through which memory must be broken into shards. When Cornelia Rasch and White-Mason agree to exchange their photographs of the late Mary Cardew, the subtle shift in perspective between the two variations speaks "across the years, straight into [his eyes]" (1909, 1972: 220).

It is in this context that we may now return to the lessons of *The American Scene*. When James finds himself aboard yet another train, speeding toward Palm Beach, Florida, the cinematic perspective[6] offered by the movement is given more attention than anything else: "It is the penalty of the state of receiving too many impressions of too many things that when the question arises of giving some account of these a small sharp anguish attends the act of selection and the necessity of omission" (1907, 1994: 311). James here cannot, or does not, focus on "objects" but, rather, on those inanimate "things" and reflections.[7] The perspective from the window of the moving Pullman car recasts James's vision on the very question of the now disappeared nation itself.

Somewhere between Charleston, South Carolina, and Florida is a spectral presence—an "effect" (317): America itself. The American girl, or rather "the effect of the American girl as encountered in the great glare of her publicity, her uncorrrected, unrelated state," speaks to him: "'Ah, once place me and you'll see,'" the specter says to the author, somewhere and everywhere in this long book without dialogue. If we think back as far as *Daisy Miller* (1878), we may have a sense of how this "unrelated state" has now fully detached from national referents. Daisy Miller is no longer an expatriate, far afield, but she is here uncorrected, illegible, and unseeable. James figures this remarkably in a particularly long and multiprismatic sentence, the last few clauses of which I quote:

> . . . I did no more, at the moment, than all pensively suffer it again to show me the American social order in the guise of a great blank unnatural mother, a compound of all the recreant individuals misfitted with the name, whose ear the mystic plaint seemed never to penetrate, and whose large unseeing complacency suggested some massive monument covered still with the thick cloth that precedes a public unveiling. We wonder at the hidden marble or bronze; we suppose, under the cloth, some attitude or expression appropriate to the image; but as the removal of the cloth is perpetually postponed the character never emerges. (1907, 1994: 318)

Perpetually postponed, like "some massive monument covered still," the figure of the nation is ever deferred. James does not return, or rather is not a figure of return.

"Algebraic figures?": Hitchcock's *Strangers on a Train*

Speaking with Francois Truffaut (1967), Hitchcock readily admitted to the flaws in *Strangers on a Train*: "the ineffectiveness of the two main actors and the weakness of the final script" (he means the dialogue) (Truffaut 165). Hitchcock goes on: "The great problem with this type of picture, you see, is that your main characters sometimes tend to become mere figures" (165). Truffaut, who has already stated that he is fascinated by "the bold manipulation of time, the way in which it's contracted and dilated" in the film (164), follows up with a provocative question: "Algebraic figures?" Truffaut's interest in the algebraic quality of the film relies precisely on the weakness of the characterization and the acting: "*Strangers* is actually mapped out like a diagram. This degree of stylization is so exciting to the mind and to the eye that it's fascinating even to a mass audience" (165). The flaws may provide an opening to something different about the film.

Hitchcock and Truffaut move on to discuss the early shot of "the separating rails" on the tracks of Washington D.C.'s Union Station and how they mirror the collision of the two men's feet that opens the film (see Figure 3.1). "Isn't it a fascinating design?" Hitchcock asks. "One could study it forever" (164). This seems to be Hitchcock's answer to Truffaut's question, substituting trigonometry for algebra. It is an intriguing parlay that hints at this film's obsessions and techniques. The "social life of things" in *Strangers on a Train* (e.g., the pair of eyeglasses that both Miriam (Kasey Rogers), Guy's (Farley Granger) estranged wife, and Barbara (Patricia Hitchcock), his soon to be sister-in-law, wear), the association of doubling and crossed paths with motive-free (thus perfect) murder, and the volleying of the tennis ball itself (in one of the most famous shots of the film) suggest, particularly in the light of James, a rich meditation on circulation. *Strangers on a Train* is obsessed with these objects, which seem to adhere with "thingness" in the Jamesian sense as

FIGURE 3.1 The abstract image of train tracks.

they mediate and collapse the space between individuals and consciousness—that is, these objects and figures are less important as physical objects and more important as stand-ins or prisms through which to view social relationships.[8]

Robert Corber (1999) provides a strong reading of objects in *Strangers on a Train* in the service of an argument about the film's relationship to national questions. Corber historicizes the film's relationship to homosexuality and the national panic of sexuality in McCarthyist America and takes a psychoanalytic approach to the film's scopophilia and self-reflexivity about the gaze. He begins by noting that "the images of the federal government . . . bear no obvious relation to the plot" (100). For Corber, at the heart of the film's choice of setting in Washington, D.C., is, instead, a meditation on the relationship of "the homosexual" and national security. Guy Haines—tennis star with a political future in Washington—travels on his own Oedipal journey within a Lacanian frame. In his dangerous double Bruno Antony (Robert Walker), Guy moves through the "mirror stage"; confronted with the fragmented shards of himself by encountering himself as object—seeing himself in the other (Bruno)—Guy can ultimately consolidate himself as finite.

This is a way for Corber to engage the powerful feminist psychoanalytic readings of Hitchcock's structured gaze and to see how Miriam's challenging sexuality is figured through the most loaded of objects in the film: her eyeglasses, via which the audience sees her murder and through which Miriam sees more than she is seen. Miriam "circulates freely among men" (115) and is thus linked to the camera's own interplay with the glasses. First this is because her glasses operate as a kind of fetish object, and when they are cracked, and carried around by Guy, "they are a kind of trophy or prize . . . [and] the mark of her castration and thus guarantee Guy's totality and coherence" (116). But when Hitchcock moves his camera to show us Miriam's murder via the reflection of her own glasses, in a famous shot, Corber sees this as a moment of self-reflexivity. Corber argues that this exhibits a crisis in the film's system of representation; it is a sign that the film "distrust[s] the logic of its own specular regime" (118). Corber sees the move ultimately as conservative, claiming that Hitchcock attempts to contain the very political and sexual indeterminacy he has discovered. That indeterminacy is signaled by other objects as well: Corber goes on to read the lighter and Bruno's shoes as clues to (homo)sexuality—as style, as objects handed between men, as potential substitutes for physical interaction.

As useful as it is, we can move beyond Corber's psychoanalytic, historicized frame in search of a post-Americanist Hitchcock. It is here that Truffaut's suggestion that the film works algebraically and Hitchcock's trigonometric rejoinder reveal great insight. For if the two principal characters become algebraic substitutes for one another (Guy equals X, and Bruno equals Y, but X = Y), the film's relentless movement through space operates via these substitutions and its continual return back to the same locations. If Bruno = Guy, this is a threatening equation since Bruno follows Guy continually, as stalker, as substitute, forcing Guy into motion. Guy will eventually follow Bruno through the same landscape that we have already watched Bruno traverse (the amusement park where Bruno has murdered Miriam), and the suspense builds as Guy rushes to beat Bruno to precisely the location where Bruno committed the murder, in order to stop him from planting yet another object (a cigarette lighter, inscribed with the pseudo-algebraic formula "A to G"). That this is more than merely a chase scene is indicated by the strange temporal lag that Hitchcock inserts into his screenplay (something missing from Patricia Highsmith's original novel, on which the film was based): a tennis match. Before Guy can race Bruno to the amusement park, he must first win a championship round at Forest Hills, New York. It is precisely here that Truffaut points to the expansion and collapsing of time in the film. And there is a spatial, circulating logic at work as well. As we watch Guy play tennis, we also watch the spectators at the match move their heads back and forth to follow the ball. (Hitchcock draws our attention to the oddity of tennis spectatorship in an earlier famous shot, in which Bruno's head alone is fixed amid a crowd of oscillating heads, figure 3.2.) Spectatorship is doubled here, of course, but tennis spectatorship is also the impediment to the film's forward momentum, the antithesis of train movement.

The film ends in circulation of a different sort: a vortex, a merry-go-round that spins out of control. Or, rather, the suspenseful part of the film ends here (there is a coda). That is, a spiral ends the film that begins and ends (in the coda) on a train hurtling through space, back and forth between New York's Penn Station and Washington's Union Station.

In the film's mysterious and haunting coda, Bruno and Guy's opening shoe bump is doubled. Guy bumps shoes with a priest, who looks up from his paper and asks, as Bruno did, whether Guy is *the* Guy Haines. It might seem that the

FIGURE 3.2 Bruno's head alone is fixed amid a crowd of oscillating heads.

circuit is going to repeat all over again. For Corber, the importance of this moment is that Guy's Oedipal journey has been resolved, though a hint of "homosexual menace" remains (1999, 116).

But the priest does something more than reference the "institution that sanctions monogamous heterosexuality," as Corber would have it (116). The priest also signals Hitchcock's very next film, *I Confess* (1953), in which Montgomery Clift would play a priest who receives the confession of a murderer. The priest on the train is a hint by the filmmaker who constantly moved back and forth between subject and object of his camera—as most powerfully seen in his own cameo appearances in his films—that the future of his filmmaking was now visible in the present, though no one might yet know as much.

As Truffaut notes, *I Confess* would be something of a failure, but one of the best things about it is "the way Montgomery Clift is always seen walking; it's a forward motion that shapes the whole film" (Truffaut 1967, 171). Truffaut is fascinated by a moment when Clift leaves the courtroom, surrounded by a crowd, when a "fat and repulsive woman eating an apple" looks on the scene with "malevolent curiosity" (173). Hitchcock jumps in: "I especially worked that woman in there; I even showed her how to eat that apple" (173). In the interview, Truffaut and Hitchcock agree that this is part of the "whole tapestry" of a film (the word is Hitchcock's), but the apple, too, exists in its own temporal register: "That's why, when these films are reissued several years later, they stand up so well; they're never out of date" (173).

There's no explanation for how the inclusion of the apple keeps the film from being out of date. But we may recognize that this *thing*—the apple, which here mediates the relationship between the crowd of onlookers gawking at Clift as he leaves the courtroom and allows Hitchcock to make one of his signature critiques of the horrors of the legal process itself—operates in its own temporal register, inside and outside of the time of the film.[9]

Thus, the presence of the priest at the end of *Strangers on a Train* suggests the intrusion of the future (Hitchcock's next film) and is akin to Giorgio Agamben's sense of the potentiality of the work of art, discovering in its own fragments the work of art it might become. Hitchcock's hint about the future of his work is neither algebraic nor trigonometric, nor even fractal.[10] Rather, it suggests affiliations outside the work of art (or literature) read merely for its discrete meaning, whether that meaning is historicized or disciplined. It is Hitchcock's gesture outside his own film toward nonreturn.

Brought together, and considered in light of their doubled transnational movement, James and Hitchcock suggest a *multilateral* consciousness that eludes the logic of the "American Century" and its coincident forms of readings.[11] In *The American Scene,* James discovers or reveals that the diasporic figure cannot—or can choose not to—return home. This Jamesian lesson resists the provincializing tendencies of American Studies, which negotiates challenges to its reading practice by reincorporating the diasporic subject as always capable of return, with the national frame reasserting its powerful center of gravity. The ways in which James reveals otherwise, his concatenation of arguments and images, in turn provoke a new reading of Hitchcock. The primary lens through which to discover this aspect of James is *circulation*, as that which James is doing (both as diasporic subject and as traveling subject), as a technology of looking, and as the means by which we might link James and Hitchcock.

4

Colonial Discourse and the Unheard Other in *Washington Square* and *The Man Who Knew Too Much*

Alan Nadel

The ambiguous title of Hitchcock's *The Man Who Knew Too Much* (1956) suggests what the film will confirm: the epithet does not mean what it sounds like it means. The man, in fact, did not know much; rather, he knew a little, which was more than was good for him. Nor, in James's *Washington Square* (1881), is Catherine Sloper as she sounds, at least not what she sounds like to her father, Dr. Sloper, a man who similarly knows too much, that is, supposes too much about what he does not know. This simple confluence—two works in which men mistake what something sounds like for what it is—raises, in the hands of James and Hitchcock, an array of complicated questions about knowledge, authority, and gender, questions, I will try to show, that implicitly in James and explicitly in Hitchcock link these misperceptions to the kinds of gendered subordination that characterize colonialism.

The Man Who Knew Too Much revolves around two sounds unintelligible on the film's soundtrack, the message whispered by the dying Louis Bernard (Daniel Gelin) into the ear of Dr. Ben McKenna (James Stewart), and the silenced singing voice of McKenna's wife, Jo (Doris Day), formerly an internationally renowned performer. Focusing on the second of these sounds, Robert Corber (1993) makes clear that the treatment of the woman's voice is crucial to Alfred Hitchcock's 1956 remake of *The Man Who Knew Too Much*, as it foregrounds "the acoustic dimension of the bond between mother and child" (152). It thus returns the woman, Jo McKenna (née Conway) to the domestic sphere, the place where, Corber stresses, her husband had consistently sought to relegate her. Expanding on Corber, Brian Edwards (2005) astutely notes that the film exceeds the issue of voice, entailing an array of acoustic relations, in that "*The Man Who Knew Too Much* is obsessed with the ambiguities of language—with homonyms, with slang expressions, with translation, with foreign language beyond translation, with dialects—and more generally with sound and noise as they relate to knowledge" (185).

Of the critics who have written on the film, Edwards is most attentive to the crucial homophone, "Ambrose Chappell/Ambrose Chapel," which he sees as more than a plot device or a bit of Hitchcockian wit. Rather, it indicates a breakdown in the auditory information system that permits the subordination of North Africa (or, by extension, the colonized world) to the desires of an American imaginary. The film's acoustic relations make clear, in other words, the United States's obtuse complicity with European colonial interests in the Cold War period. The film's homophones thus call attention to the general practice by which comprehension results from not hearing alternative meanings. Thus, they emphasize a systematic process of subordination endemic to colonialism, as well as—Corber's point—to American Cold War gender relations.

To some degree, Corber could be talking about James's *Washington Square,* a novel in which homophones underscore the idea that Dr. Sloper's beliefs about his daughter rely on his delimiting her possible meanings. The novel's crucial issue, accentuating the general scope of Sloper's paternity as a widower raising his sole surviving child, is whether Catherine will choose to marry her first suitor, Morris Townsend, an attractive ne'er-do-well drawn, at least in part, to the shy, somewhat overweight Catherine because of her potential inheritance. Rather than forbid the marriage, Sloper withholds approval, thereby constructing a contest between himself and Morris for Catherine's allegiance. Delighting in being more clever than either she or Morris, Sloper approaches that contest with self-confidence and amusement. His initial pleasure, however, gradually morphs into resentment as he fails to evoke from Catherine the assurances he desires, and, more significantly, as he allows the game to test definitively Catherine's affection for him.

In this context, much has been made of the silences in *Washington Square* as expressions of power, control, and resistance.[1] Melissa Valiska Gregory (2004) points out, furthermore, that if "withholding speech . . . is the ultimate power . . . obvious displays of linguistic prowess function by contrast as crude weapons, almost as brutally as physical domination" (152). But equally important in the novel are the silences that result from disallowing possible meanings in the speech of the other. Although Sloper may finally admit that his test fails (meaning that Catherine fails his test), he never comprehends his culpability in that failure, the direct function of his promoting this second kind of silence. Sloper silences Catherine, in other words, by refusing to recognize what she means. His expectations, in effect, preclude any possibility that Catherine will show affection in terms they both can recognize. Sloper cannot see that the way Catherine expresses her determination to marry Morris demonstrates the very affection for her father that he desires. If "it had become vivid to [Catherine] that there was great excitement in trying to become a good daughter" (1881, 1985: 79), Sloper can perceive neither Catherine's fidelity, nor his role in rendering it obtuse. Missing Catherine's intention when she promises, "If I don't marry before your death, I will not after" (97), he responds, "Do you mean that for an impertinence?" (97).

Artists pervasively concerned with the relationship between interpretation and perception, both James in *Washington Square* and Hitchcock in *The Man Who Knew Too Much*, use homophones to foreground this issue. Juxtaposing the two works, therefore, may show how suppressing the meanings of the Other reflects the oppressive paternalism of Victorian and of Cold War neo-Victorian America. Hitchcock's resituating the initial episodes of his film from the 1934 version's Switzerland to Morocco (in 1955 still a French colony) suggests, as well, I believe, how the discursive practice of suppressing alternative meanings typifies the relationship between colonialist and colonized subject. Finally, thinking about how Dr. Sloper attends to Catherine and how Dr. McKenna attends to Jo, in conjunction with the way people attend to the use of homophones and, as well, to the demands of a film soundtrack, may indicate something structural about the power relations in which we participate when we assume—however tentatively—the role of moviegoer, especially when watching films in the mainstream Hollywood style.

Fidelity

Film theory helps us understand the important role sound plays in creating knowledge and distributing power in James's novel and Hitchcock's film because a film soundtrack participates in the system of cinematic representation that also silences the meanings, rather than the voice, of the other.[2] If homophones make more apparent a general principle of language—to construe one meaning, we must suppress other possibilities—, with a film soundtrack we must more aggressively deny what we hear in order to privilege what we see.[3] This is because the film soundtrack provides an independent set of auditory information that shapes, anticipates, comments upon, interprets, or expands the realm of the visual information, in conjunction with which our of knowledge of the film world emerges.

"If the viewer takes the sound to be coming from its source in the diegetic world of the film," David Bordwell (2008) explains, "then it is faithful, regardless of its actual source in production." The meaning that film sound produces, in other words, comes not from external reality, but rather from a resemblance, a structured misprision, because the audience is really hearing two things: the perceived sound—for example, an egg frying—and the material that produced that sound—perhaps cellophane being crinkled. With a statement that might echo or at least intrigue James, Bordwell concludes that "fidelity is thus purely a matter of expectation" (278). From this perspective, film sound requires the same kind of interpretation as do homophones, that is, the negotiation of two things with different meanings, which sound alike.

This problem of fidelity—things might not be as they sound—is extensively thematized in *Washington Square*, where each of the characters constructs a test of fidelity based on an expectation of what resembles it. To Catherine's aunt, Mrs. Penniman, Morris Townsend sounds like the earnest hero of a romance novel; hence, her own conception of the romance between Morris and Catherine:

> Mrs. Penniman took too much satisfaction in the sentimental shadows of this little drama to have, for the moment, any great interest in dissipating them. She wished the plot to thicken, and the advice that she gave to her niece tended, in her own imagination, to produce that result. (1881, 1985: 123)

From this perspective, she consistently mistakes Morris's behavior, inferring Morris's fidelity even in his planned break with Catherine: "Ah but you must have your last parting!" urged [Mrs. Penniman], in whose imagination the idea of last partings occupied a place inferior in dignity only to that of first meetings" (148).

More significantly, Catherine and her father attempt to assess Morris's fidelity to the role of faithful lover, gauging his intentions by the extent to which his actions resemble their specific expectations. In trying to ascertain what actually produces Morris's effects and affects, Sloper seeks exactly what, under Bordwell's definition, sound fidelity must suppress: to presume we hear thunder, we must not see the wobbling metal sheet. We must not summon the second component of the homophone. Sloper concludes that what sounds like Morris's affection is actually selfishness, at the same time failing to recognize that a similar disparity between production and affect could describe the fidelity of his own affection for Catherine. Invested in testing Catherine's fidelity to him, Sloper selfishly puts his experiment ahead of his daughter, and that affect convinces Catherine that he does not like her, not simply that he does not like losing.

As the novel progresses, Sloper, in fact, becomes more obsessively concerned with victory or, as he puts it, whether Catherine will "stick":

> "By Jove," [Sloper] said to himself, "I believe she will stick—I believe she will stick!" And this idea of Catherine "sticking" appeared to him to have a comical side, and to offer a prospect of entertainment. He determined, as he said to himself, to see it out. (99)

This introduction to the term "stick" is ripe with homophonic implications, even more comic than Sloper's image of his daughter as embracing, metaphorically, a tar baby. For Sloper's narcissism allows him no idea of what, beyond the girth of his eminence, Catherine could stick to. She could stick to Morris, to a plan, to her word, and to a set of ethical principles. She could also endure, that is, stick it out, in the same way that Sloper determines to "see it out." In that phrase, moreover, the antecedent noun for Sloper's pronoun, "it," is ambiguously, infelicitously, the gerund "sticking," making Sloper determined to "see it sticking out."

Catherine also obtains skewed perceptions because initially she, too, does not understand how fidelity operates. Taking the affect as synonymous with its source, she misconstrues her father's investment in controlling her perspective. *Washington Square* thus can be read as Catherine's (double) lesson in fidelity. You can tell, she explains to Morris about her father, when a person speaks to you "*As if* they despised you!" (137, emphasis added):

> He spoke that way the night before we sailed. It wasn't much, but it was enough, and I thought of it on the voyage all the time. Then I made up my mind. I will

> never ask him for anything again, or *expect* anything from him. It would not be natural now. (137, emphasis added)

Catherine's emphasis on privileging nature over expectation rejects the idea that fidelity is a matter of expectations; instead, believing herself misled by her expectations, she renounces them as unnatural.

Despite this renunciation, Catherine's search for fidelity continues to be informed by the dual meanings produced by a single sound, such as the word "everything," in the following exchange. When Catherine says, "I have given up everything," Morris responds, "You shall have everything back" (154). For Morris, "everything" refers to Sloper's estate, so that in breaking the engagement Morris is returning to Catherine her entire inheritance—everything. For Catherine, Sloper's love and approval were everything, comprising both the history and predication of her life. The third, and worst, meaning is that her loyalty to Morris has caused her to lose, not her father's affection, but the illusion that it ever existed: everything.

That the word "everything" could sound like the same thing and be something completely different suggests that Morris is as deaf as her father to Catherine's meanings. Just as, with increasing adamancy, Sloper contends that Catherine will adhere to him—to his society, his desires, his judgment—while with equal adamancy Catherine adheres to a set of ethical principles, so when Morris early on asks that Catherine "cleave," meaning to cling to him, in the end she does cleave, that is, sever from him. One does not have to be clever to use a cleaver.

The Homophones of North Africa

The Man Who Knew Too Much begins with the intertitle: "A single crash of Cymbals and how it rocked the lives of an American family." Given the odd capitalizing of "Cymbal," "it's tempting," as Donald Spoto (1979) states, "to see the epigraph as offering a pun on 'symbols'" (242). One might also read "crash" as a pun on "clash," as suggested by the film's astonishing opening episode on a bus traveling from Casablanca to Marrakech. Dr. McKenna, from Indianapolis, his wife, Jo McKenna, and their son Hank (Christopher Olsen), are on vacation revisiting the area where McKenna was stationed during World War II. When the bus jerks, Hank accidentally grabs and thus removes the veil from an Arab woman, initiating a clash of symbols at several levels. Citing Frantz Fanon, Edwards (2005) points out that the Arab woman's veil is inextricably related to French colonization:

> [Fanon] notes that before the [Algerian] revolution, the "veil was worn because tradition demanded rigid separation of the sexes, but also because the occupier was bent on unveiling Algeria.". . . Thus Hank's unveiling of the Moroccan woman identifies him with the French obsession with unveiling, one ineluctably linked with colonialism in Algeria and Morocco. . . . [Hank's]

> unveiling suggests a desire for the American to occupy the place of the French. (190–1)

What for the Americans signifies fashion or custom for the Arabs represents both public decency and resistance to colonial subjugation, so that the outrage of the woman's husband finds its commensurate opposite in McKenna's abashed ignorance.

This ignorance points us toward the other capitalized word in the opening intertitle, "American." Technically not a homophone, it certainly functions here to foreground both the nationalistic impetus of Stewart's consciousness and the utter invisibility that accrues to the suppressed alternative meanings of some homophones. Ostensibly, what could have a more transparent meaning, in 1955, than "American"? From the American perspective, the West's position in the Cold War, as I have argued elsewhere, demanded that "American" stand for a singular set of values, a pervasive set of norms, facilely reduced to such phrases as "the American way of life," or "the American Dream," or simply "democracy."[4] The preservation of "American" as a unitary term thus required domestic suppression of alternative perspectives, values, or lifestyles.

When Hank removes the Arab woman's veil, he initiates the film's unveiling of the suppressed meaning of "American." "American" means McKenna need not understand the veil's significance, implying the ignorance resides instead in the Arab's failure to comprehend what it means to be an American. He should know that veiling is alien to someone whose national identity, American, symbolizes equality. Yet McKenna's wife is also veiled: the internationally renowned singer, Jo Conway, subordinated to her husband, travels under a permanent alias, Jo McKenna, Indianapolis housewife.[5] Like the Arab wife, her voice—literally her singing voice, and figuratively her voice in the decisions that delimit her identity—has yielded, in accord with the custom of her country, to the will of her husband, the father who knows best (to cite the title of one of the most popular American television shows in the mid-1950s).[6]

When the Frenchman, Louis Bernard, who extricates the American is confused by the homophone "Jo," the woman's nickname that echoes a man's name, the resulting gender confusion masks Dr. McKenna's more significant colonization of his wife: "I've called her that for so long nobody knows her by anything else." Furthermore, if the one name, Jo, can refer to two people, the less acknowledged issue is that the two names, McKenna and Conway, can refer to one woman. The homophone "Jo" also momentarily focuses Bernard on the wrong person, Hank, suggesting how the English-speaking McKennas are temporarily focusing Bernard on the wrong couple, making Bernard the man who knows too much. Bernard, too, is two, doubling as an agent of the French "FBI" looking for two English-speaking people who are in Morocco to hire an assassin. But there are two too many people who sound like something else, which is too much for Bernard, and, when he imparts information of the assassination plot to them, too much for the two McKennas, too, too much, that is, for the two McKennas to handle, in that it requires them to ascribe the duplicity they suspected in Bernard to the Draytons, too, of whom they, themselves, are the unwitting doubles.

But this is too much information, and I am going too fast. This opening scene reveals even more about what it means to be American: not only to know too little about other cultures, but also to assume a more generically homophonic relationship with the other. The McKennas can, as Sloper does with Catherine, manifest the mindset of the colonizer, reducing Morocco to something that sounds American. As Wlad Godzich (1986) explains, "Western thought has always thematized the other as a threat to be reduced, as a potential same-to-be, a yet-not-same" (xiii).

This act of reducing the other to the same also can be found in the opening scenes of *The Man Who Knew Too Much*. Looking out the bus window, Jo says, "Of course this isn't really Africa . . . it's the French Morocco," and even though McKenna corrects her—"Well it's northern Africa"—Hank replies, "still seems like Las Vegas." When McKenna mentions Marrakesh, Hank says, "sounds like a drink," to which McKenna replies, "sure does." Later, in the Arab marketplace Hank can say: "Look: sewing machines. Looks like a television commercial." The authority for these conversions lies in part in Hank's assertion that his father had liberated Africa, making North Africa a subsidiary space, reduced to the liberator's terms and meanings.

Here Hitchcock is using a device Sharon Cameron (1989) accurately identifies in James:

> In *The American Scene*, James empties out the landscape, marginalizes the people, so that consciousness, a pure subject becomes empowered outside the structures of psychological realism whose limits and conditions it is free to disregard. Here power is a consequence of the ability of consciousness to dominate objects, which are repeatedly subordinated to its interpretive reassessments. . . . The travelogue provides the generic conditions for the disengagement of consciousness from psychological realism, conventionalizing the disassociation in terms that make it falsely recognizable. (7)

This false consciousness acquires comic proportions when the McKennas reduce the North African travelogue to the body parts of McKenna's patients and the medical procedures with which he controls those parts:

> "You know what's paying for these three days in Marrakech?"
>
> "Me."
>
> "Mrs. Campbell's gall stones, and you know the purse I bought in Paris—Bill Edward's tonsils."
>
> "You know I never thought of it that way before. I'm wearing Johnny Matthews' appendix."
>
> "What about the boat trip. Let's see: It took two boys, and one girl, and two sets of twins, didn't it?"
>
> "And Mrs. Morgan's hives."

"All the way home we'll be riding on Herbie Taylor's ulcers."

"And Alieta Margle's asthma."

"Now if we could just get four cases of the seven-year itch, we could retire, or if Mrs. Giles is really going to have triplets, we can completely redecorate the house."

Like James, Hitchcock employs the travelogue to explore the consciousness of the American, which is what makes this film so quintessentially American (even though, Stuart McDougal [1998] points out, "none of the movie takes place on American soil" [59]). But Hitchcock also challenges the American travelogue/tourist sensibility by turning "American" into a homophone, meaning liberator *and* appropriator, proponent of democracy *and* suppressor of difference, owner of superior knowledge *and* victim of crass ignorance.

Astutely identifying how James represents the violence in this mode of consciousness, "What is bracketed in the fiction," Cameron contends,

> is not others but their otherness. Or, in terms more congenial to the violence of this phenomenon, James posits otherness so that it can then be bracketed by his characters and so that we can be made to bear witness to the consequences of that bracketing. (30)

This is exactly what happens in the marketplace immediately after McKenna describes his dismembering people, bracketed as "patients," who have supported his return to the place he formerly "liberated." At that point, Bernard, disguised as an Arab, is chased by a man in identical garb and fatally stabbed. The night before, the McKennas had seen Bernard in a restaurant, after he had broken his dinner date with them, driving McKenna to the verge of confrontation with the Frenchman. Instead, however, McKenna displaced his anger by violently tearing the chicken apart, using both of his hands, a direct affront to the manners of the Moroccan restaurateurs. If McKenna's petty violence against the chicken and against Moroccan manners asserts what it means to be an American—that is, asserts the asymmetrical prerogatives of American consciousness—that violence returns directly to McKenna the next day on a much grander scale, when two objects of that violence—the Arab on the bus and Bernard in the restaurant—merge into one stabbed man staggering toward McKenna in the marketplace.

Through this figure McKenna discovers the "native" is not what McKenna took him for: Bernard's Arab disguise means that as a Frenchman, too, Bernard had been disguised. As both stabbed Arab and government agent, he violently reasserts himself into the American's now disoriented consciousness, cuing him to yet another violence—a planned assassination—the secret to which is found in (or disguised by) the homophone, "Ambrose Chapel" (a place that McKenna takes in as person, "Ambrose Chappell"). What was too much knowledge for Bernard to live with becomes, because it is a homophone, too much knowledge for McKenna to understand.

That moment also puts Morocco in brackets, rendering it peripheral to the film's knowledge by revealing all the contending parties in the assassination plot to be Anglo-American-European. As the opening scene suggested, North Africa is just a travelogue, the real dispute being among the people who "liberated" North Africa by returning it to French rule. In the consciousness of those people, the "Dark Continent" (which Hank on the bus had qualified by saying it is "twice as bright as Indianapolis") is only a resource, a place from which an assassin may be extracted, in the same way that any natural resource may be appropriated for domestic (i.e., Anglo-American-European) use.

The film thus produces a world that employs North Africa as a nonproductive appropriation. When McKenna's fingers smear the dark cosmetics of Bernard's disguise, the knowledge the Frenchman imparts to the American is that North Africa is a masquerade (see Figure 4.1).[7] This is why, as Fanon (1963) points out, the "native" is an entity produced by the settler through an act of violence, reenacted and displaced in a series of asymmetries that construct national identity out of, to use heuristically the vocabulary I am employing, homophonic conflations. Not an indigenous entity, the "native," in Fanon's analysis, is the product of a doubling effected by settlement, which is always a violent activity. This doubling renders the "native" a member of a preexisting social order, which must be destroyed to make the native part of the settlement. The settler does not conquer a sociopolitical space but rather creates such a space through the obliteration of historical antecedents.

As the settler's creation, therefore, the word "native" is always a homophone, simultaneously meaning colonial subject (member of a population organized and informed by the settler's terms, definitions, and values) and everything that the colonial enterprise has destroyed, the trace of the history that has been subsumed.

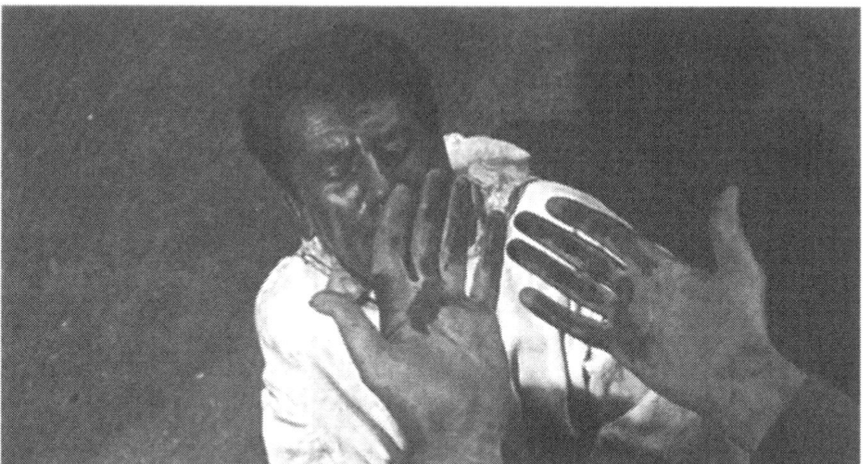

FIGURE 4.1 The cosmetics of Bernard's disguise impart the knowledge that North Africa is a masquerade.

"Native" refers as well to a person whose festering resentment constitutes the position of a subject inculcated in a system of value whose benefits she is barred from enjoying. From this perspective, the name of the colony is also a homophone, to which the secret agent, Louis Bernard, has given a double face, while the actual "native" in the marketplace, who stabbed his double, remains a silent figure in the discourse of the settler, and the violence that Fanon finds endemic to colonialism is exposed, from the Anglo-American-European perspective, as itself a resource of, not a fault in, the colonial system.

Further, because these presumptions are axiomatic to McKenna's consciousness, they cannot stand outside of it as a knowledge produced by his experience. The colonial status of Morocco, like the status of his wife, functions as a known and, therefore, cannot also operate as unknown, an emptiness that in its filling produces new knowledge.

The man who knows too much thus becomes the American whose consciousness—to echo a basic James motif—is not commensurate with his comprehension, a point made by McKenna's repeated misprision of fidelity, exemplified by his mistaking the Draytons for the congenial English couple they sound like. When the Draytons kidnap Hank, before McKenna tells Jo what has happened, he suppresses her consciousness with pills that she does not know are heavy sedatives. McKenna's treatment of his wife reflects the limitation of his own consciousness, already suggested by the way he subordinated North Africa to the meanings of its liberator. Hitchcock dramatically underscores those limitations, for Jo McKenna, whom McKenna had rendered unconscious, eventually unveils the homophone's second meaning, that Ambrose Chapel names a place rather than a man. In that place designated by the homophone's other meaning, moreover, Hitchcock renders McKenna literally unconscious.

Ward and Protectorate

Yet, despite his momentary silencing, McKenna remains the guardian whose charge is mandated by exactly the silence he generates. In this regard, he emulates Sloper, who repeatedly alludes to Catherine's silence as the grounds for his authority over her. He must protect her from Morris, he explains to Mrs. Penniman, because "the position of husband of a weak-minded woman with a large fortune would suit him to perfection!" (1881, 1985: 46). To Morris's sister, Mrs. Montgomery, he says,

> I am sure if you were to see Catherine she would interest you very much. I don't mean because she is interesting in the usual sense of the word but because you would feel sorry for her. She is so soft and simple-minded, she would be such an easy victim. (72)

Regarding his daughter as a protectorate, Sloper further explains that he believes Morris ill suited to be "a protector and caretaker of my child, who is singularly ill-adapted to take care of herself" (74). Sloper behaves as though her character were a (somewhat crude) product of nature. Andrew Scheiber (1996) discusses at length Sloper's treating her as though she were a biological specimen, and, indeed, Sloper's perceived expertise in the natural sciences figures greatly in his assessments. Sloper claims to understand nature, and, Ian F. A. Bell (1991) notes, "If any word dominates Washington Square, it is 'natural' or its variants" (57).[8] But Bell also points out that Catherine is treated as a commodified object (23), in light of which it is possible to see Catherine's place in Sloper's discourse as a natural resource, a raw product, so to speak, for which he had hoped there might be some use: "Try to *make* a clever woman of her" (1881, 1985: 8, emphasis added), he instructs Mrs. Penniman. And when Mrs. Penniman asks, "do you think it is better to be clever than to be good?" (8), Sloper replies in strictly utilitarian terms: "Good for what?" (8). Eventually, however, he finds this natural product has negligible value, concluding that "she is about as intelligent as a bundle of shawls" (123). That Catherine thus stands in Sloper's discourse for both the native and the raw materials the native must produce to sustain the colonial system brings additional ramifications to Susan Griffin's (1989) important insight that Catherine's "body is a social and cultural construction" (125), even though, as Scheiber (1996) stresses, she "is not the figure inscribed by her father's various discourses" (257).

If these discursive practices give Sloper warrant for his governance, however, they also make it impossible for him to hear Catherine indicate what her principles mean to her and for him. When Catherine says, for example, that if she lives with Sloper she should obey him and, conversely, "If I don't obey you, I ought not to live with you—to enjoy your kindness and protection" (1881, 1985: 117), Sloper immediately divorces her from his admiration for her reasoning: "This striking argument gave the doctor a sudden sense of his having underestimated his daughter. . . . But it displeased him deeply, and he signified as much" (117). First Sloper attributes the argument to Morris, but when Catherine owns it, Sloper immediately banishes it to silence: "Keep it to yourself, then" (117). And Catherine does. Her alterity remains so permanently beyond his comprehension that it becomes, James tells us, "his punishment" (169). Regardless, Sloper uses his power to convert Catherine's silence into his meanings, refusing to concede "to the idea that she ever had a right to think of Morris" (170). "'I put my foot on this idea from the first, and I keep it there now', said the doctor. 'I don't see anything cruel in that: one can't keep it there too long'" (170).

In the domestic arrangement antedating the film's action, McKenna has similarly subordinated Jo, the film implies. When McKenna actually sedates her, the violence this subordination entails become visibly explicit. In what Corber (1993) identifies as McKenna's projecting his own hysteria onto Jo, McKenna misrepresents Jo's conditions as nervous and hyperbolic. Then, first invoking his authority as a physician, and finally bribing her with the promise of new information about Bernard, McKenna coerces Jo to take pills, the purpose of which he also misrepresents. They are, in fact, heavy sedatives that render Jo helpless when McKenna finally reveals that the Draytons have kidnapped Hank. Jo, even though sedated, responds, at least at first, aggressively. Rising from her bed, she pushes against McKenna, then hits his arms with her clenched fists, while shouting "I could kill you!" Realizing simultaneously that that her son is missing and that her husband has lied to her and drugged her, she struggles against him with all her remaining strength, while crying hysterically. She even tries to bolt for the door and resists McKenna so forcefully that he must pin her to the bed until the sedatives take hold.

Corber is correct that she has now become the hysteric McKenna accused her of being, and that this action "forcibly returns Jo's voice to her body" (142). But what makes his means of doing so particularly horrifying is that Hitchcock shoots the scene to resemble a rape, a point emphasized by the concluding shot (see Figure 4.2). Jo is lying on the bed, her faced turned away from the camera, which is located behind her neck, where the edge of her pillow might be. The upper body of McKenna dominates the shot, his chest against her torso. He still has her arms pinned, and he is leaning forward as though he were about to mount her. "I'm sorry," he says, as her resistance gives out.

Hitchcock, too, in the conclusion, "apologizes" to Jo, not simply by averting the assassination and rescuing her son, but by extracting her from silence. In a brilliant twelve-minute segment without dialogue, in Albert Hall where the assassination is set to take place, the film foments a complete revolution, first emulating a return to the silent era, and then returning back to the sound era, with a violent scream emitted by the tormented Jo. The conditions that produce this scream are unique, not only because the silent film conventions suspend the issue of fidelity introduced by the soundtrack, but also because in this space of suspended fidelity, Jo participates in a personal revolution. At the outset of the sequence, she occupies a place in Albert Hall diametrically opposite the stage on which she had formerly

FIGURE 4.2 Shot to resemble a rape.

performed, a place where her helplessness is evident, a place that makes visible the suffering that her alterity produces (see Figure 4.3). Visually, acoustically, and thematically, therefore, the advent of Jo's scream revolves the attention 180 degrees, to change her from a silent member of the audience (the role assigned her by her husband) to the object of the audience's attention. That revolution gives agency to Jo's voice by restoring the other referent of the homophone, "Jo": Conway replaces McKenna when her scream disrupts the assassin's aim. As Jo Conway, she gains access to the embassy, and, by singing very loudly, virtually shouting, she signals to her son and thus effects his rescue.

Jo's scream is the scream Catherine Sloper is never allowed, as Sloper's prerogatives inform his repression of the meanings that the subaltern's voice echoes: the second referent of the homophone. In his most violent assertion of that prerogative, after isolating her at an Alpine precipice, Sloper seethes with barely restrained violence, as he warns her, "I am not a very good man" (1881, 1985: 125). So intense is his acknowledged passion that Catherine perceived him as "dangerous, but Catherine hardly went so far as to say to herself that it might be part of his plan to fasten his hand . . . *in her throat*" (125, emphasis added).

Sloper's demonstration creates for Catherine an indelible spectacle, ironically anticipated by an interchange between Sloper and Mrs. Almond at the outset of Catherine's involvement with Morris. When Mrs. Almond says, "very possibly you are right [about Morris]. But the thing is for Catherine to see it" (41), Sloper cleverly replies, "I will present her with a pair of spectacles!" (41). For the attentive Catherine, however, one spectacle—the spectacle of the Alps transformed into the abyss that her father's violent will portends—is quite enough to fulfill the augury of the spectacular homophone's other meaning. It will take Hitchcock to complement

FIGURE 4.3 Jo's place in Albert Hall diametrically opposite the stage on which she had performed.

James with a pair of violent spectacles, the first in the marketplace and the one that responds to it, in the auditorium, literally the place for (at last) listening.

But James gives Catherine no such place, so, in the end, Sloper can tell Mrs. Almond, in terminology that precisely evokes the colonialist blindness and deafness, "I don't at all recognize your description of Catherine . . . [S]he seems to me much better than while the fellow was hanging about" (170-1). Denying his daughter any capacity for interior life, he views her contentment solely in terms used for a colonial subject, those of activity and productivity: "She is perfectly comfortable and blooming; she eats and sleeps, takes her usual exercise, and overloads herself, as usual, with finery. She is always knitting some kind of purse or embroidering some handkerchief, and it seems to me she turns these articles out about as fast as ever. She hasn't much to say; but when had she anything to say?" (171).

Framed this way by James and Hitchcock, the issue of fidelity and its homophonic infidels suggests a dynamic of cinematic representation, which, at least in mainstream cinema, creates knowledge out of resemblance and misprision. At their basic level, moving pictures make a series of still shots to resemble motion, synchronize an audio track with those moving stills to resemble speech and action, and sequence shots to resemble the passing of time and the arrangement of space. The issue always is whether the sagebrush or the rocket ship or the faithful wife or the obedient child resembles what we imagine them to be. But the price of the complacency with which we enjoy our imagined reality is the unhearing of meaning and the tacit endorsement of suppression. To the extent that we, as moviegoers, share in the kind of entertainment that Dr. Sloper constructs out of his misprision of Catherine's character and motives, we may be engaging, however slightly and however pervasively, in a colonial practice that, as Hitchcock makes clear, mandates violence.

5

Bump

CONCUSSIVE KNOWLEDGE IN JAMES AND HITCHCOCK

Mary Ann O'Farrell

In an episode of the television show *Oz*, Stella, the civilian librarian (played by Patti LuPone) who has just taken over management of the Emerald City prison unit's spotty collection of books, is both pleased and puzzled when she discovers that Henry James's *The Ambassadors* (1903) has been taken from its shelf. She has not thought of the prisoners as exhibiting such sophisticated tastes and has not been accustomed to thinking of *The Ambassadors* as appealing even to her own taste: she had had to be "force fed" indigestible James in college. Encouraged by the prisoner who serves as her assistant to examine the returned book more closely, Stella turns it over, noting that its red is a little redder than it ought to be and its cover may even be a little bit dented. The librarian comes to discover, that is, from impressions left upon the book, that—read or not—it has been used as a weapon; a prisoner has been concussed with the full force of Henry James (see Figure 5.1).

What, a viewer might ask, could Henry James be doing in prison? *Oz*'s quick and felicitous reference works to identify James in several ways. Certainly the prison reader's choice of one of James's most densely homosocial fictions reflects the show's interest in the homosociality of prison life, as well as its powerful and popular fantasy that in prison queer romance exists alongside violent sexual force feedings. Certainly, too, the scene is readable as an account of comparative cultural capital. Books have different uses in prison; a prisoner has earlier requested from the library an especially long novel—he needs toilet paper, he reports. The inclusion of James's text is also an invocation of the novel of manners, a tip of the hat to manners as a textual mode recognizable in the prison drama; the buzz and the novelty of life in the Oswald State Penitentiary (Oz) depend upon visible hierarchies and on a hothouse intensity produced by pressures and disciplines, strictures and demands, that order and give consequence to a social world surprisingly familiar to readers of the novel of manners. But, even as it invokes it, the show seems also to mock the novel of manners, to slap at the genre's egotistical fantasy of its uses in the world and at liberal notions of the value of culture and literacy. The novel of conscious hesitations might seem unable to speak to the swift, sudden, and conclusive

FIGURE 5.1 The full force of Henry James.

actions of HBO's violent prison fiction, and the television drama might be understood by including it to supplement the novel with violence, with that of which the Jamesian novel of manners—for all its knowing—is supposed to be ignorant.

No less mocking in her choice of weapon, and no less certain in her fantasy of what her object fails to know, the psychiatric patient Miss Carmichael (Rhonda Fleming) in Alfred Hitchcock's *Spellbound* (1945) also takes a book for a weapon, chucking one at the head of her psychiatrist, Dr. Constance Petersen (Ingrid Bergman). The busty and leering Miss Carmichael is set by the film in opposition to the white-coated and buttoned-up Dr. Petersen, who is chided by her colleagues no less than by Miss Carmichael for her presumed sexual ignorance, their chidings attempts to compensate for their various inadequacies in the presence of a smart woman. Her work is cold and devoid of instinct, the lecherous Dr. Fleurot (John Emery) tells Dr. Petersen, and hugging her is "like embracing a textbook." Like Miss Carmichael, he'd like to throw a book at Dr. Petersen, he says, though she is a book herself—target and missile at once in the fantasy of the amorous doctor. Throwing the book at her, both Dr. Petersen's colleague and her patient would shock her into knowledge with the force of the projectile; her psychoanalysis may be too processual, too immaterial, and too slow in its readings to come to terms with the force of the world.[1]

The scenes in the *Oz* library and in the sanitarium office point usefully toward an account of that most Jamesian and most Hitchcockian of topics—knowledge.

The prison librarian and her assistant, Bob Rebadow (George Morfogen), will have an affair of the institutions (sex in the prison and in the library at once), and in the library scene, viewers come to anticipate their romance through the pleasure each obviously takes in guarding and displaying what he knows or what she doesn't; knowing is of the body in its flirtatiousness as well as in its violence. Knowing that a book may be a weapon, Rebadow milks his epistemological advantage, encouraging Stella to turn over the book, to learn for herself that a prisoner has "clubbed his cellmate" with it by seeing that the book is reddened and damaged. Stella, though, is elaborately unfazed, unflappable, nonchalant—brassy, even, in her ability to go, conversationally, on. Which inmate did it, she wants to know, and "what cellblock is he in?" His choice of book is no less telling for his eccentric use of it. Amazon.librarian, she wants to make recommendations based on his prior selections. Knowing that a book may be a weapon, Stella knows nothing she did not know before; a book on which an impression has been made is a book that makes an impression, and it may be no less read for all that. And, if a woman at whom a book is flung is herself a textbook, she may yet be more impressive than she is impressed by a violent knowledge that doctor and patient alike would force upon her.

"Just beyond the threshold of the drawing-room she stopped short, the reason for her doing so being that she had received an impression. The impression had, in strictness, nothing unprecedented; but she felt it as something new, and the soundlessness of her step gave her time to take in the scene before she interrupted it" (James 1881, 1981: 442). Let *Portrait of a Lady*'s (1881) Isabel Archer, then, "struck" (443), in James's words, by a vision she will remember, "that of her husband and Madame Merle unconsciously and familiarly associated" (473), before *they* comment upon *her*, permit herself to be used to comment upon the scenes in *Oz* and in *Spellbound*: what Hitchcock depicts in his evocation of the book as projectile and what *Oz* produces in its invocation of a blunt force Henry James is the characteristically Jamesian and characteristically Hitchcockian fantasy dramatizing the immediacy of an impressive knowledge that claps one upside the head. The televisual reference, that is, makes it possible to see something about those scenes in James and in Hitchcock when characters just *know* and to begin to understand something about how such scenes figure an experience of coming to blunt force knowledge.

Early in Hitchcock's *The Lady Vanishes* (1938), when the film's heroine Iris (Margaret Lockwood) realizes that a lady traveling with her has disappeared, she asks the other travelers in their shared train compartment where her companion is, identifying the absent woman as "the lady who looked after me when I was knocked out." Having been conked on the head by a flower box, Iris is susceptible to the response given her query by the fellow across the way (Philip Leaver). "Maybe," he says with the accent of a stage Italian, "it make-a you forget." The Italian remark misleads not only about the whereabouts of Iris's new friend but also about how knowledge works in texts by Alfred Hitchcock and Henry James, where the opposite seems as often to be the case: that former of impressions, *the concussion*, Hitchcock and James suggest, is what makes it possible to know. While its everyday symptomology as a head injury—including dizziness, confusion, sleepiness—might suggest a diminishing of awareness, the concussion of Hitchcockian fantasy may also heighten awareness, and the Jamesian concussion—more figurative and, even in its most concretizing figurations, less localized somatically—may, by means of its disorientations and dislodgings, likewise facilitate a startling coming to knowledge.

Starting from a strong sense of James and Hitchcock as alike in figuring and articulating through their works an everyday epistemology, this essay examines coming to knowledge as a topic in their novels and films and suggests that both the novelist and the director render the experience of knowing and the nature of knowledge as sudden, violent, material, and concussive. And, in undertaking this examination, I mean as well to consider what it is we have come to know about knowledge from reading James and from watching Hitchcock.

Iris's concussion in *The Lady Vanishes* is portrayed with specificity and care as an injury and an event leading to physical and cognitive consequences. The flower box's impact is audible, and it leaves a bump on Iris's head, causing her to black out. Camera lenses help viewers partake of Iris's symptoms. Her blurred vision is briefly identical with the film image, as a watery whirlpool reorganizes what Iris sees in the minutes after her injury and as her nearly interchangeable friends appear with train station personnel in triangulating triplicate. A suave and courtly brain specialist (Paul Lukas) offers an account of how "even a simple concussion" can produce "curious effects upon an imaginative person": hallucinations in the form of "a vivid subjective image." But the brain specialist is villainous and his evaluation suspect. Iris's vivid subjective image proves not to distort but to match the odd reality of the world as it exists in miniature on a train,[2] and, knocked into an accurate perception of that reality, she alone among the travelers both knows and acknowledges it. The vivid impression produced by the concussion may well be subjective, but it need be no less a kind of knowledge for its injurious origin and its subjective being.

Alongside Hitchcock's literalization of the bumpy acquisition of a concussive knowledge, James's articulation of the impression strongly received, which might have seemed merely metaphoric, takes on a physical dimension, and the Jamesian concussion, if it is not actually a blow to the head, may still be a physical event effecting the transfer of knowledge—a blow to the brain, as it were. In *The Golden Bowl* (1904), James writes about Charlotte's perception that her friend Mrs. Assingham is attentive to Charlotte's relations with the Prince: "What had just happened—it pieced itself together for Charlotte—was that the Assingham pair, drifting like everyone else, had had somewhere in the gallery, in the rooms, an accidental concussion; had it after the Colonel, over his balustrade, had observed, in the favoring high light, her public junction with the Prince" (1904, 1983: 185). Colonel Assingham has seen Charlotte and the Prince together and has just *known*—read the social signs and deduced from them with the rapidity and force of an instantaneous knowing—the nature of the relation between the two. The social movements and encounters of the party are physicalized in James's language as events generated by crash and crush and impact. In the swirl and the "squash" of the party, with its "vague, slow, senseless eddies," entities bump and thump and jostle (183). In James's terms, the squash just *is* the party, another name for it, and the bumpings and jostlings its reason for being. And in the squash, Bob Assingham has encountered his wife, in their concussion letting her know what he has seen and, seeing, known—"the way one of her young friends was 'going on' with another" (186). In James's rendering, the concussion is both the knowledge (Bob's recognition of a relation, Fanny's knowing what he knows) and the coming together. Condensing their meeting, their talking, and their knowing into "the accidental concussion" they "had had," James registers the shock, the impact, and the materiality with which the transmission of knowledge may be experienced and felt. And he registers as well the capacity of knowledge to move both ways, to affect both parties to its transmission. Bumping and jostling, transmitter and receiver alike are subject to impact, and, knowing this, we know something about the social relations around the transmission of knowledge; we recognize that the progress of social knowledge is achieved as much by the nudge as by the word, and that the nudge of knowing effects a temporary social union heated by physical contact, even when that union is undone as the jostler inevitably detaches and moves on. Contemporary technology, too, knows what James knows: the Bump Technologies app for Apple's iPhone transfers contact information from one device to another when the gadgets or the hands holding them are bumped into one another. Supplementing the apparent disembodiment of wirelessness with the apparently intimate manual interaction, the app speaks to a fantasy like James's that would embody, sometimes, the transmission of knowledge and that enjoys the mutuality of knowledge's reverberations. But while the Bump of the iPhone is necessarily deliberate and disregards or disavows the role in knowledge of accident and of surprise, the bump of concussive knowing in James and in Hitchcock registers the material consequences of knowing, which change the world of money and relationships and things, of what bodies do and don't. Knowledge works by startling and dislocating, and, when they attend to its capacity to dislocate and startle, James and Hitchcock emphasize the way knowledge disorients and disturbs as *knowing* (an act in motion) before it settles into a *knowingness* (a condition or a characteristic in stasis).

The accidental concussion of Bob and Fanny Assingham follows on Bob's own moment of revelation—the moment when he sees Charlotte wait for the Prince and greet him on the stairs. In seeing them together, Bob just knows—knows, that is, to construe their meeting as a "public junction," a relation, a "'going on'." And Col. Bob's just knowing is the product of a certain kind of scene appealing to James and to Hitchcock, in which a coming to knowledge is given the content of heterosex; in such scenes, someone, seeing a man and a woman together, speed-reads their relationship and knows it to be or to have been erotic. In *Dial M for Murder* (1954), for example, the cuckolded Tony (Ray Milland) tells the ne'er-do-well he blackmails into the attempted murder of Tony's unfaithful wife about his following her to an assignation with her lover. "I could see them in the studio window as he cooked spaghetti over a gas range. They didn't say much—they just stood very natural together. You know, it's funny how you can tell when people are in love." Tony's musing highlights the oddity of the *just knowing* moment in James and Hitchcock, which depends upon an ability to read and to identify relation (through inclinations and postures and silences) in a way that both acknowledges and obscures the reading process that produces the knowing in favor of an occulting that privileges the instantaneousness of coming to knowledge; that people are in love, that they've had sex or that they have it, that they have had a child, is a thing that, funny, you can just tell.

Tony's manner and tone as he describes this incident are themselves funny. He is expansive and expository, the pleased maker of a casual observation that he knows to be apt, elaborately unbothered by its content. But the very elaboration of his exposition denegates his denial. The scene has been disturbing and injurious for him. As a motive for the planned murder, his desire for his wife's money might screen a motive for murder in the injury of her infidelity. And confirmation of an affair he suspects is taking place comes not from the physical evidence of love letters in his possession but from the impact of watching two people stand, "very natural together" over a gas ring. The distaste with which sophisticated Tony comments on the lovers' low-rent meal, "spaghetti" distanced from his table by careful enunciation, alone reveals the somatic content of his experience of this scene of his knowing. Far from funny, his *just knowing* as a response to what he witnessed has been dislocating and deranging.

In Hitchcock's *Shadow of a Doubt* (1943), the sight of a man and woman in relation is, rather than the acknowledged cause of a concussive knowledge, its figuration. The film suggests an etiology for the derangement that has turned visiting Uncle Charlie (Joseph Cotten) from the sweet-faced and sailor-suited boy of a middle-aged sister's (Patricia Collinge) cherished photograph into the adult Merry Widow Killer. Just days after the childhood photograph was taken, the boy Charlie rode his new bicycle on an icy road into a streetcar. The resulting skull fracture, viewers are led to think, changes him from a quiet boy (a reader) into a worldly peripatetic, hard to pin down. His mother "wondered if he'd ever look the same. She wondered if he'd ever *be* the same," his sister recalls. Uncle Charlie's concussion, the film suggests, has made him who he is, and who he is is a man who thinks he knows something you don't know. Talking with his niece, young Charlie (Teresa Wright), he is obsessed with his knowing and with hers: "Charlie, what do you know?" he asks, and the question is not entirely rhetorical. "You think you know something, don't you? You think you're the clever little girl who knows something. There's so much you don't know, so much. What do you know really? . . . How do you know what the world is like?" Questioning her, Uncle Charlie tells young Charlie what she doesn't know—"Do you know the world is a foul sty?"—but, in their repetition, his do-know/don't-know questions suggest an obsession with knowing itself as a form and an event.

The content of Uncle Charlie's obsession, though, belongs as much to the film as it does to him and is reflected in a film clip, shot by Hitchcock himself for use as a citation of Uncle Charlie's deranged view and showing what the scene of just knowing so often shows: men and women in relation. When we first see Uncle Charlie, lying fully clothed on his boarding house bed, smoking and musing, we may understand the images that have run under the film's credits as the content of his thoughts. Accompanied by a version of Franz Lehar's "The Merry Widow Waltz" that sets the melodic confection above a sometimes sinister undercurrent, they are images of men and women waltzing. Figures reproducing themselves through repetition as they dance in a circle, the men and women appear several times throughout the film (see Figure 5.2). Seeming sometimes to be Uncle Charlie's imaginings, they are also—in their disconnection from the diegesis—the film's musings.

Though what Uncle Charlie thinks he knows is the greediness and perfidy of women (men's "silly wives" deplete them), the film knows marital depletion to work the other way as well; it is Uncle Charlie's neurotic sister who has been diminished and exhausted by her marriage. What, together, Uncle Charlie and the film know and revisit in the reduplications and recurrences of the dancing image, is what Bob Assingham knows and what *Dial M*'s Tony does: the fact of the sexual relation, just visible beneath the romance of dancing or the assertion of love. The boy Charlie's concussion is isomorphic with the shattering consequences of knowing. Seeing the men and women in looping relation seems to have followed on his concussion, and, in adulthood, his repeated do-you-don't-you-knows mime the repeated circulations of the dance, alike obsessions for a mind concussed into something it can't get out of its head.

FIGURE 5.2 "What Uncle Charlie sees."

"I'm trying to keep my mind free of things don't matter," young Charlie's little sister Anne (Edna May Wonacott) remarks, refusing a telephone operator's proffered message early in the film, "because I have so much to keep on my mind." What to do with one's knowledge—with what occupies one's head—is much a subject of the film. "I think tunes jump from head to head," says young Charlie, unable either to identify or to dismiss from her head's keeping the Lehar tune. While for James in *The Golden Bowl*, the transmission of knowledge has required the literal concussiveness of bodies in social motion, for Hitchcock, the transmission of knowledge, though no less concussive in its dislocating effects, is independent of the physical. The tune in Charlie's head, later picked up by her mother, is Uncle Charlie's obsession—and the film's—made aural. And like the tune, the hallucinatory image of the dancers jumps from head to head, from Uncle Charlie's to young Charlie's to the viewer's, with a stop in the director's along the way. What Uncle Charlie has seen becomes young Charlie's way of seeing; Hitchcock's, ours. The "vivid subjective image" that follows upon concussion is transmissible, and from Anne's refusal of intrusive information, we might learn how to convert and preserve such an image as an obsession. The maintenance of the vivid subjective image depends upon the rejection of that which would take up its mental space. The transmissibility of the subjective image as a way of knowing we cannot get out of our heads, while it is what's most disturbing about Uncle Charlie's vision, is also what films and novels depend upon and what Hitchcock's films and James's novels so often depict by means of a concussive bump or the impression it leaves behind.

Hitchcock's tracing of Uncle Charlie's derangement to the concussion he experienced as a small boy may remind us of other little boys shocked into knowledge, other naive child-observers who learn through the thunderclap of sudden knowledge that they have not always been part of the story. (No Charlie, uncle or niece, is to be found among the waltzers.) All these moments about which Hitchcock and James are so expert are, that is, little primal scenes, rehearsed and reduplicated among adults. Later in Hitchcock's career, the scene may be at its most baroque. As Scottie Ferguson (James Stewart) drags Judy (Kim Novak) upstairs in the bell tower in *Vertigo* (1958), he seems to want and to need to recreate the scene of his exclusion; his repeated characterization of Judy in relation to her lover-Pygmalion Gavin Elster ("You were a very apt pupil! You were a very apt pupil!") insists upon the willingness with which she participated in a knowing of which he was not a part. Not having witnessed the scene that determined his present self, Scottie attempts to remake and, as any Freudian observer-child might, recast it to include himself. But if Hitchcock is able so to refine the primal scene, this may be because he has considered it in its most elemental form—two people standing naturally together—in *Dial M for Murder* or because culture has learned it so well and so thoroughly not only from Freud but from life and from Henry James.

Readers of James recall the most famous instances of these scenes in his novels: Isabel's sighting, mentioned above, of Gilbert Osmond at ease with Madame Merle in *The Portrait of a Lady*; Lambert Strether in *The Ambassadors* seeing a couple in the same boat, "in their own boat," and, on that seeing, knowing them "expert, familiar, frequent" (1903, 1985: 389). We know these scenes from life, too, whether from high school cafeterias or from what (to know them this way) would have to have been excessively Freudian childhoods; we know them from observation, or we know them (as one may know them more skeptically in James and elsewhere) because, no less than any observer of the sacred fount, we produce them as lovers for their novelty, for their ability to attenuate and to debanalize desire, perhaps for their imagined ability in our own imaginative fictions to keep away by anticipation's charm their nonfictional equivalents. What's striking to me always is how much the world, too, knows that these scenes are Jamesian. Writing about her instantaneous comprehension of her husband Ted Hughes's relation to a student with whom she has seen him walking, for example, Sylvia Plath notes that she is able to be no Maggie Verver in response.[3]

As a reader and viewer of the primal scenes in James and Hitchcock, I become my most pathetically naive reader-self, attached to denial and wondering how it is one knows what one just *knows*. But James and Hitchcock outline an answer to this question. The relative postures and gazes and relaxations noted by Isabel—like the natural stance of a couple watching a pot boil observed by Tony, like the face-covering undertaken by a parasol wielded in a boat, like the "shirt-sleeves" and startings and responsiveness recorded by Strether (388)—are no more than the instantaneous registrations habitual for superreaders of manners, whose reading, if it is sometimes too fast for their self-conscious awareness of their knowing, is not too fast for their concussive encounter with what they know.

In their family resemblance as primal scenes, then, these moments in James and Hitchcock and in the world may suggest a way to reread and to reconfigure what's important in the primal scene. What makes them primal scenes are their status as sites where sex and knowing cohabit and their structuring of a event in which an observer witnesses a relation and knows—if nothing else—that he or she is excluded from it. In these striking encounters, a protagonist (only by virtue of the accident of witnessing) comes to know that he or she is not a protagonist after all—that people have sex and it's not with you. If we could, though, reverse our sense of this discovery (old and repeatable as it is, it feels new every time), we might understand that, for Hitchcock and for James, the interesting part of this equation is not about sex but about knowledge. I mean to suggest, that is, that we might understand these primal scenes as places where sex figures knowledge, where the secret isn't sex but knowledge, and the violent surprise of coming to knowledge needs to be managed and contained.

From James and Hitchcock, we might then learn to reread a reconstrued primal scene as the apprehension of a relation that is crucially an apprehension of one's prior state of unknowing. The experience of coming to know for the novelist and for the director—figured as it is in their works—is multiply structured and includes (a) knowing the thing you now know, (b) knowing that you did not know it a minute ago, that you never knew it until now, and (c) knowing your exclusion from the ranks of the knowing. No wonder, then, that sudden knowledge—striking and impressive—as a coming to learn, is also confrontational and concussive. A sadness accompanies coming to knowledge in James and in Hitchcock—perhaps in life—because even as knowledge includes one among the knowing, knowledge is always also the knowledge of one's exclusion.

So it is these things that Isabel learns when she comes upon Osmond and Madame Merle together, and James's great scene, along with its contemplative aftermath for Isabel, fulfills the demands of the primal scene while it can be made also to comment further on the very idea of it. All the required elements are present. The couple in relation: returning home to her drawing-room, Isabel finds her husband with his old friend in a "familiar silence" (1881, 1981: 442–43), in a "desultory pause," "musing, face to face" (443). Of "their relative positions," James writes that they "struck" Isabel "as something detected" (443). "[U]nconsciously and familiarly associated" (473), the man and woman might as well be making spaghetti. The sex is present in the ease of their bodies together, in their postures and inclinations, and perhaps even, briefly, in James's diction; the "nudity" (442) of Osmond's antechamber flickeringly undresses the fully clothed man and woman in the next room. And the primal scene is present in the concussive knowing: watching them, Isabel is all impressions and strikings, and she knows herself to be *de trop*; "she instantly perceived that her entrance would startle them" (443). In its aestheticization, the arrangement seems complete, the silence a rounding off and enclosing. Excluded, Isabel is struck by a sense of herself as disruption, as the projectile that would (and does) break the scene. The suddenness of her just knowing might reverberate.

Still, Isabel's unknowing is complicated, and her relation to what she has come to know by means of her impression ("she had received an impression" [442]) is implicated in her disavowal of the plot by which she has been married to Osmond. Isabel's insistence that she has not been the object of a plot has been important for her. Considering how the marriage came about, Isabel thinks, "There had been no plot, no snare; she had looked and considered and chosen. When a woman had made such a mistake, there was only one way to repair it—just immensely (oh, with the highest grandeur!), to accept it" (440). Isabel's pride is audible in her claiming responsibility for her own unhappiness and for the unhappiness in her marriage. But a textured unknowing inhabits this very pride, and Isabel's insistent negative of "no plot" and "no snare" is overturnable by the Freudian logic that finds "not" inadmissible by the unconscious. To assert that there has been no plotting is to know that there might have been. Madame Merle's intimations of a prior relation to Osmond come awfully close to telling Isabel about their past. She reminds Isabel and herself in saying, "I must not forget that I knew your husband long before you did; I must not let that betray me. If you were a silly woman you might be jealous" (437). And Osmond's assessment of Madame Merle ("I liked her once better than I do to-day" [438]) exhibits all the duplicity of irony: read with one emphasis, it tells that he dislikes her; read with another, it tells that he once did like Serena

Merle. Isabel's coming to concussive knowledge, that is, suggests that such knowledge tells her what she has known but has refused, and the long night of contemplation that follows on this scene is a coming to terms with this recognition. The scene of concussive knowledge embarrasses as well as pains by complicating unknowing with the notion that one should have known and that not knowing may be a refusal to know.

Isabel's other crucial "not" unites her husband Osmond to her former suitor, Caspar Goodwood, in their effects on her. "She knew of no wrong he had done; he was not violent, he was not cruel . . ." (462), she thinks of Osmond, and, of Goodwood, "He had not been violent, and yet there had been a violence in the impression" (528). In pulling together the not-violence of Isabel's assertions with her sense of "a violence in the impression," James rewrites Freud *avant la lettre*. In Freud's primal scene, the boy who sees his parents having sex takes the sex for violence; this mistake is the embarrassment that afflicts the newly knowing in the primal scene. James's primal scenes, and Hitchcock's, make it possible to rewrite the boy's mistake yet again. He has not been wrong to perceive violence, but it inheres, not in the sex, but in the violence of the impression left by sudden knowing and by the force with which one recognizes one's exclusion.

"But the thing made an image, lasting only a moment, like a sudden flicker of light. Their relative positions, their absorbed mutual gaze, struck her as something detected. But it was all over by the time she had fairly seen it" (443). In representing Isabel's receipt of the violent impression of Osmond together with Madame Merle, James reaches beyond the medium of words in the direction of a flickering visuality. The inexorable past tense of his verbs—the time taking of language—is necessarily inadequate to the instantaneousness of what he would represent. To understand the white light of knowing, as James does, in terms of an impression left is to attempt to catch, to materialize, to render evidential the knowledge of a moment. To understand the impression—as James also does—as an image, immaterial and uncatchable as "a sudden flicker of light," is to gesture toward the photographic or perhaps to imagine the cinematic as a site for the representation of concussive knowledge, perhaps to imagine Hitchcock.[4]

Charlotte Stant's is a primal scene that is scenic only in her imagination, represented as it is in language and made visual by her thinking about it. Some rotation among the subjectivities in a scene of concussive knowledge might recast it.[5] Seeing Charlotte with the Prince has been a scene of knowing for Bob, but Charlotte's imagination of Bob's party concussion with his wife and its attendant transmission of knowledge constructs a scene of concussive knowledge for Charlotte. Their concussion is not something she has witnessed but something that has "pieced itself together for Charlotte," something she builds out of her knowledge of the ways of parties and of her friends. She has come to talk to Fanny about her relation with the Prince and, in doing so, to "convert it to good" (1904, 1983: 182). Charlotte wants something from her friend—her company and her judgment. But the disappointment and shock of knowing that Fanny already knows lead to Charlotte's credible fantasy of the concussion between the husband and wife and lead to her recognition that the concussive constitution of "the inimitable couple" (186) marks her own exclusion and leaves her profoundly alone.

In considering the scene of concussive knowledge in Hitchcock's films and James's novels, I have found myself wondering what it is that makes coming to know so violent, so scary, so "anxious-making" that it need be represented by the blow that shatters and disorients. The shattering concussion that comes near the end of *Spellbound* provides one way to think about that question. When she discovers that Dr. Murchison (Leo G. Carroll), the head of the sanitarium, has shot his would-be replacement and when he turns his revolver on her because she has revealed her discovery, Dr. Petersen (she of plodding textbook learning) responds by slowly, carefully, and deliberately leaving him alone with his gun. Viewers of the film know what happens. Dr. Murchison turns his gun on himself, as Hitchcock turns the gun on the audience. Today, the effect looks mildly cheesy: the hand holding the gun is big and waxen; it moves mechanically; and death—it turns out—is a blast of orangey-red. But something about it remains powerful as an account of what frightens in the moment of just knowing. Like those cops in TV shows who leave corrupt buddies alone to kill themselves, Dr. Petersen leaves Dr. Murchison to himself. Though in her best analyst voice, she tells him what he will do (he'll turn himself in for a life of scholarship in prison, she says), she is wrong and one suspects that she knows it: she's finding a way for herself to leave the room unharmed. But, while there's no question that she has to go and that viewers of the film want her to escape, there is some requisite heartlessness, too, in the desire for self-preservation that makes her leave Dr. Murchison alone to the concussion of the bullet and to the concussive knowledge that puts a stop to knowledge—the knowledge of death. Admitting the audience to the prospect of that violent knowing, Hitchcock gives Dr. Murchison the gift of our company and rewrites the exclusions of the scene of just knowing as the inclusiveness of death. Everyone will know it. Everyone will be (like Chad and Madame de Vionnet, the couple seen by Strether) in the same boat, but everyone will be in it alone. The anxiety about knowledge that understands it as striking and violent figures knowledge at its logical extreme. For James and Hitchcock, all knowledge points toward the suddenness and conclusiveness of that concussive knowledge that it is impossible finally to know and from which it is impossible to recover.

6

James's Birdcage/Hitchcock's Birds

Patrick O'Donnell

For Hugh Kenner in *The Pound Era* (1971), Henry James's shepherding in modernity and seeing out the nineteenth century, James's "unimagined labyrinths" conspire with "art's antipathy to the impercipient" to produce a body of work that combines obsessive reflexivity and compulsive attention to detail (4). We might also say the same of Hitchcock films from, roughly, *The Man Who Knew Too Much* (1934 version) on, in proximate relation to the latter epoch of cinematic modernity as James stands in relation to the earlier epoch of literary modernity. More pointedly, James and Hitchcock reflect in unprecedented ways on the relation between detail and labyrinth, both signature elements of their collective opus. They employ a specificity that intensifies relative to the degree of reflexivity signifying consignment of the real to the realm of the utterly indeterminate, marked above all by endless simulations of the factual, the reduplicative. Meanwhile, the work of the text, literary or cinematic, is to attempt a mapping of social labyrinths by means of a dissemination and gathering of myriad details. Sometimes this dissemination and gathering falls under the heading of the representation of a "consciousness"; sometimes it is purely iconic, a vast field of birds of every species, birds on every wire, intimating the apocalyptic failure of culture's plot to rule nature. In both instances the hidden agenda is to bolster a notion of human subjectivity as escaping, via a sleight of hand, the net of reality by becoming paradoxically trapped in what James figures in the Preface to *Roderick Hudson* (1907, 1934) as the skein of social "relations" that "stop nowhere," the "exquisite problem of the artist" being "eternally . . . to draw, by a geometry of his own, the circle within which they shall happily appear to do so" (5).

So much depends in James and Hitchcock on the perception of detail, on the ability to sort out between two or several equally valid logics which one is most consonant with "reality," or to exist, impossibly from the perspective of ideological critique, in both or all at once, though it is certainly pretty to think so. "Everything counts," writes James in the Preface to *Roderick Hudson*, "nothing is superfluous . . . the explorer's notebook . . . [is] . . . endlessly receptive; thus, an obsessive attention to every detail—what he describes as "the beguiling charm of the accessory facts in a given . . . case"—marks the high moment of revelation for many a James protagonist (3–4). Similarly, for Hitchcock, as Tom Cohen (1994) remarks, we can observe the manner in which Hitchcock "turns film into a surface amalgamating a multitude of material and technological markers beyond the mimetic images," thus generating a cinematic text that operates via a host of myriad details to deflect our attention from the narrative, while signifying the same narrative's overdetermination (237). In the odd figure he develops for his early work as an author for whom everything comes to count, James writes that as a "young embroiderer of the canvas of life," he "began to work in terror . . . of the vast expanse of that surface, of the boundless number of its distinct perforations for the needle, and of the tendency inherent in his many-coloured flowers and figures to cover and consume as many as possible of the little holes" (1907, 1934: 5–6).

This lure of detail that, extending James's figure, is a fetishistic excrescence upon the grid of reality—in effect, what makes it mesh, the net of its network, the parceling out of the big hole of the real into the "little holes" that constitute both its narratability and its being-narrated—this seduction by the nitpicky, intimates the larger investment of modernity in what Slavoj Žižek in *The Ticklish Subject* (1999) terms the splitting of "the subject of desire" from "the subject of drive."[1] The former, Žižek writes, is "grounded in . . . constitutive lack," whereas the latter—the subject of drive—"is grounded in a constitutive surplus, that is to say, in the excessive presence of some Thing that is inherently 'impossible' and should not be here, in our present reality—the Thing which, of course, is ultimately the subject itself" (304). In a preliminary sense, what is happening with detail in James and Hitchcock, what has transpired under modernity according to Žižek, is the evolution of identity as fundamentally voyeuristic: filling in the blanks, as it were, by perversely observing the holy and unholy acts of others; assuming that the real action is always elsewhere, but only real if observed unobserved, or observing and observed with both parties feigning ignorance of observability.

This condition of the "impossible" modern subject has nothing to do with desire as such, but everything to do with the splitting of desire from drive and, analogously, within the more confined realm of modernist aesthetics, the splitting of the capacity for reflexivity from the capacity for representation. James despairs in his Preface: you can never fill in all of those tiny holes, you can never see or know enough. Hitchcock despairs in a similar manner: despite all the clues, repetitions, doublings, details, symbolic and logical chains, and technological gimmickry of his films, the narratives themselves never add up to anything. Thus, *Vertigo* (1958), in which a man falls in love with and witnesses the death of the same woman twice, once for practice, once for real; *The Birds* (1963), an essay on the apocalyptic incidental; *Psycho* (1960), which argues that not only can you go home again, but you can't go, nor have you ever been, anywhere else; *Rear Window* (1954), in which a man sees exactly what he sees, the point of the film being that he must convince others that he sees exactly what he sees. What you see in Hitchcock is what you get—a succession of loosely associated images reflecting his sense that life is an entirely metonymical affair, an endless procession of contingencies, images, objects, events, and persons. Both Hitchcock and James compensate for this narrative despair—this sense that the more you immerse yourself in the texture and weave of detail, which is the only thing of interest to do in any case, the less sense it will all make, or, in Žižekian terms, the closer you come to the Thing of subject, the more it vanishes before your eyes. Narrative itself, of course, conceived as drive pure and simple, its ends irrelevant and inaccessible in any case, is the solution to its own inadequacy. James writes; Hitchcock films. They construct hyperreflexive stories and subjects in those stories who look everywhere for some Thing until they find or lose it. It is this compensatory strategy in James and Hitchcock that underwrites the formation of subjects whose desire is entirely constrained, in an oddly formal sense, by the, supposedly, globally capacious libidinal pulsion that enables the manufacture and acquisition of desire's objects, which is supposed to get us where we want to go but only and always takes us where we've already been.

In typically Jamesian fashion, the story behind *In the Cage* (1898) is so insubstantial as to cause the reader to reflect ironically on its "aboutness" or the essential hole at the center of event. The protagonist is an insignificant post office clerk whose dull life and prospects of a dull marriage to her fellow clerk and future grocer, the dully named Mr. Mudge, are elevated only at work, behind the cage of the telegraph counter, where she has the opportunity to observe how the other half lives as she checks the steady flow of telegrams being paid for by her rich customers before they are handed over to the telegraph operator. Privy to a network of communications between multiple parties entangled in the vast, but seemingly singular, web of circumstances that constitute the social order of late Victorian London aristocracy, "our young lady," as James refers to her throughout, stumbles upon a conspiratorial affair between one Captain Everard and a married woman, Lady Bradeen (1898, 1969: 77).[2] Because both are clients, James's protagonist is able to track the affair, the secret meetings, the forwarded and rerouted messages, the beards and screens that must be deployed in order for the affair to progress in that mode of secrecy which is obvious to everyone. Of course, behind the cage, taking his messages and returning his change, she falls in love with Captain Everard herself but must live out her passion vicariously as the "friend" who facilitates matters.

"Our young lady" is, thus, a hermetic figure, a voyeuristic message-sorter at the center of a narrative about sorting messages; as the telegraph clerk, she both purveys and purloins information—coding and decoding it—such that in her labor the relation between subjects and objects of knowledge is collapsed. As she increasingly gathers "clues" about the Everard/Bradeen affair, she perceives herself leading a "double life . . . in the cage" (186)—that of the grocer's fiancée, the anonymous clerk, and that of one who is at the panoptic center of a global system of communication and exchange:

> There were times when all the wires in the country seemed to start from the little hole-and-corner where she plied for a livelihood and where, in the shuffle of feet, the flutter of "forms," the straying of stamps and the ring of change over the counter, the people she had fallen into the habit of remembering and fitting together with others, and of having her theories and interpretations of, kept up before her their long procession and rotation. (186–87)

It is likely that only voyeuristically, in one who aspires to megalomania, could bureaucracy and the mundanity of message transmission be romanticized in this fashion—only if what is overseen, peeked at, or looked into can be woven into a systematic, yet diffused narrative whose point, as it were, is not the code but the coding. Like her friend, Mrs. Jordan, who has constructed for herself a boutique career as a floral arranger for the rich, James's protagonist "more than peeped in—she penetrated" (192); into the "immensity of th[e] intercourse" between her clients, she reads in "stories and meaning without end" (189).

James thus confers upon this unnamed heroine the power to assemble out of overwrought "clues" shreds of evidence, and sporadic messages (for her clients, including the beloved Captain Everard, frequently take their messages elsewhere), a "whole" narrative discourse that is both self-contained and scattered. It is both replete with "facts and figures" in a communication system where money and information are exchanged at an increasingly furious rate, yet so empty of content that the real "story" of *In the Cage* is not what the protagonist discovers—for she only finds out the whole story behind the affair second (voyeuristic) hand from Mrs. Jordan, who "hears things" while arranging plants in mansions—but what she accomplishes as a kind of stand-in who brings a putative totality to the semi-random, scattered, and partial fictions she "peeps into." Performance, not disclosure, is the sign of narrative "success" in James's tale.

The contradictions of "our young lady's" position are revealed in the novella's climax, when Captain Everard has reached a crisis point in his relationship with Lady Bradeen and visits the telegraph office to see if a copy has been kept of a telegram she has sent through a third party to him, and Everard fears there is something in the message (or not in the message; it is not clear) that might give them away. Taken aback by Everard's imperialistic attitude in this tense episode, "our young lady" takes the opportunity to engage in some sadistic play with the captain, for, though the copy of his telegram has been discarded long ago, she retains perfect memory of every message he has sent through her, but she prolongs revealing her recollection to him while he squirms. She thus takes revenge upon him as part of her dawning recognition that: (a) after all, she is but a civil servant to him and the aristocratic world that he embodies, though her voyeurism has allowed her to imagine herself at its center, empowered as the gaze that sees it and controls the flow of its information from behind the cage; (b) she actually knows very little about Everard and his affairs; (c) the more she does know, or manufactures as known, the more she realizes the contingency of his story to hers, her eccentricity in his narrative, which is why she must seize this fleeting instant when she becomes central to his destiny.

Well, only on rare occasions is James quite so frank about who holds or has the capacity to squeeze, manipulate, and even break the Thing, though, it is obvious that for James the Thing is nothing, a constitutive surplus, as Eric Savoy (2001) argues in his reading of James's objects. Captain Everard explains that the telegram "'fell into the wrong hands, but there's something in it . . . that may be all right. That is, if it's wrong, don't you know? It's all right if it's wrong'" (1898, 1969: 249). His dilemma is that Lady Bradeen can't remember what she put in the message, so that it is not known if she put the wrong thing (an unintentional bit of misinformation); the right thing (coded correct information), he fears, will provide a telling clue to whomever has intercepted the message about the nature of their relationship. What is actually contained in this purloined letter remains obscured. Finally letting him off the hook, after tortuous minutes in which she plays the role of "some strange woman at Knightsbridge or Paddington" (247), what she provides to Captain Everard as confirmation that the original telegram contained a mistake is a code written on the back of his card:

> He took the whole thing in with a flushed intensity . . . "By all the powers—it's wrong!" And without another look, without a word of thanks . . . straightened his triumphant shoulders and strode out of the place.
>
> She was left confronted with her habitual critics. "If it's wrong it's all right!" she extravagantly quoted to them. (251)

794961: what could it be? A date? It does not parse. A telephone number? Possibly, but it is a stretch given that in 1900, two years after the publication of *In the Cage*, the London telephone system was using simple four digit numbers and did not have the need to move to a larger three-letter prefix and four digit number system until the 1920s (Historic London). An address? A mathematical subroutine? A "cipher code," as John Carlos Rowe (1998a) queries, potentially as legible as the code cracked (complete with instructions) in Poe's "The Gold Bug" (161)?[3] In terms of the narrative, it is pure code, pure "constitutive surplus," and the clerk's power lies in her ability to reveal or conceal it. Her mistake, however, is to think that she acquires some form of agency in the larger world outside the cage of class and reduced expectations because she controls the dissemination of information. Here, I wish to distinguish between power and agency, just as I wish to distinguish between drive and desire, for the postal clerk's function in both possessing and yielding up the code is remarkable for its disabled effects. It doesn't provide her with a larger view into the affair to which she has only a kind of hieroglyphic access; it has no effect on the outcome, for what would have happened or not happened as the result of the interception of the message has already happened or not happened, and it completely and finally removes the postal clerk from the realm of contingency to the social order that Captain Everard inhabits, for in the process of giving him the Thing, the code, she is reduced to the role of alien menial to the upper classes (the "strange woman at Knightsbridge or Paddington") rather than being confidante to the demigods of the London aristocracy. The delivery of the code reveals the extent to which her power as informant is reliant upon her position as a kind of switching mechanism in a digital system of communication and exchange, an operant whose province is limited to the bytes of information flowing through her, and only one of many such mechanisms that might be used, randomly or not, under given circumstances (as the narrative makes clear, Captain Everard and his ilk tend to deliver their messages at whatever local telegraph office suits their convenience). "Our young woman's" access to information—the quanta of her mobility as subject—is thus inextricably linked to her placement or entrapment in the cage/matrix of the social order. There is no agency here, but only a drive-function, a routing mechanism for desire in a situation where drive is, as it were, everywhere (there are untold thousands of messages screened by hundreds of such postal clerks in late–nineteenth century London every day), and desire—or what I would term the narratability of drive—is nowhere, no thing, the aftermath of drive.

The anonymous postal clerk's plight is that of the modern, post-Hegelian subject, or as Žižek (1999) states it, "the subject [which] is the very gap filled in by the gesture of subjectivization" (158). Enter Alfred Hitchcock. *The Birds*, Hitchcock's forty-eighth feature film and arguably the one that, technically, posed the most difficulty for him, could be seen as an *In the Cage* expanded to global proportions. The postal clerk's delusional centrism regarding her "little hole-and-corner" is blown up to gargantuan dimensions in *The Birds* as the cage of Bodega Bay comes under attack from fowls of all species whose presence is attributed to the arrival of Melanie Daniels (Tippi Hedren), a San Francisco socialite more of the order of Lady Bradeen than "our young woman." Melanie comes to the fishing village in order to play a practical joke on a man she has just met in the city, Mitch Brenner (Rod Taylor), and ends up staying for dinner and much more. As is the case with James's novella, one wishes to ask what this film is about, beyond surplus of detail: so many birds, so many Things flocking together, that even in their specificity (one or two crows per child in a scene where children are attacked in a schoolyard) they become indistinguishable, a single big Thing, a parliament of fowls acting in concert, orchestrated by forces unknown as it comes out of the sky at random moments portending the end of the human world (see Figure 6.1).

The Birds is a Cold War film, released only months after the Cuban missile crisis, but whether the allegorical apocalypticism of the film can be read as the self-destructiveness of technology with its bird-missiles raining down without warning out of the sky and the *On the Beach* atmosphere of Bodega Bay and the Brenner family estate, or as the revenge of nature on culture, closer to the script's origins in the Daphne du Maurier story, is indistinguishable and largely irrelevant. For *The Birds*, I contend, is not about Cold War paranoia, scapegoated women, nature's revenge, or the incidence of evil. It is, allegorically, about nothing in particular. That is, it is an allegory of particularity or symptomaticity per se: the real, in James's metaphor of the carpet, only comprehensible as a series of holes or gaps to

FIGURE 6.1 *The Birds*: so many Things flocking together that even in their specificity they become a single big Thing.

be filled in; a thousand gulls and black birds coming suddenly out of the sky, as a manifestation of that order, sheer contingency writ large that we struggle to organize into a narrative of something, anything.

Something of a pastiche in this regard, *The Birds* is encyclopedic in fetishistic detail and its provision of partial, compensatory narratives that attempt to explain what is happening in a film where nothing is happening except sheer event, the Big Other's surprise attacks on the humble citizenry of the planet. In one of the film's key scenes, taking place at The Tides bar and restaurant, opinion and information are exchanged offering leads to an explanation for events, but they are all red herrings, dozens of inoperative codes changing hands, as if Hitchcock had decided to enact a reprise of all of his MacGuffins in one film. What is, in effect, a town meeting in the local hangout turns into a parodic enscenement of the social order attempting to cope with that which lies completely outside the range of its narrative methods and compensations; but none of these logics—scientific, mythological, theological—offers any real purchase upon the questions of what has gone wrong in Bodega Bay, and why. In a flurry of reference, visual puns, and general hermeneutic excess, we see children, fearful that the birds are going to eat them, eating fried birds; we hear two citations from the Old Testament and one from the New; we witness expert testimony on the difference between blackbirds and crows, the size of bird brains, the flocking habits of fowls, and the numbers of birds and species in North America and the world; we see a bevy of signs and details—multiplied liquor bottles on the wall, two matches lighted to ignite one cigarette (a foreshadowing of the bird attack in next scene, where the man having the Scotch at the bar drops a lighted match while getting into his car, which ignites a trail of spilled gasoline, causing a spectacular explosion of cars and gasoline pumps), the "no credit" and "no checks accepted" signs, the Gallo wine sign, the reversed neon sign in the bar window, the Bodega Bay welding sign across the street, photos of Bodega Bay and impressionistic paintings of rural scenes, the cigarette machine with its mirror that reflects the waitress's movements, the symmetrically arranged ashtrays lined up at the bar, Rod Taylor's cargo pants and salt and pepper sports coat ensemble. And then there are the stereotyped roles: the drunken prophet; the neurotic mother; the salty sea captain telling tales of monsters at sea; the amateur ornithologist/detective Miss Bundy, sticking to the facts and looking for all the world like Miss Marple; the cynical outsider. One can attribute all of this to realism or the weaving of plot, but it is all provided, here and everywhere in *The Birds*, to activate an intention behind the eruption of the real in the film instantiated by the bird attacks—an intention that never arrives or hits its mark.

The film does invite explanation, as if it needed to elicit from the viewer the ontological foundation for its own making, but the list of possibilities, from which I select a few highlights, is self-contradictory and fragmentary. *The Birds* offers no motive or reason for itself, no explanation, whole and intact, for the events—planned or random, orchestrated or merely "documented"—screened therein:

1. Melanie Daniels is an evil, alien presence who consciously or unconsciously brings destruction to the rural landscape with her from the big city (San Francisco), representing the corruption of nature by culture in modernity. Humankind has angered an anthropomorphized nature;
2. A paranoiac subset of one: Melanie Daniels is a reformed embodiment of *la dolce vita* (or *la vida loca*)—a rich girl, having once been falsely accused of running through fountains in Rome in the nude, she now does volunteer work for children (figuratively, the same ones attacked by the birds) and takes a course on General Semantics at Berkeley (yet she's the worst reader in the movie: the student of the human science that studies the formation of meaning is, at every turn, as in the clip, speechless or tautological when confronted with the question of what it all means). Though she's changed her life (here, Hitchcock's Catholicism comes into play), she's guilty forever, and the film is "about" the eternal exacting of retribution;
3. It's an antismoking movie! (Drinking is bad, too). Melanie Daniels smokes incessantly during the film, lighting up twice with Mitch's old flame, Annie Hayworth (Suzanne Pleshette), the local schoolteacher; Melanie is smoking outside the schoolyard as birds assemble to attack the children and drinking martinis with Mitch just before they attack children at a birthday party; and then there is the punishment exacted upon the man at the bar for lighting up a cigar—he gets blown up and burned to death. In fact, eating, smoking, drinking, sex, and talking in general are regarded in this film as punishable behaviors. All, of course, can be read as assaults upon nature, illustrative of the nature versus culture thematic of the film—but nature conceived as what? If everything other than any form of

human social interaction is nature, then nature is a kind of zero since the film makes it clear that "nature" is a series of representations emerging from the social imaginary. The birds, on the other hand, are aberrations of the natural order, or rather, in this narrative where the flocking and squawking of birds serve as parodic embodiments of the human, and the violence and appetites of humans, always on display, serve to demonstrate our base, birdy nature, the birds represent the self-cancellation of the social order, human desire hoist with its own petard.

4. It's all about the (postmodern) Oedipus complex where everybody must get castrated. Mitch Brenner can't be released from Mom's (Jessica Tandy's) clutches (what might be called in other terms her Oedipal attention span) until he undergoes the trials of manhood, which include bringing Melanie home to roost and protecting the family keep: we see his victory when Lydia, returning in horror from a neighbor's farm where she has seen a corpse with its eyes pecked out, drives up to the house to see Melanie and Mitch in what is clearly a postcoital embrace, she dressed in flannel nightgown (bought from the local general store) and fur coat (a remnant of her days of Roman decadence). As Mitch & Co. drive out of paradise in final, apocalyptic scene where the sun sets over birds covering the landscape as far as the eye can see, a shocked, wounded Melanie, visually raped by a flock of birds, lies in the sympathetic arms of that tough old survivor bird, Lydia Brenner, her gaze now directed at her new (recastrated) daughter and away from her (postcastrated) son, her Oedipal attention now "properly" redirected. The nuclear family is redeemed, renucleated, though in an asymmetrical way: son becomes dad (who died years ago, and whose picture is shredded by the birds when they attack the family homestead); the bad mother becomes the good mother; the bad, rebellious daughter becomes the good, supplicant (raped) daughter, though there is the curious twist that Lydia now has two daughters, in other words, a surplus of daughters and no sons, unless one counts Mitch reconstituted as both castrated son and father now that the threat of the castrating daughter is out of the way.

The laundry list of explanations, intentions, and motives could go on, but none of these results in a total logic or economy that can be said to undergird the film. The birds in *The Birds* are for nothing and no one, or for everything and everyone. They are both just birds and avatars of everything from the coming apocalypse and Russian missile strength to nature, guilt, the sublime, the other to technology's other (what can be characterized as the revenge of Nietzsche's superman upon itself), the exteriorization of the Oedipal, the reinternalization of the exteriorization of the drive per se. This movie is what happens, to invoke Žižek again, when the subject of drive is split from the subject of desire, when constitutive surplus is delinked from constitutive lack; that is, it portrays the formation of modern subjectivity as an attack on subjectivity, or more precisely, subjectivity under attack from itself. This is not the "divided self" of existentialism nor the split subject of classic Lacanian analysis; it is not the celebrated mobile subject of happy postmodernism nor the paranoid subject of sad postmodernism; it is neither the ethnic subject nor the white subject; it is neither regional nor global; neither imperialized nor imperialistic. Or, rather, it is not only one or more of these. All are, rather, symptomatic features of modern subjectivity per se, which among other things is to be recognized as a series of semblances in which the ratio between constitutive surplus and constitutive lack is negotiated as and through these symptoms.

In conclusion, I want to focus on how the modern subject is fundamentally voyeuristic, noting the different voyeuristic logics that exist between James and Hitchcock. (Certainly, part of the difference to be marked here resides in the different media, but I am concerned here with a conception of subjectivity that has found its medium in film, but which is by no means coterminous with that medium). It is already clear from my commentary how the protagonist of *In the Cage* is literally voyeuristic: she lives her life—her only life, for it is clear that marriage to Mr. Mudge and removal to the London suburbs is, for her, a form of death—through the messages exchanged between amorous parties; she studies the semiotic codes of the aristocracy in order to spy out and play a role in their affairs in the only way she can, as a switch point in a system of communication and exchange. The postal clerk's voyeurism involves peering through the screen of code to the events beyond those that she perceives being experienced by others, but of course this activity is an integral part of a larger system of proliferating urban semiosis and commodification (a telegraph station in every neighborhood, a computer in every home) that can only operate by means of subjects occupying the position of voyeur. Spying on the rich in *In the Cage*, an occupation engaged more forthrightly by Mrs. Jordan, is integral to the ongoing work of the social order of pre-Fordist capitalism represented in the novella, for such voyeurism symptomatically recirculates the desire for status, wealth, sex, and beauty that structurates that order. But equally important, James makes clear, is the absolute separation of this system's "drive"—the flow of information and gossip, the libidinality of class envy that motivates "our young lady's" momentary sadism in withholding information from Captain Everard—from what can be viewed as its content, the objects of desire existing within it, but only by means of a contingency, incidentally or accidentally, opportunistic lacks recognizable only through the surplus value of discerned codes.

In *The Birds*, the world of *In the Cage* is turned inside out, for the voyeurism of Hitchcock's film resides entirely in the eyes of the birds and the bird's-eye of the camera, as if the semiotic surplus of the drive was looking to the specific and localized play of desire for its energy, its constitution. In one shot only in the film—when the birds have attacked the townspeople of Bodega Bay with ensuing explosions, wrecked cars, broken windows, and general mayhem—do we see the town from far above, from the height of the hovering birds, viewing the drive to meaningless

FIGURE 6.2 In one shot only in the film do we see the town from high above.

violence and global destruction at its source, as if, metaphorically, gazing on the social order from within the eye of the drive, the center of absolute nonintentionality, would explain it (see Figure 6.2). But this distance shot, this inverted voyeurism, merely serves to confirm, spatially, the gap between the birds as embodiments of "sense-less" drive and the surplus of intentionality it magnetizes as the humans, below, enact their mythemes, practice their hermeneutics, and perform amazing escapes from and reattachments to the embodiments of Oedipal desire. Subjectivity, in this scenario, is the attempt to elide the violence of the separation between the constitutive surplus of the drive and the constitute lack of desire by discerning its logic, which, if nothing else, offers the illusory predictability of the return of that violence upon itself in the subject. *The Birds*' excess and fetishizing of detail and action represent the degree to which drive has separated from desire in this realm where information has replaced knowledge in a narrative that commences with a scene of commerce (the purchase of lovebirds in a gilded cage) that leads, both inevitably and by hook or crook, to a scene of apocalypse now.

To close in a different register, I refer to Henri Lefebvre's "First Prelude" in the *Introduction to Modernity* (1995) where he considers the mode of modern historical being as that of "maieutic irony." Reading Marx's famous passage from "The Eighteenth Brumaire" on repetition and revolution in history, Lefebvre writes that:

> For Marxists, the Hegelian cunning of the idea in history becomes the objective irony of history acting within subjectivities. This irony comes from the fact 'men,' social forces and ideas, masses and individuals, act in ways contrary to their intentions; and moreover, they express their actions by ideologies, signs and symbols which are frequently misleading. Sooner or later even the best-laid plans will come to grief; such is the law. There is always an element of the unforeseen in history, even though history is not absurd, devoid of meaning,

> undetermined. The foreseen and the unforeseen, chance and necessity—these are the constituents of dialectical movement in history, and doubtless in nature too; the determination of becoming. (21)

There is much to concern us in this dense formulation, but it is worth regarding it, simply, as symptomatic rather than constative, and to ask how it is that a revealing conception of modernist subjectivity in history could arrive at the notion that "social forces and ideas, masses and individuals" have achieved an ironic status in which they can "act in ways contrary to their intention." Where does this counterintention come from? How do we, as a mass or individually, register this contrariety? How do we know we are acting contrary to intention, and not just intentionally acting contrarily? Such questions could only be posed toward a definition of semifree historical subjectivity (contrary to Lefebvre's intentions, I am sure!) in which the split within the subject between drive as constitutive surplus and desire as constitutive lack has already occurred in history. Certainly in these narratives by James and Hitchcock we encounter the question of how it is possible for acts and events to occur contrary to intention, at the crossroads of contending intentions, and at the extremes, without intention or without occasion altogether. The putatively free modern subject, existing as a mode of reflection upon or observance of, act as manifestation of drive and act as fulfillment of desire, constitutes itself, like capital, as a single embodiment of lack and surplus, too much freedom, too little agency, replete with intention and short on options. This is the return of the solitary "romantic self"—"the bird on a wire"—to its true home in modernity, infinitely multiplied, always the voyeuristic observer of its own nefarious agency.

7

Sounds of Silence in *The Wings of the Dove* and *Blackmail*

Donatella Izzo

Hallucinatory Adaptations

Parallel reading is a risky business. Placed side by side and allowed to cross-examine each other, texts have a way of circumventing the single-mindedness of the investigator's intention. Rather than yield the "truth," however provisional, about their mutual relationship, they sometimes establish adventurous, possibly illicit new liaisons. In what follows, I will read Alfred Hitchcock's *Blackmail* (1929) as a creative screen adaptation of Henry James's *The Wings of the Dove* (1902). This is, of course, a totally unwarranted move: no document grounds such a notion, nor has Hitchcock ever manifested an interest in James's work that would make the notion tenable as a serious scholarly hypothesis. I will therefore offer it as a hallucinatory one: the result of a paranoid interpretation induced by the joint impact of two abysmal Masters of bafflement on a reader's impressionable mind.

The Vulgar Little Street

The social world of *The Wings of the Dove* is predicated on a spatial split introduced at the very beginning through the references to the "vulgar little street" that Kate Croy takes in from the "small balcony" of Lionel Croy's shabby room (1902, 2006: 217). What this opening scene creates for the reader is an immediate and lasting sense of the character's precarious standing: Kate Croy's social background, which the heroine is required to abject if she is to enter her rich aunt's world and make her fortune there, is colored by her father's unspoken crime, which has tainted his name and created a wide discrepancy between his delinquent "truth" and his facade as "so particularly the English gentleman and the fortunate settled normal person" (220). Exactly such a discrepancy between "truth" and appearance will become the key to Kate's whole strategy of self-rescue in the novel—a strategy constantly haunted by the troubling shadow of the "vulgar little street" ready to engulf her if she fails.

Blackmail similarly opens on a slum scene—a police squad irrupting into the room of a suspect to arrest him—that creates a spatial, temporal, and social elsewhere framing the apparently respectable world of the rest of the story. The spinning wheel in the very first shot, the van rushing through the city streets, the distant communication technology in the van, all convey a sense of the fast pace of modernity, of which the flying squad, in its impeccable speed and effectiveness, becomes the fitting epitome (see Figure 7.1). This modern world is abruptly suspended with the squad's entrance into the slum: beyond the arch, they walk into the nineteenth century. In sharp contrast with the police van, a carriage and a horse are standing by; the hanging laundry, the children playing in the court, and the disheveled woman in a shawl that tries to stop the squad on the threshold all belong in a Dickens novel (or in James's Chirk Street). This indexes a different chronotope than the rest of the film, connected to nineteenth-century social realism—a noisy, unruly world that resists being disciplined and repressed by the law's emissaries (as witness the object thrown in by the crowd outside during the arrest).

The slum sequence looks back to earlier forms not only of social organization but also of artistic representation. As is well known, *Blackmail* was originally shot

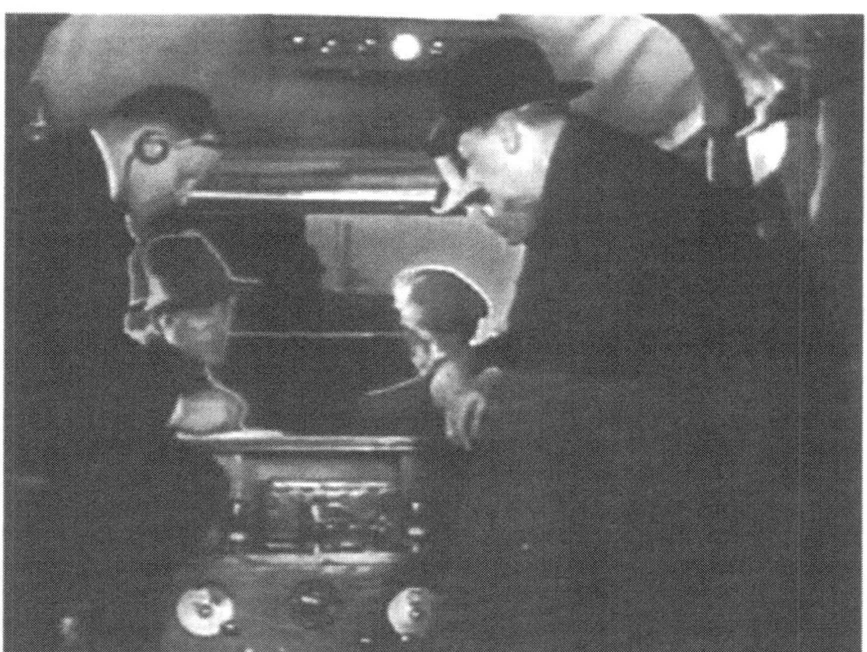

FIGURE 7.1 A new world of superior technology, order, and truth-producing rationality.

as a silent movie, then immediately shot again as a talkie using the new technology that had just become available and circulated in both versions.[1] The opening sequence, though, is entirely shot using the silent movie technique, throwing in sharp relief the sudden introduction of sound in the dialogue that follows, when the scene moves back to the present-day world of Scotland Yard, and the focus shifts from the impersonal operation of law enforcement and the teeming world of the urban underclass to the private lives of the film's protagonists. What the opening sequence of *Blackmail* stages is nothing less than a confrontation between two social and historical worlds, with one ostensibly prevailing over the other by virtue of its superior technology, order, and truth-producing rationality. And yet, despite the efficiently scientific, sanitized operation of the law—the implacable succession of the suspect's interrogation, identification, fingerprinting, and jailing, followed by the whole police department collectively and suggestively *washing their hands*—the "low life" ushers in the story, announcing the way it will keep haunting the legality of its surface, threatening to engulf the petty-bourgeois respectability and the veneer of modern sophistication of its protagonists.

She Waited, Alice White

Like Kate Croy in the much quoted incipit of *The Wings of the Dove*, Alice White (Anny Ondra), the protagonist of *Blackmail*, is first introduced in the act of waiting for a dilatory male—her fiancé, Frank Webber (John Longden), one of the policemen in the preceding scenes. Much is made of this waiting in the sequence that follows: Alice peevishly uses it as an excuse for her capricious behavior, causing an argument that induces Frank to leave her alone in a tearoom. This in turn enables her to spend the evening with the artist (Cyril Ritchard) from whom she has secretly received a note, and to whom she addresses a number of complicitous, seductive signals. While the triangle established here is more conventional than the one enacted in *The Wings of the Dove*, the woman character's role in both texts belies the lack of agency suggested by the passive attitude of waiting. Far from appearing as the passive object of the two men's attentions, Alice is figured—in her very capriciousness, as well as in her maneuvering to get rid of Frank—as a free agent, wishing to act out her desires, however ambivalent these may seem. The polarity offered by the two men is significant: an artist and a policeman, the former alluring her with his (allegedly) uplifting intellectual conversation, the latter proposing to spend the evening watching a movie on Scotland Yard—a narcissistic replica of his own job, confirming him in his self-importance—the former trying to seduce Alice into embracing his sexualized notion of herself—the naked body with which he completes her playful drawing of a face, the skimpy dress he makes her wear, purportedly to paint her portrait[2]—the latter trying to reinstate her in a traditional role as housewife by offering to make her a present of needle and thread to mend the holes in her glove (a detail suggestive of carelessness and sexual availability, later to resurface in the dead artist's room as an incriminating sign of her misplaced sexuality). In other words, one man is unleashing, the other one is policing Alice's imagination, each in his own interest: the prospective husband no less than the would-be seducer and attempted rapist. Alice White, though, is—at least in this sense—truly a "Miss Up-to-Date," as the artist mockingly sings immediately before attempting to rape her. Through her breach of traditional feminine codes of behavior, she is claiming an agency and a freedom to experiment; she is trying, however self-deludedly, to engineer a path for herself that will allow her *not* to have to choose between the symbolic roles and social destinies embodied and prescribed by polarized male figures. "I shall sacrifice nobody and nothing, and that's just my situation, that I want and that I shall try for everything" (1902, 2006: 264), famously declares Kate Croy, examining her options near the beginning of *The Wings of the Dove*. Like Kate Croy, Alice White wants to have her cake and eat it, too.

Such an attempt is of course futile, and both women will be forced to learn anew about the binding quality of their positions within the world's existing gender and class relations. Like a veritable cautionary tale, *Blackmail* seems to be inspired by a patriarchal pedagogy aimed at teaching the heroine the fatal consequences of her lack of discretion. After repeatedly taking her to the very brink of catastrophe, the film finally leads the delinquent heroine back into male custody and the limiting but protective fold of the Law, by now thoroughly epitomized by the man-husband-policeman in his manifold functions. Ironically, Alice is spared the legal consequences of the murder she has committed by her very lack of importance within the patriarchal structure: repeatedly silenced by Frank during his confrontation with the blackmailer, and then once again kept waiting in the police station, she cannot get the inspector to listen to her confession and finally gets away with her crime.

Or does she? Immediately after revealing the truth to Frank—a revelation appropriately taking place inside Scotland Yard—we see Frank leading her by her arm along the corridor, like the arrested man in the earlier sequence. Everything in the story converges to suggest that her real crime was not killing her attempted rapist, but imprudently accepting his invitation in the first place. By confessing both crimes to Frank, she has effectively put herself in his hands. And we are left to wonder whether after all, with Alice's secret now firmly in her future husband's possession, a new, lifelong kind of blackmailing is not going to begin.[3] Can it be an accident that both Frank and Tracy, symmetrically, each hold one of her gloves? For Alice and Frank no less than for Kate and Merton, "We shall never be again as we were!" (see Figure 7.2).

Blackmail

If I were to choose a single word to describe the dynamics of *The Wings of the Dove*, that word would now have to be "blackmail"—to such an extent does Hitchcock's geometrical rendition of character relations in his movie throw into relief the underlying logic of every interaction in James's novel.

FIGURE 7.2 "We shall never be again as we were!"

The blackmailing that goes on everywhere in *The Wings of the Dove*, of course, is not always literal: in the OED sense of "a payment extorted by threats or pressure, esp. by threatening to reveal a discreditable secret," the word only applies to Tracy's attempted extortion in the movie, based on his possession of one of Alice's fateful gloves. Still, in the broader current sense of making demands by exerting moral and emotional pressure through overt or covert menace, blackmail saturates James's story no less pervasively than Hitchcock's: indeed, few notions are more relevant to the minute machinery of characters' relations in the novel. Kate is morally blackmailed by her father and by her sister, who see her position as "a value, a great value, for them both" (1902, 2006: 263), demanding that she become rich for their sakes. She is morally and economically blackmailed by her rich aunt, who demands that she give up both her family and Densher if she wants to inherit, eventually, all of her money. She is blackmailed by Merton Densher, when he requires that she seal their pact by having sex with him, and then again in the final dialogue of the novel, when he demands that she give up Milly Theale's inheritance if he is to marry her. And of course, reciprocally, Kate is herself putting pressure on the reluctant Densher to win Milly's affections in order to finally get both her money and Kate. Milly's illness, no less than her wealth, wields an enormous power over all other characters, extending to the momentous—and paralyzing—consequences of her final bequest. And finally, Lord Mark's fateful revelation to Milly of the existence of a secret engagement between Kate Croy and Merton Densher is, seen in this light, perfectly in line with a blackmailer's behavior, trading secret information in exchange for supposed personal advantage.

The entire interpersonal network of *The Wings of the Dove* operates according to this economic principle of mutual instrumentalization—"the working and the worked were in London, as one might explain, the parties to every relation. . . . The worker in one connection was the worked in another; it was as broad as it was long—with the wheels of the system, as might be seen, wonderfully oiled" (333). This is a principle of universal convertibility based on universal commodification, and its overarching logic is succinctly stated by Lord Mark: "'Nobody here, you know, does anything for nothing'" (321). In its array of indefinite pronouns, equally dematerializing subjects and objects, and voiding them of any referentiality but their role in an abstract economy of exchange, this sentence captures the novel's situation with wonderful subtlety. In the world of *The Wings of the Dove* literally anything, however intangible, can be commodified, sold, and converted into monetary advantage—family ties, friendly affection, love found or lost. The intellectual abstraction of James's late world is, in fact, thoroughly saturated with capital and with the power games that keep it in circulation, albeit in an apparently disembodied form—the very essence of reification.

Blackmail, then, is especially relevant to such a world not just by virtue of the mechanism of exchange it epitomizes, but exactly because it is eminently a way of converting the intangible into the tangible—information into money, affection into leverage—epitomizing the process whereby under the conditions of advanced capitalism, material and immaterial values are incessantly transformed and made interchangeable. It is of course in the treatment of Milly Theale that the process is fully explored: the bare fact of her enormous wealth is constantly transmogrified into an array of immaterial qualities, subjected to the very end to an idealization that, try as it might, can never wholly suppress its material base. This is made even more evident, paradoxically, at the moment of her death, which on the one hand completes her retrospective idealization, while on the other proving, once again, through the legacy, the universal axiom of the convertibility of love into currency. And vice-versa: Merton Densher, even while trying to deny it, unwittingly reinforces this convertibility, not just in his final exchange of money for marriage with Kate, but in his retrospective falling in love with Milly. What this disembodied, idealized love actually effects is changing back the money into feeling: by reciprocating Milly's gift, it activates the structure of exchange underlying the gift.[4] Indeed, the elaborate rituals of nonknowledge, evasion, and rejection that he performs *exactly* in order to extricate himself from the inescapable awareness of these cumbersome facts—universal equivalence and ubiquitous commodification—only manage to foreground the ultimately financial character of Milly's "spread wings."[5]

Secrets

If the basic economy of blackmail is an economy of exchange, its specific field of application is the cognitive one. As Alexander Welsh has argued in his analysis of this plot motif in George Eliot, a thematized preoccupation with blackmail bespeaks the rise of a culture of information and publicity where knowledge and reputation have acquired a wholly new social prominence, giving new significance and value, in turn, to such terms as privacy and secrecy. In order for blackmail to exist, there must be a secret and somebody's unwarranted knowledge of the secret; in order for blackmail to work, though, the secret must be kept. Hence the paradoxical status of these secrets, perceivable as such exactly because they are known, but remunerative both in economic and in narrative terms exactly because their knowledge is restricted or conjectural, like the exact import of Milly Theale's illness or of Kate Croy's relationship with Densher.[6] To that extent, the cognitive structure of blackmail closely resembles the paradoxical one D. A. Miller (1989) described in *The Novel and the Police*: "I have had to intimate my secret, if only *not to tell it*; and conversely, in theatrically continuing to keep my secret, I have already rather *given it away*" (Miller 194). Or, as phrased just as strikingly in *The Wings of the Dove*: "What was behind showed but in gleams and glimpses; what was in front never at all confessed to not holding the stage" (1902, 2006: 397).

This paradox is nicely captured in the scene of *Blackmail* when Frank asks Alice to join him in the phone booth at her father's shop, to avoid being heard by her family, and shows her the glove he found on the crime scene (see Figure 7.3). Unknown to them, Tracy (Donald Calthrop), the blackmailer, is watching them from outside, and before Alice has a chance to reply he interrupts the scene by mockingly asking to place a phone call to Scotland Yard. He has already surmised what happened the night before and is even in possession of the other glove, so he did not need to watch the couple to know Alice's secret; still, in the dialogue that follows he draws attention to Frank's behavior by offering this remark: "By the way, you are the detective? Let me give you a tip. Don't wave the important clues inside of phone boxes: they've got glass doors. You know, detectives in glass houses shouldn't wave clues."

The most interesting implications of this exchange revolve around the question of secrecy and disclosure.[7] How are we to read the blackmailer's warning, momentarily subverting not just the power relations, but the very structure of authority? Addressed not to the guilty party but to the detective *as* detective, this remark does not concern the secret, but rather its knowledge. By extending the literal visibility entailed by the glass door into a metaphorical reminder of the proverbial vulnerability of those who accuse others while being themselves open to reproach, the blackmailer hints at the guilty reciprocity of the secret and its unveiling and exposes the danger that comes not with detaining the knowledge of a secret, but with threatening to reveal it (as Tracy's own subsequent career will also go to show). "[T]he social function of secrecy—isomorphic with its novelistic function—is not to conceal knowledge, so much as to conceal the knowledge of the knowledge," as D. A. Miller puts it (1989, 206). Careful indirect disclosure of the secret is the engine as much of successful blackmail as of narrative suspense, and indeed of narration itself. To my mind, what the imperfect privacy of a phone booth with a glass door figures is exactly the paradox of the always already public

FIGURE 7.3 In the phone booth, Frank shows Alice the glove.

nature of the secret, of its structural *need* for visibility and for communication (what else is a phone booth for, after all?), of the theatricalization of knowledge as disclosure. With the glass door of the booth operating like the "fourth wall" of a proscenium theater or the eye of the camera, and spectatorship signaled by the reverse shot with which the blackmailer's face suddenly breaks through that invisible wall, the episode works as a *mise en abyme* that foregrounds not just the interdependence of secret and knowledge, secret and narrative, but the shared position of both the director and the spectator as blackmailers (see Figure 7.4).

Silences

The paradoxical structure of secrecy is not just an engine of narrative development. The demand for truth and the will to know it are capable of being immediately deployed in the field of power relations. Keeping one's secrets is a way of evading the other's will to know by keeping to oneself the "truth" of one's self. Learning secrets is a way of creating and managing a power differential, of retaining or redressing an existing power imbalance: Kate Croy's strategy of keeping her engagement secret while appropriating the secret of Milly's illness and of her love for Densher is in this sense an exemplary combination of defensive and offensive use of one's own as well as of others' secrets. This value of knowledge in structuring relations is made all the more evident, in the two texts under examination, by the setting

FIGURE 7.4 The blackmailer's face breaks through the phone booth's invisible wall.

of each story in what might be termed an "information society":[8] a fact underscored by Densher's profession in *The Wings of the Dove*, pointing to that exchange value of information, which is more covertly attested by the machinations going on everywhere in the social and interpersonal sphere; but also made explicit in *Blackmail* by the prominent presence of newspapers and news headlines, with the scene at the tobacconist's displaying their evident impact on the public's imagination.

In its abstract operation, blackmail is simply a structure of power-knowledge, or, rather, a structure that makes the relation of knowledge to power explicit.[9] Unlike ordinary discursive apparatuses, though, blackmail structures a system of relations that is based not on the play of statements but on *silence*, in its twofold quality as *both* an effect *and* an instrument of power—that is, both silence as the silencing of the disempowered, *and* silence as the reserve of the powerful or of those seeking empowerment.

This is nowhere more evident than in *The Wings of the Dove*, whose plot is entirely predicated, as I have suggested above, on the use of silence as an offensive and defensive weapon within an economy of mutual blackmailing. The prominence of silence in the novel, though, exceeds even this function: there is hardly a page where it is not mentioned, foregrounded, examined. Illustrations would be virtually endless, and examples would of course have to include, besides secrets proper and reticences about things "too terrible to name" (1902, 2006: 508), such well-known instances as Milly's "turn[ing] her face to the wall" (599), her refusal to speak after

Lord Mark's fatal visit, and her finally unread letter. Silence is literally made tangible in the novel—"silence was gross and thick" (487)—and endowed with qualities and activities of its own: "a silence that looked out for them both at the far reach of their prospect" (281). Thus made palpable, it becomes perceivable as the veritable soundtrack of the novel: "It was mostly in stillness [things] spoke to her best; amid voices she lost the sense" (507); "it was . . . something that, for the spiritual ear, might have been audible as a faint far wail. This was the sound he cherished when alone in the stillness of his rooms. He sought and guarded the stillness, so that it might prevail there till the inevitable sounds of life, once more, comparatively coarse and harsh, should smother and deaden it" (683–4).

Silence, however, is not just an exceptionally emphasized thematic presence in *The Wings of the Dove*. Communication and interpretation are effected through a pervasive hermeneutics of silence, whose uppermost example is possibly provided by Books IV and V, largely devoted to Milly's analyses and discussions of the "abysses" and the "labyrinth" (338) of Kate's and Densher's silence about their acquaintance. Silence in the novel is the universal currency of numberless interactions, supplementing, contradicting, or replacing verbal exchange: "her silence was itself too straight an answer" (519); "the subject was made present to them . . . only by the intensity with which it mutely expressed its absence" (678). Thus, as the ubiquitous medium of signification,[10] it engenders a semiotics of its own, dispensing with verbal exchange: "Kate had positively but to be there just as she was to tell her he had come back. It seemed to pass between them in fine without a word" (396); "What he hadn't in the least stated her own manner was perpetually stating" (647).

In *The Wings of the Dove*, James seems to be simultaneously investigating the operation of language as a tool of manipulation and a token of social exchange, and straining beyond words toward an unprecedented form of verbal narrative—one where the sounds of silence take center stage as vehicles of knowledge, understanding, and communication, while words recede to the role of background noises or take on the theatrical quality of self-aware performances. What more is needed to envision *The Wings of the Dove* as the virtual script of a silent movie?

Sounds

A similar tension is embodied in *Blackmail*. It is wonderfully fitting, to be sure, that a film thematically revolving around such a machinery of silencing and disclosure as blackmail is also, technically as well as historically, a unique cinematic embodiment of the tension between sound and silence as means of producing, conveying, mastering, and policing meaning. A self-aware experiment with the innovative technology of sound cinema, *Blackmail* seems to be staging a metalinguistic debate over its potential and limits.

In striking contrast with the wordless operation of the law that frames the story—the opening sequence and the final pursuit of the blackmailer, both accompanied only by music—the dialogues in the movie seem meant to exemplify the unreliability of speech as a means of effective or truthful communication: in scene after scene words lie, seduce, and mislead, contradicted by facial expressions, gestures, movements, and a whole semiotics of places, objects, and images comprising an array of Hitchcock signature pieces. These include, of course, such a favorite Jamesian devices as the painting *en abyme*, of which *The Wings of the Dove* provides perhaps the most celebrated example in the Bronzino portrait. Of the two paintings in the artist's room, the one begun by Alice in a part-flirtatious, part-serious attempt at trying her hand at artistic self-expression develops, as I mentioned above, into a male representation of her as a sexualized being that she first undersigns and then repudiates. The second, the jester, recurs as a leitmotif in the scenes that follow, mocking Frank during his inspection of the dead man's premises; appearing again after the blackmailer has comfortably installed himself in Mr. White's chair, effecting the transition to the police station, where he is going to be identified by Crewe's landlady; and finally sealing the film with a half-derisive, half-threatening final note troublingly addressed to the saved but not guiltless heroine, as well as at the horrified fiancé and now dishonest policeman, at the unknowing and deceived police, and of course at the audience.[11] Equally expressive is the framed photograph of a uniformed Frank that looks reproachingly on Alice from the room of her bedroom the morning after the murder, while the wordless sound of the bird's warbling in its cage, for all its melodiousness, recalls the more troubling implications of cages that Frank will make explicit in his later appellation of Tracy as "a jailbird."

Only right after the murder, when sounds become expressionistically charged with the subjective dimension of Alice's obsession, do the aural and the visual dimensions converge, albeit at the cost of a repudiation of verbal communication, erased in the long night Alice spends wandering through the city, or relegated to background noise in the subsequent conversations during breakfast at her parents'. Finally, what emerges in the second half of the movie is the salvific role of silence, or, rather, the salvific role of woman's silence when she obeys patriarchal injunctions. Throughout the confrontation between Frank Webber and the blackmailer, she tries in vain to interrupt, only to be repeatedly silenced. And later, at Scotland Yard, her attempted confession is deferred until she effectively escapes the consequences of having killed a man. The heroine's (qualified) happy ending is thus ironically secured through denying her the right to speak, that is, through the very gendering of roles that makes woman powerless and woman's speech culturally irrelevant within a patriarchal institution.

Confessions

Alice White's speech in the second half of the movie coincides with a repeated failure to confess. And, indeed, this is hardly surprising: structurally, confession is the very opposite of blackmail, the antidote that, by making the secret known, voids it of its exchange value and therefore of its economic power—as well as of its cognitive and narrative drive. No wonder, then, that the protagonist is only allowed to carry out her confession in the very last sequence.

The deferral of confession, though, is not just a device for regulating suspense and keeping the blackmail going, nor does it operate exclusively along the cognitive axis. In its very essence, confession produces a narrative of guilt vis-à-vis the law. What remains to be determined, however, is the nature, respectively, of guilt and of the law.

If, as I have suggested, Alice's true crime in the story, within the patriarchal framework, is her attempt at an independent exercise of sexuality, Alice's final disclosure becomes paradigmatic of Michel Foucault's argument that in Western culture, sex is construed as *the* secret of the self, so that in the ritual of confession "truth and sex are joined, through the obligatory and exhaustive expression of an individual secret" (Foucault 1978, 61)—Alice's individual secret literally coinciding, in this case, with sexuality. What is more interesting, in light of Foucault's observations on the structure of authority at work in confession, is that this is a secret that Frank *already knows*, since he witnessed Alice's meeting with the artist in the first place. A veritable Foucauldian ritual, Alice White's confession is not so much a truth-producing moment, either for Frank or for the audience, as a subject-constituting performance and a ritual of subjection—or rather, a ritual of subjection as constitutive of subjectivity. Through her confession, Alice is thus (re)constituted, after her attempt at rebellion, as a dutiful female subject within a patriarchal system: as an act of subjection addressed to her prospective husband, her confession reinstates him anew as her lawful judge and authority, the recipient of her loyalty and from now on, it is to be surmised, the exclusive manager of her (otherwise risky) sexuality.

Authorities, though, are themselves problematic in the movie; in this sense, it is highly significant that the protagonist is hindered from making her confession to the police. In its coming too late, Alice's disclosure produces an ironic twist in the movie's structure of authority: by correcting its false conclusions about Tracy's guilt, it exposes Scotland Yard's mistake and creates a crisis in its credibility that subverts its earlier representation in the story. By revealing to Frank his own unwitting complicity in sheltering a murderer and causing the death of an innocent man, it undermines the masculine self-assurance, based on the impregnability of his professional status, that he had exhibited during the scene in the tearoom, and then again in the Whites' parlor. In other words, creating a split between private and public figures of patriarchal authority, the confession only has value within a private dimension, where it produces a bizarre structure of mutual (dis)empowerment based on an intricate mutual dependence, which models the man–woman relationship on the complicity linking partners in crime (or, for that matter, a blackmailer to his/her victim). On the other hand, the public and official authorities are (as is frequently the case with Hitchcock) devalued and ridiculed, and so is the woman's attempt at claiming for herself a public conscience as a citizen subject to the rule of law. Ironically, the downplaying of the importance of woman, as manifested in the sequence at Scotland Yard, results in the simultaneous disempowerment of man. And the policeman's final joke backfires, unwittingly revealing a literal truth: "'Ah ah, so you found him, Miss? Did she tell you who did it? . . . You want to look out, or she'll be losing your job, my boy!'"

That confession may play a prominent role in a thriller by a Catholic director whose interest in the theme is also attested by countless similar scenes in other movies—including one titled *I Confess!* (1953)—is, of course, only to be expected. That it may emerge as a perceptible leitmotif in *The Wings of the Dove* is perhaps more surprising. Used as a declarative verb, as a participial adjective, as a quintessentially Jamesian adverb—"Recognition . . . sat confessedly in her own eyes" (1902, 2006: 408)—confession and its derivatives pervade the novel, with the automatic effect of construing every utterance, perception, or aspect as the revelation or discovery of something hidden. Thus, every interaction is constituted as a potentially truth-producing exercise in investigative cross-examination, as an effort at opacity to avoid giving oneself away ("To meet her now with the note of the plaintive would amount somehow to a surrender, to a confession" [385]), or else as a free gift of self-revelation offered as a token of friendship and confidence—Milly's "theory of intimate confessions" (511) bringing her and Kate together and offering them relief from their shared need to be constantly wearing a mask. Appearing as it does in the middle of an elaborate and much-quoted analysis of the manifold layers of reserve and concealment between the two women, however, this mention of confession only serves to underscore their mutual holding back: "They flourished their masks, the independent pair, as they might have flourished Spanish fans; they smiled and sighed on removing them; but the gesture, the smiles, the sighs, strangely enough, might have been suspected the greatest reality in the business. . . . It was when they called each other's attention to their ceasing to pretend, it was then that what they were keeping back was most in the air" (511). In a world where secrecy and duplicity are the very foundation of everybody's identity and behavior, the continuous rehearsal of the notion of confession stands as a *foregrounding* of the act of revelation or discovery itself and, simultaneously, as a perpetual reminder of its delusional quality and of the mutually constitutive nature of concealment and disclosure.

Confession in *The Wings of the Dove*, however, is not just a matter of lexical recurrence. No less than *Blackmail*, the novel features a major confession scene. Perhaps surprisingly, its protagonist is not the scheming, duplicitous, sexually active Kate Croy—in regard to whom one even finds such an unmistakable trace of the detective story villain as the repeated mention of her need of an "alibi" (400–1)—but the "dovelike" Milly Theale. The scene is of course the episode of her second visit to Sir Luke Strett, the distinguished physician, whose impression on Milly on the occasion of her short first visit had been emphatically described to Kate as a regenerative Catholic ritual: "'I feel—I can't otherwise describe it—as if I had been on my knees to the priest. I've confessed and I've been absolved.

It has been lifted off'" (368–9). During the visit that follows, we learn, "She told him, . . . straightway, everything" (369); while, in his turn, Sir Luke is said to have known everything beforehand by virtue of his having "found out simply by his genius—and found out, she meant, literally everything" (370). Again in line with the Foucauldian pattern, confession does not produce knowledge, but rather acknowledgment of and subjection to an authority who "requires the confession, prescribes and appreciates it, and intervenes in order to judge, punish, forgive, console, and reconcile" (Foucault 1978, 61–2).

One may well wonder, though, what this portentous "everything," the object of Milly Theale's confession and of her absolution, may be, especially at a point in the novel when her subsequent secrets—illness and love—are still merely conjectural. If every confession is confession to a guilt that coincides with subjectivity, Milly's guilt lies perhaps in the very facts that constitute her distinctive identity: young, immensely free, immeasurably rich, afflicted by an indefinite illness, romantically infatuated with her own unique predicament, and very consciously American.

Ethics

What kind of authority is James installing at the heart of his novel through Milly's confession? Impotent to avert death, unwilling to provide explicit truths, unable to offer any comfort or support but understanding and encouragement, and yet presented throughout the novel as a luminous figure and a moral paragon, Sir Luke Strett is a very unusual authority. Even as a patriarchal figure, he is a somewhat anomalous one, and not just because he appears to be unattached to any spouse.[12] His advice to Milly Theale is, basically, that she should dare to live and unleash her desire—a desire whose sexual implications are at one point frankly discussed by Susan Stringham and Maud Lowder—and this suggestion puts him strikingly at odds with the kind of authority figures we meet in *Blackmail*. His universally acknowledged authority is possibly an effect of a feature that sets him apart from the rest of the characters. He is the only figure in the novel—paradoxically, since he is presumably a well-paid professional—to be presented as alien to the circuit of universal exchange in whose stalemate all characters will be finally caught; a powerful figure of knowledge whose knowledge is nevertheless not immediately translatable into a bid for power over others, but rather deployed as a recognition of their ethical claim; a possibly idealizing (and, for once, definitely anti-Foucauldian) representation, which might perhaps be taken as James's closest approximation to a moral judgment over the novel's world.

Let me then, by way of wrapping up this parallel reading of underlying affinities and unlikely relations, compare the ethical framework that this creates for *The Wings of the Dove* with the one offered in *Blackmail*.

Both texts display ethical complications: in *Blackmail*, these relate not only to Alice's choice to confess, but also to Frank's (protective or self-protective) decision to hide Alice's glove from his colleagues and later to his attempt to prevent her confession and to his final acceptance of her guilt. The ending, in fact, spreads guilt more than it purges it. It only makes sense ethically as a happy ending if we are convinced of the heroine's fundamental innocence, if we see her guilt as primarily sexual and therefore as redeemed by her final deferral to Frank's authority, if we assess attempted extortion as a worse crime than taking a man's life, and if we share the view that private affection takes precedence over the law. In other words, it creates an irreconcilable paradox, a fissure within the ethical system.[13] The jester's laugh in the final image thus simultaneously involves the police, the law, and each of the characters—as well as the viewers—in the short circuit that comes from having created a putative happy ending that unsettles the very possibility of ethical choice by hinging on a set of impossible alternatives.

Impossible alternatives are, of course, exactly the keynote running, from beginning to end, through *The Wings of the Dove*. Critics have confronted the ethical entanglements of *The Wings of the Dove* for decades. Most recently, Slavoj Žižek (2006) has produced an analysis of the intricacies of the novel's ending, proposing a reading of Kate as the true ethical character in the novel and of her final choice as the only ethical one, "possible only within an atheist perspective" (139).[14] Significantly, Žižek's reading of James's novel insistently relies on an extended parallel with Hitchcock's themes and devices—a parallel he takes to the point of inviting us to visualize Kate's and Densher's confrontation over the letter announcing Milly's bequest "as a scene in a Hitchcock's film: first the exchange of gazes; only then, slowly, does the camera approach the object, the focal point of the scene . . ." (1902, 2006: 134).

Perhaps this might go some way towards retrospectively justifying my claim for a hallucinatory adaptation. Too bad, really, that the Masters only meet in critics' fantasies.

8

The Perfect Enigma

Judith Roof

> There are insects which "escape the eyes of hungry birds by living and dying in the shape of a flower," a flower whose coloring is "a design made up of hundreds of tiny insects"
>
> —Mark Rutland, *Marnie* (1964)

> . . . the plain moral that a young embroiderer of the canvas of life soon began to work in terror, fairly, of the vast expanse of the surface, of the boundless number of its distinct perforations for the needle, and of the tendency inherent in his many-colored flowers and figures to cover and consume as many as possible of the little holes. The development of the flower, of the figure, involved thus an immense counting of holes and a careful selection among them. That would have been, it seemed to him, a brave enough process, were it not the very nature of the holes so to invite, to solicit, to persuade, to practise positively a thousand lures and deceits
>
> —Henry James 1984, 5–6

Alfred Hitchcock's 1964 film, *Marnie*, and Henry James's 1895 short story, "The Figure in the Carpet" both offer enigmas for their multiple audiences to resolve. Dramatizing overtly the practices of psychoanalysis and literary interpretation, each text affords an explicit subject for analysis. *Marnie*'s subject appears to be Marnie Edgar (Tippi Hedren), a bookkeeper-cum-professional thief whose larcenous impulses are motivated by more than simple greed. Marnie becomes the love interest of the rich young entrepreneur, Mark Rutland (Sean Connery), who from the very beginning knows of her propensities. Apprehending her after she steals cash from his stationery company's safe, Mark declares his love, blackmails her into marriage, and becomes her analyst, trying to discover the underlying trauma that has left Marnie frigid, dishonest, equinophilic, terrified of thunderstorms, and paralyzed by the color red. The mystery of "The Figure in the Carpet" is the central pattern or "figure" animating the novels of the esteemed author, Hugh Vereker. Vereker's "figure" is the critical prize obsessively sought by a trio of young literati—the story's narrator, his competitor, Corvick, and Corvick's fiancée, Gwendolyn. Conflating the man Vereker with his work, the critics embark on a competitive quest for Vereker's meaning, endeavoring to penetrate Vereker's secrets, believing the figure they seek, as the author himself has assured them, is the key to his art.

Bound up in the seductions of knowledge, neither text points to a single answer; instead, they each contrive multiple frames of looking and finding which suggest that both texts catalyze and perpetuate shifting, polymorphous desire as a necessary mode of consumption and perhaps an end in itself. Apparently focused on a single enigma, both texts invest much less obviously but far more insistently in a secondary quest—the stolid and quietly spectacular desirings of the various layers of questers. Although *Marnie* includes what appear to be occasional glances into Marnie's psyche as the screen suddenly flushes red or flashback memories erupt from what we assume to be her point of view, these clues do double duty, giving the film's audience information sufficient to empathize both with Marnie's plight and Mark's search, drawing the audience into the film's observing economy as a third frame of questers. "The Figure in the Carpet" traces not Vereker, who disappears after the first few pages, but the critics' attempts to discover Vereker's key as well as the narrator's efforts to track and benefit from the success of the other critics. The story provides neither direct clues nor evidence from Vereker's texts themselves, focusing entirely on the narrator's prolonged and frustrated observations about the other critics. Neither having read Vereker's work nor having any basis upon which to form any kind of judgment, the readers of James's story have no vested interest in Vereker's figure at all but instead have an interest in the dynamics of the quest itself and the desire for knowledge that catalyzes it.

The trick of both texts is that the object of any quest is not what it seems to be; it is not a figure, an answer, a childhood trauma, or meaning.[1] Instead, these decoys screen systems of circulation in which objects, desires, and identifications substitute for and displace one another, producing a dynamic of deferral and perpetuated desire. In this economy, the greatest lure of all is the idea of knowing. Knowing itself in both *Marnie* and "Figure" is deadly. In *Marnie*, knowledge is literally knowing about a murder; in "Figure," Corvick's triumph precedes his own rapid demise. The entry point into this dynamic of perpetuated desire is not the lurid enigma itself—Marnie's or Vereker's secrets—nor even some discernible or predictable lack in the questers, but is instead the provision of vectors of desiring—the multiple positions and dynamics that organize the various modes and possibilities of seeing and knowing (where the two neither constitute nor guarantee one another). These seductive structures draw the audience's attention to a specific discourse—psychoanalysis, literary criticism—among several as the appropriate mode of both interrogation and pleasure. They also invite their audiences to assume a position in relation to the ostensible secret, which seduces audiences into one of several other quests defined in terms of identifications with their enigmatic objects and their questers, emotional transferences, and degrees of critical consciousness displayed in the texts and deployed by audiences. Protagonists and audiences desire despite themselves and desire that desire.

Ultimately, although both texts seduce and mislead through their provision of a misleading enigma that produces ambiguity upon ambiguity, they enact and make visible the frustrating and paradoxical processes by which desire and knowledge are perpetually at odds with one another, resulting in desire perpetuated for its own sake. One cannot have both desire and knowledge at the same time, which means that the desire that drives the layers of telling—of narrative—that comprise both of these quests actually works to forgo knowledge in favor of maintaining the drive—the desire to tell—where telling offers itself as a means of knowing and mastering. Wanting to solve the puzzle of Marnie or discern Vereker's figure makes acquiring an answer increasingly impossible, not because the answer is not there to be known, but because it doesn't matter and, because the more one wants to know it, the less likely it will be that any answer would suffice. Desire rather than knowledge is the point; in both texts curiosity is driven less by an actual answer than by a desire to desire. The knowledge imagined to fulfill this curiosity neither secures desire nor permits a pure pleasure in consumption. Instead, the desire to know turns back upon itself, reverberating through the proliferating layers of textual consciousness, suggesting but veering away from the lacunae that would seem to incite desire to ricochet endlessly as the telling that subtends questing for its own sake.

Deferrals

Although James's story precedes Hitchcock's film by seventy years, the film's visualizing of the multiple, entangled lines of analysis and desire intrinsic to the very processes of watching and interpreting film reads the ambiguities of "The Figure in the Carpet" back on itself. The film exemplifies the ways the seductions of a projected pattern hide the constitutive fracture at the intersection of knowledge and desire. The incommensurability of knowing and wanting produces narrative as the effect of a drive to tell masquerading as the desire to know. *Marnie*'s complex circulation of multiple systems—cinema, psychoanalysis, transgression, trauma—simultaneously produces, provisionally fulfills, and perpetually fuels the desire for the answer that would secure some mastery, some cessation, some desire of the other. It appears, in other words, to work according to Freud's pleasure principle of seeking quiescence in closure.[2]

But the film counters this impulsion toward an answer. If anything, *Marnie*'s mode of enunciation (the specific means by which the cinematic apparatus produces the illusion of a source and presents the narrative) consists of perpetually shifting and deferred looks that signal and stand in for a desiring that becomes increasingly complex. The lines of sight are entangled with confused, displaced, and deferred lines of desire. Marnie watches in order to plan her thefts, her mysterious desire compelling her forays, her object revealed at one point to be her horse, Forio, who might substitute for her mother. Mark watches Marnie, desiring her, desiring to know the motivations of her desire, desiring her desire. Lil (Diane Baker), Mark's sister-in-law, watches them both, desiring Mark's desire, perhaps desiring Marnie, desiring the knowledge that might master the situation. We watch them all, desire them all, caught up in all manner of desiring dynamics masquerading as analysis, narration, identification, curiosity. The apparent end points of these chains of deferred looks and layered desire are Marnie's mother (Louise Latham), who persistently averts her look, and Forio, whose response is indeterminable ("You can bite me anytime, Forio," Marnie comments ecstatically). Both mother and horse ricochet the looks back around, neither absorbing the accrued investment of interest offered them. Mark watches Marnie engage with both her mother and her horse, not as the envious competitor, but waiting in line for what will inevitably shift again.

Marnie deploys its complex system of looking as the register of this network of desirings, especially as watching also seems the only route by which knowledge about others' desires might be gained. The film opens with a sequence that maps the transference of a look at the retreating Marnie (who has just stolen from her employer, Strutt) from the camera to Strutt to Mark Rutland, and finally to Hitchcock, enacting from the beginning the shiftiness of point of view and the elusiveness of its object, while simultaneously establishing watching as the key vector of knowing. Each look—the camera's, Marnie's, Mark's, Lil's, Strutt's, or Marnie's mother's curious look away—enables simultaneously several possible, but generally fleeting modes of engagement. Posing characters both to be seen and to see, *Marnie* permits every schematic mode of identification (being or having), and every economy of desire—voyeurism, fetishism, heteronormativity, homosexuality, lesbianism—to operate in relation to any character because all participate in the circulation of questing observings motivated by their own lust and desire for knowledge while they offer sites for investment. Mark, Marnie, Lil, and even Forio are the camera's beloved objects.

Pleasure in *Marnie* comes only with refusing to occupy a single position or settle for even partial knowledge of Marnie's or Mark's or Lil's motivations, an economy that may partially account for why the film was commercially unsuccessful.[3] Narratively, Mark's motives are as enigmatic as Marnie's; and in the hom(m)osexual transfer of looks at the film's opening, Mark would seem to stand out as Marnie's fetish correlative. None of the characters—Marnie, Mark, Lil, Marnie's mother—is who he or she appears to be; all masquerade. And if Marnie flees and strikes back below the money belt, Mark blackmails her into marriage, asserts his marital rights against her will, and attempts to control and own her. At the same time, he identifies enough with her to know where she is going before she gets there. Lil is also a part of the observing economy, standing outside of Mark's ongoing struggle while wishing to be inside, watching voyeuristically, seeing through both Mark and Marnie, trying to manipulate their narrative by inviting yet another looker, Strutt, to the prehunt ball (see Figure 8.1). Lil is the film's audience correlative, desiring Mark, identifying with both Mark and Marnie, embodying a

FIGURE 8.1 The observing economy.

bisexuality that the film links with desire and illusive knowledge and doing what the audience cannot do—meddling with events to try and force an end to the circulations.[4] Lil also operates as an object of desire herself, as the camera lingers on her longing face. The circle of observers and knowers in the film is never complete, as Strutt's appearance catalyzes yet another round of revelations, which then force the confessions of Marnie's mother in Baltimore.

Mark also models another mode of engagement. His analysis of Marnie sets up a complex psychoanalytic model of transference and countertransference as another mode of consumption and unresolved desiring. Allied with the film's deferral of looks, the engagements of transference—one character taking the place of another in a series of emotional deferrals—puts feelings and emotional investments into circulation. Marnie, finding herself trapped by Mark Rutland, refuses to transfer her desire to him. This may not only be a motivation for her objectification; it is also a reason for an identification with her, if we regard Mark and the film's opening *glissement* of male observers as oppressive. Whatever desire has encouraged her kleptomania and frigidity, she keeps it to herself, even as the narrative continually spectacularizes the leakage from her unconscious as she suffers nightmares, overreacts to thunderstorms, and is overtaken by the color red. While Marnie invests feelings in her mother and her horse (neither of these investments is a transference), Mark, from the start the studious behaviorist, has already fallen victim to a countertransference, putting himself into what he imagines is Marnie's place, being what he imagines she would want him to be, anticipating her desires in a quest to locate her mystery. In the end, although Mark calms a Marnie who has found out the ostensible source of her trauma, there is no resolution, no cessation of desiring. We still do not know, for example, whether the revelation of Marnie's gallant homicide will actually make her less frigid, more accepting, and more wifely, nor do we know whether Mark will continue his attendance on a spouse who may no longer refuse to look back. We do not know if Marnie's mother will become more tender or if Lil will continue to haunt the edges of Mark and Marnie's truce. Knowing what we know does not halt the desire for desire at all.

Who knows what when, how each character's observations frame the others, and what desires append to their observations are all shifting possibilities in *Marnie*. In the end, though we may know some of the traumatic events that may have induced Marnie's behaviors, we still do not know Mark's motivations nor Lil's nor the mother's nor even our own. We have been sent on a chase, seeking knowledge, offered the vision of shifting sources, investments, fetishistic sites of cathexis, duplicitous performances of masquerade, and the confusions of transference, but all multiply the possibilities instead of leading to any singular answer. If Marnie is the film's lure, what she screens is precisely the complex richness, delusive mastery, perpetual frustrations of a desiring catalyzed by a delusive knowing. In the end the film's seduction is its constant perpetuation of desires, prolonging and putting off through its skeins of other-directed looks that induce an audience to crave a focus more often than it offers it one.

Grounding the Figure

Like *Marnie* (or *Marnie*, like it), James's "The Figure in the Carpet," defers and ultimately withholds any solution to the quest posed to its narrator. Like *Marnie*'s Mark, the interested and emotionally cathected sleuth, "Figure's" first-person narrator is triangulated with the object of his quest through a series of male relationships—his with the author, Vereker, and Vereker with the other critic, Corvick. But unlike Mark, the narrator in "Figure" gains neither associational advantage nor authority by virtue of his function as "enunciator"—as the apparent origin of the story. Instead, "The Figure in the Carpet" persistently denies the narrator the knowledge he seeks, producing, as in *Marnie*, the seductive lure of a persistently deferred desire. The story narrates the narrator's failure; the story's readers work to supersede the narrator's own limited vision, perceiving what the narrator narrates though fails to perceive, but, in the end, knowing no more about Vereker's "figure," than the narrator does, though suspecting perhaps more.

Marnie's desiring circulations are perpetuated by the film's constant shifting of the look among characters and the camera. In "The Figure in the Carpet," circulation is less perpetual than it is oscillating, back and forth between what are constructed as the incommensurate perceptibilities of figure and ground. These are "completeness; continuity; finite form," according to J. Hillis Miller (1980, 61). They are the "ambiguity" of "incompatible, yet equally tenable possibilities" that "renders choice impossible and frustrates the reader's expectations of a univocal, definitive meaning" according to Shlomith Rimmon-Kenan (1980/81, 108, 186). The impetus of economies of both texts, however, is to shift persistently the site where the lure—that which seems to offer both question and answer—is imagined to operate. In *Marnie*, although the more obvious lure seems to be what makes Marnie tick, each character offers its own enigma, at least insofar as each character presents a mystery about what he or she desires or why he or she watches (or does not watch in the case of the mother) the others. While the main lure of "The Figure in the Carpet" seems to be the question of Vereker's demystifying figure, the seductive impetus splits into, on the one hand, the answer, claimed by Corvick, which the narrator continues to seek, and, on the other, the increasing provision of a potentially self-reflective insight about the nature of the quest for meaning and the desire that grounds such a quest. If in *Marnie*, lurid figures substitute for one another, in James's story, the levels of perception and query split and proliferate, chasing through and producing frame after interpretive frame, eliciting and putting off a desire that cannot be accounted for by the pretext of intellectual curiosity.

The desiring economy of "The Figure in the Carpet" consists of the interplay of its accumulated, mobile frames of query and provisional insight. The initial encounter between the narrator and Vereker occurs as a compensation for the narrator having overheard Vereker's disparagement of the narrator's review of Vereker's new novel, a review written as a favor for the narrator's friend Corvick, who did not have time to write it. This first favor frames a set of frames—Vereker's novel, the narrator's review, Vereker's comment—that recede to some unknown origin in Vereker's writing itself, posed by Vereker as the pattern that animates all of his works. The novel, the favor, the review, the conversation are then framed successively by Corvick's and Gwendolyn's obsessive researches for Vereker's figure, Corvick's removal to the East, Corvick's claim to have discovered Vereker's figure, Corvick's marriage, his death, Vereker's death, Vereker's wife's death, Gwendolyn's remarriage, her death in childbirth, and finally a return to a scenario reminiscent of the first framing encounter between the narrator and Vereker, the fruit of the originary quest still up in the air, as the narrator confronts a man as clueless as he is. The narrator waits and looks for the insights of each new movement, each part of the quest's trajectory, hoping to gain secondhand what he cannot find himself. Aligned with this derivative, but increasingly imperceptive, look, readers forge their own patterns from events, but the patterns that appear, like those of a shell game, only suggest where the answer has not been revealed. All of this promising lack of fulfillment perpetuates desire. All of the framings and multiplications of seekers—the narrator, Corvick, Gwendolyn—"invite endless redoublings" (Miller 1980, 109). In the end as the narrator sits with Gwendolyn's widower, desire is all that remains, as unassuaged as ever.

R(enunciation)

Splitting desire and proliferating sites of investment, the economies of *Marnie* and "The Figure in the Carpet" persist through critical analyses of the texts, each text producing in its accumulated critique the economy of desiring desire that haunts the texts themselves. The texts' complex perpetuations reproduce themselves in criticism that reiterates, not only their framing quests, but also a critical tendency to try to reduce the texts' complexities to a singular, mediated, definitive scenario. In the end, the problem catalyzed by both texts is a problem of interpretation itself as the potential destroyer, but also the source of the pleasures of desiring.

Interpretations of *Marnie* try harder to be more definitive than readings of "The Figure in the Carpet," which seem to be content resting between the indeterminate conclusions of J. Hillis Miller and Shlomith Rimmon-Kenan. *Marnie*, one of the more mysterious of Hitchcock's productions, offers perhaps less in the way of systematizable semiotics and more in the complexities of visual frustrations. For this reason, *Marnie*'s critics tend to focus on how the film secures connections between seeing and knowing—precisely the connection the film ultimately denies. In perhaps the most famous essay written about the film, Raymond Bellour, for example, overtly links seeing to what he imagines are vectors of authority. His "Hitchcock, The Enunciator" (1977) closely reads the film's opening sequence, showing how it aligns the viewer with a series of doubles "irregularly distributed on a trajectory at the origin of which there is Hitchcock, the first among all his doubles, a matrix which allows their generation, and his own image of himself as pure image power—the camera-wish, of which the object-choice is here the woman" (73). This argument demonstrates how specific practices of point of view, editing, and narrative appear to construct an ultimate site of knowledge, the fictive enunciator or vantage from which we imagine we scrutinize Marnie.

Like the film, however, Bellour's argument is already seduced by the lure of potential knowledge apparently afforded by the activity of watching. The flip side of his argument suggests the ways that *Marnie*'s enunciative structure might also persistently defer these identifications. Even though the string of deferred looks would appear to produce a set of single-minded male substitutes, the apparatus itself is already split between Freud's two inapposite modes of identification—that of wanting to be a character or wanting to have a character. Parsed precisely around these processes of desire, identifications fragment any kind of enunciative unity insofar as every film image inscribes two looks—that of the camera and that of the character—each of which might operate within one of several different identificatory economies. The alignment of the camera with the enunciator with the protagonist's desires competes with the proliferation of varied scenarios of looking, knowing, and desiring that persistently diverge attentions and investments.

Bellour's attempt to deploy a process of enunciation to secure critically the alignment of looks and desires at the beginning of *Marnie* defends against too much perversity in a film in which the apparatus constantly shifts from one character's perspective (i.e., via a specific point of view) to that of another to that of the camera, and in which the relationships among the characters consist largely of multiple, overlapping observings. Bellour understands this complexity as the film "delegating the look," which "makes the splitting of vision possible, in which the enunciation is inscribed across the multiplicity of textual systems from a base at once constant and shifting" (82–83). In other words, by defining the source of a master look, the film's perverse directions can be interpretively, if only imaginarily, controlled, quelling the film's polymorphous, perpetuated desirings.

Beyond this organizing enunciative function, *Marnie*'s very system of looks, displays, watching, observing, and observing observing install widely varied modes of knowing and engaging, ranging from identifications to fetishism, masquerade, and transference. In addition, the film deploys multiple underlying affective economies (the heterosexual, homosexual, lesbian, familial, interspecies), each of which invites a completely different set of consumptive processes. The result is precisely Mark's "flower" made up of a masquerade of wholeness invested in the lure of Marnie herself instead of a single masterly investigation of what woman wants.

Just as Bellour locates the figure of Marnie as the intermediary figure for the organization and transference of these multifarious looks, other critics adapt Bellour's suggestion of multiple deferred inscriptions, initially reading these as more open and mobile, enabling multiple identifications that operate more thematically. Dominique Sipière (1996), for example, seconds Bellour's observation of *Marnie*'s shifting focalizations, noting as well that the film's focalizations "do not have a mechanical rapport with one another" (28, translation mine).[5] In her book on Hitchcock, Tania Modleski (2005) suggests that "Hitchcock's fear and loathing of women is accompanied by a lucid understanding of—even sympathy for—women's problems in patriarchy" (112). The contradictory posture Modleski attributes to the filmmaker finds its way as well into readings that understand *Marnie* as illustrating precisely that set of contradictions as a way of resolving its system of deferred looks. John Fletcher's (1988) analysis of *Marnie* follows the insights of such feminist film theorists as Joan Copjec (1982), who sees patriarchy itself as "the effect of a particular arrangement of competing discourses, not as an expressive totality which guarantees its own interests" (58). *Marnie*, thus, becomes a different kind of answer: an example of how a film can challenge both the hegemonic character of enunciation and the possibilities for cooperative, yet resistant strategies.

Fletcher's resolution of *Marnie's* difficulties comes by specific recourse to this gendering, a division apparently reified by the film's animation of the ur-plot of heterosexual difference inscribed in modes of seeing. In other words, Fletcher tries to sort out perversities by denying them and realigning seeing with knowing gender itself. Instead of locating mastery in a masculine enunciator, Fletcher sees the film as a gender battle whose undecidability ultimately accounts for the film's indeterminate feel. Fletcher defines the film's clashing modes of viewing as "the relation of the male scenario of fetishism to the female scenario of masquerade" (58). Fetishism, a predominantly male mode of viewing in which an object is taken as both the substitute for the missing organ and assurance of its continued presence, offers in itself an intrinsically self-contradictory posture of disavowal—"I know but all the same . . ."[6] Masquerade, as Joan Rivière (1929) formulates it, is a predominantly female posture in which women hide masculinity behind a display of hyperfemininity. It operates primarily from the side of Marnie in the guise of a subject. As a self-contradictory posture, masquerade enacts, according to Fletcher, "the different relations between its elements of 'mask' and 'transgression' and the differing meanings they accumulate" (1988, 58).

Fletcher's model may indeed neatly account for some of the ways desire itself is confabulated and perpetuated in the film, but it does so precisely by not really focusing on desire at all. Containing desirings within structures of deceptive and self-deceptive, gendered vision displaces the film's economy of desire symptomatically back into the activity of watching as again the site of mastery and knowledge. Because the film deploys multiple modes of watching as a decoy in which layers of watchers fail to know, the criticism, too, has missed part of the point, which is that watching is finally more about the watcher's desire than about any kind of knowability and that perhaps such watching is itself a deviant activity, unpredictable and unorganizable. Even trying to reorganize the vectors of desire in the film into more homosocial or lesbian and homosexual lines still tries to parse out and recoup the imagined relation between knowing and seeing.[7]

Critical responses to the absence of answer in "The Figure in the Carpet" echo critics' responses to *Marnie*, but with a crucial difference. Although many of the story's interpreters arrive at an "answer," one central critical dispute manages to enact the desiring economies of the story itself. In general, as might be anticipated by the decoy of the "figure," there is disagreement about whether or not the story's mystery has ever been solved and who solves it. As with *Marnie*, critical discussion shifts from the possibility of any diegetic solution to a reading that focuses more on the consumption of the text—and what in the text produces its varied modes of consumption—than on any narrative or characterological mystery. Of course, the two—diegesis and consumption—are entwined, perhaps constituting the same thing, as the story forces its readers into repeating its narrator's misapprehensions even as readers and critics might defend themselves against the failure of solution by raising other questions. As in *Marnie*, readers of "Figure" occupy multiple sites of identification—with the narrator, with the narrator's quest, with Vereker, or with an ironic knowing position produced as an effect of the narrator's various blindnesses. Narrative itself drives toward the idea of finding a solution, even if that solution is empty, paradoxical, silly, or cruel. But, unlike in *Marnie*, the identifications and quests in "Figure" are secondhand. Readers do not seek the pattern themselves but seek the narrator's and Corvick and Gwendolyn's seeking, caught not in the singular quest for the meaning of Vereker, but in the questing, desiring economy of the questers.

As both J. Hillis Miller and Shlomith Rimmon-Kenan have argued (but in different and clashing ways), "The Figure in the Carpet" constitutes itself through ambiguity. Miller argues that the very conditions of representation force a constitutive split or "catachresis" inherent to any telling. All literature exists as a figure in that "there is no 'literal' language for the representation of states of consciousness and interior experience" (1980, 111). The "figure" that is, thus, a necessary operation in the rendition of a story never correlates with some supposed realistic referent, producing narrative that is what Miller calls "'unreadable,' undecidable, irreducible to any single equivocal interpretation" (111). "The Figure in the Carpet," which Miller sees as "mim[ing] this unreadability," produces "incompatible readings" that produce an inevitable enigma. This enigma motivates "multiple ambiguous readings" that "are not merely alternative possibilities. They are intertwined with one another in a system of unreadability, each possibility generating the others in an unstilled oscillation" (112). Rimmon-Kenan (1980/81) reads ambiguity as a more limited phenomenon: "By providing incompatible, yet equally tenable possibilities, ambiguity renders choice impossible and frustrates the reader's expectations of a univocal, definitive meaning" (186). As in Miller's version, this ambiguity produces "an insoluble oscillation between the opposed members of a logical contradiction" (186).

The oscillation appearing even in the critical encounter between a deconstructive and a structuralist reading plays out the tensions produced by the constantly shifting nexus of knowledge and desire in the story. Like *Marnie*, "The Figure in the Carpet" perpetuates its desiring economy beyond itself into commentary, theory, and understandings of positionality and meaning, which, in Miller's terms, merely extend the catachretic operations. Wanting to find in the core of both texts some germ about the truth of life and death, the insightful illuminations of sexuality and reproductive processes, the animating factors of guilt and love, the ultimate bases of art and existence, the texts, their characters, and their critics submit to the mysterious economies of mobile desire in order to find the mooring point of it all. Perpetuating ambiguity and desire does not provide an answer. Or, in the alternative, such perpetuation provides, as some critics suggest, an answer in the process of looking itself, or it replicates the texts' dynamics as an effect of consumption (of reading, watching, or identifying), the secret providing answers that, like the texts themselves, merely displace and substitute process for desire, appending an artificial end to potentially ceaseless oscillations.

Both an unanswered question and the frustrations of no answer lure audiences on through a series of splits produced by the nature of the questions themselves. Both the mystery of Marnie's psychic trauma and the key to Vereker's art situate what appears to be a single answer in place of a complex process. Both of these enigmas go to the heart of meaning—of persona and art—which in the end have no single answer at all, but which instead instigate an endless chain of associations that themselves lead to and from the splits (split subjects, divided attentions) by which any impression of singularity or subjectivity persist. And in catalyzing the searches, these delusively simple keys raise as many questions about the questers as about the enigmas, including the texts' audiences themselves. Insofar as Mark searches for the key to Marnie's kleptomania, he, too, searches for the impossible key to his own desire, and the audience to the search looks for both and their own. Insofar as the narrator in "The Figure in the Carpet" narrator looks for the key to Vereker's art, he seeks both his own significance and that of the others who search in competition with him, as does the reader. The texts' enigmas never hide in a single spot but generate economies of desire that implicate all of the texts' consumers as their ultimate seduction.

In the end, even desire itself is not an answer, but a clue to what cannot be known. It is a metonymy operating within an infinite cascade of substitutions. The ambiguity of the texts maybe unresolvable and may shift the impetus of meaning and pleasure to process or desire itself, but even that is "unreadable" and undecidable, shifting with every consumption, emerging and working differently depending on which tack one takes. One may "know" some things and not others, but different things, partial knowledges, different quests. The texts' ambiguity means not that no one can know anything, but that no one can know everything—no one can know precisely the pattern that organizes all. Even if a single character (or two) is imagined to have "it," it may not even be the point. Instead, the looking, the being, the enacting, the processes of reading, telling, and engaging themselves, as other critics point out, may be as much a part of the seduction as any potential figure, which is always already a substitute anyway for that which we do not know and cannot tell. Whatever foundational ambiguity persists in these two narratives animated by ambiguity, that foundation does not precede or catalyze the narratives; it is not originary. Instead, ambiguity emerges out of the condition of desiring knowledge itself. What this means is that whatever it is that audiences and critics think is at the core of these texts only exists by being put into motion as an effect of—instead of the cause of—desire. Telling is generated to generate tellings.

Both *Marnie* and "The Figure in the Carpet" produce an economy of perpetuated desire that repeatedly enacts the incommensurability of knowing and wanting. Neither film nor story offers mastery, closure, or quiescence, though both texts flirt with a version of mastery as either deferred (as in Bellour's model of enunciation) or delusive. Both enact what neither seems to be enacting: the proliferated splits—in identification, knowledge/desire, modes of watching, the genesis of narrative—by which we know we will never know and watch anyway as the very heart of narrative itself.

9

Hands, Objects, and Love in James and Hitchcock

READING THE TOUCH IN *THE GOLDEN BOWL* AND *NOTORIOUS*

Jonathan Freedman

Criss-cross: can we imagine James and Hitchcock meeting in an airport lounge (there's one in heaven, I'm told) and having a long, meditative conversation, expatriate to expatriate, transplanted American to transplanted Englishman? What would they talk about? Well, what *wouldn't* they talk about? They'd want to discuss technique, of course, with respect to their own medium or one another's. They would share a laugh at their too-reverent ephebes, like Percy Lubbock or François Truffaut—much less literal-minded academics like me or, quite possibly, you. They might chat about the nuts and bolts of their business, whether the publishing markets in the United States and England that so frustrated James or the succession of studios and studio heads that Hitchcock juggled so brilliantly. Or perhaps they would exchange tales like a pair of small-town gossips, swapping stories of the doings of Edith Wharton or Jonathan Sturgis for those of Tippi Hedren or Cary Grant. Or maybe, in a meditative mood, late in the evening, having had one or two too many, they would confess their deepest fantasies: "I . . . like to watch," Henry might say (considerably more polysyllabically). "Me, too," Hitch might rumble in return.

Or maybe, just maybe, they would confess their deepest preoccupation. Maybe they would talk about love.

Love in all its many manifestations is Henry James's great theme, and Hitchcock's as well.[1] The project for each of them was, we have all come to assume, to trouble that most mysterious of emotions, to crosshatch it with omnibus forms of desire, or to kink it up, to disconnect it from its immediate object and reconnect it with others, or to no object, or even no-longer human ones, like a mother's corpse. Love for each was notoriously connected as well with mastery—mastery of others, mastery of form, mastery of others through form. We know this: Hitchcockians and Jamesians alike have spent the last twenty years patiently teaching us this moral, but it's pretty clear they learned their lesson from the masters. Yet there is also a countermovement in the works of these figures, a push against the hermeneutics of suspicion that each has, in his own way, generated.[2] I want briefly to talk about two moments in two works in which these two let go of their career-long skepticism about the nature and possibilities of love. Each is fraught. Both are keyed to displacements of their concern with vision, that faculty usually associated with James, theorist of point of view, and Hitchcock, master of point-of-view shots, respectively. In *The Golden Bowl* (1904) and *Notorious* (1946), Hitchcock and James pay attention to other parts of the human body than the eyes—specifically, to hands, and hence metonymically, and often actually, to the sense of touch—in ways that challenge the grim logic of their shared, discourse-shaping ocularcentrism.[3] Indeed, within each of these works, a sensuous phenomenology of touch emerges, and it is this touch that turns us back from a world of things to the human and from the human to love in ways that ultimately raise powerful questions about James's and Hitchcock's representational endeavors—and our responses to them.

To turn first to *The Golden Bowl*: what's striking about the critical response to this novel is the perdurability of the interest in the relation between the subject (however conceived) to the object-world in which that subject is forced to live. There's not all that much difference between Laurence Holland's state-of-the-art reading of the novel of 1964 and Bill Brown's state-of the art reading of 2003. For both, the novel is engaged with the struggle of Maggie Verver and hence Henry James to make meaning via recalcitrant objects in a thing-strewn world, most notably of the bowl itself (triumphantly for Holland, less so for Brown).[4] And it's further received wisdom that the bowl, like all objects, like all people, in this novel, is understood and interpreted *visually*—by the Antiquario for Charlotte and the Prince (who has only to glance at it to know that it is cracked), by Maggie for Fanny, and then, after it is broken, by Maggie for the Prince, whom she bids to gaze at and interpret the meaning of the bowl's shards. Knowledge and vision, insight and eyesight, semiosis and visuality, are one, or at least significantly aligned, in a way that James and Jamesians alike have trained us to see.[5]

True enough. But also true and less significantly reflected in the criticism is the appeal of things in the novel to the other senses, an appeal that also gets registered through the career of the bowl.[6] Over the course of *The Golden Bowl*, the bowl is not only commented on, discussed, quarried, raised into an object of symbolic significance (it is, after all, referred to as the "gilt cup," pun fully intended) and magical properties, turning it at times into a walking, talking fetish ("that cup there has turned witness," Maggie says at one point [1904, 1909: 24:164]), the bowl is also *handled*—touched, caressed, carried from shop to home, held, pinged, elevated into the air, shattered on a marble floor, and pieced back together. And as it is so multiply deployed, it is the hands that handle the bowl that James persistently emphasizes.

This process begins with the Antiquario, who not only takes the golden bowl out of its square box, "covered with worn-looking leather"—leather that at least appears to bear the marks of many hands' touch over time—but also "handles it with tenderness, with ceremony" as he presents it to Charlotte and Amerigo, then "hold[s] it aloft" for Charlotte's inspection, tapping it with a key to demonstrate its soundness (1904, 1909: 23:112, 117). The bowl is handled by Charlotte, too, who holds it "in both her fine hands, turning it to the light," noting as she does so its heaviness, its (misleading) solidity (23:113). The bowl is implicitly touched again when the Antiquario sells it to Maggie, then by Maggie, who takes it home and places it on her mantlepiece. When we next see the object, it is not only put on display but grabbed by Fanny, who

> casting about her and whose inspiration decidedly had come, raised the cup in her two hands, raised it positively above her head and from it solemnly smiled at the Princess as a signal of intention. So for an instant, full of the thought and of the act, she held the precious vessel, and then with note taken of the margin of the polished floor, bare fine and had in the embrasure of the window, dashed it boldly to the ground, where she had the thrill of seeing it lie shattered with the violence of the crash. (24:179)

Notice how protracted is Fanny's holding the bowl in her two hands before she breaks it, a gesture that mimics but negates the Antiquiaro's holding it aloft as he shows it to Charlotte. Yet even after the bowl is broken, its tactile career continues. Maggie carries its pieces to the mantel and sets them there, and, as she places them before Amerigo, it's again the physical contact between her and the object that is emphasized:

> the split determined by the latent crack was so sharp and so neat that if there had been anything to hold them the bowl might still quite beautifully, a few steps away, have passed for uninjured. As there was nothing but Maggie's hands during the few moments the latter were so employed, she could only lay the almost equal parts of the vessel carefully beside their pedestal and leave them thus before her husband's eyes. (24:182–3)

We note again how the performance of Maggie's hands is foregrounded in this briefly enacted action of a "few moments" duration, for even in that limited period of time, they shape the visible demonstration of the bowl's fracturedness and of the knowledge of marital rupture it proclaims. By pointed contrast, throughout the entire scene, Amerigo stands with his hands in his pockets—that is, touching nothing, neither Maggie nor the bowl, unless like the similarly inclined (and aptly named) Ralph Touchett he is touching himself.

This emphasis on the handling of the bowl reminds us that objects in this novel exist not just as static *things* to be read and reread, interpreted and reinterpreted, but as concrete objects that can be—and are—held, touched, moved about, lifted in the air (twice), broken, put back together. To this extent, the novel comports to the outlines of so-called "thing theory," that way of reading that (reductively put) stresses the mutual construction of objects and the humans who encounter and perceive them.[7] But to invoke thing theory here is to note, by contrast, how insistently James emphasizes the contact between hand and object, how persistently he focuses on the juncture between the human and the material, people and things, wrought through touch. The same quality extends, at a particularly crucial moment, into the novel's patterns of figuration, where even the mentalistic representations of objects participate in the novel's emphasis on tactility. Indeed, it is in one of James's elaborate figures that the connection between the human and the material via touch is represented most thoroughly. I am referring to the second-most commented-on object in the book, the image of the pagoda by which the novel depicts Maggie's response to the relations in which she, her father, her stepmother, and her husband are enmeshed. This is one of the most remarkable passages in all of James, one in which we witness a rhetorical figure, an extended, curlicuing metaphor, representing the thought processes of a character in the act of figuring out her situation. As one might expect, the language of visuality seems to dominate the passage, as it habitually does in Jamesian moments of imaginative self-inquiry—one thinks here especially of the famous scene of Isabel staring into the fire in Chapter 42 of *Portrait of a Lady* (1881), or even of the language applied to Maggie later in this passage ("her watching by his fireside for her husband's return . . . fell for retrospect into a succession of moments that were *watchable* still") (1904, 1909: 24:9, 11). But here, the metaphor has Maggie give up on seeing before she is able to approach the pagoda: "at present, to her considering mind, it was as if she had ceased merely to scare and scan the elevation, ceased so vaguely, so quite helplessly to stare and wonder" (24:4). Rather than motionlessly *seeing*, as James describes Isabel Archer's fireside vision in *Portrait*, Maggie actively circles the pagoda, and rather than motionlessly *see*, she "sounded . . . one of the rare porcelain plates" then "applied her hand to a cold, smooth spot and waited to see what would happen" (1881, 1909: 3:xxi; 1904, 1909: 24:4). And what does happen is a fantastical effect out of the *Arabian Nights*: "it was as if a sound, at her touch, after a little, had come back to her from within—a sound sufficiently suggesting that her approach had been noted" (24:4).

What we are dealing with here, of course, is metaphor piled on metaphor, trope troping trope[8]; my point in focusing on such an effect is to ask why the metaphors turn at this moment beyond sight to the other senses and to observe that, again, it is touch that takes primacy among those senses. Indeed, we note again not only how insistently James emphasizes the power of touch—it's the application of Maggie's hand to the pagoda that produces the reciprocating sound, not her rapping on it—but also how tenaciously touch lingers: like Fanny holding the bowl in her hands for a prolonged time before dashing it to the ground, or Maggie holding the pieces together, this (figurative) touch is protracted, its duration enacted both by the verb "apply" and then the waiting game that follows. This passage goes even further than the other two moments of contact in rendering the feel of the object at hand—its temperature and texture, "cold" and "smooth"—and in suggesting the complex phenomenology of touch itself. Touched, the pagoda also *touches*; it makes a sensual impression on Maggie's hand even as Maggie "applies her hand" to it. The result is a juncture mediated by the sense of touch between things in the world and the bodily being that touches them, one that takes us outside the familiar Jamesian dialectic of consciousness and vision into a different relation between being and world, one organized by the feeling-and-being-felt hand as well as the imperious

Emersonian eye. As such, the metaphor figures a different attitude not just toward things, but toward the way one interacts with them. If vision works on the figurative as well as the narrative level as a trope for cognition, touch similarly figures not just engagement in the phenomenal world but also efficacious action in it. "By a mere touch of her hand," the narrator tells us, Maggie makes "a difference in the situation so long present to her as practically unattackable" (1904, 1909: 24:3).

"A mere touch of her hand," the phrase that on first glance or hasty reading seems to denigrate the sense of touch actually inflates it, suggests the power that accrues to touch throughout the novel, a pattern that holds in figure and narrative alike—a juncture enacted just a few pages later, when Maggie's goal as she articulates it to herself, "is to bring about a difference, touch by touch, without letting any of the three, and least of all her father, suspect her hand" (24:33). "Touch" here, of course, is itself touched with the sense of the artist's "touch," a sense that predominates in many of the references to touch that gather through the novel; so, with reference especially to writing, is "hand." But I want to insist on the physicality, the embodied quality, of the novel's deployment of touch and hand, for it is here, I think, that James's work might best be thought of in tandem with (and put in perspective by) that of philosophers who, starting about the same time as he was writing *The Golden Bowl*, brought touch back into prominence. Touch (relegated to the lowest of senses by Aristotle and Plato, frequently denigrated thereafter) was often appealed to by twentieth-century phenomenologists and their deconstructive successors as an alternative way of being and knowing to those on offer in the Western philosophical tradition, a tendency that begins with Husserl, continues through Merleau-Ponty, and augments in the work of Edith Wyschogrod, Jean-Luc Nancy, Jacques Derrida, and Michel Serres.[9]

This may be because touch deconstructs the ways we understand sense experience itself. Touch is not reducible to, or locatable in, one organ or another the way vision is identified with the eye, hearing with the ear, smell with the nose. Touch is multiple, employing nerve endings, receptors, skin, different parts of the body—it can be involved with the fingertips, or the palm of the hand, or any part of our skin that touches anything else, or for that matter other body parts, like the genitals and lips. Moreover, Mark Paterson (2007) reminds us that "touch" in the broadest sense of the word extends from the cognitive to the emotional, the affective, the erotic, a fact registered, as Paterson points out, in the English language, in which touching or being touched by are synonyms for being moved emotionally. (The same is true of the French *toucher* and the German *berühren*.) But touch's chief philosophical appeal is that it allows for, even demands, a different, more fluid model of inwardness and outwardness than do models built around the other faculties, most especially (and most relevantly to James) vision. If in Western ocularcentric culture, vision is closely linked to cognition, and hence to a distancing from and an attempt to master the world, touch by contrast brings us as bodily beings into close contact with a world that defies our attempts at mastery. As Merleau-Ponty (1962) writes: "In visual experience, which pushes objectification further than does tactile experience, we can, at least at first sight, flatter ourselves that we constitute a world, because it presents itself with a spectacle spread out before us at a distance, gives us the illusion of being immediately present everywhere and being situated nowhere . . . [But] as the subject of touch, I cannot flatter myself that I am everywhere and nowhere; I cannot forget in this case that it is through my body that I go to the world, and tactile experience occurs 'ahead' of me, and is not centered in me" (316).[10] Moreover, we know and hence inhabit our body with special immediacy but in a wholly different way through touch, either when we touch ourselves (Merleau-Ponty's example, revising Husserl, is that of the left hand clasping the right one, in which one becomes both subject and object) or when we touch other things, thereby becoming aware of the part of the body that is doing the touching as well as of the thing it touches.[11] Similarly, we know the world in a more intimate way when we touch it than we do through the other senses, especially vision, as we feel the textures or the temperatures of objects (or air, or water) through our fingers, or hands, or skin. What Serres (2009) writes of skin per se applies equally to the first two of these, which are, of course, wrapped by and ontologically implicated in skin itself:

> The skin is a variety of contingency: in it, through it, with it, the world and my body touch each other, the feeling and the felt, it defines their common edge. Contingency means common tangency: in it the world and the body intersect and caress each other. I do not wish to call the place in which I live a medium, I prefer to say that things mingle with each other and that I am no exception to that. I mix with the world which mixes with me. Skin intervenes between several things in the world and makes them mingle (81).

This paradox applies, *mutatis mutandis*, to any body part involved in the act of touching: it exists to establish a margin between the body and world and yet enacts their mingling, a doubleness captured in Serres's oxymoronic trope of the "common edge."

I mention this body of work not to enlist James in the phenomenological army,[12] but rather to suggest some of the distinctive qualities of his invocation of touch. Jamesian touch doesn't just refer to or even gloss a richer, more complex account of the relation between bodies and world—although it does that; it also suggests the projection of will and desire into that world by means of the body, whether in fact or in figure. Hence, touching for James is both particularly powerful and particularly fraught: since the Jamesian world is a world, par excellence, of others as well as things, of subjects making their claims on other subjects as well as objects making their claims on people, touch is fully caught up in the games of social will to power that are persistently anatomized in his fiction. This is truest as we move—as the novel wishes us to do—back from the world of objects to that of subjects, from things to people, and from consciousness metaphorized as vision to bodily engagement mediated through touch, specifically by the erotic touch, and the touch of hand on hand or even skin on skin. Here, especially, touch turns as problematic as anything else in this book, especially as it moves from focusing on the object-world to parsing the human. Indeed, the conundrum at the center of touch—its simultaneous establishment and undoing of firm lines of difference and clear markers of distinction between body and world—becomes the basis for James's interrogation of intimacy, which can be reductively but not inaccurately described as what happens to subjects when people start touching one another.

We see this most clearly through the character in the novel who does the most physical touching, the Prince. Two moments in particular stand out. One is his first embrace, at least his first diegetical one, with Charlotte. Here, of course, the contact is rendered in precisely the terms of mutuality that the trope of Maggie's hand touching the pagoda evoked, but in this case it's a highly problematic contact—touching other people is different from touching pagodas, in figure or in fact, especially when the touchers have been lovers and are flirting with the possibility of becoming so again. Charlotte and the Prince more or less seduce each other in the act of pledging to "protect" Maggie from knowledge of their own past. "Each hand instinctively found the other" and the erotic charge gathers—"only facing and faced, only grasping and grasped, only meeting and met"—until it is discharged: "everything broke up, broke down, gave way, melted and mingled. Their lips sought their lips, their pressure their response and their response their pressure; with a violence that had sighed itself the next moment to the longest and deepest of stillnesses they passionately sealed their pledge" (1904, 1909: 23:312). Note how what's enacted here is the breaking down not just of physical boundaries but of any boundary whatsoever between these two. Led by hand touching hand—touch touching touch—they move into a oneness that annuls their separate corporeal selves, a breaking down that is, as we have seen, implicit in the act of touch itself. James's language itself accomplishes this merging as each is rendered by indistinguishable participles and then by the even more indistinguishable pronouns "theirs" and "they."

Tellingly, James's tropes of meeting, mingling, and melting here are similar to Serres's (2009) invocation of "mixture" in his description of skin, but where Serres is invested in breaking down the distinction between the body and world, James is interested in the human dynamics of this merging or mixture: he sees the experience as a inter- or even transpersonal one, and hence one open to manipulation, gulling, and abuse as well as a gorgeous overcoming of the body's boundaries through intimate contact. For the loss of a bounded self is what the Prince brings to both of his women—another reason to note the power of, and distrust of, this form of touching. When Maggie makes her move to alter their relationship—when she applies her metaphorical "mere touch of a hand"—the Prince responds by holding "her close and long, in expression of their personal reunion . . . He rubbed his cheek tenderly and with a deep vague murmur against her face, that side of her face she was not pressing to his breast" (1904, 1909: 24:19). Indeed, he turns into a kind of a New Age hugging machine—he takes "possession of her hands and was bending towards her," "then draw[s] her to his breast . . . for a third time," "keeping her close for their slow return together to the apartments above" where they can, and presumably do, make love (24:28, 29).

That the Prince is trying to distract Maggie is obvious, and that he uses the erotics of touch to do this equally so. No wonder that, for the rest of the novel, the wising-up Maggie shies away from his touch, recognizing that the full activation of this sense would undo her utterly: "A single touch from him—oh! She should know it in case of its coming—any brush of his hand, his lips, his voice, inspired by recognition of her probable interest as distinct from pity for her virtual gloom, would hand her over to him bound hand and foot" (24:142). Or again: "he was so near now that she could touch him, taste him, smell him, hold him; he almost pressed upon her" (24:352). Here, just before Charlotte and Adam's departure, she sends the Prince away having almost succumbed to his touch—"she closed her eyes to it and . . . put out her hand, which had met his own, and which he held" (24:352). But she demonstrates her mastery of even the haptic realm, as she communicates her will to Amerigo through precisely this gesture: "Then it was that from behind her closed eyes that the right word came. "Wait!" She kept her eyes shut, but her hand, she knew, helped her meaning" (24:352–3). Touched physically and emotionally through the contact with Amerigo's hand in what she nevertheless understands to be his effort to manipulate her, Maggie touches back, her countertouch (significantly distinguished from the register of vision by the anatomically impossible clause in the first sentence I have quoted, "from behind her closed eyes . . . the right word came") communicating her meaning along with, and perhaps in excess of, her words.

Despite her own mastery of the touch with which Amerigo attempts to reseduce her, Maggie's erotic yearning for Amerigo is palpable, and moving; the mutuality of touch as a key to intimacy, its breaking down of the barriers between self and other as well as self and world, is precisely what James is trying to find a place for in his novel. But at the same time, this breaking down of barriers is something about which he's deeply worried, since it is so very powerful as to be rife with the potential for abuse. One solution to this problem is to leverage touch—to use touch so as not to be used by it. Maggie adopts precisely this tactic by accepting Charlotte's embrace after the card game at Fawns as a visible sign that she accuses Charlotte of "nothing" (24:250)—an embrace that both echoes and parodies Charlotte's and Amerigo's soul-merging embrace, enacted here deliberately rather than spontaneously, publicly rather than privately: "her husband and her father were in front, and Charlotte's embrace of her—which wasn't to be distinguished for them, she felt, from her embrace of Charlotte—took on with their arrival a high publicity" (24:252). And after she convinces her father that it is in her best interest as well as his for him to return to American City, she again accepts an embrace, this time in private: "[H]e drew her to his breast and held her. He held her hard and kept her long, and she let herself go; but it was an embrace that, august and almost stern, produced for all its intimacy no revulsion and broke into no inconsequence of tears" (24:275). These embraces—loaded in different ways, and not untouched by the erotic in either case—show Maggie's adopting Amerigo's deployment of touch as a kind of social weapon. Each of these embraces, as is the nature of touch, involve the breaking down of physical boundaries between bodies, a Serres-like "tangency" between them. Maggie enters into these embraces, however, in order to convince people of the sincerity of that about which she is lying, to reify her impersonation of a daughter happy to sacrifice her father, a friend successfully gulled by her friend. No wonder Maggie, who earlier had thought to herself that she held them "all in her hands" now feels that "there was nothing left to do and that she could thereupon fold her hands"—hand touching hand, here, as in Merleau-Ponty's (1962) trope of touch rendering self as other, a sign that she is at once the same and different: at once her old self—Maggie as object for her father and Charlotte, to whom she remains the same—and the new Maggie she has morphed into—Maggie as willing, willful subject, known as such to herself, to Fanny, and the Prince (1904, 1909: 24:329).

It's with all these multiple and overlapping understandings of touch—as bodily action, as seduction, as engagement with the world, as a challenge to the coherence of the subject, as source of manipulation, as erotic fulfillment—that we can approach the final page of the novel and attempt to make sense of Maggie's final gesture there:

> It kept him before her therefore, taking in—or trying to—what she so wonderfully gave. He tried, too clearly, to please her—to meet her in her own way, but with the result only that close to her, her face kept before him, his hands holding her shoulders, his whole act enclosing her, he presently echoed "See? I see nothing but *you*." And the truth of it had with this force after a moment so strangely lighted his eyes that as for pity and dread of them she buried her own in his breast. (24:369)

I have always viewed this scene as a nihilistic one, concentrating as I did so on what the text foregrounds, the play of eyes. The Prince's glittering gaze combined with his echoing words has until recently seemed to me to indicate that he is a hypnotized automaton; the echo of Aristotelian "pity and fear" suggests a sense that Maggie doesn't quite know what to make of the drama her own hand has made and of which she now claims to be a spectator; Maggie's burying of her eyes in his chest betokens a denial of agency if not an outright death of the heart. But this is to read the novel as focused on eyes and eyes alone, and what I have been proposing throughout this section is that we need to emphasize the novel's invocation of other senses as well. And these, too, are engaged by the Prince. Although the Prince tried "too clearly" to please Maggie, and although the "truth" of the final words he utters elicit "pity and dread," nevertheless he offers Maggie what the novel has been covertly privileging: the consolations of touch, and especially erotic touch, imaged both as fulfillment and oblivion ("his hands holding her shoulders, his whole act enclosing her"). This embrace can be read as mutually self-abnegating, but their previous selves are ones that might well be annihilated, given the disastrous outcomes they have wrought. An alternate reading of the passage would thus focus instead on the potentialities of the embrace itself, and of the shifting of amatory registers from the head to the body, from the eyes to the skin, from reason to touch, and from one subject acting alone to an erotic merger James both fears and celebrates. The haptic route, the route through touch and hand and skin to the final embrace, reminds us of how much is at stake for both Maggie and James in this final clinch, and hence of how much a hermeneutic that remains suspicious of that embrace is forced to leave out. What is thereby brought in I will leave until later—until after we compare and contrast this embrace with others effected in Alfred Hitchcock's 1946 film, *Notorious*, embraces that resemble those in James's novel but transpose their dynamics into a different register.

> One wonders whether in Aristotle's *Peri psuchēs [De Anima, On the Soul]*, his treatise on touch, there was room for *blows* (for striking blows in all their multiplicity, a multiplicity that may not be reducible to a general blow) or *caresses* (all stroking caresses, which may not be accessible either by way of any subsumption under one concept of caress in general) . . . And let us not exclude either that certain experiences of touching (of "who touches whom") do not simply pertain to blows and caresses. What about a kiss? Is it one caress among many?
>
> —Jacques Derrida, *On Touching—Jean-Luc Nancy* (2005, 69)

Early on in *Notorious*, government agent Devlin (Cary Grant) finds himself in a roadster with a drunken Alicia (Ingrid Bergman). They're stopped for speeding by a policeman; Devlin shows the cop an I.D., and he lets them go, saluting as he returns to his motorcycle. Alicia is furious. As she yells at Devlin, he covertly prepares to take the wheel—there's a series of close-ups of his hands moving toward it. She resists, grabbing the wheel, and he delivers what looks like a karate chop—a quick, hard, angled, aggressive movement—that forces her to relinquish it. She fights back, flailing with both arms, attempting to deliver a series of slaps. He holds her arms in his to prevent this, then delivers another sharp, staccato blow, this time to her head or neck—shielded by his head and back, we can't see exactly where—that leaves her senseless.[13]

At the end of the film, Alicia is almost senseless again, this time as the result of drugs administered by her mother-in-law (Leopoldine Konstantin) and husband, Alexander Sebastian (Claude Rains). This time, she reaches out to Devlin and lays her head on one shoulder, her hand resting on the other; he takes her gently, one arm around her back and the other supporting her arm, as he leads her slowly down the staircase, joined by Sebastian who ineffectually puts his hand on her back, hoping to convince the Nazi spectators, already suspicious, that she is sick and that he is helping Devlin take her to the hospital. As they reach the car, Devlin helps Alicia in; Sebastian begs to be taken with them rather than face the wrath of his fellow spies. Devlin refuses—a refusal emphasized as it is enacted by the end of the shot, which shows Devlin's hand pushing down the button in the same decisive, angled motion he used to detach Alicia's hands from the wheel. The car speeds off; Sebastian returns to his certain death.

Hands are never far from Hitchcock's interest—think of the last scenes of *North-by Northwest* (1959)—or from that of his critics, from the heyday of the *Cahiers du Cinema* to our own moment.[14] But even in his hand-haunted oeuvre, this film stands out both in the extensiveness and the richness of meaning Hitchcock generates from hand and touch. The latter in particular becomes clearer when we juxtapose the film with James's endeavor in *The Golden Bowl*. Indeed, the film emphasizes not just the connection of hands to things in the world and other people, but also the ability of the hand to master or govern things in a way that exceeds Maggie's wildest ambitions. The wheel of the car, the lock, Alicia's body: these are all means to Devlin's end, machines he steers or turns on or off by one means or another. Hence the hand and hence touch are intimately connected by Hitchcock with the process of objectification in its most phallic, masterful mode, one that renders the female body into just another object, albeit one put to a socially useful end—in this case, the breaking up of the spy ring. Moreover, Devlin's deployment of his hands—especially the short, staccato-like gestures he makes near the beginning and at the end of the film—suggests a realm of touching left out of the accounts given by theorists I have relied upon for my understanding of *The Golden Bowl*. Like Maggie's touch, Devlin's attempts to make a difference in the world; unlike Maggie's, the contact between hand and hand, or hand and body, or hand and Other, is nasty, brutish, and short.

But as my second example suggests, this is not the only use of hands, or of touch, that we encounter. Devlin's touch at the end of the film is no less efficacious, but it is different. It, too, is undeniably effective—without his hands holding Alicia, she would never have made it out of bed or would have collapsed on the floor if she tried—but here it is also gentle, almost generous. The transformation of Devlin can be measured by the movement between these two uses of his hands. For just as *The Golden Bowl* might be said to be a novel about the education of Amerigo, touch by touch—his metamorphosis, at Maggie's hands, from a somewhat bemused object contemplating his own vending on the appropriately named Bond Street into a full-fledged adult capable of embracing, and being embraced by, another human being—so, too, *Notorious* might be read as a film about the education of Devlin by means of touch. "I couldn't see straight, couldn't think straight," Devlin tells Alicia at this moment, in words that almost precisely echo Amerigo's last words in the book—"I see nothing but you." And the similarity does not stop there: just as it is Maggie who leads Amerigo to a new role through the use of touch—as it were, by the hand—so it is Alicia who teaches Devlin to become more compassionate, and so teaches him through her hand and her touch.

For as opposed to Devlin's, Alicia's hands are in constant motion and perform a wide variety of tasks. Initially, as we have seen, they flail at Devlin, but when the two arrive in Rio, they attempt to seduce him. In an outdoor restaurant, her long black-gloved hand dances about, turning toward her right temple to illustrate her ascription of his thoughts about her ("You're thinking, once a kook, always a kook, once a tramp, always a tramp"); then both hands get laid down on the table as she invites him to hold them (his telling response: "I've always been scared of women)"; then one dances to the side of her face, then back down again as she plaintively inquires, "why won't you believe in me?" All the while, in marked contrast, Devlin's hands remain crossed in front of him, only activating themselves when, a scene later, he finally grabs and kisses her, in another one of his sudden, violent, staccato gestures. Her active, seductive deployment of the hand turns from alluring to touching as they return to their hotel room: she enters after him, pauses, puts the key away and takes off her long gloves, then moves out to the balcony where he has again preceded her, reaches out to him while speaking somewhat taunting words ("they'll all say you fell in love with a tramp"). When he again suddenly embraces her, she pushes her body fully against his, then wraps her arm around his back as they kiss, caressing his ear, then invites him to stay for dinner ("I have a chicken in the icebox"). When he protests that they'll have to wash up afterward, she responds: "We'll eat with our fingers!" Not only does Hitchcock visually associate hands with sexuality, so does his dialogue, the two deliciously complementing as they comment on each other.[15] But more than that: fingers are not only metonyms for sex organs, but also for the entire repertory of bodily being itself, a being in which appeals to the senses (touch, taste, even hearing) cross, complement, and enhance each other.

Hand as metonym of sexuality, intimacy; touch as a form of contact that breaks down barriers between sense and sense, self and body, and self and other: Hitchcock is on territory familiar to us from James. But the deployment of Alicia's hands goes further, in ways that bring Hitchcock closer to James and Alicia closer to Maggie. In the middle third of the film, Alicia's hands become yet more active, doing things other than touching or being touched. They becomes not just a sign of the projection of will into the world, but the means by which that will is effectuated, and not metaphorically or figuratively, but, as befits film, with visual immediacy. Indeed, Hitchcock's camera frequently draws our attention to hands as metonyms for Alicia's agency, especially in the crucial scene in which Alicia steals the key to the wine cellar from Alex. As Alicia enters their bedroom on the night of the party, her hands are, as usual, in motion—she is putting on her earrings—when she spies the keys on the dressing table, rendered in the traditional Hitchcock idiom of point-of-view shot. As the sequence continues, the point-of view shots of the bathroom from which Alex speaks and threatens to emerge combine with close-ups of Alicia's face looking toward the bathroom and other close-ups of her hands touching the keys, drawing back, then touching them again as she slips the key to the wine cellar off the ring and prepares to leave the room. The emphasis on hands augments as Alex emerges. He extends his hands to hers—in this, as in all ways, he shows himself to be a generous and loving partner, the very antithesis of close-handed, tight-fisted Devlin. Alicia, of course, is in a pickle: she must meet them or betray her act of theft. She does so with clenched fists, the right one containing the key. Alex then kisses with a mixture of intimacy and gallantry, her left hand, which she is forced to open, and prepares to kiss the right, this in apology for his suspicions of her—suspicions that, of course, are completely justified. Alicia saves herself by flinging her left arm around his shoulders in exactly the same gesture of embrace that she used with Devlin. Mid-clinch, she is then able to transfer the key from one hand to the other, drop it on the floor, and push it (which we see, again in close-up) under the bed with her foot (see Figures 9.1, 9.2, and 9.3).

Her hands are the means through which she acts out her dual role as loving spouse and secret agent; like Maggie's, they are the means through which she dissimulates, again like Maggie not so much the touch but via one variant of it, the embrace. But the emphasis on the hand doesn't end here. The next sequence begins with one of Hitchcock's most dazzling and justifiably famous shots—a crane shot beginning on the top of the staircase and sweeping down into the crowd of partygoers being greeted by Alicia, ending with a spectacular close-up of her closed hand, holding the key. In this sequence in particular, Alicia's hands intervene in the world—and in so doing, as with Maggie, it is her skill and subtlety, her mastery of "touch" in every sense of the word, that comes to the fore. For like Maggie, Alicia knows how to use touch in all its manifestations—physical, psychological, as a means of manipulation—making Devlin's, by contrast, appear to be crude and therefore of limited value in the extraction of the secret from Alex and his group. But—whether explicitly or implicitly—Devlin seems to follow her lead in the very next sequence, to adopt both her haptic strategy (touch in the physical sense) and subtlety (touch in the metaphorical sense). To be sure, his own directness comes to the fore—while looking in the wine cellar at a manifest at the back of the row of

FIGURE 9.1 Alex extends his hands to Alicia.

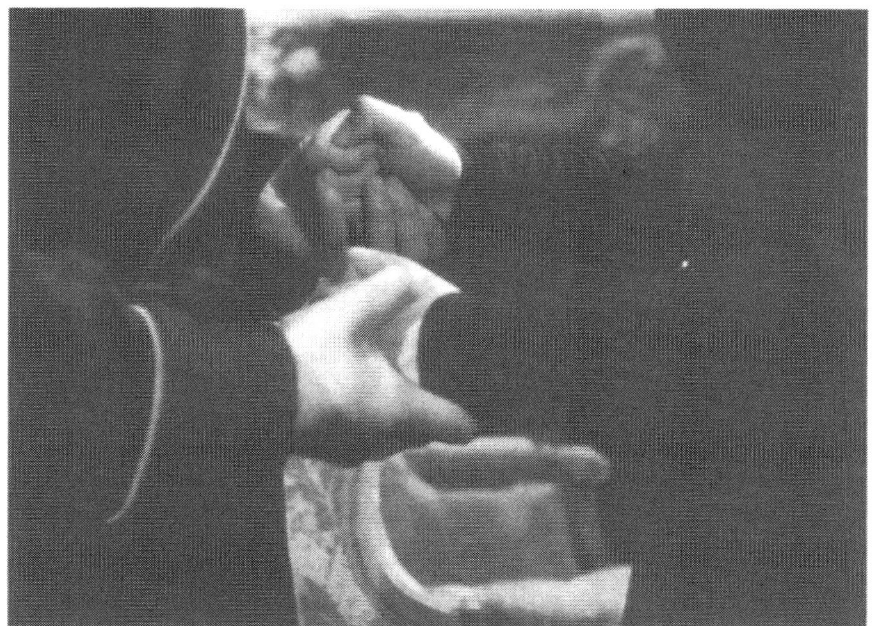

FIGURE 9.2 Alicia meets Alex's hands with clenched fists, the right one containing the key.

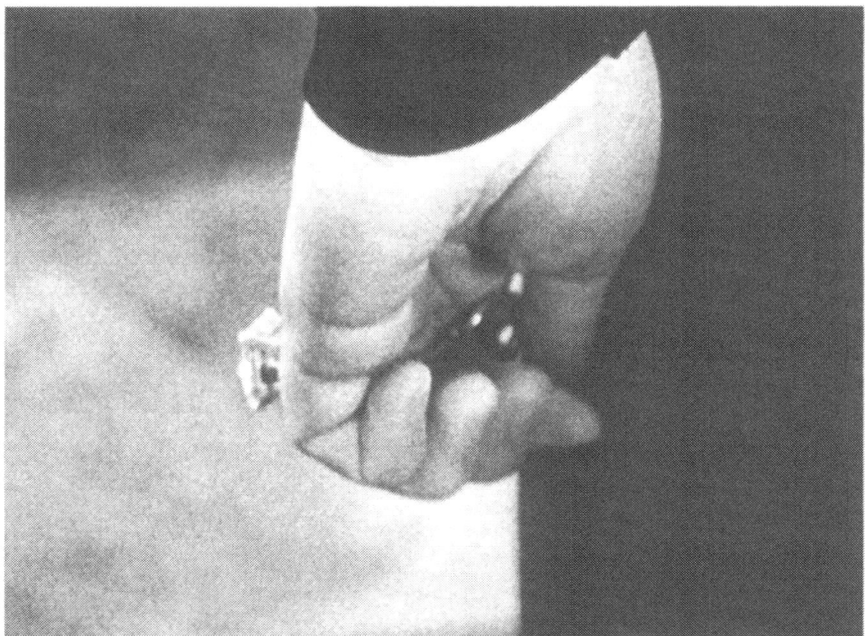

FIGURE 9.3 Alicia switches the key to her left hand.

champagne bottles, he brushes against them, causing one to fall; this of course reveals the uranium sands concealed therein, which he scoops up and puts in an envelope—thereby solving the mystery but also, in the end, inculpating Alicia. A potentially more troubling inculpation impends, however, as the butler Max and Sebastian arrive to look for more champagne. Devlin grabs Alicia, tells her that he is going to kiss her, then puts his arm behind her back and does so framed by the lit doorway, precisely imitating both the tactics and the body language of her embrace with Sebastian[16]—and for that matter, the tactics of Maggie, who publicly stages the embrace with Charlotte "for them," for the eyes of her father and husband.

From this moment on, the trajectories of Devlin and Alicia cross, a process registered visually by the differing trajectory of hands and their uses. Her hands prove to be her undoing—at least visually: they bring her the poisoned coffee, again in a striking close-up that makes a telling counterpoint with the close-up of her removing the key from Sebastian's ring. (Complementing them in another sequence is a close-up of Mrs. Sebastian's hands pouring the coffee, then handing it to Alicia, who takes it and brings the poisoned cup to her lips.) As she grows weaker and weaker, so do her hands—they flutter in front of her face as she complains about the light when she first feels the effects of the poison; they are almost entirely motionless during her last meeting with Devlin at the park; thereafter, they only serve to deliver poison to her mouth or to signify her illness, rising to her temples, for example, just before she collapses. Devlin's hands, hitherto largely immobile, now begin to stir. In their final park bench meeting, Devlin plays with his newspaper with one hand, then drapes the other over the side of the bench; when he later has a conversation with Colonel Pickering, his superior officer, he fiddles with a cigarette—here in marked contrast with the other scene in which he smokes, that of the party sequence, in which a cigarette is held in one motionless hand while the other hand is kept in the pocket of his dinner jacket. When Devlin comes to the Sebastian mansion to rescue Alicia and is kept waiting in the foyer, his hands are crossed in front of him. Then they're extended to propel him around a column at the top of the stairs, with catlike grace, and as he walks down the hall, his fingers twitch slightly with excitement. As Devlin enters her bedroom and moves to her bed, Alicia can barely stir but—in a moving gesture—she extends her hand. For the first time in the film, he takes her hand in his, then moves his face close to hers as he confesses his worry, avows his love, and prepares to move her to the hospital. The use of hands with which I began this section of the essay—he both supports her and urges her forward by the shoulders, as she begins to walk to and then down the stairs—follows naturally from this one; further underlining the significance of this gesture, it's made in the same form that embracing has taken since Alicia first embraced him in their hotel. (It's also the precise inverse of that of the haptic strategies of the spies: when they help Alicia into her bed after her final attack, they first move her forward by pushing the small of her back, then lead her to the bed by holding her wrists, as if they were manacling her, which, without knowing it, they are.) Embrace has come full circle: first a sign of her love for the emotionally blocked Devlin, then used by both her and Devlin as means of manipulation, it now becomes a means for him to demonstrate his affection for a sick Alicia—and to save her life (see Figure 9.4).

Perhaps for these reasons, the conclusion has struck many as poorly motivated, a turn to wish fulfillment in what is otherwise a film that is quite harsh in its depiction of romantic love. If, as *New York Times* critic Bosley Crowther had written in the aftermath of *Notorious*'s success at the box office, "love conquers all," that discovery seems to be limited to the last reel (1946, 49); Devlin's return to the house and his rescue of the sick maiden seem like gestures out of fairy tale or, as per Lesley Brill (1988), romance. To read it this way, *pace* Brill's cheerful Frye-like take on Hitchcock, is to be caught up in the hermeneutic of suspicion that generates out of Hitchcock's career-long anatomization of amatory kinks and quirks. But it is also to ignore the haptic threads I have been tracing throughout the film, the ways that Devlin and Alicia's relation develops by a progression of gestures, caresses, and more utilitarian deployments of the hand and of touch, both strategic and otherwise, until its end, where these merge together into the molding of their bodies into one via the conflation of self and other, the touching of skin on skin, that is wrought by embracing. As in *The Golden Bowl*, focusing on the hand, reading through the touch, gets us to a different point with respect to the film's representation of romance than we would arrive at if we merely focused on the eye with its cinematic equivalents, the gaze and the look. It transports us to that place where Hitchcock

FIGURE 9.4 Embrace has come full circle.

suspends his own skepticism and opens himself up to the same possibilities James evokes at the end of his narrative, the mingling of bodies and subjects that is effectuated by love.

To be sure, this is only one moment in the unfolding of the film's final sequence. The ending is not all sweetness and light—far from it. Devlin is holding a gun (or pretending to hold one) in his jacket pocket while supporting Alicia in the other: he is at once a cynosure of old-fashioned masculinity and the new man she has taught him to be. The use of point-of-view shots of the Nazi onlookers as they pass down the stairs brings a strong dimension of suspense to the scene even as the embrace of Devlin and Alicia enacts the end of the suspense of what is to happen between *them*. As we have seen, further, Devlin deploys the staccato touch to close the car off from potential escape by Sebastian, perhaps to his detriment as an intelligence officer (it has always seemed to me a sign that Devlin is acting as a jealous lover rather than a professional that he leaves Alexander to face his fate); surely Sebastian would yield valuable information in exchange for his life. The final shots, moreover, leave very much open the question of Alicia's fate: suspended as she seems to be between life and death, Alicia might well not make it to the hospital to which Devlin is bringing her, although the wan smile she gives Devlin after he has shut the door on Alex suggests that she may well do so.

It's here that the comparison with *The Golden Bowl* might prove even more helpful. The concluding moves I have been describing in *Notorious*—the push toward an embrace that brings the love plot to a climax, the subsequent open ending—are equivalent to those in James's novel, where the even more spectacular gestures of closure are followed by the opening of questions by these very same gestures. In *The Golden Bowl*, the sense of an uncertain future extends beyond the final words of the book into the empty space that fills the rest of the page, designating not only an open space for the reader but also a space of newly built relation neither the glittery-eyed Prince nor the buried-eyed Maggie can envision, but which they both must now enter. In Hitchcock's case, that double ending is wrought when Devlin and Alicia drive off to an uncertain future and Alex returns to the house that he has tried to turn into Alicia's tomb and that is shortly to become his own. In both, then, a newly restored relationship opens out into the space of sheer potentiality while a more troubled, if not perverse one—the childless and apparently sexless coupling of Adam and Charlotte and the emotionally fraught coupling of Alex and his mother—is definitively closed off from any further growth, change, or development, in the case of one by exile, in the case of the other, presumably, death. The embrace in either case thus marks the end of one kind of relation and the opening of another—but this latter relation is not, cannot be, represented not (or not only) because James and Hitchcock have no language for or vision of an adult relationship but because it is one that these two couples, like any couples, need to forge together, to make with their own hands.

And it's here, perhaps, that we touch on the greatest affinity between these two works—and between the third, odder couple with whose hypothetical meeting I began this essay, Hitchcock and James: the ways both *The Golden Bowl* and *Notorious* extend the representational media in which they're embedded. The combination of closure and opening with which each ends, and the movement beyond their own form of representation—words in one case, images and sound in another—to not only the hypostatization of vision but the evocation of touch define the robust and persistent experimentalism of both of these artists who were persistently interested in expanding the form they were working in (and working to shape). "Touch" in this sense, for each of them, is ultimately a metonym for the ability of print or visual media to reach out beyond their own limitations and engage the reader or viewer in a space beyond language or screen, to challenge us to move beyond representational forms so as to touch us—to move us, to make an impression—even after we are finished with them. Through their invocation of touch, both of these texts thus leave matters in reader's or viewer's own hands, preparing us to move back into the world that opens up before us as touch by touch we feel our way through its manifold varieties of contingency.

10

The Touch of the Real

CIRCUMSCRIBING *VERTIGO*

Eric Savoy

> Every real signifier is, as such, a signifier that signifies nothing. The more a signifier signifies nothing, the more indestructible it is.
>
> —Jacques Lacan, Seminar 3 (1955–6, 1993: 185).

Henry James and Alfred Hitchcock were avowed, even obsessive, formalists, and if this observation is self-evident to the point of banality, it is nonetheless true that a sharp critical attention to craft and method can clarify and particularize the common ground they share. Generally in the late work of James and Hitchcock, form inheres not merely in the careful calculation of point of view—that is, in camera angles or the narrative eye—but also in the disposition of bodies in scenic space. "Disposition" here signifies the physical arrangement or distribution of characters in a given scene, which functions at once as individuating (that is, indicative of specific temperament, inclination, tendency, or propensity) and as an index of relationality (that is, of intersubjective dynamics and of role within the overarching emplotment). Relationality in both James's novels and Hitchcock's films tends to assume a fairly static architectural design wherein what matters most is not proximity but distance—a seemingly untraversable space charged with static: visual impercipience, illicit desire, and a formidably apprehensive mode of apprehension. Cumulatively, and in strikingly similar ways, the formal rigors of distantiating constitute for both James and Hitchcock the intersubjective as such.

It is not surprising, then, that the disposition of bodies, or architectonic relationality, is realized, framed, and confined by the poetics of architecture and interior design in the work of both artists. The seating arrangement in train compartments, for example, was endlessly interesting to Hitchcock. The placement of the telephone in *Dial M for Murder* (1954)—or of the coffer in *Rope* (1948)—provides a focus for suspense, if it does not indeed initiate it. *Rear Window* (1954) would have been inconceivable without architecturally distantiating voyeurism. What transpires on staircases is often mortifying—literally so in Hitchcock's work. The classic example of relational disposition occurs in *The Portrait of a Lady* (1881): in Chapter 40, Isabel Archer stops short on the threshold of her drawing room, arrested by the still, silent tableau of Madame Merle and Gilbert Osmond engaged in—well, nothing: "their relative positions, their absorbed mutual gaze, struck her as something detected" (1881, 1986: 458). With geometric precision, James renders visible the entire plot of the novel in the silent space between Madame Merle and Osmond, between Isabel and the others, and in their triangulated disposition. In order to take the measure of this scenic tableau, and of the emplotment for which it serves as synecdoche, the reader must not only visualize but also—paradoxically—animate this stillness by bringing a cinematic eye and a formalist curiosity to interior design. Placement, arrangement, disposition, and distance are everything.

A certain scenic topography that recurs frequently in James's late work is utterly foundational to the dynamics of performance in Hitchcock's 1958 film, *Vertigo*: the protracted, repeated circling movement of one character around another, who remains stationary and is usually seated. In climactic moments, particularly when this tableau shifts into the register of allegory, the center about which circles are described is not another character per se, but rather a spectacular figuration of the intersubjective drama in which the protagonist has become enmeshed. At issue in this progression from literal to figurative registers is the larger meaning of a character's circular movement: on the one hand, it may be said to enact performatively—to literalize and, simultaneously, to allegorize narratively—the circuits of nonarrival that are endemic to James's notorious circumlocution. This bodily gesture renders periphrasis visible and, to that extent, dramatically realizable. On the other hand, it seems to schematize intersubjective relationality in a silent space, beyond the logics of rhetorical figuration.

Broadly speaking, the figure, situation, or agent at the center of circular inscription sustains a deceptive relation with the circling protagonist. Consequently, that figure is an object of an obscure and ambivalent desire that resists direct articulation. In order to keep desire in the air, and the plot in motion, scenic method must preserve that distance between the object and the hovering subject. What remains constant is the sense that desire—and indeed all forms of relationality—are profoundly dangerous. In the formalist vision of both James and Hitchcock, to desire is to broach the territory of the gothic: that is, to solicit the return of the repressed, to stage the encounter with the traumatic Real,[1] to encounter the void at the center of subjectivity, to become unhinged. In proportion to the movement of narrative toward the gothic, the disposition of the circling body stages the precarious, imminent undoing of the subject—fascinated, yes, but also fearful, with defenses on high alert. This scenic economy, then, stages not only a striking and entirely visible geometry of intersubjectivity, but also a force field of attraction and repulsion—an encounter with the Real that is imminent, yet deferred—as the psyche is drawn somatically. If James's and Hitchcock's protagonists are suspended between the desire to know all and the fear of that knowledge, it is also true that the deferral of the subject's traumatic undoing generates our pleasurable suspense in proportion. By the logics of Hitchcock's cinematography, the temporality of deferral requires a mode of repetition that is manifested spatially and scenically: again and again, we observe the protagonist circling the object that will be in time the locus of his traumatic undoing.

Leo Bersani (1976) argues that James's narrative methods constitute "a richly superficial art" (132), for despite their density of psychological detail, they are "remarkably resistant to an interest in psychological depth" (130). James's indifference to "psychological depth" accounts for the fortunate paucity of reductive narrative explanation—the summary character sketch; the accounting for desire's origins, traumatic or otherwise; the explicit linking of this event to that—in his best work. Concomitant with this authorial reserve is the severing of any totalizing relation between narrative and story: in James, there accrues over time a remainder, a stubborn residue of story. James's logical axis of composition is resolutely horizontal, eschewing obvious profundity, Jamesian significance inheres in the recurring patterns of circumlocutionary dialogue and bodily disposition, both within the frame of individual scenes and in their repetitive linkages. Central to this matter of disposition is the reiterated dramatization of the circling body.

Narrative gambit with Hitchcock, by contrast, unfolds along a vertical axis. In his most celebrated films of the 1950s and early 1960s, not only does narrative work toward a full realization of story, but, in the cultural climate of American Freudianism, story is also often a matter of case history—that is, the deep underpinning, in the archive of the protagonist's unconscious, of the original trauma that has set in motion the film's emplotment. Story, then, is often a matter of the subject's, and the narrative's, prehistory.

Despite its reliance upon deep explanation of the narrative prehistory and upon intricate emplotment, *Vertigo* remains a formalist tour de force, the power of which is explicable in Jamesian terms—that is, by way of the symmetry of scenic construction along a horizontal axis of temporality. If symmetry is largely a matter of highly stylized, gestural repetition, then the temporal *déroulement* of this film is framed by a spatial poetics—an architectural configuration of rooms, rooftops, and, spectacularly, staircases—in which the compulsions of circling, ascent, and descent gather momentum. In the film's diegesis, considerable emphasis is placed upon the unaccountable impulse to "wander about": both Scottie (James Stewart) and Madeleine (Kim Novak) cultivate the pose of aimless *ennui* and frequently proffer in their rather stilted conversations this vague account of their activities. Diegetic *wandering* coalesces not only in Scottie's rapt *wondering*, but also in an architectural design that gives precise form to his circuitous routine. For all the explanatory contrivance of *Vertigo,* Madeleine (or, more precisely, the *idea* of Madeleine) remains the mesmerizingly empty center of Scottie's wandering-and-wondering-about: enclosed in a mystical other world, remote and inaccessible, and haunted by the dead, she—and Scottie's repetitive revolution around her—may signify the vertiginous Real of the death drive, but the "thing" that *is* Madeleine remains recalcitrant, impervious to articulation. I suggest, then, that the act of describing a circle about this tantalizing center constitutes this film's *parti.* In architectural criticism, the *parti* is the "big idea," the originary and often highly abstract graphic concept that relates function (the relationship of the parts to the whole) to aesthetics, to realizable form.[2] A *parti* serves as the organizing, unifying force, at once abstract idea and material form, upon which the work is constructed. In James's textual topography, the circular *parti*—as diagrammatic supplement to circumlocution, or as visible rendering of overarching relational design—is necessarily two-dimensional, as broad as it is long, and is constrained both by the obvious flatness of the page (so far, no pop-up book is in the works) and by James's horizontal axis of composition. In *Vertigo,* however, the cinematic medium allows the circular *parti* to acquire a third, vertical dimension as it culminates in the figure of the ascending spiral: in these climactic moments, Hitchcock's most innovative camera work registers and induces precisely the affect of vertigo, generated diegetically by an imminent fall into the Real.

In its opening frames, *Vertigo* announces its formalist *parti* in abstract, spiraling images that seem to emerge from and to return to the eye; this clever construction, at once simple and intricate, not only situates the malaise associated with vertigo in fearful optics but also prefigures the restless scopophilia, beyond the pleasure principle, that will drive the film. Beginning with a close-up of a woman's face and moving quickly from her lips to her eyes as she glances uneasily from left to right, the camera settles on a tight, sustained shot of her right eye; then, Saul Bass's abstract designs emerge as the camera seems to enter the woman's pupil. During the credits, multicolored spirals unfold and swirl against a black background (presumably "deep inside" the eye), culminating in a blazing red spiral as the camera pulls back from the pupil. The eyes, nominally the center of the subject and the seat of subjectivity, are utterly vacant, and thus are entirely resonant with that empty center that Scottie will revolve around. Such vacancy also suggests that vertigo is occasioned by the close encounter with this void.[3]

Any critical project that brings literature and film into dialogue will focus, to some degree, on visual economy in the field of object relations; my particular linking of James and Hitchcock takes up an excessive fascination with the object that Lacan theorized as "captation," as well as a narrative emplotment that shatters captation with "a touch of the Real." Such shattering is properly traumatic: it redeploys a prior traumatic history, leaving the subject in the clutches of a melancholia that admits no continuation of narrative. Captation and its circuits are basic to the *other* dimension of this project, which is formalist: a tendency in late James—a recurring allegorical tableau in which the characters are diagrammed as turning around the Real, a gesture that steps outside the flow of narrative in order to explain and to consolidate it—and a kind of architectural turning or circularity of the camera in *Vertigo* that at once represents the vertiginous in relation to the traumatic Real, and—like James's work—oddly literalizes the movement of circling around. This formalist dimension of my argument—the narrative work that circulates, in circular fashion, *around* the Real—attempts ultimately to demonstrate a progression from the "symptom" upon which figural subjectivity is founded toward what Lacan, in the last stage of his teaching, called the *sinthome*.

Freudian practice understands the symptom as a coded message to be deciphered by the analyst with reference to the unconscious. In the early 1960s, however, Lacan began to argue that the symptom does not call for interpretation; rather, it is better conceptualized as a pure *jouissance*—the particular modality of the subject's enjoyment of the unconscious—addressed to no one. A decade later, Lacan arrived at the term *sinthome*, which, as Dylan Evans (1996) explains, "designates a signifying formulation beyond analysis, a kernel of enjoyment immune to the efficacy of the symbolic." Beyond discourse, beyond diagnosis and the talking cure, the *sinthome*, "far from calling for some analytic 'dissolution,' it is what 'allows one to live' by providing a unique organization of *jouissance*" (189). In other words, the *sinthome* is what allows the subject to cohere: in the words of Slavoj Žižek (1991), "this point functions as the ultimate support of the subject's consistency, the point of 'thou art that,' the point marking the dimension of 'what is in the subject more than himself'" (32). The *sinthome* marks, as Žižek argues, "the last Lacanian reading of Freud's motto *Wo es war, soll Ich werden:* in the real of your symptom, you must recognize the ultimate support of your being. There where your symptom already was, with this place you must identify; in its 'pathological' singularity you must recognize the element that guarantees your consistency" (137).

What might such a "signifying formulation" look like? Broadly speaking, the *sinthome* is an embodied gesture or a nonsensical "tic" that is thoroughly grafted onto a repetition compulsion. Žižek's most helpful location (if not "definition") of the *sinthome* is perhaps his distinction between "acting out" and what Lacan calls *passage à l'acte*. A symptom is an "acting out," "an attempt to break through a symbolic deadlock (an impossibility of symbolization, of putting into words) by means of an act [which] still functions as the bearer of some ciphered message" (1991, 139). The *sinthome*, as a "passage to the act," "entails in contrast an exit from the symbolic network, a dissolution of the social bond. . . . By "'*passage à l'acte*,' we identify with the *sinthome* as the pathological 'tic' structuring the real kernel of our enjoyment" (139).

Hitchcock's cinema has compelling affinities with psychoanalysis, and in taking up the continuum of motifs that *auteurist* theory locates as central to this body of work, Žižek is singular in avoiding interpretation. A prime example is the motif of "the person who is suspended from the hand of another," a scene that was introduced in *Saboteur* (1942) and recurs in *To Catch a Thief* (1955), *Vertigo* (1958), and in *North by Northwest* (1959). These are among Hitchcock's most iconic scenes. Žižek argues that if we search in this repeated motif for a common meaning, "we *say too much*." If we see them as merely empty signifiers that accrue meaning only in relation to each film's context, "we *don't say enough*." We strike exactly the right balance, Žižek concludes, "when we conceive them as *sinthoms* in the Lacanian sense: as a signifier's constellation (formula) which fixes a certain core of enjoyment, like mannerisms in painting—characteristic details which persist and repeat themselves without implying a common meaning (this insistence offers, perhaps, a clue to what Freud meant by 'the compulsion to repeat'" (1992, 126). Žižek's account of the Hitchcockian *sinthom(e)*,[4] and the analogy he sustains between this cinematic motif and painterly mannerism as gestures that "fix a certain core of enjoyment," are directly related to what I have been presenting as a topographical formalism, beyond interpretation and depth psychology, that is common to both Hitchcock and James. The subject's inveterate habit of circling around its elusive object, recurring throughout late James and central to the cinematography of *Vertigo,* is obviously related to the larger themes of the works, which are concerned with the subject's baffled relations with his or her object. But circularity itself, as a purely formal gesture, cannot be entirely accounted for as an allegorical intrusion into narrative, because allegory is primarily an explanatory mode by which narrative comments on its own deeper implications. Circularity is, rather, a manifestation of stylistic, formal excess: it grips us visually, as pure surplus. Like all forms of repetition, it condenses something without representing it—and that something, if it exists, remains recalcitrant to interpretive inquiry. As such, the *sinthome* of the embodied gesture is pure form, and to the extent that it is "about" anything, it illuminates the kind of authorial signature that James and Hitchcock may be said to realize.[5] At issue, then, is what we mean by literal.

Captation: "The Museum Mood"

Lacan began using the term "captation" in 1948 to refer to the imaginary effects of the image: on the one hand, it has the sense of captivation, thus expressing the fascinating, seductive power of the image. On the other hand, the term conveys the idea of "capture," which evokes the more sinister power of the image to imprison the subject in a disabling fixation (Evans 1996, 20). If captation confers upon the object an illusory presence, a plenitude of meaning based on nothing, it also promises, deceptively, the wholeness of the subject. Captation underlines the contingency of the object and the void of subjectivity. In both *The Ambassadors* (1903) and *Vertigo,* the protagonist experiences captation as the moment of his entry into a narrative that is already in progress. That narrative is a lie, or more precisely a cover-up,[6] and is perhaps suspected by the reader or viewer of being so, yet it exerts a powerful fascination. The result, predictably, is that we at once identify, yearningly, with the protagonist's "captivation" and, in order to experience the pleasure of narration, attend with some distance the unfolding drama of *méconnaissance*. Captation demonstrates the great formula of classic Hollywood cinema: woman is the symptom of man.

I begin my survey of James with Strether in Paris, at the exact midpoint of *The Ambassadors.* He has made the journey, famously, as the emissary of Woollett, Massachusetts, and of the formidable Mrs. Newsome, with the plain purpose of rescuing her son, Chad, from the clutches of a *femme du monde* and returning him to New England, where he will take up his role in the family business—a factory that manufactures MacGuffins. Woollett knows what it is about, and so does Strether, until he falls under the charm, the lure, of Paris itself—a vertiginous place, where "what seemed all surface one moment seemed all depth the next" (1903, 1994: 64). Seduced by glamour, by vistas, by *omelettes aux tomates*, and by dresses very much *décolletée*, Strether collaborates gleefully in his own manipulation and undoing. And, according to James's paradoxical calculus, Strether must indeed be wrong in order to be right, he must fail in order to succeed. To succeed, that is, in detaching himself from the residues of American puritanism, which requires in turn the undoing of identity, a dissolution into homelessness and radical alienation. All of this requires captation—the paralyzing fixation upon the object of Madame de Vionnet, by which Strether takes up the threads of a story that runs counter to Woollett's line: that Chad's relation with Madame de Vionnet is a "virtuous attachment" (112). Strether, at least initially, dutifully parses the adjective in relation to the noun, but Little Bilham's formulation circulates in the novel as a catachresis, admitting so many interpretations and glossings that none can emerge into referential clarity—a clarity that, in any case, would be merely the vanishing point of "woman" on the horizon of incalculable desire.

At once duped and knowing—such is the peculiar nature of Jamesian "double consciousness" (1903, 1994: 18)—Strether attaches to Madame de Vionnet the entire matrix that we signify, metonymically, by "Paris." By matrix, I mean a visual economy in which scopophilia supplements the reticences of discourse, a place in which the tacit is dealt with tactfully. "'I dare say,'" says Miss Barrace at Gloriani's garden party, "'that I do, that we all do here, run too much to mere eye. But how can it be helped? We're all looking at each other—and in the light of Paris one sees what things resemble. That's what the light of Paris seems always to show. It's the fault of the light of Paris—dear old light.'" If "'everything shows,'" Strether rejoins, do things "show" "'for what they really are?'" Miss Barrace, tactfully, avoids a question that is both impercipient and importunate: "'Oh I like your Boston "reallys!"'" (126). This conversation induces a certain semantic and epistemological vertigo in the oscillation between "to resemble" and "to really be." If captation requires both the suspension of their difference and their insertion into the circularity of *différance*, then Strether is primed for his own investment in a virtuous attachment. What he attaches to this atttachment is subject to the logics of chiasmus: Paris is embodied in Madame de Vionnet, just as Madame de Vionnet *is* Paris. For it is in the vicinity of Madame de Vionnet that Paris seems, and indeed is, itself. The one is the index of the other—the index, that is, of authenticity, of the real thing.

When Strether visits Madame de Vionnet's house in the Faubourg St.-Germain, for example, every beautiful object signifies for him its deep continuity with the past; they serve to anchor Madame de Vionnet, "passive under the spell of transmission" (146), as the antithesis of restless American acquisition. Everything in the scene coalesces for Strether under the sign of authenticity. Subsequent encounters with

Madame de Vionnet consolidate the stability of the signifier: her arrangements to marry her daughter, Jeanne, strike him, "through something ancient and cold in [them]–what he would have called the real thing" (240). The reiterated grammar of the conditional ("he would have come nearest to naming," "he would have called") suggests Strether's positioning Madame de Vionnet as the *point de capiton,* the signifier that stablilizes and arrests the shifting and vertiginous play of the sign that is Paris. James's careful construction of the *point de capiton* makes possible and inevitable—indeed, it may be said to be the precondition of—the very Hitchcockian scene of captation in the midpoint of the novel, to which I now turn.

At the beginning of Book 7, Strether pays a visit to Notre Dame, where he watches with increasing fascination a lurking figure around whom he constructs not a narrative, exactly, but a figure worthy of Victor Hugo, a seventy-volume set of whose works he had acquired on his honeymoon trip to Paris:

> . . . he suddenly measured the suggestive effect of a lady whose supreme stillness, in the shade of one of the chapels, *he had two or three times noticed as he made, and made once more, his slow circuit.* She wasn't prostrate—not in any degree bowed, but she was strangely fixed, and her prolonged immobility showed her, while he passed and paused, as wholly given up to the need, whatever it was, that had brought her there. She only sat and gazed before her, . . . and she had lost herself, as he could easily see, as he would only have liked to do. She was not a wandering alien, keeping back more than she gave, but one of the familiar, the intimate, the fortunate, for whom these dealings had a method and a meaning. She reminded our friend—since it was the way of nine tenths of his current impressions to act as recalls of things imagined—of some fine firm concentrated heroine of an old story, something he had heard, read, something that, had he a hand for drama, he might himself have written, renewing her courage, renewing her clearness, in splendidly-protected meditation. *Her back, as she sat, was turned to him, but his impression absolutely required that she be young and interesting, and she carried her head moreover, even in the sacred shade, with a discernable faith in herself, a kind of implied conviction of consistency, security, impunity.* But what had such a woman come for if she hadn't come to pray? (174, emphasis added)

"All of this was a good deal to have been denoted by a mere lurking figure" (174) is James's conclusion to this still, silent tableau in the center of Paris, this turning point in both the spatial and temporal dimensions of the novel. Strether's belated recognition of the "lurking figure" as Madame de Vionnet is both timely for James's plot and, in a sense, too late for the safety of the protagonist, for what *turns* in this turning point is the *point de capiton* toward, and indeed into, the captation of the subject. There is a certain chiastic relation here between perceiving subject and perceived object, for the "strangely fixed" quality of the object is transferred to the subject. Strether, consequently, is "fixed," or transfixed, in this rather cinematic economy of *le regard,* precisely at the "turn" where the narrative of the "virtuous attachment" intersects with other, and older, romantic stories derived from Strether's desultory wanderings in the French novel.

Every element of what James calls the "method and the meaning" of Madame de Vionnet's strange presence in Notre Dame—the woman "wholly given up to her need," itself unfathomable and alluring; the turned back; the woman's "implied conviction of consistency"—will recur in an equally important scene in *Vertigo:* the scene in the art gallery of the Palace of the Legion of Honor where Scottie gazes, transfixed, at the spectacle of Madeleine, herself transfixed by the portrait of Carlotta Valdez. I shall turn in due course to this scene as a replay of what James calls "the museum mood"—the unchecked flourish of the Imaginary in the field of observation. For the present, I have more to say about the position of the spectator in the scene of captation—the oddly literal and gestural *turning* of Strether *around* the riveting object. Like a camera, Strether focuses on the lurking figure as the center point of his revolving perambulation around the cathedral: he "notices" as "he made, and made once more, his slow circuit." This might strike one as a minor detail in the tableau, but I would argue that it is intimately related, as a repetition of repetitive circling, to identical instances in other narratives in late James. In every instance, James allegorizes the captation of a fixated and bewildered subject in relation to an unknowable lurking figure—in relation, that is, to the traumatic Real. If the pull toward diagrammatic allegory oddly exteriorizes the conscious movement of the subject, it also oddly literalizes the circumference of Jamesian circumlocution as an embodied movement around. Indeed, James seems, late in his career, positively to require such coherently visible diagrams in order both to figure his subjects' hermeneutic bafflement and to distance himself from his habitual and more labyrinthine modes of figuration. Drawing or describing circles in words, then, is both an allegorical supplement *to*, and a strange literalization *of*, the great Jamesian symptom: circumlocution. And it is precisely here that the *sinthome* may be said both to describe and to inscribe.

The *Sinthome*

The classic example of the Jamesian *sinthome* occurs at the outset of Book Second of *The Golden Bowl* (1904), where Maggie's "situation had been occupying, for months and months, the very centre of the garden of her life, but it had reared itself there like some strange, tall tower of ivory, or perhaps rather some wonderful, beautiful, but outlandish pagoda." To develop the metaphor into allegory, a certain *movement* must animate the tableau; accordingly, "she had walked round and round it—that was what she felt; she had carried on her existence in the space left her for circulation, a space that sometimes seemed ample and sometimes narrow." No figurative door gives access to the referential content of the pagoda or the situation that it allegorizes. If the "great decorated surface had remained consistently impenetrable and inscrutable," then Maggie finds herself, finally, having "ceased merely to circle and to scan . . . to stare and to wonder" (1904, 1985: 299–300).

Intersubjective inscrutability is the keynote, too, of a strikingly similar tableau in *The Wings of the Dove* (1902) where James figures forth the paradox that governs the relation of Milly Theale and Kate Croy, namely, "it was when they called each other's attention to their ceasing to pretend . . . that what they were keeping back was most in the air." Thus, James writes,

> was a wondering pitying sister [Kate] condemned wistfully to look at her [Milly] from the far side of the moat she had dug round her tower. . . . We have positively the image, in the delicate dusk, of the figures so associated and yet so opposed, so mutually watchful: that of the angular pale princess, ostrich-plumed, black-robed, hung about with amulets, reminders, relics, *mainly seated, mainly still,* and that of the upright restless *slow-circling* lady of her court who exchanges with her, across the black water streaked with evening gleams, fitful questions and answers. The upright lady . . . *makes the whole circuit, and makes it again,* and the broken talk, brief and sparingly allusive, seems more to cover than to free their sense. (1902, 2006: 512, emphasis added)

In the final installment of this catalog of the allegorical *sinthome*, the revolution of a captated subject around a figure "mainly seated, mainly still" images, even as it literalizes, the baffled movement of John Marcher around the grave of May Bartram, toward the conclusion of "The Beast in the Jungle" of 1903:

> The open page was the tomb of his friend, and *there* were the facts of the past, there the truth of his life, there the backward reaches in which he could lose himself. He did this, from time to time, with such effect that he seemed to wander through the old years with his hand in the arm of a companion who was, in the most extraordinary manner, his other, his younger self; and to wander, which was more extraordinary yet, *round and round a third presence—not wandering she, but stationary, still, whose eyes, turning with his revolution, never ceased to follow him, and whose seat was his point, so to speak, of orientation.* (1903, 1964: 398, emphasis added)

This is the Jamesian *sinthome*: a recurring gesture that is iconic in James's writing, which condenses James's pleasure as an artist. Across this series of rather diverse narratives, it returns as a distinctive compositional signature. If his characters' embodied acts of turning about their respective objects may be said to allegorize narrative circumlocution—that is, to represent diagrammatically, as a kind of metanarrative, James's world of oblique discourse that turns about but never arrives—this recurring gesture is more than a symptom, more than the bearer of a coded message. The *sinthome* exceeds the parameters and the requirements of representation as such. It is primarily, I would argue, an inveterate habit that renders coherent, for the reader, the Jamesian—and perhaps James's own—body. Less an "acting out" than a *passage à l'acte*, it has the qualities of a physical movement, as much on James's part as on that of his characters. Insistent in its repetition and return, the circular gesture accrues a palpability, a materiality, that cuts through the elaborate textures of James's lexicon and syntax in order to transcend narrative language itself—or rather, to seem to do so. Its power is its visual appeal, which approximates the cinematic. And it is precisely this narrative *sinthome*[7] that may be said to bind fiction itself, and to do so in a perverse manner that thwarts all expectations of realist closure and resolution operative under the laws of the novel's Symbolic constitution.

I would argue that the Jamesian *sinthome* that emerges in Notre Dame determines the "spell" under which Strether operates, for he devotes himself to policing the perimeter of his captation and to preserving his explanatory fiction. When it crumbles, it does so in a precisely parallel tableau, in a correspondent scene of disenchantment. This occurs in the French countryside, where Strether recreates his memory of a certain landscape by Lambinet: the scene, like its counterpart in Notre Dame, demonstrates the excesses of the Imaginary in the quest for French authenticity. The rural village "affected him as a thing of whiteness, bluenesss and crookedness, set in coppery green" (1903, 1994: 307), and his nostalgic "return" to a French painting—for he had "not once overstepped the oblong gilt frame" (307) occurs in conditions that "were *the thing*, as he would have called it" (308, original emphasis). At the height of his pleasure, Strether becomes aware of a boat on the river, with a gentleman and a lady with a pink parasol, and "it was suddenly as if these figures . . . had been wanted in the picture" (309). James's technique at this point shatters the static and iconic pictorialism of the Imaginary—of this thing called "France"–as the "tableau" becomes suddenly animated: the lady's parasol "shifting as if to hide her face, made so fine a pink point in the shining scene" (310). As the mark of the *punctum,* the parasol might be said to "puncture" the canvas and its wholly Imaginary elaborations, and to mark the irruption of the traumatic Real. It is important here that a distinctly feminine object serves as the focal point of the uncanny, of the return of all that has been repressed.

On the other side of the tableau, punctured by the parasol, is "the deep, deep truth of the intimacy revealed." This spatial economy of the reality principle gives way to the temporal, as Strether takes the full measure of his Imaginary elaborations: "he had dressed the possibility in vagueness, as a little girl might have dressed her doll" (or as Scottie dresses Judy to return Madeleine to life). Belatedly, Strether recognizes that his imprisonment in the "museum mood" had required that he "try all along to suppose nothing. Verily, verily, his labour had been lost" (315). If nothing is the realm of the Imaginary in general and of captation in particular, requiring as they do the disavowals and repressions of competing narratives, then the Imaginary collapses *not* in a salutary return to reality or a reintegration in the Symbolic order, but rather, into nothing. And since nothing can come of nothing, the narrative closes on the desert of renunciation and disenchantment that is Strether's life. If the *sinthome* and its turnings are synonymous with the temporality of captation itself, then the *sinthome* is exposed as having turned around, as having circumvented, the void that it its center, the emptiness of the Real.

From Circle to Spiral: Hitchcock's *Sinthome*

Whereas the irruption of the real is deferred in *The Ambassadors* and marks the dead end of narrative, in *Vertigo,* the traumatic real is the point of departure: when Scottie slips on a steep roof during a police chase and hangs suspended, clinging precariously to a rain gutter several stories above the street. Vertigo is induced rather than represented here by Hitchcock's simultaneous use of the vertical zoom with the backward tracking shot, a technique he will exploit repeatedly to mark the return of the traumatic primal scene. If, as every theorist of trauma after Freud has emphasized, trauma is characterized by the unconscious repetition of an event that remains unfathomable, then *Vertigo* is an exemplary trauma narrative. Essentially, it grafts onto the traumatic residue of Scottie's vertigo—the chronic fear of falling— the plot of falling in love with a ghostly illusion.

In terms of character alignment, too, Hitchcock's film recalls the quadrilateral emplotment of *The Ambassadors.* Strether falls into the web of deception woven by Chad Newsome and Madame de Vionnet, and this triangulated relationship is brought to discourse in his conversations with Maria Gostrey, the *ficelle* and the woman to whom he would have done better to attach himself. In *Vertigo*, Scottie is the dupe of his old college friend Gavin Elster (Tom Helmore), who needs a credible witness to the "suicide" of his wife, Madeleine, whom we never see. As Scotty falls in love with the woman whom he takes to be Madeleine Elster, he attempts to evade the knowing scrutiny of his close friend, Midge (Barbara Bel Geddes)—the woman he would have loved, if desire (or at least cinematic desire) were not so perverse and bent on dangerous captation. Elster's plan is that Scottie will track his deranged wife, who believes she is possessed by the suicidal spirit of an ancestor, Carlotta Valdez, to the bell tower of the Mission of San Juan Bautista; because of his vertigo, he will be unable to ascend the staircase of the tower and to prevent "Madeleine" from throwing herself off. The role of "Madeleine" is played by Elster's mistress, Judy, who—and this is the kernel of the plot—channels the unspecifiable *thing* that is "Madeleine" so perfectly that Scottie becomes utterly captivated by her. Madeleine is, from the get-go, an illusion, a pure allegory of cinematic desire itself; her function in the plot is to braid together the fearful fascination of Scottie's vertiginous trauma of the primal scene with its unconscious repetition in the captation of that thing we call love. That "unspecificable thing" that inheres in Madeleine we might hazard to specify as the death drive: the fatal attraction of the Real that, concealed by displacement and condensation, by the cinematic dreamwork that *is* Madeleine, is less a character than a locus of representation. Spectral and otherworldly, Madeleine's suspension between the living and the dead returns to visibility the appallingly attractive *motif* of falling, which marks every climactic turn of the narrative: Madeleine dreams of falling into her grave; she falls into San Francisco Bay; she "falls" from the bell tower of San Juan Bautista. We learn, of course, of the conspiracy by which "Madeleine" does not fall; rather, Elster throws his murdered wife from the tower. If this illusory fall marks the return of Scottie's severe trauma as he stands paralyzed in the stairwell of the bell tower, it also makes possible the larger plot of return and repetition: Judy returns, is remade by Scottie into Madeleine, and the revelation of Judy *as* Judy marks not only the final death of the illusion, but also the literal death of Judy, when the narrative closes upon the repetition of the ascent up the bell tower and her accidental fall.

Much of this plays out under the rational gaze of Midge, the Maria Gostrey figure in this film, the confidante and chum who was once engaged to Scottie but whom the film represents as an impossible love object. As one of those bespectacled Hitchcock women who know too much, Midge's role is not only to puncture the *particular* fixation of Scottie's captation, but also to ridicule the mystique that attaches to the female body. Midge earns her living as an illustrator for lingerie advertisements, and we first meet her as she draws a new kind of brassière that Scottie refers to as a "doohickey": it guarantees "revolutionary uplift . . . based on the principles of the cantilever bridge," she explains. There is nothing about feminine glamour that Midge does not know or eschew, and she thus serves as the reality principle: as a foil not only to "Madeleine" as pure figment, but also to the entire assembly of Hitchcock's blondes. For if "Madeleine" is, as I have suggested, an allegory of cinematic captation, then Kim Novak takes her place in a signifying chain—Janet Leigh, Grace Kelly, Tippi Hedren—each of whom is a radically empty presence, at some level indistinguishable from the others.

The plot of *Vertigo* is advanced by Scottie's repeated circulation *around* the void of the Real that is Madeleine. The alluring center of Scottie's circumference is not merely the illusion of an illusion of an illusion (that is, Judy as Madeleine as cinematic woman), itself entirely vertiginous, but also a spectral woman who is at once a *revenant* and already in the embrace of death, and thus the grounding figure (much like John Marcher's "point of orientation" in the graveyard) of Scottie's recall to the primary scene of trauma. This compelling *sinthome* of Scottie's circling around the Real moves sharply from the horizontal axis to the vertical—that is, the circle extends into a spiral—in the culmination of each half of the narrative, when Scottie pursues Madeleine up the staircase that winds around the deep well of the Mission's bell tower. To mark the return of primal trauma as Scottie gazes deep into the stairwell, Hitchcock redeploys his opening camera technique of the vertical zoom into the depth overlaid by the reverse tracking shot—a move that, as I have suggested, induces rather than merely signifies vertigo. If this complex shot grafts the sensation of falling onto the "rise" of the abyss, then it may be said to signify not only the upward "surge" of the repressed primal scene but also the paradox that *is* vertigo: "the fear of falling and the desire to fall; . . . the desire to die and the terror of death" (Spoto 1979, 277). The vertical spiral may be said to *literalize* the circuits of the death drive that are allegorized in Scottie's horizontal circlings around the illusory object.

In drawing Scottie into the plot, Gavin Elster tells him that his wife spends her days "wandering about," and this phrase circulates in the film, picked up by both Madeleine and Scottie, as a means of deflecting interrogation about how they spend their time. Its repetition brings into focus the missing noun that ought to follow the preposition, a noun that might stand for the unaccountable center of such peripatetic circulation. Scottie's first sighting of Madeleine at Ernie's Restaurant establishes the visual logics of the gaze: Madeleine is seated with her back turned toward the camera, and this distinctly Jamesian image heightens our curiosity, drawing us into the spell of the glamour that attaches to the undead, haunted woman. Again and again, as Scottie follows Madeleine about San Francisco during the first pursuit narrative, Madeleine appears with her back turned toward us—at the flower shop, at the grave of Carlotta Valdes in the cemetery of Mission Dolores, and in the art gallery of the Palace of the Legion of Honor. This latter is Hitchcock's most extensive and detailed scene of captation; it repeats exactly the terms of Strether's elaboration of the lurking figure at Notre Dame. This scene is remarkable for its slowness, its silence, its stillness. Stationed at the perimeter of the gallery, Scottie gazes at Madeleine, who in turn gazes at the portrait of Carlotta Valdez (see Figure 10.1).

A series of close-up shots underscores the depth of Madeleine's identification with Carlotta: she holds an small bouquet identical to Carlotta's, and her hair is dressed in Carlotta's manner—gathered behind her head and drawn into a tight spiral. Indeed, the close-up on the dark center of Madeleine's hair knot is so prolonged that it not only suggests Scottie's fascination with dark depth—the center *of* the center—but it seems to supplement the museum mood by recalling Gustave Courbet's painting, *l'Origine du monde* (1866): a canvas in the Musée d'Orsay that depicts the close-up view of the genitals and abdomen of a woman, lying back and spreading

FIGURE 10.1 Madeleine gazes at the portrait of Carlotta Valdez.

her legs. Hitchcock's sustained close-up on the empty center of Madeleine's spiraling hair marks the termination, or the point of arrival, of this first pursuit sequence, a downhill journey from Madeleine's apartment on Nob Hill that has taken the form of what Donald Spoto (1979) calls "a descending spiral" (283) (see Figure 10.2). Here, at bottom of cinematic descent, where the camera can go no further, Scottie's captation is firmly bound and where the void at the center of the gaze solicits our fascinated fall.

Hitchcock's plot turns upon the premise that a subject who is haunted by a traumatic event is driven ineluctably to repeat that event. Scottie's descent through the vertical city, culminating in his falling in love, can be but the intermediary stage between one terrifying ascent and another. The first half of the narrative is framed, then, by the relation between two traps: Madeleine's captivating spiral of hair in the Palace of the Legion of Honor into which Scottie, and the subjective camera, "fall," and Scottie's nauseating ascent of the spiral-like staircase of bell tower at San Juan Bautista in pursuit of a "Madeleine" whom he believes is intent upon suicide. In this economy of fearful symmetry, Scottie is paralyzed in midascent by the steady grip of vertigo. As I have noted, this climactic scene is both a repetition and a return of the primal scene of trauma. But there is another repetition upon which the narrative logic depends, and this repetition has a new twist: once again, Scottie is witness to the death of another. Whereas in the primal scene, the other detective falls into and *inside* the abyss upon which our attention is riveted, Madeleine plunges to her death (or so we believe) *outside* the perimeter of the bell tower. Indeed, nothing in the film is more shocking than the fall of Madeleine's body, visible through the aperture of the staircase wall, rushing past the frame for a split second. Such exteriority is traumatic because it marks the collapse of the *sinthome* as a defensive strategy, as a means by which the subject can cohere.

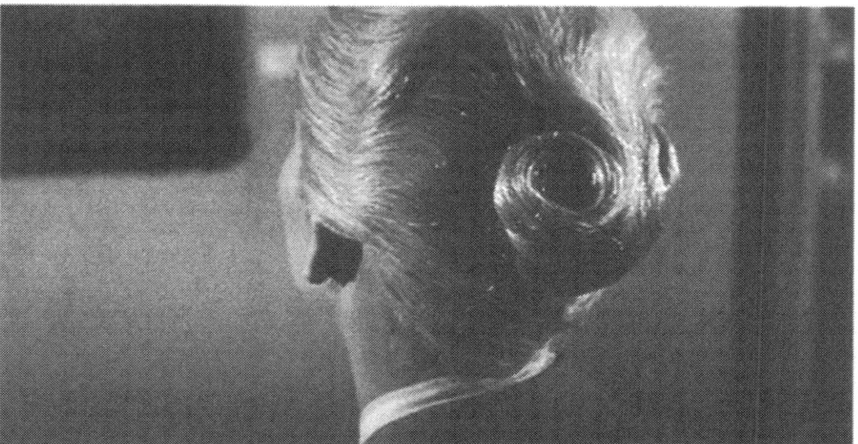

FIGURE 10.2 The dark center of Madeleine's hair knot.

All along, Scottie has circled around Madeleine in what emerges, retrospectively, as the attempt to contain or to frame the terms of captation and to localize cinematically the site of the void of the Real. Suddenly, the illusion of the fixity of the Real is decentered; it spirals out of the illusion of control. This, I think, explains both the severity of Scottie's catatonic trauma, his doctor's diagnosis of "acute melancholia accompanied by a guilt complex," and the desperation to recover or to "refashion" Judy as Madeleine in the second half of the narrative, which makes sense now only as the repetition of a repetition of a repetition. In terms of plot, what this requires is the incorporation of Judy into Madeleine, herself an incorporation of Carlotta, and the repetitive return to the bell tower at the film's conclusion, where "everything" is now "out in the open"—entirely exteriorized. What is unmasked in the final scenes of *Vertigo* is not merely the radical decentering of "Madeleine"—as the woman who was never there—but also the shattering of the illusion that the trauma of the Real has a content or attaches to a "thing," that it has a center about which we can circulate defensively. It is this shattering of the Real as locus, as locatable, as *event*, that is "the touch of the Real."

Throughout the preceding argument and analysis, I have attempted to bring Lacanian concepts into dialogue with complex cultural production—in particular, with formal and stylistic aspects of fictional and cinematic narrative that ought to be understood as authorial, or *auteurist*, signatures. But Lacan insists that the *sinthome*, as the act by which the subject embraces his symptom as self-constituting, embodies a seamless coherence that remains beyond interpretation. It doesn't ask to be decoded; it refuses translation into the cause-and-effect logics of the symptom; it has no language. Rather, it *is*. I have to concede that my attempt to "circumscribe" *Vertigo* in the wake of Henry James, to track those formalist resonances, is itself an excessive gesture that refuses to follow Lacan literally or, one might say, slavishly. Yet I have no recourse but to insist upon interpretive reading—that is, to approach the Jamesian or the Hitchcockian *sinthome* both as complete in itself and, at the same time, as an element of composition that points to something. To something *else*. How might that something be articulated, in its potential and its limitations? Is the *sinthome* an index of authorial mastery, of the pleasures of pure form? It demands our attention, but does it require a response in language? Is to circumscribe *Vertigo* by way of James merely to perform, through a repetition of circling about, my own captation by a cultural object? The only certain conclusion is that relations really don't stop anywhere. One thing leads to another, and these things, cumulatively, make a precarious kind of sense. If to move at all, as a critic, is to move around, then the spiraling *sinthome* that I have traced points ultimately to the shower scene in *Psycho*, which once again is the story of a person possessed by the dead, and to the swirling mixture of blood and water that spirals around and down the drain. I conclude with this critical close-up, in that recurrence of the Hitchcockian *sinthome*, in that place beyond words to which all connections point.

Acknowledgments

I wish to express my thanks to Donald Pease, who organized the Symposium on James and Hitchcock at Dartmouth College in 2008; to Daniel O'Hara, who first introduced me to the possibilities of the Lacanian *sinthome*, and who was helpful in the evolution of my argument; and to my fellow panelists, particularly Frances Restuccia, whose astute, corrective insights have given me much to think about in working with Lacanian concepts in the field of cultural representation.

11

Specters of Respectability

VICTORIAN HORRORS IN *THE TURN OF THE SCREW* AND *PSYCHO*

Aviva Briefel

In the promotional trailer for *Psycho* (1960), Hitchcock invites his audience into a world in which propriety is always on the verge of becoming improper. He adopts the role of a sensationalistic and prim tour guide who arouses our curiosity (among other indelicate responses) by hinting at gruesome events while refusing to fill in the details. Upon describing Detective Arbogast's (Martin Balsam) violent death in the Bates mansion, Hitchcock tells us with fascinated distaste, "It's difficult to describe the way that the, the twisting of—the—well, I won't dwell upon it." When he takes us to the site of Marion Crane's (Janet Leigh) murder, the motel "bathroom"—a word that he articulates very carefully—he resumes his prudish tantalizations: "You should have seen the blood. The whole place was—well it's too horrible to describe." His playful reluctance leaves us wanting more. Henry James uses a similar strategy to draw his readers into *The Turn of the Screw* (1898) when Douglas promises his fireside companions a tale that "nobody but me, till now, has ever heard. It's quite too horrible" (1898, 1995: 22). His refusal to tell the story right away sends his audience into an anticipatory frenzy that we as readers are compelled to model. In Neill Matheson's (1999) words, James constructs a "readership whose respectability fails to mask the cruelty of its desires, desires fully as perverse as any that circulate within the story" (710).

Respectability—particularly Victorian respectability—is an essential part of the gothic nature of both narratives. Critics frequently discuss the horrific respectabilities of the novella and film through the return of the repressed. Since Edmund Wilson's 1934 interpretation of the ghosts as fabrications of the governess, a "frustrated Anglo-Saxon spinster" and "poor country parson's daughter, with her English middle-class class-consciousness, her inability to admit to herself her sexual impulses" (1934, 1999: 173, 172), *The Turn of the Screw* has often been read as a narrative that exemplifies the "cruel and destructive pressures of Victorian society, with its restrictive code of sexual morality and its strong sense of class consciousness" (Nardin 1978, 132). Likewise, analyses of

Psycho typically isolate the Victorian repressiveness of Norman's mother as the source of his degeneration into a moralistic serial killer. Most famously, perhaps, Robin Wood (1989) argues that Mrs. Bates's influence is visible in the "Victorian décor" of her house, which "intensifies the atmosphere of sexual repression" that is essential to understanding Norman (Anthony Perkins) (147). In this light, Mother seems antithetical to the revolutionary nature of a film that refuses to keep sex and violence offscreen. Such critical assessments associate respectability with an outmoded past whose rules and formalities produce monsters. Ironically, they perpetuate their own versions of the repressive hypothesis as they seek to unveil the uncanny things that lurk within the "monotonous nights of the Victorian bourgeoisie" (Foucault 1978, 3).

In what follows, I contend that *The Turn of the Screw* and *Psycho* offer related yet distinct narrative challenges to the myth of Victorian propriety. The novel and film feature dangerous repressions but present these as self-conscious fantasies about the Victorian period. Repression in these texts is not a solution that the astute critic must identify in order to decipher their mysteries; instead, it is a self-conscious rendition of what "Victorian" might signify to fin-de-siècle and mid-twentieth century audiences who are willing to believe in and define themselves against it. While James identifies Victorian repression as a literary cliché, Hitchcock acknowledges the horrors that result from the discovery that Victorian repression is in fact a cliché. Their joint suspicion of the myth of repression is mitigated by a shared acknowledgment of its effectiveness as a gothic trope. For these auteurs, the dangers of Victorian propriety are as seductive as they are fictitious.

Ghosts of Victorians Past

In his 1908 Preface to the New York Edition of *The Turn of the Screw,* James describes his novella as a "piece of ingenuity pure and simple, of cold artistic calculation, an *amusette* to catch those not easily caught" (1908, 1995: 120). But by what, exactly, are we meant to be caught? Based on the avidity with which critics discuss the nature of the apparitions of Miss Jessel and Peter Quint, the main challenge seems to lie in determining whether these ghosts are real or fantastic projections from the governess's disturbed mind.[1] In her canonical reading of the novella, Shoshana Felman (2003) posits that trying to impose a single meaning on this text is itself evidence of entrapment. We need to take Douglas's advice seriously when he cautions one of his listeners that "The story *won't* tell . . . not in any literal vulgar way" (Felman 152; James 1908, 1995: 24; italics in original). Felman warns against Freudian readings of the novel such as Wilson's that try to solve the problem of the ghosts by insisting that the governess suffers from sexual hysteria. To decipher the text in this manner is to ensnare it, to make it say only one thing: "The literal is 'vulgar' because it *stops* the *movement* constitutive of meaning" (Felman 153; italics in original). While repression is an essential part of this narrative, it does not provide the key to the governess's identity. Instead, it functions as one of many Victorian stereotypes that confirm the literary nature of this story, which readers must encounter as representation rather than reality.

The impulse to decipher the *Turn of the Screw* as illustrating the negative effects of Victorian repression is itself illustrative of Foucault's critique of the repressive hypothesis. Drawing on Foucault, John Kucich (1987) writes that the pervasiveness of the myth of Victorian prudishness allows us "to see ourselves, by comparison, as part of a teleological movement toward freedom and authenticity" (4–5). At first glance, there may seem to be something anachronistic in the suggestion that James resists this oppositional use of the Victorian. To do so might imply that the late-Victorian author is "doing" Foucault before Foucault, and before Freud's writings about repression and the uncanny. Yet, James's suspicion of the idea of Victorian morality seems less anomalous in light of the climate in which he was writing. Michael Mason (1994) contends that, while negative associations around the term "Victorian" did not flourish until after Queen Victoria's death in 1901, the sense of hostility toward and superiority over high-Victorian values emerged at the fin de siècle: "The cliché was indirectly prepared in the 1880s and 1890s in people's feeling that very great changes, perhaps so great that they beggared the historical imagination, had occurred in the recent past" (16). This period set the stage for the "reactive" nature of our "modern sexual consensus . . . impossible even to state without the notion of an ideological enemy being brought into play" (Mason 3). Written when these ideas against the high Victorian were beginning to crystallize, James's gothic novella exposes the construction of the Victorian, and particularly the dangers of Victorian repression, as a convenient bogey.

James's narrative looks to the Victorian period as the golden age of the ghost story, drawing from such prime examples of the genre as Elizabeth Gaskell's "The Old Nurse's Story" (1852) (Allott 1961). Rather than a straightforward homage, however, the text purposefully reproduces Victorian literary and cultural clichés. In Marianne DeKoven's words (1998), "Like the 'governess' and the beautiful, angelic-demonic orphan children, [Miss Jessel and Peter Quint] are stock types of Victorian melodramatic fiction. Peter Quint, with full name but no title, is the licentious, drunken, presumptuous seducer, with red hair and a bold expression. Miss Jessel, with no first name but the 'Miss' of her own governess position, is the tragic, doomed, darkly beautiful female victim-monster" (145). As soon as DeKoven establishes these characters as clichés, she implies that they embody a tangible Victorian presence: "They are apparitions of the Victorian past of narrative and political possibility. Quite literally, they represent the past of this narrative: the dark secret of this haunted house" (145).

In his analysis of the novel, Stanley Renner (1995) also addresses the clichéd aspects of the narrative, while nonetheless insisting on the authenticity of some of its elements. He explains that Quint resembles the physiognomic type of the Victorian seducer, which the hysterical governess projects onto her new surroundings: "What the governess sees on her first encounter with the famous 'ghosts' of Bly, the experience that sets in motion the story's central line of development, is thus not the ghost of a dead man she has never seen but the projection of her own sexual hysteria in the form of stereotypes deeply embedded in the mind of the culture" (223–4). Renner's analysis of Quint as an accumulation of clichés relies on the assumption that the governess's repression-produced hysteria is real. He writes, "Not only does James's governess fit the classic profile of the female sexual hysteric, she also experiences the 'hysterical fit' observed by turn-of-the-century clinicians" (227). Renner also references James's "technical knowledge of sexual hysteria," which he "faithfully . . . reproduces" in the governess (225, 226). In this reading, Quint's fictionality contrasts with—and, in fact, depends on—the authenticity of the governess's madness.

This willingness to believe in the governess's repression, despite the recognition of the obvious fictionality of the rest of the novel, attests to the pervasiveness of this Victorian myth. Clearly, while James's familiarity with sexual hysteria does not necessarily signal his intention to craft a clinical case study, it is comforting to hold onto the governess's propriety and resulting madness as truths. The author challenges these assumptions by using his narrative to emphasize their constructed nature, representing Victorian respectability as an empty term that can be inhabited by a range of meanings. In his account of the governess's interview with the children's uncle in London, Douglas paraphrases the man's rationale for sending the children to Bly, "the proper place for them being of course the country":

> There had been for the two children at first a young lady whom they had had the misfortune to lose. She had done for them quite beautifully—she was a most respectable person—till her death, the great awkwardness of which had, precisely, left no alternative but the school for little Miles. Mrs. Grose [the housekeeper, "an excellent woman"], since then, in the way of manners and things, had done as she could for Flora; and there were, further, a cook, a housemaid, a dairywoman, an old pony, an old groom and an old gardener, all likewise thoroughly respectable.
>
> So far had Douglas presented his picture when some one put a question. "And what did the former governess die of? Of so much respectability?" (1898, 1995: 26)

As John Carlos Rowe (1998b) has argued, the term "respectable" is so overused in this passage that it loses its meaning. While it starts off as a "moral quality" intended to describe a person ("most respectable"), it eventually defines the functional and service-based elements of Bly, including the pony and staff (67). We might initially read the auditor's question about the cause of the first governess's death as a skeptical reaction to this confusing barrage of respectabilities. Surely, things couldn't have been *that* respectable if the governess died in dubious circumstances. Douglas tries to staunch this question by saying, "That will come out. I don't anticipate," to which the listener responds, "Pardon me—I thought that was just what you *are* doing" (1898, 1995: 26; italics in original). This interchange offers another reading of the question; if we assume that the listener does interpret Douglas's comments about respectability as anticipatory, then perhaps we can also read his/her question as straightforward rather than cynical. The rest of the story confirms that respectability is, in fact, the place in which trouble is likely to occur.

The first appearance of a ghost in this narrative is accompanied by the governess's meditations about her own respectability. Walking through the estate, she considers how proper she would look to an observer:

> I could take a turn into the grounds and enjoy, almost with a sense of property that amused and flattered me, the beauty and dignity of the place. It was a pleasure at these moments to feel myself tranquil and justified; doubtless perhaps also to reflect that by my discretion, my quiet good sense and general high propriety, I was giving pleasure—if he ever thought of it!—to the person to whose pressure I had yielded. . . . One of the thoughts that, as I don't in the least shrink now from noting, used to be with me in these wanderings was that it would be as charming as a charming story suddenly to meet some one. Some one would appear there at the turn of a path and would stand before me and smile and approve. (37)

It is at the moment when the Victorian governess attains a heightened consciousness of herself as an image of Victorian propriety that the ghost emerges. Quint appears for the second time when she performs another typically respectable task, looking for the gloves she had been mending while taking tea with the children in "that cold clean temple of mahogany and brass, the 'grown-up' dining-room" (42). (It is perhaps a testimony to the precariousness of her respectability that she never finds these gloves.) Likewise, she first catches a glimpse of Miss Jessel after she takes on the "happy and highly distinguished sinecure" of playing an exaggerated version of herself—"something very important and very quiet"—for one of Flora's games (52). These examples align respectability with the ambivalence and horror of the ghosts, whose appearance is likely to produce "change . . . like the spring of a beast" (37). The narrative conditions the reader to anticipate the terrors that come with propriety.

The link between propriety and horror is so pervasive in the novel that it takes on the status of a cliché. We come to expect this association as much as Douglas's listener, who models our role as readers. The governess's tale trains us to recognize the danger that lurks behind the extreme propriety of Victorian persons and things. Hence, she revises her initial interpretation of the white curtains of Flora's bed as sheltering "the perfection of childish rest" (65) with a sense of their deceptiveness in helping the little girl run away: "I dashed at the place in which I had left her lying and over which—for the small silk counterpane and the sheets were disarranged—the white curtains had been deceivingly pulled forward" (66). Later on, after Flora denies seeing the ghost of Miss Jessel, the governess uses the child's apparent respectability as evidence of her deception: "She resents, for all the world like some high little personage, the imputation on her truthfulness and, as it were, her respectability" (102). Likewise, it is when Miles reaches a peak of social propriety that the governess becomes most convinced of his alliance with Quint. Commenting on his impeccable table manners, she observes, "Whatever he had been expelled from school for, it wasn't for ugly feeding. He was irreproachable, as always, today; but was unmistakably more conscious" (109). The abundance of these examples produces the repetitive association between respectability and its demise that comes to define the Victorian world of the novel.

Given that these associations emanate from the governess, we might read them as symptoms of her paranoia as she projects her dangerous propriety onto the world around her. But, in doing so, we need to make clear that James presents this paranoia as a literary construction that rivals the other Victorian tropes of the narrative. Before seeing the ghost of Quint, the governess does not fantasize about her inherent respectability, but about the *image* of respectability she would project to an outside observer. This image is laden with assumptions about what a Victorian governess is supposed to look like while taking a late-afternoon stroll in the lavish grounds. Her reaction to Quint's appearance also bears the mark of a gothic literary construction. She observes that "an unknown man in a lonely place is a permitted object of fear to a young woman privately bred" (38) and ponders, "Was there a 'secret' at Bly—a mystery of Udolpho or an insane, an unmentionable relative kept in unsuspected confinement?" (39). The governess has read her Radcliffe and her Brontë. While Renner interprets her projection of gothic tropes as evidence of her hysteria (233), I view these as confirmations of her own status as a literary construct. James signals that the image of the hysterical governess is already a narrative cliché, one that Douglas's auditor acknowledges in anticipating that the first governess probably did, in fact, die of so much propriety.

The visual nature of respectability in the novel draws attention to its status as a representation. What the governess craves above all else is to be seen executing her duties, until respectability takes on the status of a performance. This is evident in how she defines her impulse to protect the children: "I was a screen—I was to stand before them. The more I saw the less they would" (52). While screens tend to be defined by what they conceal, it is their own visibility that allows them to perform this function. The governess explains later on, "I greatly preferred, as a safeguard, the fulness of my own exposure" (77). Whenever her respectability is at its peak—and is thus in jeopardy—she conveys a fantasy of her visibility. This is the case when she first sees Quint on the tower and before she spots him inside the house. Sensing that something is amiss as she reads Fielding's *Amelia* by candlelight, she notes that she sets off on an exploration of the house "with all the marks of a deliberation that must have seemed magnificent had there been any one to admire it" (65). Similarly, before her final showdown with the ghost, which results in Miles's death, she tells us, "I welcomed the consciousness that I was charged with much to do, and I caused it to be known as well that, left thus to myself, I was quite remarkably firm. I wandered with that manner, for the next hour or two, all over the place and looked, I have no doubt, as if I were ready for any onset. So, for the benefit of whom it might concern, I paraded with a sick heart" (106–7). In another telling instance, the governess anticipates the uncanny events at Bly in the following terms: "I dare say I fancied myself, in short, a remarkable young woman and took comfort in the faith that this would more publicly appear. Well, I needed to be remarkable to offer a front to the remarkable things that presently gave their first sign" (37). Her observation attests to the link between two meanings of "remarkable": something that demands to be seen and something peculiar or uncanny.

Dangerous respectability in *The Turn of the Screw* thus takes on the status of an image or representation rather than a concrete identity. It corroborates Mary Ann Doane's (1996) view—drawn from Joan Riviere's 1929 essay "Womanliness as Masquerade"—that "To masquerade is to manufacture a lack in the form of a certain distance between oneself and one's image" (139). While Doane's definition of the masquerade refers to a donning of femininity through costume and makeup, it can also be applied to the "putting on" of respectability in James's novel. The governess's desire to be *seen* as respectable signals that this respectability is a disguise rather than an inherent identity. James conveys the Victorian nature of the disguise by showing its intimate connection to Bly, with its staff of servants, angelic children, and ornate towers of "gingerbread antiquity" (1898, 1995: 38). The governess first develops the image of herself that she wants others to see in the mirrors of the mansion: she describes "the large impressive room, one of the best in the house, the great state bed, as I almost felt it, the figured full draperies, the long glasses in which, for the first time, I could see myself from head to foot" (28). This moment of self-creation in front of a mirror, which resembles the beauty rituals required by masquerade, anticipates the other mirrorings that occur at Bly. The house functions as a hall of mirrors in which the governess confronts and ultimately occupies various manifestations of Victorian types. When she enters the schoolroom, for instance, she stumbles upon an apparition of Miss Jessel that looks like a warped version of herself: "Dark as midnight in her black dress, her haggard beauty and her unutterable woe, she had looked at me long enough to appear to say that her right to sit at my table was as good as mine to sit at hers" (85). Miss Jessel is the gothic double of our governess, fully transformed into one of propriety's monsters. This mirroring effect also occurs when the governess sees Quint through one of the windows of Bly and explains that, "his face was close to the glass" (43). The double meaning of "glass" as window and mirror comes to the fore when she steps outside to where the specter had appeared, and terrifies Mrs. Grose, who notices her ghostly visage, "white as a sheet," looking into the house (44).

Victorian respectability's illusory nature in James's novel does not make it any less frightening. Inasmuch as its spectacular aspects exist as representations, they demand our fixed attention; we are right there every time the governess expresses a desire to be watched fulfilling (or, as the case may be, violating) her duties. Our susceptibility to being taken in by these Victorian visions confirms James's pronouncement in his 1908 preface that "To bring the dead back to life for a second round of badness is to warrant them as indeed prodigious" (1908, 1995: 10). There is something of "*Je sais bien, mais comme même*" in the novel's demystifications of Victorian stereotypes. *The Turn of the Screw* is a transitional text that exposes the artificiality of the emergent fin-de-siècle construction of the Victorian while recognizing its effectiveness as a gothic literary device. As I will argue, Hitchcock's *Psycho* uses the medium of cinema to shift the site of horror from these outmoded tropes to the shock that comes with exposing their inauthenticity.

Through the Looking Glass

The opening scene of *Psycho* rivals the dismantling of respectability found in James's first description of Bly. Marion and her lover, Sam (John Gavin), engage in a postcoital interchange that systematically divests the term of its propriety. After Sam tells Marion he wants to see her again soon, she responds, conscience-stricken, that they can only do so "respectably, in my house, with my mother's picture on the mantle, and my sister helping me broil a big steak for three." He attenuates his proposal that "after the steak" they might "send sister to the movies [and] turn mother's picture to the wall" by agreeing to see her "under any circumstances, even respectability," all the while approaching her in a suggestive manner. Marion then taunts Sam with a line that might function as a tagline for the film—"You make respectability sound—disrespectful." Her accusation seems justified when he answers that he is "all for it. . . . It requires patience, temperance, and a lot of sweating out." Like a puzzle that involves altering one word to another by changing a letter at a time, their exchange transforms respectability from stodgy to sensual.

This redefinition of respectability is an appropriate way to begin a film that defied censorship codes. As Linda Williams writes, *Psycho* marks the "moment when the experience of going to the movies began to be constituted as providing a certain generally transgressive sexualized thrill of promiscuous abandonment to indeterminate, 'Other' identities" (2000, 361–2). The opening scene sets the stage for this rupture of cinematic convention through Sam and Marion's sexual play, the first time in mainstream cinema that lovers were shown in bed (Williams 2000, 355). The formal properties of the film also convey its illicit nature. It begins with our voyeuristic intrusion through the open window of the hotel room in a shot that links cinematic and sexual transgression: "The viewing subject is made acutely aware of the impossibility of this shot—not just the technical but the 'moral' impossibility, since the shot in question effects a startling breach of privacy" (Silverman 1986, 223). Marion's sudden turn to moral conscience appears out of place in this liberatory context, a fact that may have led Hitchcock to tell Truffaut, "Janet Leigh is playing the role of a perfectly ordinary bourgeoise" (Truffaut 1967, 282). It can also be argued that Marion, like Miss Jessel, ends up dying of "so much respectability" (1898, 1995: 26). Her quest for this elusive condition leads her to steal $40,000 with the hope of marrying Sam, an objective that is thwarted by her arrival at the Bates Motel and her death at the hands of Norman/Mother (Gordon 2008, 119). Given that Norman himself may have been victimized by too much respectability under his mother's oppressive regime, *Psycho* seems to present an object lesson in the horrors produced by repression. According to Paul Gordon, "Hitchcock's films consistently demonstrate that the desire for respectability, which in Freudian terms is modeled on the incest-taboo, that has its symbolic origins in the uncanny *(unheimliche)* house, is nothing other than the repression of the contradictory, illicit desire which is its truth" (121).

The *unheimliche* Bates mansion exposes this particular notion of repression as a MacGuffin that traps viewers who are eager to believe in the Victorian myth (see Figure 11.1). The imposing structure, which Hitchcock described as "California gingerbread" (Truffaut 1967, 269), shares the "gingerbread antiquity" of Bly. In the theatrical trailer, the director warns us that, "in this house, the most dire, horrible events took place. I think we can go inside because the place is up for sale. Oh, I don't know who's going to buy it now." Can we really *buy* its role as a solution to Mrs. Bates's overbearing nature and to Norman's insanity? It is certainly tempting to do so, given its structural role in the resolution of the film's mysteries. The suspenseful climax of the narrative involves Lila's, Marion's sister's (Vera Miles), infiltration of the mansion. Like James's governess, she is stricken with a "detective fever" that compels her to discover the secret of the house.[2] Unlike the governess, however, she succeeds in her enterprise: her search anticipates the shocking revelation that Norman, dressed like Mrs. Bates—not Mrs. Bates herself—is the psycho of this film. Robin Wood (1989) writes that "Lila's exploration of the house is an exploration of Norman's psychotic personality. The whole sequence, with its discoveries in bedroom, attic, and cellar has clear Freudian overtones" (147). But Hitchcock's trailer, in reconstructing Lila's tour of the house while self-consciously withholding useful information, asks us to interrogate its revelatory role. When we watch the scene in question, we realize that the trailer is an accurate representation of how little we do find out about Norman and his mother.

FIGURE 11.1 The *unheimliche* Bates mansion.

While the form of the sequence suggests full disclosure, its content is empty. Much of the editing consists of eyeline matches and reaction shots that convey a sense of progressive revelation as the camera alternates between Victorian objects and Lila's shocked or perplexed reactions to them. Hence, a shot of Lila entering the room is followed by an establishing shot of its ornate furniture and decorations; a shot of Lila leads to a view of a porcelain sink adorned with an elaborate soap dish and pitcher; another shot of Lila leads to one of the fireplace and accompanying chair. The sense of revelation is heightened by the crosscutting of Sam's frantic interview with Norman in the motel office.[3] And yet, neither investigation reveals anything. As George Toles (1999) puts it, "In no other Hitchcock film does the camera close in on so many objects that refuse to disclose their significance" (173). This point is best illustrated by Lila's discovery of a book in Norman's room, whose toys and twin bed suggest that it is occupied by a child rather than an adult. While she reacts to the book as if it were another piece of the puzzle, we are left in the dark: the binding is blank, and the camera cuts away just as she opens its pages. The men's tense conversation in the motel office concludes with a comparable blankness—also evinced by a Victorian object—as Norman knocks out Sam by hitting him with a bibelot.

Even more than the editing, what makes the nothingness of Lila's tour of the Bates mansion so easy to overlook is its Victorian mise-en-scène. Steven Jacobs (2007) argues that the ornate objects of the house correspond to David Stove's term "*Victorianarum:* 'that horror which even nowadays is felt, at least to a slight degree, by almost anyone who visits a display of stuffed birds under glass, for example, or of Victorian dolls and doll's clothes'" (129). In *Psycho,* horror is linked to a return of the repressed in which traces of Victorian respectability are tainted by their opposite. Like James, Hitchcock relies on his audience to fill in the blanks of the narrative with its assumptions about this recognizable trope. These projections allow us to interpret the objects in the room as signaling the disreputable aspects of Mrs. Bates's respectability. The sink, an allusion to the Victorian value of cleanliness, also conveys smuttiness as it features a soap dish held up by an assemblage of naked nymphs. The stuffy tapestries and sinister bodily impression of the bed express the lusts that may emerge from Victorian propriety: it seems "that one of the occupants spent more time recumbent than upright" (Dick 2000, 241). Likewise, the statues of winged figures strewn throughout the house evoke dark angels or Cupids (Hendershot 2001, 29; Wood 1989, 147). The visit to Norman's room, with its eerie tokens of Victorian childhood, uncannily communicates a sense of lost innocence that would be at home in James's novel. Taken together, these things entice us to interpret them as emblems of the horrors of repression.

At one point during the sequence, however, Hitchcock challenges our interpretation of these Victorian objects. One of the eyeline matches reveals a bronze statue of primly positioned hands, an artwork that looks like the sculptures of the hands of Queen Victoria's children made by the artist Mary Thornycroft (Millar 2001, 36) (see Figure 11.2). At once dainty and creepy, both sets of objects capture the uncanny repressions that we readily ascribe to the Victorians. The camera dramatically (and perhaps heavy-handedly) zooms in on the hands to convey Lila's shocked gaze; it isolates them as worrisome things, the keys to Mrs. Bates's secret. The next shot undermines this interpretation by showing Lila swiftly looking up from the sculpture to the mirror in front of her, in which, through an optical illusion caused by her own reflection in another mirror behind her, she mistakes herself for an intruder—quite possibly, Norman's mother (see Figure 11.3). This moment recalls an incident that Freud describes in a footnote from "The Uncanny" (1919):

> I was sitting alone in my *wagon-lit* compartment when a more than usually violent jolt of the train swung back the door of the adjoining washing-cabinet,

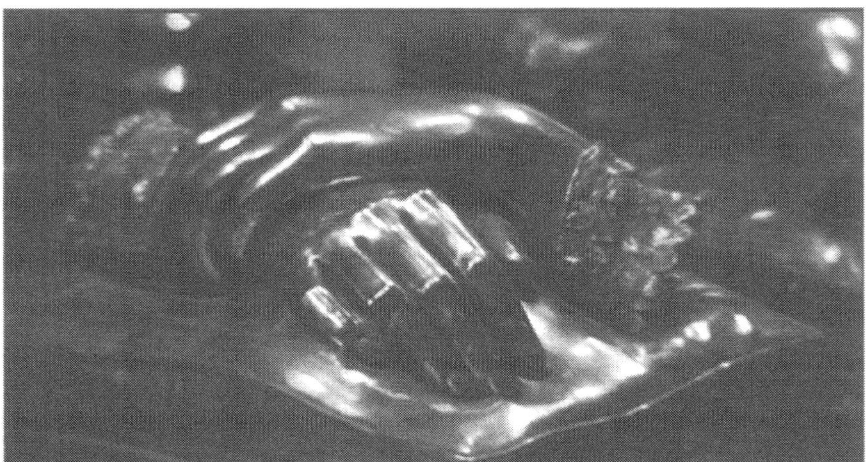

FIGURE 11.2 From sculpture . . .

FIGURE 11.3 . . . to mirror.

> and an elderly gentleman in a dressing-gown and a travelling cap came in. I assumed that in leaving the washing-cabinet, which lay between the two compartments, he had taken the wrong direction and come into my compartment by mistake. Jumping up with the intention of putting him right, I at once realized to my *dismay* that the intruder was nothing but my own reflection in the looking-glass on the open door. (1919, 1981: 248; emphasis added)

Both Freud and Lila temporarily mistake their reflections in the mirror for someone else's, only to realize that no intrusion has taken place. In each case this realization is not met with relief, as might be expected, but with consternation. While Freud refers to his "dismay" in finding out that he was the source of his own fear, Lila's reassurance that she is alone in the room is interrupted by the shocked look she gives to Mrs. Bates's bed, thus continuing her metonymical chain of (empty) associations with the Victorian repressed. These responses signal the consequences of paranoia, of realizing that one has created a monster in one's own image. They are the next logical step to the masquerade performed by James's governess and the enthusiasm with which she takes on the Victorian persona she sees reflected there. While the governess does not recognize that she has constructed Miss Jessel from her own image, Lila is made to confront the horror of her projections. Similarly, just when viewers of *Psycho* may sense that they have stumbled upon a clue in discovering the Victorian hands, we are confronted with a frustrating moment of self-reflexivity, which exposes our own desire to see these things as uncanny signs of repression.

Fittingly, the trope of the mirror emerges frequently in recent critical accounts of how notions of the Victorian have been crucial in constructions of the modern self. John Kucich and Dianne Sadoff (2000) describe "our contemporary contemplation of Victorian sex" as "a dizzying hall of mirrors, in which it seems impossible to decide whether Victorian sexuality lies behind us in the dust, or whether, in their passionate struggles with sexual repression, the Victorians were somehow the harbingers of sexual self-realization" (xix). Simon Joyce uses a similar image of reflective sandwiching in his book *The Victorians in the Rearview Mirror* (2007) when he posits that "The iconic warning we see when driving, that 'objects in the mirror are closer than they appear,' thus nicely expresses a feeling we may have about a period that no longer seems as distant as we might like to think, but instead forms the horizon for many of our most pressing debates" (16). Hitchcock shows us that there is something profoundly frightening about these double visions in Lila's response to being caught between the two images of herself projected by the ornate furniture of Mrs. Bates's room. Her fear comes both from her misrecognition of herself as Victorian monster and from the subsequent recognition that she has done so.

In its demystifying role, the mirror in the bedroom scene from *Psycho* can also be read in the context of Foucault's account of Philippe Pinel's late-eighteenth century asylum. One of the primary functions of this asylum was to convince patients of their madness, an enterprise for which mirrors were crucial: "The asylum, in this community of madmen, placed the mirrors in such a way that the madman, when all was said and done, inevitably surprised himself, despite himself, *as a madman.* Freed from the chains that made it a purely observed object, madness lost, paradoxically, the essence of its liberty, which was solitary exaltation; it became responsible for what it knew of its truth; it imprisoned itself in an infinitely self-referring observation; it was finally chained to the humiliation of being its own object" (1965, 264–5; italics in original). Both Lila and the audience are subjected to the terrifying prospect of perceiving our delusions about the Victorian, which, like madness caught in the mirror, becomes the "spectacle of itself as unreason humiliated" (Foucault 264). This moment of realization constitutes one of the essential differences between James's and Hitchcock's narratives; while the mirror marks the beginning of the governess's self-construction into the Victorian identities found at Bly, Lila's view of herself at the end of the film signals a rupture to her Victorian identifications.

It is this realization that Lila's double, her sister Marion, overlooks. Ultimately, Victorian repression does not kill her—as critics like Gordon would have it—but her inability to detect its fictionality does. Indeed, she seems to find great comfort in the familiar trope. In contrast to her fear of the police officer who pursues her on the highway, she is nonplussed by Mrs. Bates. Standing by the open window of her motel room, she hears the old woman inside the mansion berating her son for entertaining his female guest "in the cheap erotic fashion of young men with cheap erotic minds." Marion appears more concerned than frightened by what she hears, and, when Norman returns, she condescendingly tells him, "I caused you some trouble" and invites him to dine with her in her room, despite Mother's interdiction (always a good boy, Norman declines). In her subsequent conversation with Norman in the parlor—whose Victorian decor marks it as an extension of the Bates mansion (Jacobs 2007, 127)—she confidently makes assumptions about Mrs. Bates's overprotectiveness. She offers Norman words of sympathy ("If anyone spoke to me the way I heard"), urges him to escape, and suggests that he place his mother in an asylum. Marion cannot detect her own complicity in constructing the myth of Mother. In suggesting that Mrs. Bates belongs in an asylum, she resembles those patients in Pinel's institution who had not yet been subjected to the mirror treatment and only saw madness in those around them: "Madness, as simple delirium, is projected onto others" (Foucault 1965, 263). Interestingly, Hitchcock presents several instances in which Marion conspicuously fails to look in a mirror that is right next to her: when she counts the money in the bathroom of the used-car dealership; after she sees Mother's silhouette in the window of the mansion and stands by the check-in desk mirror, waiting for service; when she is reflected in the motel room mirror while Norman invites her to dinner; and as she sits in her bathrobe calculating how much of the $40,000 she has spent, moments before her murder (see Figure 11.4). Unlike her sister, she will not confront her image straight on. This astigmatism prevents her from recognizing the part of herself that resembles the fantastic matron and that led her to end her tryst with Sam in the name of the sanctity of marriage.

FIGURE 11.4 Marion reflected in the motel room mirror while Norman invites her to dinner.

Marion's cognitive inability links her to Norman, who is also deluded by his construction of Victorian propriety. While the son creates—and inhabits—an image of Mrs. Bates as an oppressive Victorian matriarch who confines him to a monotonous, solitary life, Marion projects her sense of Mother onto her surroundings. Cynthia Erb (2006) identifies the fantastic aspects of Mrs. Bates's voice in the motel room: "The sound is impossible: if Marion is down at the motel, near an open window, how is [it] that she can hear a conversation between 'two' people in a closed house up the hill? Norman is psychotic, but Marion seems to be 'hearing things'" (56). The impossibility of this scene echoes the technical and moral impossibility of our flight into the hotel window at the beginning of the film; by linking these two moments, Hitchcock attaches the audience's expectations about propriety to Marion's. The sense of voyeuristic transgression we experience early on, which may leave us self-satisfied with our willingness to put prurience aside and confront the forbidden full on, is thus exposed as our own delusion. As descendants of the Victorians, we already know that too much respectability is a tenuous thing, that it will produce its opposite. It is only later in the film that we come to realize our complicity in constructing this myth through Lila's discovery that she, too, has created Mrs. Bates. Lila's view of Mrs. Bates's body in the fruit cellar imparts the horror of our having to accept Victorian repression as an empty signifier; there is nothing underneath Mrs. Bates' wig, prim dress, and empty eye sockets.

In some sense, Hitchcock goes further than James in exposing the idea of the Victorian as a masquerade, something that can be worn as a disguise rather than a coherent identity. It is tempting to draw a progressive chronology in which the director provides a complete unmasking of the Victorian about which the author was far more tentative, but to do so would be to perpetuate the "teleological movement"

(Kucich 1987, 4) from which the modern marks its distance from the Victorian. In fact, Hitchcock himself revives the Victorian myth in the final scenes of the film by restoring murderous agency to Norman's mother. As Linda Williams (1996) succinctly puts it, "In *Psycho* we learn that the mother did it" (28). The psychiatrist revives Mrs. Bates when he explains, "Norman Bates no longer exists . . . now, the other half [the "mother half"] does," which he defines as belonging to a "clinging, demanding woman." While we might dismiss this declaration as a parody of facile psychiatric explanations, the final resurrection of the voice of Norman's mother over her son's smiling face proves that Hitchcock does not let go of Victorian repression as an effective gothic trope. In the end, the film experiences a return of the repressed that brings back the idea of repression itself. Rather than trace a progress narrative from *The Turn of the Screw* to *Psycho,* then, we might view them as works in progress. They attest to the fact that it is not easy—nor perhaps is it completely desirable—to abandon the Victorian myth altogether. We are too reliant on it, both as an artistic trope and as an iconic image against which we define ourselves. We continue to believe that the governess and Mrs. Bates, armed with proper improprieties, are getting ready to scold us once again.

12

Caged Heat

FEMINIST REBELLION IN *IN THE CAGE* AND *REAR WINDOW*

John Carlos Rowe

In the classic women's prison film, *Caged Heat* (1974), imprisoned women embody the repressive state apparatus that constructs all women as subalterns in a colonial system of gender, class, and racial hierarchies. Fighting their feminine guards and each other, in the process exposing titillating body parts, these criminalized women act out the systemic violence that defines them while offering the elusive promise of feminine emancipation. Were they to succeed, the entire patriarchal system would have to be overturned, so their cinematic rebellion must be recontained by erotic voyeurism. The pleasure masculine viewers take from *Caged Heat* exemplifies Laura Mulvey's famous reading of film narrative in "Visual Pleasure and Narrative Cinema" (1975), in which she argues that feminine characters erotically fetishize the viewer's own anxieties regarding political impotence and thereby help reassert masculine authority (6–18). Projecting their profound inadequacies onto the screen, masculine viewers find feminine characters sublimating their problems, rather than providing any effective catharsis.

Like other members of the Screen group of the mid-1970s, Mulvey interpreted cinema's technical innovations as adapted to patriarchal processes of psychological socialization. In particular, Mulvey judges what she terms the "narcissistic scopophilia" of cinematic viewing to reinforce subject formation that depends on its response to the castration complex (7). From Sigmund Freud to Jacques Lacan, subject formation was interpreted as an inherently phallocentric process, in which masculine fear of castration was overcome by the gendering of women as other, lacking the phallus, and thereby representing the unconscious fears of masculine impotence. From the scantily clad feminine prisoners in *Caged Heat* to the allure of the celebrity actress, both on and off the screen, cinematic femininity *performs* masculine desire not simply by promising sexual satisfaction but more profoundly by confirming patriarchal power to reproduce social reality. Thus, second-wave feminists like Mulvey argued that mere demystification of cinematic imagery, such as criticism of the pornographic exploitation of women in *Caged Heat*, would do nothing to overcome systemic sexism in modern Western societies. Advertising for *Caged Heat* promised that "white hot desires" could melt "cold prison steel," but the feminine prisoners direct their "riot and revenge" at the feminine warden (Barbara Steele), effectively leaving patriarchal power intact ("Promotional Poster" 1974).

Feminist critics developed similar arguments about the representation of feminine gender in print narratives. Judith Fetterley's *The Resisting Reader* (1978), Sandra Gilbert and Susan Gubar's *The Madwoman in the Attic* (1979), and Nina Auerbach's *The Woman and the Demon* (1982) are three influential examples of feminist scholarship that interpreted the ways Anglo-American literature constructed feminine characters as subaltern in order to reaffirm threatened masculinity. None of these scholars judge imaginative fiction to be inherently patriarchal, but all assume the adaptability of literature to the conventions of the dominant ideology. For these analysts, feminine illness, madness, and physical or ethical weakness are symptomatic of masculine insecurities, which are especially notable in times when women organize for greater political, civil, and economic rights.

While in "Visual Pleasure and Narrative Cinema," Mulvey judges masculine desire to be integral to the cinematic apparatus, most second-wave feminists offered counternarratives to literary patriarchy. Fetterley suggests that by resisting the literary imperatives that construct an "implied reader" in Irving, Hawthorne, Faulkner, Hemingway, Fitzgerald, James, and Mailer, the feminist reader can challenge not only masculine literature but also the patriarchal order itself. Thus, in James's *The Bostonians* (1886), the resisting reader turns from James's intended protagonist, Basil Ransom, to the relationship between Verena Tarrant and Olive Chancellor, overtly satirized by James, but carrying the "latent" "revolutionary message," "whether [James] knew it or not," of "the central elements of radical feminism" (Fetterley 1978, 152). Gilbert and Gubar would follow their critical treatment of Anglo-American patriarchy with *No Man's Land* (1988), in which they construct an alternative tradition of women's literature, which becomes more visible once patriarchal assumptions of literary "value" have been challenged.

These issues may seem to belong to the bygone era of second-wave feminism, when patriarchy could be treated in a monologic way and feminism understood as a unified political and cultural movement. Third-wave feminisms, gay studies, and queer theories have complicated these questions, in part by challenging the effectiveness of the kinds of "resistance" proposed by Fetterley. Is it as easy as she suggests to change our conventions for reading, or must the text already carry within itself that tendency, as Fetterley herself hints in her interpretation of the radical feminist subtext in *The Bostonians*? If so, are such inclinations present in every text produced within the ideological dominion of patriarchy, or are certain texts more unstable than others and thus more likely to challenge both their own aesthetic and the broader social conventions on which they rely? Does it follow, as Gilbert and Gubar appear to argue in *No Man's Land*, that such critical texts tend to be produced primarily by *women*, or can such instabilities be equally, in some cases, *more* instructive, when produced as a consequence of masculine anxieties about changing social reality, especially as it affects conventional gender roles?

We are still interested in these questions, in part because we do not yet know how to answer them. The persistence of these issues helps explain our fascination with masculine artists, like Henry James and Alfred Hitchcock, who built substantial reputations on their subtle representations of memorable feminine characters and abused femininity in general. François Truffaut (1967) helped establish Hitchcock's fame by interpreting him as an *auteur* with a coherent cinematic *oeuvre* (13–14).[1] James initiates the sort of cultural modernism, distinguished both by its attention to the growing social and political importance of women that Hitchcock might be said to conclude.

Both author and director employ exceptionally self-conscious techniques, ranging from the invariable presence of the narratorial "I" in James and the signature appearance of Hitchcock in each of his films to their respective tendencies to thematize literary and cinematic production as central to their plots. What is remarkable about James's and Hitchcock's works, albeit hardly unique to them, is their interest in and sympathy for their feminine characters, as well as their tendency to represent their putative masculine protagonists as lacking the usual qualities of manliness. In the final analysis, however, neither Henry James nor Alfred Hitchcock quite surrenders his own semiotic authority to his empowered feminine characters, subordinating even the most successful of them to the specific talents and techniques commanded by the novelist and the film director. Hitchcock was certainly not joking when he recommended that actors be "treated as cattle," presumably to be herded by the director, and many anecdotes from his long career support the idea that successful filmmaking depends on the director's manipulation of his cast (Chandler 2005, 25–6). And Henry James always understood his characters as figments of his commanding imagination, verifying its power and thus his genius. Finally, James's and Hitchcock's feminine characters cannot be distinguished from their authors' very ambivalent relations with traditional masculinity. Whether or not Henry James was actively gay in his personal life, he indisputably challenges traditional gender roles in most of his fiction. Often known for his ribald wit, even sexist jokes, on the set and in his personal life, Hitchcock repeatedly satirizes conventional masculinity and represents many of his masculine characters as regressive and infantile, less interested in heterosexual romance than in repressed Oedipal fantasies. In his personal life, Hitchcock was deeply divided about his own relations to women. In his biography of Hitchcock, Donald Spoto (1983) observes that Hitchcock was "fascinated with the techniques of conventional and unconventional sex," yet "he recoiled from physical and emotional intimacy like a child before a dark and frightening forest, retreating instead into a private world of fantasies, which were exposed in his films and sometimes in impolite conversations" (28–9). As James does so often in his fiction, Hitchcock seems to split personal qualities into masculine and feminine characters in his films, projecting his regressive traits as masculine and his desired qualities as feminine.

James and Hitchcock focus on trapped, even imprisoned, women who seem at first to exemplify the fetishistic qualities analyzed by Mulvey, but who struggle dramatically to replace their commodified bodies with their own abilities to act and choose—that is, with subjective agency (see Figure 12.1). In short, James and Hitchcock undo the systemic logics of patriarchy working through print literature and cinema by enabling their feminine characters to talk back, allowing them to embody not just masculine desire but their own psychic and cognitive complexities. In so doing, these characters help expose the processes of patriarchal voyeurism, subverting it in the interests of different incorporations. A wide range of works by James and Hitchcock meet these very loose criteria, so my particular selection of James's *In the Cage* (1898) and Hitchcock's *Rear Window* (1954) should not be considered exceptional or unique cases. Each text does foreground explicitly feminine commodification and masculine voyeurism, relating both to broader processes of technological innovation and economic modernization. Both James's and Hitchcock's characteristic self-reflexivity implicates print literature and cinema, respectively, in these new technological and thus economic means of social production, offering particularly astute, albeit historically limited, interpretations of the social construction of gender, sexuality, and agency.

The unnamed telegraphist in James's *In the Cage*, patronizingly dubbed "our young lady" throughout the novella, seems to epitomize femininity imprisoned by the social, economic, and even scopic conventions of late Victorian patriarchy (1898, 1908: 372).[2] Working everyday at her post "in framed and wired confinement" in the corner of Cocker's Grocery, she is compared to "a guinea-pig or a magpie," with the added aggravation of the sexual harassment she must endure by the masculine counter clerks. In fact, she is engaged to one of the former clerks at

FIGURE 12.1 Grace Kelly as Lisa Fremont, the epitome of feminine beauty.

Cocker's, Mr. Mudge, whose unromantic name matches his matrimonial pragmatism to combine incomes, move to suburban Chalk Farm, and save three shillings per week on rent. Trapped in her working-class situation, literally caged in her everyday labor, figuratively imprisoned by her personal circumstances caring for an alcoholic mother and her future with Mudge, the telegraphist seems to be Henry James's negative response to the emancipatory promise of women in the workplace.[3]

Her position as telegraphist places her at the center of new technologies of social communication, offering her the possibility of power equivalent to James's own. Yet James was deeply anxious about the rise of new media competitive with more traditional literature, and he often links new media with the growing power of women. Journalism, of course, was one of his favorite targets, as were photography and advertising. Generally, James focuses on the form and content of the new media, but he also understood that their technologies granted their practitioners special knowledge equivalent to the novelist's insight into his craft. *In the Cage* plays with the idea that the person who understands the new technologies of communication may well have access to powers even greater than the literary author's command of style, rhetoric, and form. In the case of telegraphy, which had been developed to speed and encrypt military secrets, James selected a particularly appropriate technology, albeit one that was more than sixty years old by 1898.[4] Yet the telegraphist seems to waste her opportunity by using access to secrets of the aristocracy to fantasize some impossible class mobility. Imagining herself in love with the callous Captain Everard and able to compete for his affections with high-society women, like Lady Bradeen, "our young lady" appears only to expose her naïveté about the power of her personal charms and her command of the social capital of telegraphy. Internalizing the romantic lives of the aristocracy, she interpellates her own status as servant to their higher purposes, acting out their melodramatic affairs and thereby granting them importance. With the potential to publicize the secret corruption and triviality of the ruling class, the telegraphist instead *celebrates* their fashionable lives, anticipating the later cult of celebrity through which cinema, sports, and other late-modern spectacles would advertise themselves (Rowe 1998a, 155–180).

In Hitchcock's *Rear Window*, Lisa Fremont's (Grace Kelly's) situation resembles the telegraphist's, even if Lisa appears to have more in common with Lady Bradeen and her social circle. As a fashion model, Lisa Fremont is little more than a mannequin displaying the current fashions that help legitimate the ruling class. Lisa's elegant commodification finds its unconscious representation in the body of Anna Thorwald (Irene Winston), the invalid who is murdered, dismembered, buried, and drowned by her husband, Lars Thorwald (Raymond Burr). More obviously, Lisa's desirable body finds its double in the ballerina, Miss Torso (Georgine Darcy), who dances in her underwear, entertains only men in her apartment, and unwittingly provides the protagonist, L. B. "Jeff" Jeffries (James Stewart) with voyeuristic titillation. Confined to a wheelchair and his Greenwich Village apartment with a broken leg, the photojournalist Jeffries is surrounded by feminine characters who exemplify the prevailing stereotypes of women in the Cold War United States: the sardonic nurse, Stella (Thelma Ritter); Miss Lonelyhearts (Judith Evelyn), who will eventually connect with the songwriter (Ross Bagdasarian); the sculptor with her hearing aid (Jesslyn Fax); the newlywed woman (Havis Davenport) initially consumed by sexual desire then reduced to nagging her husband (Rand Harper). All reinforce the conventional assumption that American women are subordinate to men. The invalid Mrs. Thorwald epitomizes feminine helplessness and dependency, and her healthier avatars embody and enact masculine desire, itself a perverse *élan vital.*

In the Cage and *Rear Window* thus invite interpretations based on Laura Mulvey's thesis. Feminized through the very spectatorial dynamics of the novella and the film, either by being forced to follow the telegraphist's partial understanding of her aristocratic customers or by even more explicitly witnessing through Jeffries' telephoto lens their doubles in a series of commodified women, viewers can work out their anxieties regarding gender and sexuality in their different historical moments. At the end of the nineteenth century, James's novella offers the possible empowerment of working women and the working class in general by their access to new technologies of communication, only to reassure the patriarchal, bourgeois Victorian audience that most workers will misuse this opportunity. Hitchcock's film entertains the social impact of the increased numbers of women in the wartime workforce by giving Lisa Fremont a career in modeling and the courage to investigate the suspicious disappearance of Mrs. Thorwald. Yet the middle-class U.S. gender hierarchies are restored neatly in the film because Lisa follows the directions of her lover, Jeff Jeffries, aiming to please him in the interests of marriage. Arrested by the police for breaking and entering Thorwald's apartment, Lisa is bailed out by Stella, Jeff's nurse, using all of Jeff's available cash. When she is assaulted by Lars Thorwald, who surprises her in his apartment, she still can gesture with her hands behind her back to Jeff that she has indeed found Mrs. Thorwald's missing wedding ring. Displaying it on her own hand, Lisa delivers a clear message to her reluctant fiancé.

In *The Women Who Knew Too Much: Hitchcock and Feminist Theory*, Tania Modleski (1989) begins by challenging Mulvey's thesis.[5] Aligning her own work with third-wave feminists like Linda Williams, Modleski wants to know what happens when a "woman" is "allowed to look for herself," thereby escaping the fetishism of the cinematic image or what we might term the broader processes of feminine reification (13–15). Although Mulvey does not refer directly to Marxian notions of reification, the fetishistic use of the feminine in film to represent masculine anxieties lends itself well to the general notion of capitalist reification. In the classic analysis by Georg Lukács (1972), the alienation of the manufactured object begins in the system of capitalist production, such as the Fordist assembly line, wherein the actual cooperation of workers is fragmented into the repetitive tasks of isolated individuals. The finished product is further alienated from workers by a market system that transforms it into a mysteriously independent object of desire, now embellished by advertising, so that the worker yearns for an object he himself actually produced (83–109).

In "The Work of Art in the Age of Mechanical Reproduction," Walter Benjamin (1969) interprets film production and acting itself as further elaborations of capitalism's perverse magic. Unlike the stage actor, the film "actor's work" is "split . . . into a series of mountable episodes," which can be completed "in a sequence of separate shootings which may take hours at the studio" and combined with scenes "shot weeks later when outdoor scenes are taken" (230). Even though the production of a film is inescapably the collaboration of many workers, the actor in particular experiences the fragmentation of his or her labor in relationship to the final film. The actor's relationship to his own labor reflects that of the industrial worker; both discover the final "product" to be alien to them: "While facing the camera [the actor] knows that ultimately he will face the public, the consumers who constitute the market" (231). Benjamin offers, however, an interesting distinction between the film actor and the ordinary worker, suggesting that the cultural work of film exceeds considerably the processes of reification in industrial production: "This market, where he offers not only his labor but also his whole self, his heart and soul, is beyond his reach. During the shooting he has as little contract with it as any article made in a factory" (231). In particular, Benjamin notes how the "cult of the movie star, fostered by the money of the film industry, preserves not the unique aura of the person but the 'spell of the personality,' the phony spell of a commodity" (231). Previously understood as a mysteriously desirable and yet elusive object, the commodity form is *animated* in film, given the "heart and soul" the actor surrenders to the directorial narrative. Such appropriation extends even to the actor's personal life beyond his labor, so that the "spell of personality," subordinated to help market the film and the actor's career, is equivalent to the "phony spell of a commodity."

Jeff Jeffries tells the insurance nurse, Stella, that he cannot marry Lisa because she is "too perfect," seeming to confirm Mulvey's thesis that the cinematic feminine is unreal, a projection of masculine desire. Of course, Lisa's "perfection" is difficult to separate from Grace Kelly's well-established reputation for sophisticated beauty. Modleski argues that Lisa's "perfection" shows how she exceeds Jeff's need for a woman who is inferior to him and thus in need of his phallic supplementarity to provide marriage, children—the nuclear and patriarchal family. Modleski argues that the murder plot of the film allegorizes patriarchal desire to project its own castration anxiety onto woman, now reduced to the dismembered parts of Anna Thorwald. But she disputes the logical conclusion of Mulvey's thesis that *Rear Window* is concerned primarily with "re-membering . . . the woman according to the little boy's fantasy that the female is no different from himself" (1989, 76). For Modleski, the film's concluding representation of Jeffries "sleeping like a baby" in his wheelchair, now with two broken legs, offers us the thin veneer of a patriarchal psychonarrative, easily dismissed by socially active and independent women. Warning us not to confuse Jeffries' voyeurism with Hitchcock's filmmaking, Modleski points out that what

Jeffries views in the rear windows of his neighbors' apartments is infantile wish fulfillment or "day dreaming," whereas Hitchcock uses the cinematic frame to provide a more adult account of gender relations (143).

Jeffries learned his skills as a photojournalist during World War II, but his abilities hardly defend him against everyday urban violence. Much as he relies on his phallic telephoto lens to invade his neighbors' privacy, his scopic, psychic, and physical powers are extremely limited (see Figure 12.2). After Lisa is arrested for breaking and entering and while Stella has gone to bail her out, Thorwald forces his way into Jeffries' apartment, turning the tables on his adversary. Jeffries' famous metacinematic defense of momentarily blinding Thorwald with successive flashes from his camera is finally ineffective; Thorwald rushes Jeffries and violently forces him out the apartment's window. His fall broken by the police, his injured body cradled by Lisa and Stella, Jeffries is symbolically castrated once again and ends the film by underscoring his own identification with the invalid, Anna Thorwald. For all his technological skills, Jeffries displays little more power than that curious little dog Thorwald kills when it begins to dig in the garden where he has buried parts of his wife.

The real talents of detection belong to Lisa, who concludes that Anna Thorwald would never have left her purse or wedding ring at home while traveling to visit her relatives. Even as Jeffries imagines he is "directing" Lisa as she looks for evidence in Thorwald's apartment, viewers are encouraged by the real director, Hitchcock, to see Lisa as the capable investigator (see Figure 12.3). In his effort to save Lisa, Jeffries calls the police, causing her to be arrested by a more powerful masculine force; when Lisa and Stella "save" Jeffries, they succeed with the help of the police. Whereas L. B. "Jeff" Jeffries' very name suggests either corporate

FIGURE 12.2 Jeff's phallic telephoto lens.

anonymity—"L. B."—or the attenuated identity of someone with the same given and surnames—Jeff Jeffries, Lisa Fremont's surname evokes psychic and sexual "freedom" and the militarism of her namesake, John Charles Frémont (1813–90), western explorer and U.S. claimant of California during the Mexican-American War. Stella's Latin name, "star," connects her ironically with the Hollywood system of theatrical celebrity to which the plain-spoken character does not belong, but hints at her moral success in caring for Jeffries, saving Lisa, helping solve the mystery, and contributing to their romantic union. Indeed, their antagonist's mythic name, Thorwald (Thor's wood or wilderness), demands more aggressive defenses than are possible with Jeff's flashbulbs and telephoto lens.

Yet just what constitutes Lisa Fremont's power to defeat Thorwald and to presumably protect the neighbors from his violence, is somewhat more difficult to define. Lisa is an able interpreter of visual evidence—the dead little dog, Anna Thorwald's purse and wedding ring—and of the psychic realities behind such signs, especially masculine sexual desire's entanglement with the human will to power. Lisa is assisted, of course, by Stella, who nurses both Jeffries' body and his roving gaze. Stella's initial common sense and regular admonitions of Jeffries' voyeurism soon give way to participation in the detective work, facilitating Lisa's role in the solution. Stella is often identified with the Law—both the psychic law regulating sexual relations and the more practical "law" of the police—and thus the figure of mediation between Jeffries and Lisa as well as between the audience and the viewers within the film. Judith Roof (2002) considers Stella a double both for Jeffries and Lisa, thus suggesting a transgendered character, despite the fact that Stella is married (98). By playing a feminine sidekick to Lisa, Stella enhances Lisa's agency in the film, enabling the two of them to take over the conventional roles of the masculine

FIGURE 12.3 Lisa looking for evidence in Thorwald's apartment.

detective and his assistant (Holmes and Watson, for example). Spending long hours in Jeffries' darkened apartment, Stella becomes Lisa's alter ego, even as Stella's growing participation in Jeffries' voyeurism identifies her with him. What Roof terms Stella's "central secondariness" reinforces the instability of conventional gender roles in the film, allowing conventionally feminine stereotypes—Stella, the nurse; Lisa, the fashion model—to assume masculine powers (98).

Feminist interpreters of *Rear Window* who have challenged Mulvey's thesis often stress the bisexuality of masculine and feminine characters as Hitchcock's suggestion that we are free to view from different gender positions, as Lisa, Stella, and Jeffries do in the course of the film (Modleski 1989, 143). Judith Roof argues that the ways in which the cinematic apparatus encourages "viewers [to] pleasurably cross-identify" may not be indicative of cultural instabilities in traditional gender roles but in fact work to regulate those roles (2002, 90). The female viewer may identify with Jeffries, as Stella appears to do, primarily to control her desire for agency and independence. Men are, after all, powerless, childish, and in need of care; in these respects, men share many of the qualities feminine viewers are ideologically urged to find in themselves. Such viewers' identifications with Jeffries are thus against their own interests, insofar as they mitigate the power of patriarchy. To be sure, Jeffries is rendered curiously defenseless, vulnerable, celibate, and infantile in *Rear Window*, qualities reinforced by Stella and Lisa, whose complementary actions may perversely prompt cross-identifications by male viewers. Yet far from these possibilities offering structural changes in conventional gender roles, they work instead merely to distract us from the real source of authority in the film. With its overdetermination of metacinematic devices—it is nothing if not a film about viewing—*Rear Window* locates authority in those who can command the representational system. Lisa and Stella work for Alfred Hitchcock, who substitutes another reality for the appearances of the quotidian lives first revealed to us in Jeffries' neighbors' apartments. Hitchcock, not Doyle, is the real "law" in this film, much as Dupin, not the Prefect of Police, represents the poetic "law" in Poe's "Murders in the Rue Morgue."

In a similar manner, we can interpret James's framing of the telegraphist's romantic fantasies about Captain Everard as conventional elements drawn from late Victorian popular romances of the sort she herself reads in her spare time. Like Lisa Fremont and Stella, the telegraphist acts out a patriarchal narrative, in which she appears to confirm her subordinate status both to the upper class and its reliance on masculine rule. Even though she works to make possible communication within the ruling order, she serves merely instrumental purposes while being captivated by the romance of such communication. Jill Galvan (2001) argues that the telegraphist "thinks herself akin—in dignity and character, if not income and lifestyle—to the aristocratic set who frequent Cocker's grocery" (299). The telegraphist's view is "for the most part fictive and illusive," a fantasy that helps her forget her dreary prospects taking care of her alcoholic mother and marrying the tedious Mr. Mudge (Galvan 302). Readers are thus reassured that the upwardly mobile working class, especially women entering the new service industries of communications as secretaries, telephone operators, and telegraphists, will do little to destabilize the existing class and gender hierarchies.

Yet the telegraphist's fantasies about Captain Everard and Lady Bradeen transcend the "ha'penny romances" she reads to enter everyday reality. When she completes for Everard the numeric code about which he is so concerned—"He fairly glared. . . . 'Seven nine four—' 'Nine, six, one'—she obligingly completed the number" (James 1898, 1908: 484), she can turn to the young male clerks in Cocker's Grocery and conclude triumphantly, "'If it's wrong it's all right,'" by which oxymoron we readers are intended to understand that if there is a mistake in the code, then Everard has not betrayed his involvement in one of his many illicit liaisons. For the telegraphist to be able to play this game at all means she has begun to interpret, not simply transmit, the messages of the upper class. In this regard, she is acting out of character, as Lisa Fremont does in *Rear Window*, so much so that when the telegraphist escapes from her cage to meet Captain Everard in Regents Park, declaring somewhat uncertainly that "'Yes, I know,'" she certainly surprises, puzzles, and probably even scares Captain Everard with the threat of knowledge that exceeds her usual circuits of communication (James 1898, 1908: 437).

At the end of *Rear Window*, Lisa Fremont is shown caring for Jeff Jeffries, who sleeps peacefully in his chair with his two broken legs as she prepares for a life of adventurous travel with him by reading *Beyond the High Himalayas* (see Figure 12.4). But as the film ends, she casts aside this text and picks up *Harper's Bazaar* to suggest that Jeff's cosmopolitanism will be satisfied by her alluring, high-fashion figure. Mothering this infantile adult, Lisa can humor his romantic fantasies, only to guarantee with her dress and body that his desire will be more than engaged at

FIGURE 12.4 Lisa ostensibly preparing for a life of adventurous travel.

home. Similarly, the telegraphist serves as a surrogate mother to a wide range of characters, including her own alcoholic mother, Mr. Mudge, Captain Everard, and the male clerks at Cocker's. Like Lisa, the telegraphist does not understand maternity as strictly biological; the last thing either appears to desire is actual pregnancy. Biological motherhood would ruin Lisa's career as a fashion model, just as it would conclude the telegraphist's career at Cocker's Grocery. Both simulate maternity, transforming their masculine counterparts into the "children" for whom they care, thus reminding their audiences the degree to which motherhood depends on nurture over nature.

The conventional feminine functions of the telegraphist and Lisa Fremont as lovers, wives, and mothers are complemented by their working relations with other women. The widowed Mrs. Jordan invites the telegraphist to join her business of providing flower arrangements to wealthy clients (James 1898, 1908: 371). Lisa not only works with the insurance nurse, Stella, to solve the crime and care for Jeff, but she is clearly identified with the ballerina, "Miss Torso," both of whom are commodified by the masculine gaze and thus understand the patriarchal logic of Anna Thorwald's murder and dismemberment. Having entered the labor force and public sphere, these working women retain many of their domestic powers while refunctioning them to aid, rather than contradict, their new agency in the modern world. To be sure, each feminine character is unable to overcome the deep sexual exploitation of her respective culture. Mrs. Jordan wants the telegraphist to take over the "bachelor's accounts," using her youth and charm to build the business; Stella, Lisa, and Miss Torso work at jobs—nursing, modeling, dancing—targeted at women in postwar America.

Nevertheless, the feminine protagonists in *In the Cage* and *Rear Window* ultimately claim their identities through the command of the prevailing system of communication and representation. The telegraphist may be "wrong about everything" in her reading of the intricate affairs of her aristocratic clients and foolishly imagine she can engage Captain Everard's affections, but the telegraph's capacity to publicize the secret lives of the ruling class offers the possibility of gender and class transformations. For Henry James, of course, whoever commands the system of communication also controls social and economic power, which is part of his prophetic understanding of Western modernity (Norrman 1977, 425). For Alfred Hitchcock more than half a century later, the dominant media of representation are film and television, rather than print, but social power still depends on the interpretation and manipulation of cultural semiotics. Indeed, Hitchcock carefully negotiates a transitional era, in which print literacy continues to shape our understanding of visual signs. Jeffries is a "photojournalist," and Lisa reads illustrated travel books and magazines.

Above all, James and Hitchcock make us see events from the position of characters conventionally rendered *invisible* as human subjects (O'Donnell, Chapter 6, this volume). Whether she attracts the masculine gaze of the clerks at work or the casual glances of her clients sending telegrams, the telegraphist is thoroughly commodified in the Victorian social economy. As a fashion model, Lisa Fremont plays with just such scopic desire, offering herself as mannequin on which others' designs can be marketed. Positioning us inside the telegraphist's cage and often inside her head, even when she is wrong, James makes us assume not only her position but also that of the novelist, whose success depends on his ability to imagine another's reality. Similarly, Hitchcock uses Jeffries' incapacity to empower both Stella and Lisa; when Lisa "looks back," gesturing at Jeffries' from Thorwald's apartment, we cannot miss her effort to subvert the conventional voyeurism of the masculine gaze.

Of course, the telegraphist and Lisa Fremont do everything according to the direction of their authors, James and Hitchcock, so that their feminist achievements as well as their fatal limitations lead us finally to these two canny Masters of their media. James's ambivalent attitudes toward women's and working-class rights qualify our conclusions about the symbolic emancipation of women in *In the Cage*. For James, the real command of representation does not belong to the instrumentality of new technologies, but to authors who can adapt new media to address venerable questions about the human predicament. Similarly, Hitchcock merely plays with emancipated femininity, using it to expose the childishness and brutality of most men while reserving for himself transcendent knowledge of human nature. Neither the author nor the *auteur* radicalizes the social system of Western representation, in which individual subjectivity is measured by one's capacity to represent his or her relation to the larger world of signs.

In this situation, the common *donnée* of the Jamesian novel and Hitchcock film, characters can never overcome the literary form or cinematic frame. James and Hitchcock exemplify a practice that is most likely a general consequence of what Foucault (1977) terms "the author function" in modernity (148). Although Foucault does not specifically address the tacit gender hierarchy of the modern "author function," Continental feminists like Luce Irigaray (1975) and Hélène Cixous (1975) explicitly identify the patriarchal, "phallogocentric" qualities of such authority. Henry James replaces Captain Everard in the telegraphist's affections and Alfred Hitchcock finally controls Lisa Fremont. If these were the only expenses for such visions of empowered femininity, then we might be willing to grant these authors their powers, even mastery. But the history of modernity from the Jamesian novel to film and television is filled with this logic of substitution, whereby new social challenges and threats to the existing ideology are acted out for the sake of conventional catharses. James's feminine characters never quite reach his level of knowledge, even though James urges actual women to try, as he does in his Commencement Address to the graduating women at Bryn Mawr College in 1905: "Imitating, yes; I commend to you, earnestly and without reserve, as the first result and concomitant of observation, the imitation of formed and finished utterance, wherever, among all the discords and deficiencies, that music steals upon your ear. The more you listen to it the more you will love it—the more you will wonder that you could ever have lived without it."(James 1905, 50). Yet what he urges upon these young graduates is not avant-garde breaks with traditional means of expression, but studied practice to *imitate* the "music" of "formed and finished utterance."

As if she is following Henry James's advice to these women graduates, Lisa Fremont solves the mystery in *Rear Window*, only to normalize social relations culminating in her marriage to Jeffries. Her authority finally derives from the position of the Mother, capable of managing the neuroses of such infantile men as Jeffries, even Thorwald himself. In his biography of Hitchcock, Spoto (1983) concludes that the "confusion of mother-love and erotic love" so often thematized in Hitchcock's films—*Spellbound* (1945) and *Psycho* (1960) are the most obvious examples—reflects Hitchock's personal guilt regarding his mother, his asexual relations with his wife, Alma, and his erotic fantasies regarding his beautiful leading ladies (291). My purpose here is not to offer a psychobiographical reading of Hithcock's feminine characters, much less an interpretation based on Oedipal desire, but instead to suggest that Hitchcock's great appeal in the post–World War II era may have had something to do with the ways he imaginatively negotiated personal anxieties regarding women that are reflected in broader cultural concerns about changing gender roles.

Rear Window appeared in 1954 while the popular television shows *The George Burns and Gracie Allen Show* (1950–1958) and *I Love Lucy* (1951–1957) starred two of the most talented female comics in U.S. history, Gracie Allen and Lucille Ball. They were followed by such popular sitcoms starring women as ABC's *Bewitched* (1964–1972) and NBC's *I Dream of Jeannie* (1965–1970), in which Samantha (Elizabeth Montgomery) and Jeannie (Barbara Eden) display magical powers that transcend the wit of their predecessors. In all cases, however, these feminine protagonists reaffirm conventions of feminine domesticity while helping to legitimate the technical wizardry of television itself, that medium which allows Samantha to cause people to disappear with a wrinkle of her nose and Jeannie to grant her "master's" (Larry Hagman's) wishes without his knowledge (Rowe 2002, 160–166). Playing to feminine audiences with more time to entertain themselves than their wartime predecessors, U.S. television from the 1950s to 1970s empowers feminine characters by having them act out television's own bid for cultural and economic power (Spigel 1992, 73–98).

Between 1950 and 1970, feminine characters on popular television speak back to their husbands, claim satiric and magical powers that exceed their domestic confinement, and in many other respects anticipate the more politically directed second-wave feminism we identify with the National Organization for Women and the fight for such legislation as the Equal Rights Amendment. Yet we now recognize that the rebellions of Gracie and Lucy, Samantha and Jeannie focused on the fragile, often infantile bourgeois male, instead of on the invisible power informing the new technology of television and the broader apparatus of the postindustrial economy. Henry James easily replaces Captain Everard in our affections, just as Hitchcock makes quick work of Jeffries as he sweeps Grace Kelly off her feet. Yet these great modern Masters merely paved the way for their successors at NBC, ABC, Madison Avenue, and NASA, where the "magic" of new media, advertising, and the military-industrial complex would ventriloquize their feminine agents.

In short, Henry James and Alfred Hitchcock helped effect a transition from modern to postmodern conditions, adjusting along the way gender roles and notions of subjective agency without radically transforming them. Within the ideological constraints of late Victorian England and Joseph McCarthy's House Committee on Un-American Activities's hearings of the 1950s, Henry James and Alfred Hitchcock, respectively, challenged patriarchal authority and entertained the possibility of feminine agency. Yet insofar as *In the Cage* and *Rear Window* enabled subsequent stories of feminine identity to be framed within the existing British and U.S. ideologies, they deferred real social change by offering phantasmatic revolutions.

13

Shadows of Modernity

WHAT MAISIE KNEW AND *SHADOW OF A DOUBT*

Thomas B. Byers

Similarities between *What Maisie Knew* (1897) and *Shadow of a Doubt* (1943) run deep. Each concerns the education of a young girl—one who knows more, perhaps, than is good for her. Both educations are thoroughly imbricated with Oedipal issues, and the girls' situations are surprisingly similar in their deviations from the Oedipal script for the female—itself already a notoriously complicated "variant" on the male version. Even when things go smoothly, the girl's development hinges on displacement of desire for the mother onto the father, with the mother's difficult transformation from object of desire, through competitor for the father's love, to ego ideal, and with the accompanying complications of separation. But for both James's Maisie and Hitchcock's Charlie, matters are compounded by an abdication on the part of the biological father (and, in poor Maisie's case, by the mother as well). Each situation thus requires a substitute father who proves to be crucial. In both instances he is at once object of desire and ego ideal; one beloved and one emulated. And in both this overdetermination is signified by a gender confusion in the terms in which the daughter is addressed. It is at the end of both texts, as the protagonist separates from the substitute father, that she and he most closely mirror each other.

As their titles suggest, both narratives raise questions about the extent and accuracy of what is known, what supposed or suspected, what understood or misunderstood, what knowledge can or must be avowed or disavowed. Brian McHale (1987) argues that epistemology is the dominant concern of modern fiction (Chapter 1 *passim*), and it is as reflections of and on modernity that *Maisie* and *Shadow* are treated in what follows. My argument is that, despite their similarities, the two take quite different positions on the meaning of *substitution*, particularly substitution for the father, and that this difference reflects or constructs alternative responses—sanguine in James's text, anxious in Hitchcock's—to modernity and urbanization. Finally, the anxiety of the film reflects Hollywood's general anxiety about, and need to disavow, its grounding in a modernist technology of metonymic substitution.

"'It Hasn't Spoiled Her'"

The plot of *Maisie* begins with her home already broken, as the court decides to split her time between papa and mamma, Beale and Ida Farange. At first both parents seem to want her to themselves and try to keep her beyond their legally established turns. The affection of each for her, however, fluctuates with Maisie's usefulness in asserting his/her superiority over the other parent, and in launching assaults on the other from a distance—as, most notably, when the little girl "faithfully report[s]" papa's message to mamma, "'that you're a nasty, horrid pig!'" (1897, 2003: 404). When she stops carrying such messages and, more importantly, when her presence becomes inconvenient to the parents' developing new relationships, both pull away from and, finally, cruelly, break with her.

Maisie finds herself shuffled through a series of arrangements that include the diminishing involvement of her biological parents, the participation of various nurses and governesses, and the eventual intervention of her stepparents, first as representatives of their respective spouses, then as a couple themselves, and as individual actors. Generally these arrangements mirror the opening situation: on the one hand, someone loves or wants Maisie; on the other, that love is intertwined with her function as a means to an end—and if that function passes, so may the love. In *Maisie*, as in many fairy tales with female protagonists, the mother is the crueler (and more phallic) parent.[1] Maisie says "very simply" that "mamma doesn't care for me . . . not really" (456), and while she does not fear papa, she is more afraid of mamma "than of a wild elephant!" (477). Mamma has amply justified this fear, as once, "on the stairs, returning from her father's, she [Maisie] had . . . been dashed by Mrs. Farange almost to the bottom" (508). Mamma's "habit of brutality" (550) is painfully evident when she parts forever from her child. In a matter of minutes, she seeks to induce guilt by claiming to be "awfully ill" and telling Maisie that "one of these days . . . I hope you'll know what it is to have lost a mother" (550); claims that she has come "to sacrifice myself" and informs Maisie that her "father wishes you were dead" (551); proffers and then takes back a large sum of money; "g[i]ve[s] her one of the looks that slammed the door in her face" (553); and parts by saying, "'You're a dreadful, dismal, deplorable little thing'" (554), "turn[ing her] back and rustl[ing] away" (555).

Papa has far less force; though his teeth resemble "shining fangs," the narrator (if not Maisie) finds him merely "stupid" (524). When Sir Claude says that "No one at all is—really" afraid of papa, Maisie finds her "filial spring too relaxed, from of old, for a pang at [his] want of parental majesty" (478, 479). Though Papa, too, is cruel to Maisie when he last sees her, in his case she simply desires to be done with him so much that, when he leaves, "[h]er father had vanished and there was even yet nothing in that to reawaken the pang of loss" (535). The dynamic between Maisie and both parents helps explain her investments in various parent surrogates—especially in her stepfather, Sir Claude, and in Mrs. Wix, the governess with whom she ends up.

The first surrogate parent, Moddle, seems an exception to the rule that adults love Maisie to their own ends, for Moddle only desires that her ward not stray too far when playing; the nurse "was always on the bench when she came back" (402). As Julie Rivkin (1996) points out, "this mother figure is associated with proximity and resemblance [, and] . . . [t]his Edenic memory of an unbroken continuity between mother and child . . . conforms to a psychoanalytic account of the pre-Oedipal stage" (137). However, as Rivkin also notes, "once the father has introduced a sense of difference," once he and his friends have let Maisie know that her legs were "deficient in something that would meet the general desire" (1897, 2003: 402), Moddle can only confirm her lack (Rivkin 1996, 137).[2] From here on, Maisie faces the challenges of Oedipalization in a circumstance where the family triad is broken, her relationships to mother and father are serialized, and, worst, she has become a kind of "shuttlecock"—the pun is James's—batted by each of them at the other (James 1984, 1156).

The first substitute parent of Oedipal import is Miss Overmore, Maisie's first governess and "first passion" (1897, 2003: 411). Her relation to Maisie initially helps her to get close to Beale Farange, then to mask the impropriety of their relation, and finally to marry him (and become Mrs. Beale). Then Maisie serves as an entreé into Mrs. Beale's relationship with Sir Claude, a cover for *their* impropriety, and finally a weapon in her attempt to secure a commitment from him. When, near the end, Maisie impedes this latter aim, she becomes to Mrs. Beale an "abominable little horror" (646). Mrs. Beale ends up partially fulfilling the Oedipal mother function for Maisie, in that she is both the child's first object of desire and, ultimately, the adult to whom Maisie must surrender the (substitute) Oedipal father, Sir Claude.

Arguably the two who love Maisie most, Sir Claude and Mrs. Wix, do so not because they are better people than her parents or Mrs. Beale, but rather (or also) because the end she fulfills for each of them is most dependent on a positive relationship with her. Mrs. Wix is the one woman in the tale most suited to fill the nurturing (though not the Oedipal) role of a substitute mother because she is a mother seeking a substitute daughter (see 412). At the same time she is

> somehow, in her ugliness and her poverty . . . peculiarly and soothingly safe; safer than any one in the world, than papa, than mamma . . . safer even, though so much less beautiful, than Miss Overmore, on whose loveliness . . . the little girl was faintly conscious that one couldn't rest with quite the same tucked in and kissed-for-goodnight feeling. Mrs. Wix was as safe as Clara Matilda [her deceased daughter][.][3] . . . It was from something in Mrs. Wix's tone, which, in spite of caricature, remained indescribable and inimitable, that Maisie . . . drew this sense of a tenderness that would never give way. (414)

Sentimental and deficient in worldly knowledge as she may be, ridiculous as she seems at times, Mrs. Wix provides Maisie with stable affection and also with a "moral sense" (642)—though as John Carlos Rowe (1998a) suggests, that sense may be "woefully inadequate" (153). Rowe allows, however, that "Mrs. Wix comes to represent the whole range of other people—all variously 'nobodies' in the false society of her parents and stepparents—from whom Maisie has learned in the course of her education" (153). She also offers the child some elements of a motherly ego ideal worth emulating.

The crucial relationship for Maisie, though, and the most pertinent for a comparison to *Shadow of a Doubt*, is with Sir Claude. By Chapter 7 he is engaged to mamma, but by Chapter 11 these two have split, and mamma tells Maisie, "I've made you over to him" (1897, 2003: 459). Both Maisie's desire for him and his for her are profound, and profoundly Oedipal; as mamma says crudely: "You've gone over to him, you've given yourself up to side against me and hate me. . . . You hang about him in a way that's barely decent, and he can do what he likes with you" (460). Mrs. Wix compares him favorably "even to [the future man to] whom you may be contracted in marriage" (448). As for Maisie herself, when Sir Claude addresses her as if he has "a real indifference" to their age gap, "[i]t gave her moments of secret rapture—moments of believing she might help him indeed" (454). Later, when Mrs. Wix tells her that Sir Claude has asked to see her alone, "[t]he same as if you was a duchess," Maisie finds herself "now quite as happy as one, and also, a moment later, as she hung round his neck, [convinced] that even such a person would scarce commit herself more grandly" (492, 493). Even in her grim parting with her mother, for Maisie "[t]he great effect of their encounter had been to confirm her sense of being launched with Sir Claude, to make it rich and full beyond anything she had dreamed" (552). Shortly thereafter, when Sir Claude asks her, "Will Miss Farange do me the honour to accept my arm?," we are told that "[t]here was nothing in all her days that Miss Farange had accepted with such bliss" (555). Later "[t]hey h[o]ld each other long enough to reaffirm intensely their vows" (579), and her "gaze," which he meets "as he so frequently and actively met it," is "more than filial" (580).[4]

Sir Claude early on sees danger in Maisie's desire. He tells her "'I should be in fear of you if you were older'" (478), just as he fears both mamma and Mrs. Beale once he has become romantically entwined with them. This admission counts for more both in light of his tendency to address Maisie with "a real indifference" to their age gap (454), and because by the end of her story she *is* significantly older. In her final encounter with papa, "Maisie had her sense . . . of her having grown for him, since the last time he had, as it were, noticed her, and by increase of years and of inches if by nothing else, much more of a little person to reckon with" (*sic*, 524). One suspects that the increase in inches signifies puberty.[5] In any case, the threat of Maisie's desire may help explain why, on at least fifteen occasions, Sir Claude addresses her as "old boy," "old chap," "old man," "dear boy," or "dear man" (see, for instance, 452, 453, 456, 457, 473, 489, 561). Particularly if he is going to address her as an equal in age, he must also address her with an "indifference" regarding their sex (see also Rowe 1998a, 129).

This assertion of nondifference may also compound Sir Claude's place in Maisie's psychic economy, by installing him as a (partial) ego ideal. If Mrs. Wix has offered Maisie a moral sense, Sir Claude has, as he says, "produced life" in her (1897, 2003: 643), "the spasm within her of something still deeper than a moral sense" (643). Thus, when he looks on her as "some lovely work of art or of nature [that] had suddenly been set down among them" (644), he is seeing his own creation. Moreover, it is he who affirms Maisie's choice at the end to go with Mrs. Wix rather than with himself since he will not give up Mrs. Beale: "She made her condition,'" he says, "with such a sense of what it should be! She made the only right one" (645). He also tells Maisie that in doing this she, like he himself, has become "free" (644, 557). Desire is still at issue here—the relation is arguably that of Pygmalion and Galatea, rather than that of a creator producing his own image. Nonetheless, Sir Claude, while enabling her to complete her Oedipalization by her surrendering him to Mrs. Beale, also serves as an ego ideal for Maisie, the daughter who is also a "dear boy."

This relation is reciprocal; Sir Claude may be as much Maisie's pupil as teacher, as much the object of her agency as she of his. She brings him together with Mrs. Beale and models for him the necessity of moral choice. It is from her that he learns he and Mrs. Beale are "not good enough" to "work her in" to their domestic arrangements (647). Maisie, in short, brings out the best in him. As he declares, "You're the best thing—you and what we [he and Mrs. Beale] can do for you—that either of us has ever known" (629). His and Maisie's reciprocity of modeling and emulation helps explain why, in the end, they part not with a kiss but a handclasp, "and their eyes met" not as desiring subjects but "as the eyes who have done for each other what they can" (649).

Again, those who love Maisie best are those whose own ends are most tightly bound to their relation with her and the role(s) it gives them. What Sir Claude wants, from the outset, is "to see the thing through" (441), the "thing" being commitment to familial relations. "The truth about me," he claims, "is simply that I'm the most unappreciated of—what do you call the fellows—'family-men.' Yes, I'm a family-man; upon my honour I am!" (440). His relation to Maisie makes him one: not only does it make him a father figure, but it also brings him together with Mrs. Beale, in a match to which he ultimately realizes he must remain committed. Even in giving up Maisie he is sticking to his "truth" because he must relinquish her both to allow her Oedipal passage—thereby serving as a good father—and to remain true to Mrs. Beale, to whom he declares at the end, "Yes, my dear, I haven't given you up . . . and I don't mind giving you my word for it that I never, never will" (648).[6]

While Maisie's relationship with a substitute father parallels Charlie's in *Shadow of a Doubt*, the two substitutes are significantly different. Part of what makes Sir Claude a happy (and atypical) substitute father is that, from the outset, he more or less accepts his castration. Once mamma gives Maisie over to him, "He appeared to accept the idea that he had taken her over and made her, he said, his particular lark; he quite agreed also that he was an awful humbug and an idle beast and a sorry dunce" (459). In assuming the lark of playing the patriarch, Sir Claude recognizes himself to be a humbug—as all fathers are, in pretending to fill the position of the Father. Charlie's uncle, on the other hand, suffers such anxiety about men's castration by women that he is driven to violence.

Another crucial difference between the two texts arises from Maisie's experience of repeated (parental) substitutions as the adults around her go through their shifting allegiances. To Maisie, it all "sound[s] . . . very much like puss-in-the-corner, and she could only wonder if the distribution of parties would lead to a rushing to and fro and changing of places. She was in the presence, she felt, of restless change" (464).[7] In fiction, as in life, one might expect such a pattern to damage the child. Thus, Kevin Ohi (2004), while recognizing that the novel "does not sentimentalize," nonetheless argues that "Maisie's experience of such exchange is an experience of loss" (97), and emphasizes the "melancholia" of "her position enabling exchange" (93). Similarly, Christine Britzolakis (2001) asserts that "If, for James, the figure of the wide-eyed, wondering child literalizes the process of coming to terms with urban modernity . . . this process is coded throughout as essentially traumatic" (383), as an instance of "the Jamesian metanarrative of modernity" in which "[t]rauma, feminization of the aesthetic subject, and spectatorship are linked terms" (384).

While I agree with Britzolakis about what Maisie literalizes, I reject her diagnosis of trauma: it seems remarkable how little damage Maisie sustains. At the beginning the narrator prepares us for a tale of victimization: "[n]othing could have been more touching at first than her failure to suspect the ordeal that awaited her little unspotted soul. There were persons horrified to think what those who had charge of it would combine to try to make of it." But he continues, surprisingly, by saying, "[n]o one could conceive in advance that they would be able to make nothing ill" (1897, 2003: 399). In the New York Edition Preface, James explains that in his thinking about her initial situation, it

> became rather quaintly clear that, not less than the chance of misery and of a degraded state, the chance of happiness and of an improved state might be here involved for the child, round about whom the complexity of life would thus turn to fineness, to richness—and indeed would have but so to turn for the small creature to be steeped in security and ease. (1984, 1156–7)

As the idea developed,

> For satisfaction of the mind . . . the small expanding consciousness would have to be saved . . . by the experience of certain advantages, by some enjoyed profit and some achieved confidence, rather than coarsened, blurred, sterilised, by ignorance and pain [.] . . . [I]nstead of simply submitting to the inherited tie and the imposed complication, of suffering from them, our little wonder-working agent would create, without design, quite fresh elements of this

order—contribute, that is, to the formation of a fresh tie, from which it would then (and for all the world as if through a small demonic foresight) proceed to derive great profit. (1157)

Thus, as Julie Rivkin (1996) points out, "the family structure that is actually developed in *What Maisie Knew* . . . [is] based not on the propriety of origins or the authority of paternity, but upon a dynamic of substitution" (127), and both Rivkin and I follow James in seeing this dynamic as neither a bad thing nor a source of damage to the child. As Mrs. Beale observes, "It hasn't spoiled her" (1897, 2003: 442).

If, as realism invites us to do, we imagine Maisie as a real person, she exemplifies psychosocial "resilience" and the importance of mentors. While adults (especially her parents) do abuse and neglect her, there is always a caring adult in her life. She is resilient, able to accept love when it is offered and to ride happily on the train of substitutions, rather than fix her gaze wistfully on those who are sending her away. Of course, as a textual figure Maisie invites not a constative but a rhetorical reading. In this vein, Rivkin points out that the alternative and substitutive family structure amelioratively disrupts the stability of patriarchy. I will suggest later that *Maisie*'s affirmation of substitution also advocates a more positive disposition toward modernity than is found elsewhere in James—or in *Shadow of a Doubt*. All this helps explain why the texts' endings feel so different—particularly why Hitchcock's, though adhering to the conventional happy ending formula, nevertheless feels so much darker.

"She Is Doomed to Love her Uncle Charlie . . ."

As in *Maisie*, in *Shadow* the inadequacy of a father triggers substitution. But in Hitchcock's text, this process turns out to be anything but benign. It also links familial dynamics with the social circumstances of modernity because the substitution for the father also offers to substitute a vital urban for a stagnant small-town way of life. The film implies that this attempt is misguided; the substitute father and lifestyle deliver something far more sinister than they promised. Far from vitality, the city brings chaos, alienation, and murder; far from boredom, the town ultimately promises stability and love. Upon closer examination, however, the attempted substitution is moot because the difference between the two settings is already a difference within the small town itself. Modernity is already there.

Unlike Beale Farange, Joseph Newton (Henry Travers), the biological father of protagonist Charlie Newton (Teresa Wright) in *Shadow of a Doubt*, is not cruel. But like Beale, Joseph is, as Robin Wood (2002) says, "ineffectual . . . [and] largely ignored" (51). Indeed, the biblical reference of his first name suggests that he is not the real Father—not that this Joseph's biological parenthood is questioned, but that he is a weak placeholder for the patriarch. Thus, Charlie, like Maisie, becomes involved in a family romance with a substitute father: in Charlie's case her uncle and namesake, Charlie Oakley (Joseph Cotten).

Uncle Charlie long ago left his family and small town for the excitement and cosmopolitanism of the city, and his niece sees him as "a wonderful person who will come and shake us all up, who will save us" from what she perceives as the family's "terrible rut" in the peaceful, beautifully treed town of Santa Rosa. It's a place where "[w]e sort of go along and nothing happens," where women in particular endure tedium: "Dinner, then dishes, then bed," Charlie says. "I don't see how she [Charlie's mother, Emma (Patricia Collinge)] stands it" (the proper grammatical antecedent of "it" here is "bed"; clearly her father does not provoke Charlie's Oedipal desire). Uncle Charlie does come to visit, and at dinner on his first night he seems poised to fulfill his niece's hope for stimulation, regaling his family with tales of luxury and extravagant gifts.

Nonetheless, Uncle Charlie is far from the noble Sir Claude, or even from a Hollywood representative of urban glamour like the Thin Man. He is much more the alienated, *film noir* type. The film's opening sequence showed him lying on a bed staring vacantly at the ceiling in a lonely rooming house in a rundown urban neighborhood. He was being followed, and he went to Santa Rosa to hide from his pursuers. He wants to break with the city and reconnect to a simpler past in the "wonderful world" of his small-town childhood. "Everybody was sweet and pretty then," he tells the family that first night, and "it was great to be young." "Cities," in contrast, he says in a later dinner scene,

> are full of women, middle-aged widows, husbands dead, husbands who've spent their lives making fortunes, working and working. Then they die and leave their money to their wives. Their silly wives. And what do the wives do, these useless women? You see them in the hotels, the best hotels, every day by the thousands. Drinking the money, eating the money, losing the money at bridge, playing all day and all night. Smelling of money. Proud of their jewelry but of nothing else. Horrible, faded, fat, greedy women.

In the city, Uncle Charlie felt driven to rid the world of such women, by seducing and then strangling them. He is in fact a deeply misogynist serial killer.

He tries to seduce Charlie, too, at least metaphorically. Initially, Charlie feels a close connection to him, in which his role as substitute father and "longed-for lover" (Rothman 2003, 187) is never far from the surface. But just as Sir Claude tries to protect himself from Maisie's and his own desire by turning Maisie into a male protégé, so Charlie, sharing her uncle's masculine-marked name, tries to interpret their bond in terms of identification rather than desire:

> I'm glad that mother named me after you and that she thinks we're both alike. I think we are too. I know it. It would spoil things if you should give me anything.[8] We're not just an uncle and a niece. It's something else. I know you. I know that you don't tell people a lot of things. I don't either. I have the feeling that inside you somewhere there's something nobody knows about. . . . Something secret and wonderful and—I'll find out. We're sort of like twins, don't you see?

In reply, Uncle Charlie asks her to "give me your hand, Charlie" (as if in marriage) and puts on her finger a ring that was previously given to one of his victims by her husband. She tries to identify with him, but he (in contrast to Sir Claude) actively tries to make her desire him, so that he can manipulate her (see Teresa Wright in Raubicheck 2002–3, 41–2). Later, when he sees that his seduction has failed and she suspects him, he tries, on three occasions, to kill Charlie. Finally, in an act of self-defense she pushes him off a train into the path of an oncoming locomotive.

After his death, young Charlie keeps his terrible secret, allowing family and community to honor him and thus problematically reinstalling him, for others, in the position of ego ideal that he once held for her. To protect his memory, she must also keep a secret of her own: if she revealed her hand in his death, she would have to explain her motive, which would mean exposing him. Uncle Charlie thus occupies the position of the primal father of Freud's *Totem and Taboo* (1918). As we recall, this figure must be slain to institute the incest taboo (1918, 1960: 186), but in slaying him the sons also "carried out their wish for identification with him[,]" after which "the suppressed tender impulses had to assert themselves" (184–5) in honoring him. Of course, niece Charlie is not exactly a son—yet she is like one both in name and in her wish to identify. This wish is unhappily fulfilled when she becomes what her uncle had become: a killer with a secret.

At the end, Charlie's reunion outside the church with an appropriate love interest, detective Jack Graham (MacDonald Carey), proffers resolution of her Oedipal situation. Yet this resolution feels tenuous. As Paula Marantz Cohen (1995) points out, even though "[a]s a professional enforcer of the law, the detective is the 'proper' replacement of the father in a conventional family plot . . . [he] is hardly a weighty presence in the film; indeed he seems to be more peripheral . . ." (72), very much like Charlie's father in Wood's description quoted earlier—and quite insufficient to displace the memory of and desire for Uncle Charlie. Thus, Hitchcock reportedly said that Charlie is "doomed to love her uncle Charlie until the end of her life" (Dolar 1992, 38). As on the psychosexual level, so on the ideological: as Wood (2002) suggests, though the film has "as a central ideological project the reaffirmation of family and small-town values which the action has called into question[,]" ultimately this affirmation "is completely hollow" (48). The Hollywood closure notwithstanding, one does not feel that young Charlie, her family, and Santa Rosa have been successfully inoculated against the plagues of incestuous desire, murderous rage, and urban corruption carried by Uncle Charlie.

What's Modernity Got to Do with It?

As critics from François Truffaut onward have noted, *Shadow of a Doubt* is built on overt structures of doubling and binary opposition; hence, where *Maisie* emphasizes a chain of metonymic substitutions, *Shadow* focuses starkly on the either/or.[9] There is only a single deviation from the "proper" pattern of Oedipal/paternal substitution in Charlie's development; instead of going smoothly from father to husband, she takes a detour through her uncle. If in *Maisie* repeated substitution is a sometimes painful but finally benign process, in *Shadow* one departure from the script becomes a recipe for trauma that will last a lifetime.

According to Jean Baudrillard (1975), "[i]deology always thus proceeds by a binary, structural scission" (27). *Shadow of a Doubt*'s insistence on binaries, and on the threat posed by any "improper" substitution, suggests both that the text is highly invested in ideological projects and that these projects are embattled. Of course, the precariousness of normative gender and sexual (pre)scripts comes as no surprise in a film by a man who spent his career exploring the difficulties of such scripts and the woe in deviating from them. What is unexpected is Hitchcock's nod toward an antiurban ideology more commonly associated with Frank Capra. The opening sequences emphasize the town–city opposition, with their pans rightward across the urban wasteland to Uncle Charlie and leftward across the sunny small town to his niece, both lying on their beds, with their heads at opposite sides of the screen. As Wood points out, the contrast is both of "the fallen world against a world of prelapsarian innocence" and "the two faces of American capitalism" (2002, 298). The fallen world is emphatically the world of modernity, a pairing strongly connoted by the intensely black smoke (ordered by Hitchcock [Truffaut 1967, 153–4]) of the train on which Uncle Charlie arrives. He flees the taint of modernity even as it comes trailing after him to pollute the pastoral setting.

Yet the taint is already there. Modernity, that black-smoking train, has already pulled into the Santa Rosa station (see Figure 13.1). Both city and town contain ineffectual, castrated men with murder in mind. Herbie (Hume Cronyn), the nerdy neighbor with mother problems who plays the murder game with Joseph, is precursor to that small-town boy, Norman Bates. Santa Rosa's streets, as young Charlie rushes to the library, are as crowded, bustling, and anonymous as urban scenes (though the cop is clearly small-town). A fluttery widow, typical prey for Uncle Charlie, appears the first time he walks around town. Most telling of all is the scene at the 'Til-Two Lounge, a dive of the sort that one finds in *It's a Wonderful Life* (1946) when pastoral Bedford Falls is transformed into the urban blight of Pottersville (see Figure 13.2). In Hitchcock's film (as later in the two-faced Lumberton of David Lynch's *Blue Velvet* [1986]), Pottersville is not Bedford Falls' imaginary other; it is just around the corner. Young Charlie herself begins not in innocent bliss, but in dissatisfaction, desire for change, for something new. The dangerous fruit she longs to eat is that of modernity, substitution, and desire. And again, it is already in her.

Charlie's troubled walk through Santa Rosa contrasts revealingly with Maisie's pleasurable outings in urban space with Sir Claude. Early on,

> [t]hey rambled the great town [London] in search, as Mrs. Wix called it, of combined amusement and instruction [the city, thus, is a Horation work of art].

FIGURE 13.1 The black-smoking train at the Santa Rosa station.

FIGURE 13.2 The 'Til-Two Lounge.

> They rode on the top of 'buses, they visited outlying parks; they went to cricket matches where Maisie fell asleep; they tried a hundred places for the best one to have tea. This was his direct way . . . of making his little accepted charge his duty and his life. They dropped, under uncontrollable impulses, into shops that they agreed were too big, to look at things that they agreed were too small[.] . . . (1897, 2003: 474)

This *flanerie à deux* is Sir Claude's way of performing his self-proclaimed identity as "family-man" (440). The city is not a threat to familial relations but a field for their development.

In the crucial scene where she contemplates whether or not to "give up" Mrs. Wix in favor of Sir Claude and Mrs. Beale, Maisie walks with Sir Claude in Boulogne:

> She remained out with him for a time of which she could take no measure save that it was too short for what she wished to make of it[.] . . . They walked about, they dawdled, they looked in shop windows; they did all the old things exactly as if to try to get back all the old safety, to get something out of them that they had always got before. (634)

The window shopping symbolizes Maisie's process of sifting among potential substitutions while postponing a choice that forecloses alternatives. To choose is frightening, but the urban, metonymic structure of *flanerie* offers both pleasure and safety.

Both *Shadow* and *Maisie* invite or enact technics of deconstruction. *Shadow*'s town–city binary deconstructs in that the difference between its terms is already a difference within. Analysis of this (decon)structure is traceable through much of the poststructuralist work on gender, further back through classic deconstructive literary readings like Barbara Johnson on *Billy Budd* (1980), all the way to *Of Grammatology* (Derrida 1998), with its argument that the opposition of speech as primary presence to writing as secondary absence is always already an opposition within speech itself. Such analysis is applied particularly to texts structured by nostalgia for "the lost or impossible presence of the absent origin" (Derrida 1978 292). Interestingly, Derrida associates this nostalgia specifically with Rousseau, in whom it expresses an intense antimodernism.

In a more optative vein, deconstruction advocates what Derrida calls "the joyous affirmation of the play of the world" (292)—and the play of the signifier. In this mode one does not cling to origins but happily rides the train of metonymic substitution, with no nostalgic gaze over the shoulder for the home left behind. It would be satisfying to argue that James's text thus accepts substitution and modernity. It would make James the hero of this essay, once again anticipating poststructuralist insights and proving himself as much a postmodern as a modern master. However, I do not think it would be accurate.

Describing the joyous, "Nietzschean *affirmation*" of free play, Derrida emphasizes that it "plays without security," in contrast to another play, "a sure play: that which is limited to the *substitution* of *given* and *existing, present* pieces" (292, all emphasis in original). It is finally this latter play that I identify with *Maisie.* Here I follow Donna Przybylowicz (1986), who sees *Maisie* as exemplifying "James's realistic works of the early and middle periods," which construct "a noncontradictory and homogeneous world of truth . . . [in which] although we sense opposition between the individual and society, at the end of the book this conflict is brought to rest. . . . Here the imitation of reality is predicated on the arbitrary identity between signifier and signified, sign and meaning" (24, 25). Przybylowicz perhaps overstates the case, and a reading of *Maisie* as a more modernist and less realist novel is possible,[10] but it seems to me that one reason Maisie's story is able to come out so well is that it assumes/constructs a world in which neither the social nor the philosophical problematics of modernity have fully hit home. What makes substitution relatively benign here is not a radical surrender to contingency but an underlying sense that the ground, though shaken a bit, has not really been rent. I cannot say whether it is this sense of security that produces the relatively happy ending, or whether the ending produces the sense. But in either case, *Maisie* does not feel like a text that radically threatens security: Maisie's or the reader's.

What makes Hitchcock's text so much more anxious about modernity? I doubt the answer is biographical, since James doesn't generally seem less anxious than Hitchcock; indeed, one of their similarities is that both assert their artistic mastery as a way of controlling their well-known insecurities. The question may be unanswerable, but considering it leads me to a closing reflection on Hitchcock's medium. Hollywood films may be likely sites for anxieties about modernist metonymic substitution because, first, these films are constituted by such substitutions in specific stylistic and technological ways and, second, the project of Hollywood style is to disavow this fact. The "continuity" in the continuity editing system stands "for the smoothly flowing narrative, with its technique constantly in the service of the causal chain, yet always effacing itself" as an "indiscernible thread" (Bordwell, Thompson, and Staiger 1985, 194–5). Thus, continuity editing is at the heart of the system of suture by which, as Kaja Silverman (1983) puts it, "cinematic coherence and plenitude emerge through multiple cuts and negations" (205). If technique is to be an "indiscernible thread," it must disavow the cuts in the thread. Many of the continuity system's prescriptions exist precisely to mask its operations of substitution.

On an even more basic level, film relies on a modernist technology that "fools" us into experiencing a seamless flow of time when what is actually happening is the replacement of one discreet image for another. The film mechanism allows the regular, systematic substitution of such images, generally at the rate of 24 per second. It is the same kind of mechanism that, on a clock or watch, divides a minute into sixty discreet seconds (and embodies the concept of modern mechanistic time). Of course, in cinema the rate of image replacement is fast and regular enough to be indiscernible, so that time within a shot can be visually experienced as something much closer to Bergsonian *durée* than to the mechanistic process that is really taking place.[11] But it may be that the underlying fact of the mechanism—the fact that cinematic time is not what it seems or wants to seem to be—helps account for this very modern medium's obsessive anxiety about modernity.

One profound pleasure of James and Hitchcock, and one element of their greatness, is that their work so richly points beyond itself. To consider the two of them together may give two turns to the screw. I hope my consideration of *Maisie* and *Shadow of a Doubt* has led to some insights on the texts. But I'm even more interested in how, by submitting myself to these two modern masters, I've been led to try to think through (or at least around and about) knotty questions like the relation of modernity and metonymy, the pleasures and anxieties of substitution, or the contradictions of cinematic time. Perhaps no reader can ever know as much as what Maisie knew, or ever know anything beyond the shadow of a doubt. But surely the lesson of the Masters is that not to try is for the birds.

14

Awkward Ages

JAMES AND HITCHCOCK IN BETWEEN

Mark Goble

In a body of writings often admired for their exhibitions of embarrassment and self-reproach, Henry James's New York Edition Preface to *The Awkward Age* (1908,1984) opens on an especially apologetic note. Looking back at "so considerable a mass" of words, James hesitates to proceed ("reperusual gives me pause") before stopping to disparage a great many of his works that, aiming for economy, were "projected as small things" but surrendered to "an unforeseen principle of growth" and turned into "comparative monsters" that no author, much less his readers, could ever love (xxix). "I'm sorry to say the book has done nothing to speak of," James recalls his publisher declaring, "I've never in all my experience seen one treated with more general and complete disrespect" (xxxviii). Eve Sedgwick (2003) and others have taught us to read these shows of Jamesian abjection as crucial to the authority he fashioned for himself late in his career as he confronted his theatrical misadventures of the early 1890s, the diminished sales of his increasingly experimental fictions, and the intensity of the bonds he felt for such men as Hendrik Andersen, Hugh Walpole, and others who paid increasingly affectionate tribute to the "Master." For James, as Sedgwick argues, indulging his acutely developed sense of shame functioned as a strategy for channeling otherwise ugly or debilitating emotions into something else, whether a therapeutic mechanism for his periods of depression, or an "affecting and eroticized form of mutual display" that all but comprised his sex life (44).[1] In stressing the vulnerability of James's psychology at turn of the twentieth century, Sedgwick returns to a theme and diagnosis that Leon Edel articulated first in 1969, but where Sedgwick sees James fascinated by the "subjectivity-generating space defined by the loved but unintegrated 'inner child'" (2003, 44), Edel posits a more conventional Freudian logic of projection in James's "inner need" or "compulsion to revisit, step by step, the hidden stages of his own growth and development, within his safety-guise of a little girl" (261)—from Daisy Miller (1878) and Catherine Sloper (*Washington Square* [1880]) to Maisie (*What Maisie Knew* [1897]) and Nanda Brookenham in *The Awkward Age* [1899]. Over much of James's work, then, borrowing from his own description of Nanda's enticing and disquieting presence in the novel, "female adolescence hovered and waited" (1908, 1984: xxxii).

When Alfred Hitchcock became enamored with young girls as the protagonists of his films, he had far less to be ashamed of. Nearly finished with the run of thrillers that would, by the mid-1930s, make him one of the best-known directors in the world, Hitchcock turned from stories concerned with men and families beset by political intrigue (*The Man Who Knew Too Much* [1934], *The Thirty-Nine Steps* [1935], *Secret Agent* [1936], *Sabotage* [1936]) to stories focused on women beset by all manner of uncertainties about the intrigues they may (or may not) be facing in the first place. After the mixed reception to *Sabotage*, Hitchcock chose to make his next film not from a work of serious literature (*Sabotage* was based on Conrad's *The Secret Agent*), but from what he described as a "very, very bad" detective novel by Josephine Tey (Rohmer and Chabrol 1979, 50–1). Released in 1937 as *Young and Innocent*, it became Hitchcock's most successful film to date in the United States and set in motion the elaborate courtship by David Selznick that eventually brought Hitchcock to Hollywood. After seeing the film, Selznick offered praise for Hitchcock that, in its qualifications and double meanings, perfectly anticipates the tortured nature of their mutual esteem and animosity. Hitchcock was "the greatest master of this particular type of melodrama to be found in America or in England today," and, as if hoping to confirm the compliment, Hitchcock's next film, *The Lady Vanishes* (1938), was another example of the kind of movie that Selznick wanted *his* Hitchcock to make in Hollywood (Leff 1987, 27). Again, the source material (Ethel Lina White's *The Wheel Spins* [1936]) was a middle-brow fiction with a "young" and "innocent" heroine at its center. Yet, while the surrounding plot, as we will see, revisits the thematics of political conspiracy that marked Hitchcock's thrillers of the early 1930s, the film is equally fascinated by questions of desire and marriage that are positively Jamesian in their epistemological sophistication. Produced as Hitchcock was pursuing—and being pursued by—Hollywood, *The Lady Vanishes* was a critical triumph and, at the time, the most popular British film ever released in the United States; it was the *New York Time*'s "picture of the year" for 1938, and the New York Film Critics Circle's best picture as well.

In a Hollywood version of the story of how Hitchcock came to Hollywood, *The Lady Vanishes* would have been his final British film. But as negotiations with Selznick dragged on, Hitchcock accepted an offer to direct *Jamaica Inn* (1939), starring Charles Laughton and based on a popular Daphne du Maurier novel published in 1936. Regularly included on any short list of Hitchcock's worst projects, *Jamaica Inn*, for all its perversities and blunders in matching his controlled aesthetic to Laughton's brazen theatricality, nicely conforms to his last three British films' emphasis on young women awkwardly abandoned to their own resources. Indeed, *Jamaica Inn*—an early-nineteenth-century costume drama about an Irish orphan caught up in the scheming of a corrupt aristocrat who runs a crew of thieves and shipwreckers to gratify his artistic appetites—might even be described as, in James's terms, as "an account of the manner in which the resented interference with ancient liberties came to be in a particular instance dealt with" (1908, 1984: xxxiii). Here in Hitchcock's last work as a British filmmaker, the comforts of both patriarchy and tradition take on a pathological character that James hints at, but never quite allows to color, the much older Mr. Longdon's final embrace of Nanda Brookenham.

But I want to suggest another set of continuities between James and Hitchcock at these respective moments of transition in their own remarkably self-conscious careers, for the way each man treats his heroines in works such as *The Awkward Age* or *The Lady Vanishes* speaks to more than just suggestive psychological parallels, or similar attitudes towards sex and gender that survived in Anglo-American culture despite all that changed from James's fin de siècle to Hitchcock's arrival in the United States just before the start of World War II. *The Awkward Age* and *The Lady Vanishes* both turn on marriage plots that get pleasurably and dangerously diverted within larger networks of social contact and communication that feature older figures—James's Mr. Longdon and Hitchcock's mysterious Miss Froy—as crucial players, however marginal they at times appear. In what follows I trace a series of relays between James's and Hitchcock's narratives of female adolescence and the technologies of communication that pattern their modernity.

I am not simply suggesting that "girls on the threshold of womanhood"—as William Rothman (1984, 368) characterizes a recurring figure in early Hitchcock—provided a convenient metaphorics for two male artists, each with highly polished images as masters of their respective mediums, at liminal, if not ungainly, periods in their careers. For Tom Cohen (2005), the essential character of Hitchcock's achievement is his commitment to film not just as artistic medium, but as a technology within "a citational fabric that perpetually speculates on and marks its own teletechnic powers as an intervention in the histories of perception and writing" (xii). That James's works have something of their own to say about these histories has been proven by a range of critics—from Jennifer Wicke (1989) and Mark Seltzer (1992, 2000) to Richard Menke (2008) and Pamela Thurschwell (2001)—who have described his deep fascination with technologies of communication and representation. And so I would like to understand why young women in *The Awkward Age* and *The Lady Vanishes* are especially vulnerable to wayward information and to the material forms that give it shape and tangibility. This does not mean looking past the broad contours that help align these work with one another: two stories about young women turned out into the world, conceived by not-so-young men who themselves had to face new audiences and economies without knowing whether their eccentricities and innovations would be forgiven. This is just one more reason why the two are worth revisiting for all the ways they help us understand how James and Hitchcock grew out of their own awkward ages—though not without a few embarrassments and losses that would shadow the rest of their careers.

The Awkward Age was the first novel James completed working by dictation. James acquired his first typewriter to help him finish the manuscript of *What Maisie Knew* (1897), which he had begun by hand—as he had produced all his previous fiction, criticism, travel writing, and correspondence. But as the pain from a deteriorating wrist condition worsened, James decided to employ a new technology for putting words on paper, and, after receiving enthusiastic testimonials from William James (who had previously engaged a stenographer at Harvard), he secured both a machine and a secretary, or "typewriter," to use it for him. James found a medical stenographer, William McAlpine, to serve as the first of his three secretaries; McAlpine, the only man James ever hired in this capacity, was replaced by Mary Weld, and, when Weld married in 1907, Theodora Bosanquet came to Rye and took dictation almost to the moment of James's death in 1916. This context is familiar to critics who have examined the stylistic developments of James's later stories and novels, and, in some cases, the content of these texts as well. James was increasingly uncertain that he commanded a mass readership, but he now knew first-hand, each time he wrote, that at least one other person attended to his every word.

Leaving the British film industry for Hollywood supposedly entailed a less drastic change in how Hitchcock made movies. Already familiar with studio practices in Germany and elsewhere in Europe, Hitchcock was versed as well in the particular stress that U.S. production companies placed on centralized supervision by powerful producers like Selznick, frequent rewrites and retakes throughout the filmmaking process, studio control over the final editing process, and extensive audience testing before theatrical release. Unable to negotiate for the autonomy that directors such as John Ford and Howard Hawks had written into their studio contracts, Hitchcock, as Leonard Leff (1987) has helpfully detailed, quibbled over smaller details in his initial dealings with Selznick, RKO, and MGM (23–31). This is not a story for telling again here, but I would like to suggest that we can find in Hitchcock's films of the late 1930s—as in James's fictions from the late 1890s—moments that display a range of apprehensions about the effects of modernization on both the conditions that make individual expression possible and its legibility as the mark of an author (or *auteur*, we might say) whose status is no longer secure within the systems that make art possible. Fredric Jameson (1992) captures this historical situation in the broadest terms: writing about Hitchcock, but in a language that applies just as well to James, he insists that we should understand an artist's embrace of a "new artistic medium" in "a genealogical perspective in which the medium (along with its own history, its own technological development) is grasped less as a source of innovation in its own right, than as the material reinforcement . . . of a gradual fragmentation and division of labor within the psyche, as the latter is retrained and reprogrammed by the reorganization of the traditional labor processes and human activities" (126). And while I am pushing at the limits of the term by describing both James's turn to dictation and Hitchcock's move to Hollywood as the embrace of new "mediums," I think each man recognized that he had to brace himself for futures of more "fragmented" and "divided" modes of artistic labor. The interruptions and elaborate narrative difficulties that prevent communication in *The Awkward Age* and *The Lady Vanishes* are thus part of a network of anxieties about the degree to which modernity permits people to express themselves and a deep skepticism about communication as a practice that puts people into relation with each other. Which is why, as we will see, marriage figures so provocatively in these texts, not just as a plot device, but as a technical achievement of what Niklas Luhmann (1998) would call "interpersonal interpenetration": a relationship so "dense" as to "enable essentially improbable communications nevertheless to be made successfully" (58, 18).

According to an argument about *The Awkward Age* first pursued by Tzvetan Todorov (1977), James's experiment in producing a fiction consisting largely of conversations—conversations that are themselves about other conversations that may or may not have been depicted—requires us to address an "inadequacy to the rules of communication" that characters in the novel try to work around by attempting ever more strenuous "[acts] of interpretation" for one another (357). The novel revels in a display of "technical genius" that persuades the reader that "indirect information is not merely the predominant kind of information in this book, it is *only* kind" (369). Other critics frame the novel's failure to communicate less as a problem that inheres in James's language and more as a symptom of historical pressures brought to bear on late Victorian manners that must negotiate a "conflict between exposure and concealment" in preserving the appearance of Nanda's "innocence" (Culver 1981, 369), or, as Michael Trask (1997) argues, answer to a sense of "epistemological vertigo" that haunts the erotic transgressions with which the novel flirts (112). I am struck by the only sin to which James does confess in the New York Edition Preface. Referring to the French writer Gyp—the inspiration for the novel's quasi-theatrical form—James attributes the commercial failure of *The Awkward Age,* not to the dialogue that communicates the story ("dialogue organic and dramatic"), but rather to the textual form in which it reached his too few readers in 1899. French audiences, according to James, want to read the plays they see: "as soon as a play begins to loom at all large . . . the number of copies of the printed piece in circulation far exceeds at last the number of performances" (1908, 1984: xxxvii). But with "our own public," he continues, "horror seems to attach to any typographic hint of the proscribed playbook" (xxxvii). "The immense oddity," he concludes of *The Awkward Age*, "resides in the almost exclusively typographic order of the offence" (xxxvii). Writing of what he calls, "speaking for itself, representing and embodying substance and form," James declares that such fugitive, undocumented performances of language—the verbal medium of actors on a stage, or an author dictating to his typewriter—"is among us an uncanny and abhorrent thing, not to be dealt with on any terms" (xxxvii). The whole spectacle of the theater, or so it seems, is required to channel and sublimate the hatred that the Anglo-American reading public feels toward any language that refuses to distinguish its medium from its message, that simultaneously represents and embodies both its "substance" and its "form." But when such "speaking" is put on paper, it must be purged and punished like any other "abhorrent thing" a culture cannot abide.

These passages from James's Preface also underscore the profoundly written character of Nanda's most "abhorrent" transgression in *The Awkward Age*. I am thinking, of course, about the discovery in Book VIII of the name "Vanderbank"—put there in Nanda's hand—on the cover of the French novel whose reportedly salacious contents speak not only to the decadence to which Nanda has been exposed, but also to the double standard that makes her, for Vanderbank, something "not to be dealt with on any terms" once it is revealed that she has in fact read the offending novel, which he himself lent to her mother. Thus, while James's ostensible subject in *The Awkward Age* is the corruptions that might befall a vulnerable young girl such as Nanda "in a circle of free talk," the plot itself turns on the possession of a printed text upon which more text has been inscribed: in a moment of recognition determined by the materiality of the object, Vanderbank is "generally struck" by "a copy of a French novel in blue paper" that features "simply his own name written rather large on the cover . . . and endowed, after he had taken the volume up, with the power to hold his attention the more closely the longer he looked at it" (1899, 1984: 256). The letters of his name prompt him to vocalize something—"he uttered, for a private satisfaction, before letting the matter pass, a low confused sound"—that suggests at once a checked impulse to read aloud, and a more visceral reaction to the "matter" of the book insofar as after "flinging it down" he moves to the "chimneypiece," where he remains "intently fixed," as if weighing whether to add this paper to the flames (257).

By this point in the narrative, James's readers will remember that his plot has become almost as convoluted as the chain of custody required to trace the "French novel" back to its owner. Nanda has been effectively turned out by her mother to attract the attentions of various men, including Vanderbank, whom Mrs. Brook (as she is called) desires for herself; the wealthy, *déclassé* and homely Mitchy, on whom Nanda's brother, Harold, financially depends, and of course Mr. Longdon, an old friend and admirer of Nanda's grandmother, who sees so much of her in Nanda, that he promises an extravagant dowry if Vanderbank, who Nanda admires in turn, agrees to marry her. Given that all this melodrama must unfold in scenes of minimally narrated conversation among characters who largely sound alike—and all like Henry James—it is fitting that Nanda gets in so much trouble for an act of simple "bookkeeping" that, by her reckoning at least, she claims is innocent enough because it only tries to keep one small thing clear. By writing Vanderbank's name on the French novel, she can establish that it was never meant for a young girl; no respectable gentlemen like Vanderbank, even if he has so declined in the world that he must earn his living as a petty bureaucrat for the General Audit, would put this kind of book into adolescent hands. Thus, according to Nanda's demandingly circuitous logic, by inscribing the book as Vanderbank's, she is not acting for herself at all. The only information that she has added to this noisy exchange of disavowal and innuendo cannot possibly refer to her. She will only say privately to Vanderbank that she has read the book "for Tishy," as if she were a secretary providing coverage for a boss whose time is not to be wasted (266). But once Nanda's "hand" has been identified, the fiction of her disinterest falls apart, and when Nanda confesses that she has read the novel, everyone knows that Vanderbank's name on the cover is, so far as Nanda's innocence is concerned, the writing on the wall. Nanda is not just shamed for the message that her writing may communicate, but also for showing how unembarrassed she is to be the medium of her own desire.

Having earlier rejected Mitchy's advances because "there's a kind of delicacy" that someone of his class cannot get, and then been rejected by Vanderbank because he has this very "delicacy" in spades, Nanda ends the novel ready for "a grand public adhesion" to Mr. Longdon, and a "final, irrevocable flight" from London to his country home at Beccles (241, 342). Readers of the novel differ on how to take this ending: some see Nanda escaping from the tawdriness of her mother's circle and its mercenary culture of sexuality, thus finally finding peace and worth at Beccles, where "everything on every side had dropped straight from heaven, with nowhere a bargaining thumbmark, a single sign of the shop" (234). Others see Nanda banished to an artificial and anachronistic museum of bygone manners, a retreat into a fading past made slightly desperate by Nanda's own admission that, "everything's different from what it used to be" (366). In either case, James makes clear that, even if Nanda has only been promiscuous in her communications, this alone will have been sufficient to change her utterly. Indeed, Nanda appears to know this from the moment she asks Mitchy whether "her exposure" to all the "free talk" that surrounds her doesn't make her "a sort of little drainpipe with everything flowing through" (241). Mitchy, with perhaps more gallantry than some would give him credit for, tries to save Nanda from this telling figure of speech by suggesting a more optimistic image: "Why don't you call it more gracefully . . . a little Aeolian harp set in the drawing-room window and vibrating in the breeze of conversation?" (241). Alluding to the ancient technology that Coleridge famously enlisted to capture the full power of communication as a Romantic ideal, Mitchy wants to persuade Nanda that words alone, no matter the means by which they are spoken, transmitted, or registered, will not contaminate or corrupt her (see Peters 1999, 109–19). He and Mrs. Brook, along with Vanderbank and all the other characters whose talking James speaks into being for his typewriter to materialize, are not, as Mitchy earlier explains, "a secret society—still less a 'dangerous gang' or organization for any definite end" (1899, 1984: 83). Unlike some of the conspiracies in Hitchcock to which I now turn, no one in *The Awkward Age* means any harm with what they say; it could be argued, following Todorov, that none of them mean anything at all. But the vulnerability to new forms of information that James encodes as crucial to the socializing rituals that transform young girls into the "comparative monsters" of the modern world is not so easily eluded. This, too, Nanda knows, as her hesitancy during a curious exchange with Mr. Longdon early in the novel proves: when she worries that coming to visit Beccles will cost him the quiet to which he is accustomed, he replies with the supposedly comforting formulation, "Everybody's omelette is made of somebody's eggs" (148). That she keeps him waiting for her answer is perhaps a sign that she understands just whose are going to be broken.

As the last novel James produced in the nineteenth century—and the first he writes entirely with the new technologies that mark his twentieth-century works—the story of Nanda's mortifying "exposure" to a rapidly changing world does not suggest much optimism for the future it illuminates. *The Awkward Age* features so many failed marriages that Nanda's failure to marry anyone counts almost as a happy ending, though one structured as an embrace of nostalgia so strong it risks flowering into a regression from modernity itself (297). "If the mediation of marriage works," writes Tony Tanner (1979), "then everything is . . . at rest, all patterns moving harmoniously together" (16–17). For all that James's characters in *The Awkward Age* revel in "the perfection, almost, as it were, of intercourse"—the qualifiers suggesting James hears the innuendo, too—there is little sign that either language, sex, or any other medium of relationship has any hope of putting people together (1908, 1984: xxxiii).

Yet at a parallel moment of career upheaval and modernization, Hitchcock conceives one of his most strenuously romantic comedies from elements that evoke much the same scenario that James pursued to such despairing ends. As *The Lady Vanishes* begins, Hitchcock's heroine, Iris Henderson (Margaret Henderson), waits with a polyglot assembly of passengers for a snowbound train to resume its journey out of the fictional country of Brandrika, a nation that has entered into a secret treaty that will finally figure in the mechanics of the film's subplots about espionage and international deceit. But another dubious coupling—between Iris and Charles Featheringale, her "blue-blooded, check-chaser" fiancé—shadows the romance between Iris and the cheeky musicologist, Gilbert (Michael Redgrave), who inevitably joins her in her search for Miss Froy (Dame May Whitty), an elderly English woman who befriends Iris early on and then not only disappears but is said never to have existed in the first place by a growing number of characters who we slowly realize are part of an elaborate conspiracy behind her kidnapping. Much of the narrative that motivates Miss Froy's disappearance is technically devoted to the mystery behind the film's "MacGuffin"—Hitchcock's term for an artful narrative distraction. (Here, it takes the form of a few bars of folk music that encrypt the details of Brandrika's treaty, which Miss Froy, who is actually a British spy, must communicate to the Foreign Office.) The film's two genres (romantic comedy, spy thriller) converge when the "lady vanishes" and Miss Froy is taken captive. Trying to find and free her is one way that Iris can forestall the moment when she, like any young "lady" whose nouveau riche family hopes to trade their daughter for, as Iris puts it, a "coat of arms on the jam label," "vanishes" into a loveless marriage at the cost of her own identity. So when Iris sees Charles waiting for her at the station upon her return to London, she vanishes into Gilbert's cab instead and is eventually reunited with Miss Froy, who delivers the precious information to the proper authorities.

Hitchcock was seeking to consummate a merger of his own while working on *The Lady Vanishes*. Hollywood studios began to notice Hitchcock after *The 39 Steps* (1935), and the fascination was reciprocated: he traveled to the United States in both 1937 and 1938 (even going on a crash diet before his first trip!) and hired Selznick's brother, Myron, to represent him when the worsening economy in 1937 threatened major studio deals for Hitchcock's services. The months surrounding the production, release, and promotion of *The Lady Vanishes* were filled, as Leff (1987) details, with long-distance negotiations, offers and counteroffers, and public gestures of courtship between the American mogul and the British director who was not yet the *auteur* he would become in Hollywood. Which is to remember that the familiar imagery of Hitchcock's directorial mastery—sustained by tales of his cruel jokes on set, his cultivated disregard for actors, and his manipulations of the studio system—does not entirely apply to this period in his career. It was only in retrospect that it made sense to ask, as Francois Truffaut did in 1967, whether Hitchcock felt "destined to work in Hollywood" given that he had "dreamed of American-type pictures" throughout his years in England (88). At the time, however, the marriage between Hollywood and Hitchcock was by no means certain. Given the dramatic nature of the changes that Hitchcock was contemplating, we should not be surprised to find evidence in his final British films that the romance of modernity is shot through with intimations of the anxiety and nostalgia that make things decidedly awkward for Hitchcock's young women of the late thirties.

I want to trace a series of motifs in Hitchcock's last British works that return us to the central drama of *The Awkward Age* and in particular to Nanda Brookenham's cruel discovery that what makes her unmarriageable is the same susceptibility to information that makes her attractive. We can see Iris begin to grasp this lesson in the midst of a conversation she has with Miss Froy during a scene that prepares us for the film's most famous imagery. I am thinking, of course, about the revelation of "Froy" as it is has been written on the dusty window of the dining car, where it appears just as the train heads into a tunnel at a moment when even Iris has started to doubt the older woman's existence (see Figure 14.1). But the occasion when Miss Froy writes down her name is equally compelling for the ways that it presents Iris with a symbol—and a name—for a different version of who she might become if she were to reject the corporate merger that her marriage to Featheringale really is. While Miss Froy is not a rival for Iris's affections, she does represent an explicit challenge to the film's marriage plot: Iris stresses that she is "going home to be married," but at this point in the narrative, both she and Miss Froy are altogether single and independent, a shared condition that is manifest not only in the constant references to "Miss" Froy, but also in the monogrammed initials "IH" that recur on almost every item Iris owns, whether the silk robe she wears at the inn in Bandrika, the clutch she carries to the dining car for tea with Miss Froy, or, as we see here, the cravat of her traveling costume (see Figure 14.2). All these objects registering Iris's devotion to her maiden name will be obsolete when the train arrives and she marries Featheringale. Thus, an icon of her husband's inherited status will take the place of signs that literally tell us who Iris is—or, technically speaking, was. Since with marriage, of course, the lady vanishes.

This is not, however, the only play on words at issue in this scene. Miss Froy must write her name because the noise of the train keeps Iris from hearing it, and Hitchcock buries a joke within the soundtrack whose inaudibility conceals its obviousness: when Miss Froy says her name, it's lost almost completely in the scream of a steam whistle, which is why Iris responds with a loaded, questioning "Freud?"

FIGURE 14.1 The revelation of "Froy" appears just as the train heads into a tunnel.

FIGURE 14.2 The monogrammed initials "IH" recur on almost every item Iris owns.

before Miss Froy stands at the window and spells out her name correctly. "Froy," she clarifies, "it rhymes with joy." This Freudian slip is in keeping with the pattern of references to dreams, hysteria, and hallucination that structure the film, as several critics have established, and in particular provides much of the language that Dr. Hartz (Paul Lucas), who is a sinister Brandrikan agent and famous "brain specialist," uses in his attempt to prevent Iris and Gilbert from realizing the plot that they have stumbled into. One need not embrace a full-blown psychoanalytic reading of *The Lady Vanishes* to grasp the serious fun that Hitchcock is having at the expense of both Iris and his audience. If, as Slavoj Žižek (1992) argues, both the vanishing Miss Froy and her name suggest the "phantom-like apparition of a signifier" that follows "the logic of symptom as return of the repressed," it would seem that Hitchcock is almost as formulaic in his Freudian deployment, hiding the loaded sonic utterance so deeply within the sound mix that the viewers are barely certain they have heard it (238). And thanks to Miss Froy's impromptu spelling lesson, we see the verbal correction not only written down, but also projected onto a square vertical surface that provides a screen for displaying critical information that another medium of communication cannot adequately deliver. Thus, in a scene where the film's own status within what Michel Chion (1992) calls an "initiatory" narrative is acutely overdetermined, Iris must negotiate between markedly different versions of female identity, as well as between the technologies that register the effects of their modernity (138). For Iris to identity herself too readily with Miss Froy at once expresses a desire for independence from a marriage of mercenary convenience—the word "Froy" on screen will finally set her "free"—even as she realizes that turning away from what society demands of her and modeling herself on someone redolent of a disappearing past is to risk the same sterility that Nanda risks with Mr. Longdon. And it is not easy for someone so young to admit that maybe all her options, for the foreseeable future anyway, leave her *froid*.

To be precise, however, we never really know who writes the "Froy" on the window that propels the narrative of the film toward the happy ending Nanda is denied. Within the diegesis itself, there is, of course, no mystery: Iris later returns with Gilbert to the dining car where she had tea with Miss Froy and sees "Froy" right where her older friend had written it (see Figure 14.3). For the story to make sense, the "Froy" that momentarily reappears (before vanishing in a blast of air as the train enters a tunnel), must be the very "Froy" that Miss Froy has written. But if we look closely at the two names as they appear on screen, it is clear that the second and decisive "Froy" is slightly different; the letters are neither the same size nor shape, and are neither placed nor proportioned quite the same as those first inscribed on glass by Dame May Whitty. The differences are slight and are not supposed to register with the audience. Unlike Hitchcock's sly insertion of Freud—which anticipates the sophisticated, fast-paced banter from some of his most famous films of the 1950s—the two "Froys" are almost certainly a common side effect of the filmmaking process itself. Working quickly on a soundstage outfitted with a single coach for a set, Hitchcock shot *The Lady Vanishes* out of narrative order. The second

FIGURE 14.3 We never really know who writes "Froy" on the window.

"Froy"—inscribed by an anonymous set designer or prop man? by the cameraman? by Hitchcock?—could have been the "original," with Whitty instructed to make a rough duplicate of someone else's handwriting of her character's exceedingly fraught name.

We have come to call such mistakes continuity errors, and fastidious reviewers, devoted fans, and other scrutinizers catalog the hairstyles that change with every camera placement, the drinks that shift from hand to hand on every cut, and the stains that migrate from right leg to left leg when characters enter rooms. Continuity errors can provide cheap laughs for casual viewers when they catch them or become sources of surprising outrage for admirers who cannot come to terms with the reality of imperfections in the movies they adore. (On Nitpickers.com, for example, contributors have identified 352 errors in James Cameron's *Titanic* [1997], with 156 refuted; the score for *The Matrix* [1999] is 297 to 170.) And given the technical complexity and large numbers of people involved in modern studio filmmaking, such mistakes, while maybe awkward, are nothing to be ashamed of.

The fact that one "Froy" in *The Lady Vanishes* is not quite identical to the other "Froy" it duplicates is simultaneously accidental, unconscious, and appropriate. For not only is the true Miss Froy almost unimaginably different from the Miss Froy who befriends Iris in Brandrika, but practically every character on the train is some sort of secret operative masquerading as a normal passenger (Dr. Hartz, Signor Doppo, the magician who is part of the conspiracy, along with the Baroness and the treacherous Nun, in pumps[!], who eventually turns double agent and helps save the day for England); even the normal passengers are compromised by their duplicity (the philandering Mr. Todhunter and his "wife"), or revealed to possess resources of daring that their fussy personalities in no way disclose (the comic-relief pairing of Caldicott and Charters who take up arms and risk their lives for England). It is as if everybody's name is just an alias that does not tell us who they are but rather where to start looking for their secret identities and disguises. Even Iris's compulsory display of her initials is something of a cover for the fact that, in marrying Featheringale, she knows she will be turning into someone else entirely.

I should point out that Hitchcock's wife, working somewhat surreptitiously under her maiden name, Alma Reville, is credited with providing "continuity" to *The Lady Vanishes* (see Figure 14.4). Already an established editor when Hitchcock broke into the movie business, Reville continued to pursue her career in the first years of their marriage, and after giving birth to their daughter, Patricia, she remained an active force in Hitchcock's films throughout their remaining years in Britain and later in the United States. She was renowned for helping with the dialogue and for tightening the plotlines to make them plausible and consistent (within the limits of their genres), but I doubt that the Hitchcocks' idea "continuity" extended to catching infinitesimal visual errors before they could appear on screen. Hitchcock was also figuring out how to consummate another working marriage as

FIGURE 14.4 Hitchcock's wife, Alma Reville, is credited with providing "continuity" to *The Lady Vanishes*.

he was filming *The Lady Vanishes*, and so perhaps all the proliferating "IH"s are evidence that *A*lfred *H*itchcock ("I, Hitchcock?") was more anxious than he admitted about future of his own identity as a director now that his train to Hollywood, so to speak, was leaving from the station. And David Selznick was no Charles Featheringale: indeed, Hitchcock was more the "check-chaser" in this courtship, and while critics often frame his years with Selznick as an interlude before his major achievements after World War II, his final British film, *Jamaica Inn*, suggests that he may already have been contemplating some of the less appealing aspects of the cutting-edge technologies, financial resources, and authorial powers he soon hoped to command.

Hitchcock took the assignment for *Jamaica Inn* while he was waiting for his contract with Selznick to take effect; in his interviews with Truffaut (1967), he called it "an absurd thing to undertake," in part because in retrospect he realized the illogic of its story, but also because Charles Laughton, who had already signed to play the leading role, was not the sort of obedient line-reader that Hitchcock preferred. Again, a young girl and a conspiracy are at the center of the drama: Mary Merlyn (Maureen O'Hara) is orphaned and sent to live with her Uncle Joss (Leslie Banks) and Aunt Patience (Marie Ney), the proprietors of Jamaica Inn in Cornwall; there, Uncle Joss runs a group of thieves who lure ships onto the rocks, kill their crews, and sell the stolen cargo, all under the direction of an aristocratic and demented aesthete, Sir Humphrey Pengallan (Charles Laughton).

Jamaica Inn ends with a chase to the boat where Pengallan has taken Mary, hoping to escape with her to France. Laughton plays the role according to form, with a scene-chewing gusto that may not have been to Hitchcock's liking, but that works especially well to communicate the mix of lechery and paternal kindness Pengallan shows to Mary, who, like Iris Henderson and Nanda Brookenham, has "no one else in the world," as Pengallan puts it, to "take care of [her]." By kidnapping Mary, Sir Humphrey insists that he is saving her from marrying some "oaf" who would "father [on her] a dozen, sniveling, snotty-nosed brats"; this is a harsher fate than the check-chasing of Charles Featheringale or the *déclassé* manners of Mitchy. Pengallan, in fact, fancies himself a champion of beauty and tradition and is certainly the only villain in Hitchcock who quotes Edmund Burke in his last speech before the hero saves the day. "The age of chivalry is gone and the glory of Europe is extinguished," he is telling Mary as Jem Trehearne (Robert Newton), the agent of Crown sent to arrest him, storms the ship. But Pengallan makes for an unlikely Burkean, to put it mildly, as he is chased up to the heights of ship's rigging where, fat and disoriented, he utters the final words of Hitchcock's British career (see Figure 14.5): "What are you waiting for? A spectacle? You shall have it. Tell your children how the great age ended! Make way for Pengallan!" And then in disquieting slow motion, he jumps to his inglorious death.

In Hollywood, Hitchcock's "great age" was just beginning. Like Henry James in 1899, he was on the verge of becoming a different, even more masterly version of the Master he already was. Both men were about to embrace the full modernity of

FIGURE 14.5 Pengallan, fat and disoriented, utters the final words of Hitchcock's British career.

their artistic styles and practices, and accept, if not always agreeably, the consequences of the techniques that they adopted to achieve some of their signature late accomplishments. But only in *The Lady Vanishes* does the marriage between past and present leave us with a young woman who has survived at least relatively unscathed. Both *The Awkward Age* and *Jamaica Inn* make their young female protagonists bear the full weight of dismal futures that are imagined for them by men who could not have been entirely certain that their own careers were heading in the right direction. James might finally let us wonder whether Nanda is better off under Mr. Longdon's control and care, but there is no mistaking that her progress, at least for the present, has been arrested. The show of agency and desire she risked in writing "Vanderbank" does not go anywhere in the end, and Nanda seems ready to renounce the modern world that has already rejected her. Where Nanda's mother had once seen her daughter as hurtling forward—"I do all I can to enter into her life," says Mrs. Brook, "but you can't get into a railway train while it's on the rush" (1899, 1984: 108)—we come to realize that Nanda has always had the more realistic understanding of her prospects. As she admits to Vanderbank, "if moving is changing . . . there won't be much for me in that. . .. I haven't got what's called a principle of growth" (142).

Hitchcock leaves us with a last image of Mary Merlyn that projects dramatically less confidence in the epoch that will follow on Pengallan's fall. Though she is safe at last from his obscene paternalism, Mary's rescue does little to dispel the aura of the man whose promises of chivalry and comfort, though utterly depraved, still speak to the appeal of a familiar sense of order that has vanished and left nothing in its place. Mary appears traumatized as Trehearne walks her off the ship, and there is little sign that any romance will be flourishing between them. The last shot of *Jamaica Inn* surprisingly returns to Pengallan's servant, who is left in the center of the screen as the mute hero and heroine depart. From outside the frame—and apparently beyond the grave—we hear Pengallan calling, "Chadwyck," and when Chadwyck (Horace Hodges) turns, we know he is still haunted by the echoes of an authority that should by all rights no longer have a hold on him. It is hard not to see this moment registering some of the awkward resemblances between Hitchcock and the weirdly-mannered, overweight, and more than slightly perverse figure who comes to dominate the film. Then again, Hitchcock might have been looking forward to another demanding, outsized, and neurotic man to whom he was about to sign away the next few years. Selznick managed an operation that made Pengallan's gang of thieves look quaint, and while Hitchcock eventually came out the better of the two for their relationship, it is fitting that he ends *Jamaica Inn* with an affecting close-up on the hectored and embattled employee of an erratic mastermind—just the sort of man that Hitchcock was about to become.

NOTES

Introduction

1. It is very likely that other early James novels were purchased by Mudie's as well.

2. Horne, personal correspondence; Moon, *A Small Boy and Others.*

3. See also Paula Marantz Cohen's 1999 comparison of the two artists, as well as her comments on James and Hitchcock in her 1995 book and 2008 review.

Chapter 1

1. For postcolonial work on and "global" readings of James, see, for example, the "Global James" issue of the *Henry James Review* (2003), which includes essays by Wai-Chee Dimock, Paul Giles, Hsuan Hsu, John Carlos Rowe, and others.

2. *Saboteur* (1942) also engages war matters: "We were in 1941 and there were pro-German elements who called themselves America Firsters and who were, in fact, American Fascists. This was the group I had in mind while writing the scenario. . . ." (Truffaut 1967, 146).

3. Hitchcock himself later explained, "One of the things that drew the fire of the American critics is that I had shown a German as being superior to the other characters. But at that time, 1940–41, the French had been defeated, and the Allies were not doing too well" (Truffaut 1967, 156).

4. As Novick (2007) has most recently pointed out.

5. On Hitchcock as a specifically English "dandy," whose public life was a performance, see Elsaesser (1994), as well as Allen (1999).

6. It's possible, of course, given Hollywood practices, that Hitchcock was not the sole (or even a contributing) author of this speech.

7. Thanks to Alan Nadel for suggesting this connection and for his helpful responses and suggestions.

8. Her name was most often spelled "Minnie," but also, sometimes, "Minny."

9. There is also a verbal "cameo" when two characters talk about a film with a one-word title, the name of which they can't remember. *Suspicion*? It would certainly be an apt reference given *Lifeboat*'s interest in appearances, identities, and loyalties.

10. And perhaps further, given Bankhead's reputation for eschewing underwear.

11. Recall Connie's early speech: "I got some priceless pictures—some wonderful shots on deck of a lot of people on one of the lifeboats. They looked slow and heavy and fat with their lifebelts on—so lonesome"—a point of view that her lifeboat experience will gradually alter.

12. For a discussion of hands in Hitchcock, see Jonathan Freedman's essay in this volume.

13. On Rosanna's weight, see Tim Armstrong (1996) and Daniel Hannah (2007).

14. Indeed, the slim waists of James's female protagonists are mentioned so often as to be almost fetishized, perhaps most memorably in Prince Amerigo's knowing gaze at

Charlotte Stant: "He knew above all the extraordinary fineness of her flexible waist, the stem of an expanded flower, which gave her a likeness also to some long, loose silk purse, well filled with gold pieces, but having been passed, empty, through a finger-ring that held it together" (1904, 1909: 23:48).

15. See my "Jamesian Bodies" (1989).

16. These dynamics have attracted the attention of critics and biographers from Edel to Toibin.

17. As, for example, Andrew Carnegie transformed steel into libraries.

18. James refers to the story of Gray's bequest as "a fairy-tale" (179).

19. Graham Fielder is, of course, another stand-in for James: the refined, Europeanized American who knows nothing of money (see also Spencer Brydon in "The Jolly Corner"). That such a figure represents only one, projected, aspect of James is made clear by Henry James's avid interest in earning a living, as documented by scholars like Michael Anesko.

20. See, especially "Within the Rim."

21. See Novick (1996, 2007), 516.

22. Most fully in the ongoing publication of the *Complete Letters*.

Chapter 2

1. Characters in both these fictions express a concern with multiple identities as both a sign of criminal power and one of attractive variability. "He can look like a hundred people," says Annabella Smith to Hannay of the leader of the spy ring, warning him of how difficult it is to identify and avoid the danger this man represents. Engaged with Strether in a discussion of just what accounts for Marie de Vionnet's "difference," Miss Barrace claims "she's just brilliant, as we used to say. That's all. She's various. She's fifty women" (1903, 1994: 157). Singularity becomes an occasion for mock-serious dismay when Hannay exclaims to Pamela "20 million women on this island, and I have to be chained to you!"

2. Though in Hitchcock's thrillers the spymasters are most often European, and later in the century, specifically Nazi, in James the most adept master controllers are American. Like Maggie Verver, they find ways of making others do as they want without resorting directly to personal confrontation or violence. In *The Ambassadors*, the role of Little Bilham in Chad's plans is our first clue that despite his many changes, Chad after all has something in common with his mother.

Chapter 3

1. By American Studies, I mean an interdisciplinary approach to reading literary and cultural production that emerged coincident with the rise to geopolitical prominence of the United States during and immediately after World War II. Edel's reincorporation of an American James above is a strong example of the early American Studies imperative to foreground national questions and to order a canon.

2. "Crapy Cornelia" was originally published in *Harper's Magazine* in 1909 and is reprinted in James, *In the Cage* (1972).

3. I am tempted to juxtapose this sense of James with Tom Cohen's (2005) brilliant recent reading of Hitchcock's "teletechnics," which makes much of Hitchcock's attention to

black spots and visual interruptions, and which could encourage a link between James and Hitchcock precisely around a Jamesian sentence such as the one I have quoted.

4. See my extended discussion of *The Man Who Knew Too Much* in Chapter 4 of *Morocco Bound* (Edwards [2005]).

5. Lee and LiPuma's essay has spurred a great deal of scholarship in cultural anthropology. Povinelli and Gaonkar (2003) take Lee and LiPuma's argument a step further and argue for a reading practice that attends less to the meaning of texts or "textualized" objects in motion than to the question of what propels those objects and what is taken up in their circulation.

6. We can juxtapose this with Alan Trachtenberg's fine reading of the Ellis Island chapter much earlier in *The American Scene.* Trachtenberg (2004) is interested in two moments in James's encounter with New York: the process of spectation and what James discovers about it from his perch in the gallery above the processing center at Ellis Island, and James's New York visits to Yiddish Theater. Trachtenberg notes James's apparent anti-Semitism in the latter case, but he is more interested in James' fascination with the illegibility of Yiddish language, and his immersion in the scene. Trachtenberg's great sensitivity to spectation, to photography, and to perspective is helpful here.

7. Bill Brown's (2003) brilliant attention to the "object matter of American literature" and the "social life of things" is very useful in building this case, which is necessarily foreshortened. Brown, too, helps us make the jump to Hitchcock, whose work reflects back on James via the "thing." For Brown, reading James closely, the "thing" is distinct from the object, and (following Arjun Appadurai's earlier work) an attention to the social life of things reverses the perspective of the alienated relationships between individuals that Marx identifies in *Capital.* Here is Brown: "'Things' circulate as an idea in excess of any physical referent; the Jamesian sense of things can have nothing to do with the sensation of thingness. In the Jamesian lexicon, the word [thing] names a potent source of attraction, conflict, and anxiety; it does not (necessarily) name a group of physical objects." Brown's heroic reading of James's late novel *The Spoils of Poynton* (1896), which in its serialized first edition appeared as *The Old Things*, shows with great care how: "James was both obviously attracted to things yet somewhat embarrassed by them, eager to describe the physical object world yet eager to chart a kind of consciousness that transcends it" (141). Brown draws our attention to what he calls the idiosyncrasy of the late James of *Spoils of Poynton*: "human relationships become the medium for expressing things, for apprehending the intensity of their *being,* for recognizing that the being of things lies no more in the details of their mere physicality than does the being of humans" (155). Brown's distinction between things and objects, and his reading of James's fraught negotiation with the "object matter" of literature, allows us to associate James's own difficult late style, his manipulation of the object, of the scene, of the setting, now seen as if through a prism, with what I am calling a cosmopolitan, or multilateral consciousness.

8. In addition to Brown (discussed in Note 7 above), whom I am following, there is much recent work on James's understanding and representation of "things." See, for example, Eric Savoy (2001); Victoria Coulson (2004); Thomas J. Otten (2006).

9. Hitchcock, too, goes on to tell Truffaut at length about a film he wished to make about a ménage à trois, until Truffaut made *Jules et Jim* (1962), which has its own horrors and fascinations. But it is mostly for an object he wanted to film that he laments the missed opportunity: after a very lengthy exposition, Hitchcock concludes: "I must admit that the only reason the idea appealed to me was the scene I described to you: the husband puffing away contentedly at his pipe!" (176).

10. I am alluding to Wai Chee Dimock's (2006) intriguing reading of Henry James's *The Wings of the Dove* (1902), which provides an analysis of James that moves us simultaneously beyond the nation, even as the nation loops in and out of our understanding of his work. Dimock reads *The Wings of the Dove* for all of its "fractal" trajectories that move its reader outside and across deep time, geography, and genre. These three categories are major concerns for Dimock in the reading strategy she has been developing for rethinking American literature in the world system, and the means by which she identifies moments and directions of transhistorical and planetary exchange within literary texts generally marked (including by Dimock) as "American." Here, Dimock's theoretical inspiration comes from Benoit Mandelbrot's fractal geometry—"a geometry of nonintegers, a geometry of what loops around, what breaks off, what is jagged, what comes only in percentages" (76)—a mathematical model she leverages against Mikhail Bakhtin's distinction between epic (which he sees as archaic and defunct) and novel. Dimock wants us to understand James's text as *epic* more than *novel*, and she is provoked by moments of fracture that transport the reader's attention to other times and places and indeed genres via the author's references to Ancient Rome, to painting, and foreign (i.e., non-English) languages (Dimock 2006, 73–106). There will be a moment in François Truffaut's famous discussions with Hitchcock that resonates here. Hitchcock says: "There is a certain off-balance . . . every time a story takes place in a mixed ethnic community: Englishmen with Americans or else Americans with French Canadians. It's also true for pictures that are filmed in a foreign country when all the characters are English-speaking; I've never been able to get used to that" (Truffaut 1967, 169).

11. For other readings of James in a global or post-American framework, see Giles (2003), Hsu (2003), and other contributors to the special "Global James" issue of *The Henry James Review* 24.3 (2003).

Chapter 4

1. See: Gregory (2004), Auchard (1986), and Berlant (1987).

2. This is particularly true of soundtracks governed by the aesthetic principles associated with the classical Hollywood style.

3. Two edited volumes, Altman (1992), and Weis and Belton (1985), delineate the numerous issues related to film sound. Particularly useful are Altman's two essays, "The Material Heterogeneity of Recorded Sound" (15–31), and "Four and a Half Film Fallacies" (35–45).

4. Nadel (1995), *Containment Culture*.

5. Wood (1989) discusses this association, 367.

6. Elise Michie (1999) notes: "The difference between the first and second versions of *The Man Who Knew Too Much* perfectly illustrate the way the threatening possibility of a woman having a mission separate from the home leads almost automatically to what feels like a heavy-handed invocation of "domestic virtues" (41).

7. Focusing on McKenna's hands rather than Bernard's face, Edwards (2005) notes: "The dark residue . . . he tries to rub off . . . is a visceral souvenir of American obligation at home and abroad. It has come to race . . . The American abroad who thought he had left the domestic crisis of race at home finds it inescapable" (193).

8. Bell (1991) contends that "natural" is the most frequently used word to describe Morris, but Catherine, too, is frequently described in that way, and it is also Catherine who most frequently uses the word to describe Morris.

Chapter 5

1. Dr. Petersen is also said to "approach all problems with an icepack on [her] head," as if protecting herself from what sudden knowledge might do. Late in the film, her mentor Dr. Brulov warns her, "You can't keep bumping your head against reality and saying it is not there." Changed by her experiences, Dr. Petersen might be imagined to bump her head against reality on purpose, in search of a kind of knowing that, though bumpy, does not respond to requests for its appearance.

2. Unmistakably a model, the tiny train with which Hitchcock begins the film tells viewers immediately not only to read the train as a tiny world but to read the world itself as a miniature.

3. In Plath's description, the scene is both novelistic and cinematic, and she experiences it in "several sharp flashes, like blows," that must seem familiar in the context of James and Hitchcock (Malcolm 1995, 153).

4. Discussing James's "psychoanalytic-painterly style," George Smith (2009) examines scenes in James's works that are so close to the primal scene that the "repressed primal trauma is remembered—allegorically re-activated." For Smith, Isabel's sighting of Merle and Osmond is less flickeringly photographic or wishfully cinematic, as I suggest, than it is an instance of "the painterly representation of consciousness."

5. As Kaja Silverman (1988b) has said, "*The Golden Bowl* . . . is in many ways an extended primal scene" (161). Silverman, too, sees the primal scene as cinematic and also as strongly about knowledge. Considering the primal scene within the context of the Freudian attachment of knowledge to sexual difference, Silverman is interested in the way the primal scene is able to disrupt "conventional masculinity" (157) in part because the scene is "complicated by the possibility of the watching child identifying either with the mother or with the father . . ." (158). This possibility of multiple identifications accounts for the capacity of multiple characters to occupy the space of watching in the primal scenes of *The Golden Bowl*.

Chapter 6

The present chapter is a revision of an essay that first appeared in *Arizona Quarterly* 62.3 (Autumn 2006): 45–62.

1. On James's fetishization of objects, which can be viewed as the embodiment of "the lure of detail," see Brown (2002, 2003).

2. As far as I can determine, the protagonist of *In the Cage* remains anonymous throughout.

3. Rowe's chapter on *In the Cage* (1998a) focuses on the relationship between technology and gender in the figure of the story's telegrapher-protagonist, and James's anxiety, revealed in this encoding, about loss of authorial control over "information" as such.

Chapter 7

1. *Blackmail* was the first talkie in the history of British cinema as well as in Hitchcock's career. On the significance of Hitchcock's experimentation with sound in the film, see Telotte (2001).

2. Tania Modleski (1988) provides a brilliant reading of the gender dynamics in the film, and especially of this episode and of critics' attenuations of Alice's attempted rape.

3. In the reading of *Blackmail* prefacing his *George Eliot and Blackmail* (1985), Alexander Welsh makes this point, only to dismiss it on the ground that "The audience perceives that Frank is too good a person to take advantage of Alice" (16). While this may be seen as a rather naïve personalization of a structural and systematic unbalance of gender power in the film, Welsh's subsequent contention that blackmailing stands not just for Frank's new position of power, but for the whole police and for "the coercive power of society at large" (17) is an extremely forceful one.

4. The underlying contradiction and the manipulative quality of Milly's legacy—"She leaves her wealth to them, at the same time making it ethically impossible for them to accept her gift"—is underscored by Žižek (2006, 130).

5. For a brilliant recent reading of Milly's wings as referencing the spread wings of the bald eagle on the 1899 $1 banknote, and for an analysis of the power of capital in the novel, see Martin (2003).

6. Like Milly's visit to Sir Luke Strett and his severe, if elusive, diagnosis—simultaneously kept a secret and entrusted to both Susan Stringham and Kate Croy—Kate's engagement to Densher is consciously treated as an open secret: "No doubt she had been seen. Of course she had been seen. She had taken no trouble not to be seen, and it was a thing she was clearly incapable of taking" (James 1902, 2006: 255–56).

7. Stephen Brophy (1999) reads it as a reminder of the primacy of the visual over the aural in cinematic matters.

8. Information and publicity, and the rise of a culture increasingly revolving around them, are long-standing concerns for Henry James; such a late story as "The Papers" (1903, 1996) in particular, bears interesting resemblances to *The Wings of the Dove*. For a study of public discourse in James, see Richard Salmon (1997); for an analysis of publicity and consumption culture in *The Wings of the Dove*, see Despotopoulou (2002).

9. On structures of power-knowledge in James, expressed in the pervasiveness of surveillance as both theme and narrative technique, see Mark Seltzer's classic study *Henry James and the Art of Power* (1984).

10. The significant exception is of course Merton Densher, whose fanatical respect for the sacred character of the uttered word is repeatedly emphasized, and whose statements literally determine his subsequent actions in a constant attempt to retrospectively make true on his word. On the performative quality of speech acts in the novel, see Hillis Miller (2005). On the "pressure of the unspoken" (82–83) in verbal exchanges and the unique epistemology it creates, see Yeazell (1976).

11. See Strauss (2007).

12. Žižek's (2006) reading of the novel examines the emergence of an intersubjective ethics based on the recognition "of the ethical weight of others' claims on me" (126), ungrounded in any fixed coordinates for judgment and therefore integrally secular. For a reading of Sir Luke Strett's operation as a paragon of successful masculinity in the novel, see Fusco (2008). Gert Buelens (2001) also touches on Sir Luke Strett, noticing how he is the only character who does not try to grasp Milly within the deadening logic of metaphorical substitution.

13. For a reading of the moral question in *Blackmail*, see McCarron (2008).

14. For another Lacanian reading of James's novel as embodying an "ethics of desire" see van Slyck (2005).

Chapter 8

1. J. Hillis Miller (1980) notes the seductive aspect of James's story in his essay, offering the notion of a "single and totalizable meaning" as intrinsic to the "lure of metaphysics itself" (113).

2. In *Beyond the Pleasure Principle* (1920, 1961), Freud sets out a dynamic economy of instincts that tend either toward quiescence or "eros." Peter Brooks (1982) adapts this model in his work on narrative dynamics in "Freud's Masterplot."

3. In *Hitchcock and the Making of Marnie* (2005), Tony Moral notes that the film was "a commercial as well as a critical failure, causing the director to lose a great deal of confidence" (xiii). The film also, according to Moral, has "generated wider controversy than any other of the director's films" (xiii).

4. Robert Samuels (1998) argues that *Marnie* plays out this unconscious bisexuality openly.

5. Many essays point to the analytic situation of *Marnie*, especially feminist essays analyzing the relative power of the gendered roles. Readings of the film's gender politics range from Kaja Silverman's (1983) analysis in *The Subject of Semiotics* to Tania Modleski's (2005) readings of Hitchcock's gender politics in *The Women Who Knew Too Much* to Corinn Columpar's (1999–2000) critique of enunciation, Rebecca Bailin's (1982) reading of gender and violence, and Clifford Manlove's (2007) analysis of the "political dimension of the gaze." Yet other critics note the film's continuation of Hitchcock's fascination with monstrous maternal figures—see Paul Gordon's chapter (2008), "A Mother's Love: *Marnie,*" Bernard Dick's (2000) "Hitchcock's Terrible Mothers," and Allan Lloyd Smith's (2000) "*Marnie*, the Dead Mother, and the Phantom." Resistance comes, as Lucretia Knapp (1993) argues, in the film's provision of a separable lesbian space and discourse.

6. The concept of fetishism as a form of disavowal is Freud's version from "On Fetishism" (1927). The particular formation of "I know but all the same . . ." comes from Octave Mannoni's (1969) reading of Freud and it is the version taken over by such film theorists as Christian Metz.

7. Other critics undermine the heteronormative assumptions that ground these gendered systems. Fletcher's two economies, for example, are still dependent upon a binary, heterosexual epistemology, itself called into question by Kaja Silverman and Lucretia Knapp (1993). Silverman (1988a), like Fletcher, questions Bellour's (1977) reading of *Marnie*'s enunciative strategies and assumptions about the film's nexus of identifications with Marnie and site of control in Hitchcock. "The agency of that identification," she notes, "is the image of Marnie, which is passed from the camera to Strutt, Rutland, and Hitchcock-as-fictional-character during the opening three scenes of the film. Ironically, it is only through this radically dispersed and decentered 'hom(m)osexual economy that Hitchcock-as-director comes to be installed as the point of apparent textual origin, and as the seemingly punctual source of meaning" (204).

Chapter 9

1. Works on Henry James and love are legion: in addition to classic accounts in James scholarship as in Krook (1968) or Holland (1995) are studies which take that emotion as their central focus: see Lebowitz (1963), Sicker (1980), and McWhirter (1989). In recent

years many have turned explicitly to the question of James's sexuality, particularly as expressed in his recently published letters to young men like Hendrik Andersen; see, for example: Stevens (1998) and Graham (1999); for those letters, see Gunter and Jobe (2004). All students of love in *The Golden Bowl* owe a substantial debt to Bayley's chapter on James (1960).

As Richard Allen observes, Hitchcock critics split into those who emphasize him as an advocate of romantic heterosexual love (Allen 1999, Brill 1988); those who see him as primarily in its critique (Edelman 2004, Modleski 2005, Spoto 2008); those who see it as both (early Robin Wood 1969 vs. late Robin Wood 2002). My own view is that Hitchcock was, by and large, a passionate observer of human love independent of object choice: he critiqued as he examined both heterosexual desire (*Vertigo*) and queer affections (*Rope*, *Strangers on a Train*) with an odd mixture of detachment and passion. My sense of *Notorious*, as expressed below, is that it represents one of the few moments in his career where Hitchcock lets himself go—where he gave vent to a romance affirming, rather than critiquing, view. That he was thought by many to be in love with Ingrid Bergman—one of the few actresses Hitchcock had a crush on who was not a blonde—is not irrelevant here. See Spoto, *Spellbound by Beauty* (2008).

2. I owe this turn of the argument to Rita Felski (2008).

3. The term is Martin Jay's (1994).

4. Holland: "The symbol of the bowl helps govern the novel because the bowl and the act of buying it or possessing it, of breaking it and salvaging it later, inform each other, and the bowl itself does not stand as a merely referential or imposed symbol but as part of a profoundly creative act to constitute a field of form, a formal nexus" (1964, 348). Brown: "What is remarkable about the golden bowl in *The Golden Bowl* is that it seems to signify so much while it in fact signifies so little, precisely because it seems to signify so much. . . . In *The Golden Bowl*, a physical object gets described and redescribed, intensely framed, and doted upon, and thus becomes a thing, elevated to a significance it hardly possesses on its own, yet a significance that it seems to have autonomously assumed" (2002, 172–3).

5. A host of critics have written on James and vision; of these, the best remain Holland (1964) and Carolyn Porter (1981).

6. Among the critics who seek to construct a sensorium of Henry James, Thomas Otten (2006) is the one who has turned most fully to touch.

7. For thing theory and James, see not only Brown (2003) and Otten, (2006, 154–166) but also the yet-more-sophisticated formulation of Victoria Coulson (2004), who argues that "far from "remain[ing] conspicuously absent [as Brown argues], the 'details' of the Jamesian world symptomatize an *increasing*, and increasingly *specific*, imbrication of subject and object, idea and thing, in James's late-nineteenth-century apotheosis of realist representation."

8. The most instructive accounts of James's use of figurative language are those that wrestle with it, especially in the ubiquitous Holland (1964), Yeazell (1976), and Cameron (1989).

9. For Husserl see *Ideas Pertaining to a Pure Phenomenology and to a Phenomenological Philosophy, Second Book* (1989); Merleau-Ponty, *The Phenomenology of Perception* (1962); Wyschogrod, "Towards a Postmodern Ethics: Corporeality and Alterity" (2003); Derrida, *On Touching—Jean-Luc Nancy* (2005); Nancy, *Corpus* (2008); Serres, *The Five Senses* (2009).

10. Merleau-Ponty's account of the relation of touch and vision is quite complicated; just before this passage, he analogizes between the two in ways that seem to coordinate touch and sight, and later, in the manuscript left uncompleted at his death, *The Visible and the Invisible*, he rethinks vision on the model of touch, ultimately seeing the intertwining of these two as creating what he calls "flesh." Derrida (2005; to simplify recklessly) properly sees these turns as evidence of the essentially Christian, presence-affirming nature of Merleau-Ponty's discourse on touching, and by extension, of those in phenomenological accounts of the body at large. Paterson (2007) nicely uses this coordination of vision and touch adumbrated there to link to some medical adaptations of haptic technologies, that is the building of machines for blind people that help them to "see" via touch.

11. Husserl, *Ideas II* (1989); Merleau, Ponty, *Phenomenology* (1962). Again, this nexus proves to be of the greatest importance for critics of the phenomenological enterprise; in addition to Derrida, one might cite here Irigaray (1971), who puts a question to this passage:

> Is it still valid if the *two hands* are *joined*? Which brings about something very particular in the relation feeling-felt. With no passive-active, or even middle-passive. A sort of fourth mode? Neither active, nor passive, nor active-passive. Always more passive than the passive. And nevertheless active. The hands joined, palms together, fingers outstretched, constitute a very particular touching. A gesture often reserved for women (at least in the West) and which evokes, doubles, the *touching of the lips* silently applied upon one another. (Burke and Gill 2005, 134).

12. The most fully elaborated phenomenological account of James, that of Paul Armstrong, focuses on another wing in the phenomenological mansion, the one built by Heidigger and Sartre and inhabited by a concern with intersubjectivity, being for-itself and in-itself, and the Other.

13. Tania Modleski (2005) calls this gesture a punch to the jaw (68), which seems a possible reading of the gesture but not the only one. The point here is that it's different in nature and duration from the kinds of gestures, touches, and hand movements I've been dealing with up until this moment (68).

14. For a catalog of these, see Demonsablon, "Lexique mythologique pour l'oeuvre de Hitchcock" (1956) and *Hitchcock's Motifs* (2005). Much more has been said about hands in general in Hitchcock, the one closest in spirit to mine being Brill, who notes that "In North by Northwest (and in Hitchcock's films generally), hands are an emblem of intimacy, sometimes frustrated and always potential" (1988, 21). But hands are also used to strangle (*Frenzy*, *Strangers on a Train*, *Rear Window*), to reach for incriminating objects (again, *Strangers on a Train*), and to vainly attempt to protect from attack by beaked avians or wig-wearing psychopaths (*The Birds* or *Psycho*). And this is not even to mention handcuffs! (see *The Lodger*, and *39 Steps* for a virtuoso treatment of these as incentives to intimacy). See Barton (2002) for a different take than mine on hands—one that emphasizes the hand as power object that allows for, or frustrates, audience identification with the character.

15. Hitchcock's stated intention was to show that people could flirt while discussing such mundane things as a chicken dinner. But the double entendres here are obvious, and also of course Hitchcockian. No wonder that "it was Hitch, by the way," wrote Frank Nugent, "who planned and wrote the scene." [Screenplay writer Ben] Hecht's baffled remark was: "I don't get all this talk about a chicken" (Gottlieb 2003, 19).

16. That Devlin—who has kissed her aplenty but has not yet slept with her, due to the untimely intervention of his superior—tells her that he is going to kiss her has always struck me as a little strange; surely she wouldn't object if he just went ahead and did so. Presumably, he warns her of his intention so she won't respond with a start when he begins the embrace, and it also comports with his stage-managing of the scene for Alex and his butler's eyes. But this warning is also oddly courteous, raising the possibility that, since she is sleeping with another man, she might not be sexually available to him, despite the fact that she's helping him trap her husband. As such, it participates in that general process of the change in Devlin's character that I'm describing here.

Chapter 10

1. In Lacanian theory, the Real is one of the three categories or orders according to which all psychoanalytic phenomena may be described, the other two being the Symbolic and the Imaginary. Essentially, the Real is that which remains firmly outside the explanatory resources of the Symbolic. It has no language. As Dylan Evans (1996) explains, the Real is "impossible to imagine, impossible to integrate into the Symbolic order, and impossible to attain in any way. It is this character of impossibility and of resistance to symbolisation which lends the Real its essentially traumatic quality" (160). In critical theory, the Lacanian Real is deployed to explain the role and function of the monstrous (in the field of the Gothic, for example). The Real is important in any exploration of trauma: it denotes the event—or more precisely, the encounter with something—that threatens to annihilate the subject. It binds the subject to it, and if this 'it' demands our witness, it also defies it. In Hitchcock's terminology, the Real is that which holds us 'spellbound.' Staging the encounter with the Real is Hitchcock's essential cinematic project.

2. In French, "*parti*" is both the past participle of the verb *partir,* to depart, and a noun that signifies, among other things, a course of action: hence, *prendre le parti de faire quelque chose* means to make up one's mind to do something, just as *parti pris* designates a bias, or a mind made up.

3. As Donald Spoto (1979) has astutely observed, this initial image "of the spiral is more than an innovative and arresting design suggesting the dizziness of vertigo: it is the basic image on which the entire structure and design of the picture are based" (275). Spoto offers a comprehensive catalog of scenes and images in which "these swirling motions create and sustain the hallucinatory, dreamlike effect of the film" (275) and concludes that the essential structure of *Vertigo* is "vertiginous circularity itself" (277).

4. Note that Žižek changed the spelling of this word between 1991 and 1992. It is not clear why he did this: Lacan himself called it '*le sinthome*.'

5. It is important to distinguish between the formal deployment of the circle as *sinthome* and other narrative usages of embodied circling about. Not all examples of the latter coalesce into the highly stylized and repetitive diagram, or "narrative beyond words," that characterizes the former.

6. For a fuller outline of the deceptions upon which *Vertigo* is based, see Spoto (1979), 265–66.

7. When I presented an earlier version of this essay at Dartmouth College in May 2008, as part of a symposium on James and Hitchcock, Frances Restuccia suggested that the circularity I am describing, or rather circumscribing, is not *sinthomic* but is more likely

the manifestation of the drive. Indeed, to invoke the circle at all is to deploy a metaphor that is central in Lacan's of the drive, which is highly variable and evolves in ways that are contingent upon the case history of the subject. As Dylan Evans (1996) summarizes Lacan's language, the drives "do not aim at an object but rather circle perpetually around it. Lacan argues that the purpose of the drive (*Triebziel*) is not to reach a *goal* (a final destination) but to follow its *aim* (the way itself), which is to circle around the object (Seminar 11, 168). Thus the real purpose of the drive is not some mythical goal of full satisfaction, but to return to the circular path, and the real source of enjoyment is the repetitive movement of this closed circuit" (46–47). It would seem that the privileged status of the image of the circle in Lacan's model of the drive arises from the necessary attempt to render graphically conceptualizable a phenomenon that is not easily translatable into images, or into language at all. The circle is, after all, hardly an esoteric image; it is frequently invoked to represent or to model highly abstract concepts. The *sinthome*, by contrast, is emphatically not abstract: it is an embodied gesture, a recurring enactment, that performs a knotting of the Real, the Symbolic, and the Imaginary and thus renders the subject coherent and permits a certain *jouissance*. The circling of bodies that I locate in James and Hitchcock is surely connected in some way to the drive, but it is more immediately a figure—an oddly literal figure—of what I have called the subject's spatial and temporal disposition, and in the economy of novelistic or cinematic narrative, it is a representation. This is not, however, to argue that the *sinthomic* circle under investigation here and the circularity of Lacan's modeling of the drive is 'merely' coincidental. In subsequent correspondence with Professor Restuccia, she suggested, astutely, that "'inscription' (of the materiality of the signifier) is a superior way of putting it, although it is the case that any signifier can potentially take on the function of the *sinthome*, where enjoyment insists within language, or where *jouissance* is soldered to language" (e-mail, May 19, 2009).

Chapter 11

1. Another debate centers on the innocence or deviance of Flora and Miles. This question is related to the nature of the ghosts: if the specters are the product of the governess's madness, then there is a good chance that she endows the children with knowledge that they do not have. If the ghosts are real, we might lend credence to the governess's suspicion that the children are trying to hide their relationship to them.

2. I borrow this term from Wilkie Collins's *The Moonstone* (1868, 1999).

3. The sense of revelation is also heightened by its similarity to Detective Arbogast's earlier visit of the house, which was curtailed by his murder at the hands of Norman/Mother.

Chapter 12

1. In his own subsequent directorial work and in his famous interviews with Hitchcock included in *Hitchcock* (1967), Truffaut helped establish French New Wave Cinema, which relied on the central control of the director as *auteur.*

2. I am indebted to Patrick O'Donnell, who stresses James's use of "our young lady" in the novella in "James's Birdcage/ Hitchcock's Birds" (Chapter 6), and in the "Seeing James Seeing" issue of *Arizona Quarterly* 62:3 (Autumn 2006), p. 50.

3. For a fuller interpretation of James's use of the telegraph in *In the Cage*, see Rowe, *The Other Henry James* (Durham: Duke University Press, 1998), pp. 155–80.

4. The actual date for the "invention" of the telegraph is notoriously difficult to pinpoint, but Samuel F. B. Morse's experiments in the mid-1830s culminated in successful demonstrations of the long-distance transmission of messages by 1837. See Mabee, *The American Leonardo* (1969).

5. Mulvey herself would subsequently repudiate this position, along with a long list of other influential scholars of women's studies and film. A good discussion and bibliography of this debate is included in Bergstrom and Doane, eds., *Camera Obscura* 7.2–3.

Chapter 13

1. Mrs. Farange's phallic dominance is hinted early on, when we learn that she had "often beaten her husband at billiards, . . . [which] were her great accomplishment and the distinction her name always first produced the mention of" (1897, 2003: 400). Note the later reference to the "balls that Ida's cue used to send flying" (556).

2. Moddle performs a touching act of kindness when, for the first time in the novel, Maisie is leaving her father's home for her mother's. The nurse writes "on a paper, in very big, easy words, ever so many pleasures that she [Maisie] would enjoy at the other house. These promises ranged from 'a mother's fond love' to 'a nice poached egg to your tea'" (1897, 2003: 403). The paper becomes both a remembrance of Moddle's own motherly affection and a text that promises the presence of its signified but, as writing inevitably does, marks the absence of what it names.

3. This safeness akin to the dead suggests that Mrs. Wix's desire (including her desire for Sir Claude) poses no threat to Maisie. Note also that Mrs. Wix becomes, to Maisie, the purveyor of the law (of the dead mother?).

4. While Maisie's Oedipalization is particularly relevant for the comparison to *Shadow of a Doubt*'s Charlie, I agree with Rivkin (1996) that it is not simple; rather, Maisie's story is "at once, undecidably, a confirmation of the oedipal [*sic*] scheme and an abandonment of its logic" (159).

5. Clearly Maisie ages, as considerable time elapses in the novel. Jean Frantz Blackall (1993) claims that "[t]he first third of the novel covers about nine years," but makes no supporting argument (162). I agree with Donna Przybylowicz (1986) that "[i]n the first fourteen chapters . . . the temporal duration is not precisely defined"; rather, "the use of summary, ellipsis, and the iterative mode, causes the narrative action to melt together and makes it difficult to determine how much time is elapsing" (26–27). Perhaps the best overall accounting is Rowe's, which places Maisie somewhere between eleven and fifteen by novel's end (1998a, 218 n. 8). At any given point she may seem older than she is, for she is a wonder of precociousness so far as knowledge is concerned. I think James means for us to puzzle over her age.

6. Humorously, near the end, Sir Claude has misplaced his walking stick, and it seems he has left it with Mrs. Beale (1897, 2003: 620).

7. Dictionary.com defines "puss in the corner" as "a parlor game for children in which one player in the middle of a room tries to occupy any of the positions along the walls that become vacant as other players dash across to exchange places at a signal." Obviously the term also carries slang implications regarding the erotic nature of the "rushing to and fro and changing of places."

8. "It would spoil things" because it would muddy their identificatory relationship with a signifier of desire—which is exactly what he now attempts.

9. Among critics who emphasize the binary structure are Rohmer and Chabrol (1979), Rothman (1984), Spoto (1983), Rosenbladt (2004), and Dolar (1992).

10. For example, see Susan Honeyman (2001) and Rowe (1998a). For Honeyman, *Maisie* reveals James as "realist in his quest for accurate representation, modernist in his use of transparency, but like post-modernists as well in exposing transparency as a conventional illusion" (74). For Rowe, "Maisie will come to accept and even celebrate the instabilities of gender, class, race, and age that distinguish the modern age even as these same instabilities incapacitate the adults around her" (124). In my view Maisie can celebrate these instabilities precisely because ultimately for her they are not very destabilizing. They do not constitute the Derridean radical loss of the center (see James 1897, 2003: 280).

11. Nadel (2002, 193–6) argues intriguingly that James's realism operates like film in this regard: "[t]he coherence of the social gesture or quotidian act, broken down to its minimum thresholds of significance and then reconstituted as the illusion of itself, as an imaginary plenitude, describes equally well, I think, the fundamental trick of cinema and the sensibility of James's fiction" (194).

Chapter 14

1. An earlier version of Sedgwick's essay appeared in David McWhirter's important collection, *Henry James's New York Edition: The Construction of Authorship*. I am also indebted to Eric Savoy's insightful work on this motif in James and its always sexual implications; see his essay, "Embarrassments: Figure in the Closet," *Henry James Review* 20.3.

WORKS CITED

Allen, Richard. 1999. "Hitchcock, or the Pleasures of Metaskepticism." *October* 89 (Summer): 69–86.

Allen, Richard and S. Ishii-Gonzalès, eds. 2008. *Hitchcock: Centenary Essays*. London: British Film Institute.

Allott, Miriam. 1961. "Mrs. Gaskell's 'The Old Nurse's Story': A Link between *Wuthering Heights* and *The Turn of the Screw*." *Notes and Queries* 8: 101–2.

Altman, Rick, ed. 1992. *Sound Theory and Sound Practice*. New York: Routledge.

Armstrong, Paul. 1983. *The Phenomenology of Henry James*. Chapel Hill: University of North Carolina Press.

Armstrong, Tim. 1996. "Disciplining the Corpus: Henry James and Fletcherism." In *American Bodies: Cultural Histories of the Physique*, edited by Tim Armstrong, 101–18. New York: New York University Press.

Auchard, John. 1986. *Silence in Henry James: The Heritage of Symbolism and Decadence*. University Park, PA: Penn State University Press.

Auerbach, Nina. 1982. *The Woman and the Demon*. Cambridge, MA: Harvard University Press.

Bailin, Rebecca. 1982. "Feminist Readership, Violence and Marnie." *Film Reader* 5: 24–36.

Barton, Sabrina. 2002. "Hitchcock's Hands." In *Framing Hitchcock: Selected Essays from The Hitchcock Annual*, edited by Sidney Gottleib and Christopher Brookhouse, 159–79. Detroit, MI: Wayne State University Press.

Baudrillard, Jean. 1975. *The Mirror of Production*, translated by Mark Poster. St. Louis: Telos.

Bayley, John. 1960. *The Characters of Love: A Study in the Literature of Personality*. London: Constable.

Baym, Nina. 1981. "Melodramas of Beset Manhood." *American Quarterly* 33: 123–39.

Bell, Ian F.A. 1991. *Henry James and the Past: Readings into Time*. New York: St. Martin's Press.

Bellour, Raymond. 1977. "Hitchcock, The Enunciator." *Camera Obscura* 2 (Fall): 66–91.

Benjamin, Walter. 1969. "The Work of Art in the Age of Mechanical Reproduction." In *Illuminations*, edited by Hannah Arendt, translated by Harry Zohn, 217–51. New York: Schocken Books.

Bergstrom, Janet and Mary Ann Doane, eds. 1989. "The Spectatrix." *Camera Obscura* 7.2–3 (May/September).

Berlant, Lauren. 1987. "Fancy-Work and Fancy Foot-Work: Motives for Silence in Washington Square." *Criticism: A Quarterly Review of Literature and the Arts* 29: 439–58.

Bersani, Leo. 1976. *A Future for Astyanax: Character and Desire in Literature*. Boston: Little, Brown and Company.

Blackall, Jean Frantz. 1993. "The Experimental Period." In *A Companion to Henry James Studies*, edited by Daniel Mark Fogel, 147–78. Westport, CT: Greenwood Press.

Bloom, Harold, ed. 1988. *Henry James's* The Ambassadors*: Modern Critical Interpretations*. New York: Chelsea House Publishers.

Bordwell, David. 2008. *Film Art: An Introduction*, eighth edition. New York: McGraw-Hill.

Bordwell, David, Kristen Thompson, and Janet Staiger. 1985. *The Classic Hollywood Cinema: Film Style and Mode of Production to 1960*. New York: Columbia University Press.

Brill, Lesley. 1988. *The Hitchcock Romance: Love and Irony in Hitchcock's Films*. Princeton, NJ: Princeton University Press.

Britzolakis, Christine. 2001. "Technologies of Vision in Henry James's *What Maisie Knew*." *Novel* 34: 369–90.

Brooks, Peter. 1982. "Freud's Masterplot." In *Literature and Psychoanalysis: The Question of Reading Otherwise*, edited by Shoshana Felman, 280–300. Baltimore, MD: Johns Hopkins University Press.

Brophy, Stephen. 1999. "Use of glass in Alfred Hitchcock's *Blackmail*." *CineAction*: 20–23.

Brown, Bill. 2002. "A Thing About Things: The Art of Decoration in the Works of Henry James." *Henry James Review* 23: 222–32.

———. 2003. *A Sense of Things: The Object Matter of American Literature*. Chicago: University of Chicago Press.

Buelens, Gert. 2001. "Metaphor, Metonymy, and the Constitution of Identity in *The Wings of the Dove*." *Canadian Review of American Studies* 31: 409–28.

Cameron, Sharon. 1989. *Thinking in Henry James*. Chicago: University of Chicago Press.

Caruth, Cathy. 1996. *Unclaimed Experience: Trauma, Narrative, and History*. Baltimore, MD: Johns Hopkins University Press.

Chandler, Charlotte. 2005. *It's Only a Movie: Alfred Hitchcock—A Personal Biography*. New York: Simon and Schuster.

Chion, Michael. 1992. "The Cipher of Destiny." In *Everything You Always Wanted to Know About Lacan But Were Afraid to Ask Hitchcock*, edited by Slavoj Žižek, 137–42. London: Verso.

Cixous, Hélène. 1975, 1997. "The Laugh of the Medusa." In *Feminism: An Anthology of Literary Theory and Criticism*, edited by Robyn R. Warhol and Diane Price Herndl, 347–62. New Brunswick, NJ: Rutgers University Press.

Cohen, Paula Marantz. 1995. *Alfred Hitchcock: The Legacy of Victorianism*. Lexington: University Press of Kentucky.

———. "James, Hitchcock and the Fate of Character." In Alfred Hitchcock: Centenary Essays, ed. Richard Allen and S.Ishii Gonzales, 15–27. London: British Film Institute.

———. 2008. "Alfred Hitchcock: Modest Exhibitionist." *TLS* September 5, 2008. Accessed through http://entertainment.timesonline.co.uk/tol/arts_and_entertainment/the_tls/article4685615.ece. On March 3, 2009.

Cohen, Tom. 1994. *Anti-Mimesis: From Plato to Hitchcock*. New York: Cambridge University Press.

———. 2005. *Hitchcock's Cryptonymies, Volume I: Secret Agents*; Minneapolis: University of Minnesota Press.

———. 2005. *Hitchcock's Cryptonymies, Volume II: War Machines*. .Minneapolis: University of Minnesota Press.

Collins, Wilkie. 1868, 1999. *The Moonstone*, edited by Steve Farmer. Petersborough, Ontario, Canada: Broadview.

Columpar, Corinn. 1999–2000. "Marnie: A Site/Sight for the Convergence of Gazes." *Hitchcock Annual* 8: 51–73.

Copjec, Joan. 1982. "The Anxiety of the Influencing Machine." *October* 23 (Winter): 43–59.

Corber, Robert. 1993. *In the Name of National Security: Hitchcock, Homophobia, and the Political Construction of Gender in Postwar America*. Durham, NC: Duke University Press.

———. 1999. "Hitchcock's Washington: Spectatorship, Ideology, and the 'Homosexual Menace' in *Strangers on a Train*." In *Hitchcock's America*, edited by Jonathan Freedman and Richard Millington, 99–121. New York: Oxford University Press.

Coulson, Victoria. 2004. "Sticky Realism: Armchair Hermeneutics in Late James." *Henry James Review* 25.2: 115–26.

Crowther, Bosley. 1944. "Adrift in 'Lifeboat': The New Hitchcock-Steinbeck Drama Represents Democracy at Sea." *New York Times*. January 23: 3.

———. 1946. "Love Conquers All: Mr. Hitchcock's 'Notorious' Marks His Happy Surrender to Romance." *New York Times*. August 25: 49.

Culver, Stuart. 1981. "Censorship and Intimacy: Awkwardness in *The Awkward Age*," *ELH* 48.2 (Summer): 368–86.

DeKoven, Marianne. 1998. "Gender, History and Modernism in *The Turn of the Screw*." In The Turn of the Screw *and* What Maisie Knew, edited by Neil Cornwell and Maggie Malone, 142–63. New York: St. Martin's Press.

Demonsablon, Phillipe. 1956. "Lexique mythologique pour l'oeuvre de Hitchcock." *Cahiers du Cinéma* 11: 18–29, 54–5.

———. 2005. *Hitchcock's Motifs*. Amsterdam: Amsterdam University Press.

Derrida, Jacques. 1978. "Structure, Sign, and Play in the Discourse of the Human Sciences." In *Writing and Difference*, translated by Alan Bass, 278–93. Chicago: University of Chicago Press.

———. 1998. *Of Grammatology*. Corrected Edition, translated by Gayatri Chakravorty Spivak. Baltimore, MD: Johns Hopkins University Press.

———. 2005. *On Touching—Jean-Luc Nancy*, translated by Christine Irizarry. Palo Alto, CA: Stanford University Press.

Despotopoulou, Anna. 2002. "The Price of 'Mere Spectatorship': Henry James's *The Wings of the Dove*." *The Review of English Studies* 53.210: 228–44.

Dick, Bernard F. 2000. "Hitchcock's Terrible Mothers." *Literature Film Quarterly* 28.4 (2000): 238–49.

Dimock, Wai Chee. 2006. *Through Other Continents: American Literature across Deep Time*. Princeton, NJ: Princeton University Press.

Doane, Mary Ann. 1996. "Film and the Masquerade." In *Feminist Film Theory: A Reader*, edited by Barry Keith Grant, 15–34. Austin: University of Texas Press.

———. 1999. "Film and the Masquerade." In *Feminist Film Theory: A Reader*, edited by Sue Thornham, 131–45. 1999. New York: New York University Press.

Dolar, Mladen. 1992. "Hitchcock's Objects." In *Everything You Wanted to Know about Lacan But Were Afraid to Ask Hitchcock*, edited by Slavoj Žižek, 31–46. London: Verso.

Edel, Leon, ed. 1956. *The American Essays of Henry James*. New York: Vintage.

———. 1969. *The Treacherous Years, 1895–1901*. New York: Avon Books.

———. 1975. *Henry James: Letters II*. Cambridge, MA: Harvard University Press.

———. 1978a. *Henry James: The Untried Years, 1843–1870*. New York: J.B. Lippincott.

———. 1978b. *The Life of Henry James*. 5 vols. New York: Avon.

———. 1984. *Henry James: Letters IV*. Cambridge, MA: Harvard University Press.

Edelman, Lee. 2004. *No Future: Queer Theory and the Death Drive*. Durham, NC: Duke University Press.

Edwards, Brian T. 2005. *Morocco Bound: Disorienting America's Maghreb, from Casablanca to the Marrakech Express*. Durham, NC: Duke University Press.

Edwards, Brian T. and Dilip Parameshwar Gaonkar. 2010. "Globalizing American Studies." In *Globalizing American Studies*, edited by B.T. Edwards and D.P. Gaonkar, 1–45. Chicago: University of Chicago Press.

Elsaesser, Thomas. 1994. "Hitchcock: The Dandy." *The MacGuffin* 14: 15–21.

Erb, Cynthia. 2006. "'Have You Ever Seen the Inside of One of Those Places?': *Psycho*, Foucault, and the Postwar Context of Madness." *Cinema Journal* 45.4 (Summer): 45–63.

Evans, Dylan. 1996. *An Introductory Dictionary of Lacanian Psychoanalysis*. New York: Routledge.

Fanon, Frantz. 1963. *The Wretched of the Earth*, translated by Constance Farrington. New York: Grove Press.

Feinstein, Howard M. 2000. *Becoming William James*. New York: Cornell University Press.

Felman, Shoshana. 2003. *Writing and Madness*, translated by Martha Noel Evans and others Palo Alto, CA: Stanford University Press.

Felski, Rita. 2008. *Uses of Literature*. Oxford, UK: Wiley-Blackwell.

Fetterley, Judith. 1978. *The Resisting Reader*. Bloomington: Indiana University Press.

Fletcher, John. 1988. "Versions of Masquerade." *Screen* 39:3: 43–70.

Foucault, Michel. 1965. *Madness and Civilization: A History of Insanity in the Age of Reason*, translated by Richard Howard. New York: Vintage.

———. 1977. "What Is an Author?" In *Language, Counter-Memory, Practice: Selected Essays and Interviews*, edited by Donald F. Bouchard, translated by Stephen Heath. New York: Hill and Wang.

———. 1978. *The History of Sexuality. Volume I: An Introduction*, translated by Robert Hurley. New York: Vintage.

Freud, Sigmund. 1918, 1960. *Totem and Taboo*, translated by A.A. Brill. reprint, New York: Vintage-Random.

———. 1919, 1981. "The Uncanny." In *The Standard Edition of the Complete Psychological Works of Sigmund Freud*. Vol. 17, edited and translated by James Strachey, 217–56. London: Hogarth.

———. 1920, 1961. *Beyond the Pleasure Principle*, edited and translated by James Strachey. New York: Norton.

———. 1927, 1981. "On Fetishism." In *The Standard Edition of the Complete Psychological Works*. Vol. 21, edited and translated by James Strachey, 152–7. London: Hogarth Press.

Fusco, Gianna. 2008. "Merton Densher and Heteronormative Masculinity at the Turn of the Century." In *Tracing Henry James*, edited by Melanie H. Ross and Greg W. Zacharias, 110–23. Newcastle upon Tyne, UK: Cambridge Scholars Publishing.

Galvan, Jill. 2001. "Class Ghosting 'In the Cage.'" *Henry James Review* 22:3 (Fall): 297–306.

Gilbert, Sandra and Susan Gubar. 1988. *No Man's Land: The Place of the Woman Writer in the Twentieth Century*. 2 vols. New Haven, CT: Yale University Press.

Giles, Paul. 2003. "Deterritorialization in The Sacred Fount." *Henry James Review* 24.3 (Fall): 225–32.

Goble, Mark. 2007. "Wired Love: Pleasure at a Distance in Henry James and Others." *ELH* 74.2: 397–427.

Godzich, Wlad. 1986. "Foreword." In *Heterologies Discourse on the Other*, by Michel de Certeau, translated by Brian Massumi, vii–xxi. Minneapolis: University of Minnesota Press.

Gordon, Paul. 2008. *Dial "M" for Mother: A Freudian Hitchcock*. Madison, NJ: Fairleigh Dickinson University Press.

Gottlieb, Sidney, ed. 1995. *Hitchcock on Hitchcock*. Berkeley: University of California Press.

———. 2003. *Alfred Hitchcock Interviews*. Oxford, MS: University of Mississippi Press.

Graham, Wendy. 1999. *Henry James's Thwarted Love*. Palo Alto, CA: Stanford University Press.

Gregory, Melissa Valiska. 2004. "From Melodrama to Monologue: Henry James and Domestic Terror." *Henry James Review* 25.2 (Spring): 146–67.

Griffin, Susan M. 1989. "The Jamesian Body: Two Oral Tales," *Victorians Institute Journal* 17: 125–39.

———, ed. 2001. *Henry James Goes to the Movies*. Lexington: University Press of Kentucky.

———, ed. 2003. "Global James." *Henry James Review* 24.3 (Fall).

Gunter, Susan and Steven Jobe, eds. 2004. *Dearly Beloved Friends: Henry James's Letters to Younger Men*. Ann Arbor: University of Michigan Press.

Hannah, Daniel. 2007. "'Massed Ambiguity: Fatness in Henry James's *The Ivory Tower*." *Twentieth-Century Literature*. 53.4 (Winter): 460–88.

Harris, Richard A. and Michael S. Lasky. 2000. *The Complete Films of Alfred Hitchcock*. Revised ed. NY: Citadel Press.

Hendershot, Cyndy. 2001. "The Cold War Horror Film: Taboo and Transgression in *The Bad Seed*, *The Fly*, and *Psycho*." *Journal of Popular Film and Television* 29.1: 20–31.

"Henry James in the Ivory Tower," 1918. *The Nation*, Feb. 28: 237–39.

Historic London Database. Available at http://www.abc-directory.com/site/4317351.

Hitchcock, Alfred. 1965, 1995. "After-Dinner Speech at the Screen Producers Guild Dinner." In *Hitchcock on Hitchcock*, edited by Sidney Gottlieb, 54–8. Berkeley: University of California Press.

Holland, Laurence B. 1964. *The Expense of Vision: Essays on the Craft of Henry James*. Princeton, NJ: Princeton University Press.

Hollinghurst, Alan. 2004. *The Line of Beauty*. New York: Bloomsbury.

Honeyman, Susan E. 2001. "*What Maisie Knew* and the Impossible Representation of Childhood." *Henry James Review* 22.1 (Winter): 67–80.

Hsu, Hsuan. 2003. "Post-American James and the Question of Scale." *The Henry James Review* 24.3 (Fall): 233–43.

Husserl, Edmund. 1989. *Ideas Pertaining to a Pure Phenomenology and to a Phenomenological Philosophy, Second Book*, translated by R. Rojcewicz and A. Schuwer. Amsterdam: Kluwer Press.

Irigaray, Luce. 1975. "This Sex Which Is Not One." *This Sex Which Is Not One*, translated by Catherine Porter, 23–33. Ithaca, NY: Cornell University Press.

Iser, Wolfgang. 1980. *The Act of Reading: A Theory of Aesthetic Response*. Baltimore, MD: Johns Hopkins University Press.

Jacobs, Steven. 2007. *The Wrong House: The Architecture of Alfred Hitchcock*. Rotterdam, The Netherlands: 010 Publishers.

James, Henry. 1877, 1907. *The American*. New York: Charles Scribner's Sons.

———. 1878, 1996. *Daisy Miller: A Study*. In *Henry James: Complete Stories: 1874–1884*, 238–295. New York: Library of America.

———. 1878, 1996a. "An International Episode." In *Henry James: Complete Stories: 1874–1884*, 326–400. New York: Library of America.

———. 1879, 1901. *Hawthorne*. New York: Harper and Brothers.

———. 1881, 1981. *The Portrait of a Lady*. Oxford: Oxford University Press.

———. 1881, 1909. *The Portrait of a Lady*. Vol. 3 of *The New York Edition*, New York: Scribner's.

———. 1881, 1950. *Washington Square*. New York: Modern Library.

———. 1881, 1986. *The Portrait of a Lady*, edited and introduction by Geoffrey Moore. New York: Penguin.———. 1881, 1985. *Washington Square*. In *Novels 1881–1886*. Washington Square, The Portrait of a Lady, The Bostonians. New York: Library of America.

———. 1884, 1986. "The Art of Fiction." *The Art of Criticism: Henry James on the Theory and Practice of Criticism*, edited by William Veeder and Susan M. Griffin, 165–83. Chicago: University of Chicago Press.

———. 1886, 1985. *The Bostonians*. In *Novels 1881–1886*. Washington Square, The Portrait of a Lady, The Bostonians. New York: Library of America.

———. 1892, 1996a. "Greville Fane." In *Henry James: Complete Stories: 1892–1898*, 217–233. New York: Library of America.

———. 1892, 1996b. "The Private Life." In *Henry James: Complete Stories: 1892–1898*, 58–91. New York: Library of America.

———. 1892, 1996c. "The Real Thing." In *Henry James: Complete Stories: 1892–1898*, 32–57. New York: Library of America.

———. 1895, 1960. *Guy Domville:* A *Play in Three Acts*. Philadelphia, PA: J.B. Lippincott Company.

———. 1896, 1996. "The Figure in the Carpet." In *Henry James: Complete Stories: 1892–1898*, 572–608. New York: Library of America.

———. 1897, 2003. *What Maisie Knew*. In *Novels 1896–1899:* The Other House /The Spoils of Poynton /What Maisie Knew /The Awkward Age, edited by Myra Jehlen. New York: Library of America.

———. 1898, 1908. "In the Cage." In *In the Cage, The Novels and Tales of Henry James*, New York Edition, 26 vols. vol. XI. New York: Charles Scribner's Sons.

———. 1898, 1969. "In the Cage." In *In the Cage and Other Tales*, 174–266. New York: Norton.

———. 1898, 1972. "In the Cage." In *In the Cage and Other Stories*. New York: Vintage.

———. 1898, 1995. *The Turn of the Screw*. Ed. Peter G. Beidler. Boston, MA: Bedford.

———. 1899, 1984. *The Awkward Age*. Oxford: Oxford University Press.

———. 1901, 2006. *The Sacred Fount*. In *Novels 1901–1902*. The Sacred Fount. The Wings of the Dove, edited by Leo Bersani. New York: Library of America.

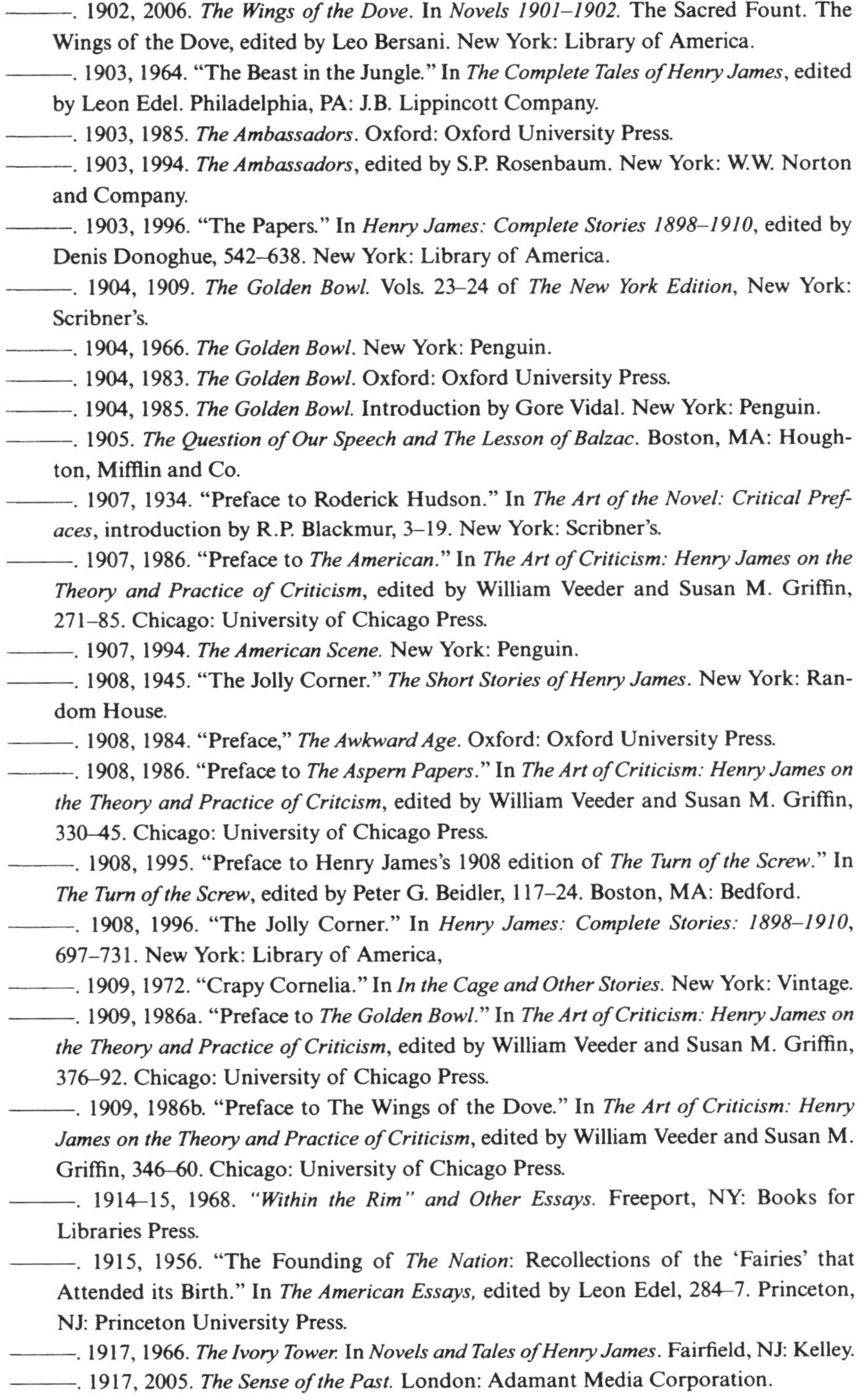

———. 1902, 2006. *The Wings of the Dove*. In *Novels 1901–1902*. The Sacred Fount. The Wings of the Dove, edited by Leo Bersani. New York: Library of America.

———. 1903, 1964. "The Beast in the Jungle." In *The Complete Tales of Henry James*, edited by Leon Edel. Philadelphia, PA: J.B. Lippincott Company.

———. 1903, 1985. *The Ambassadors*. Oxford: Oxford University Press.

———. 1903, 1994. *The Ambassadors*, edited by S.P. Rosenbaum. New York: W.W. Norton and Company.

———. 1903, 1996. "The Papers." In *Henry James: Complete Stories 1898–1910*, edited by Denis Donoghue, 542–638. New York: Library of America.

———. 1904, 1909. *The Golden Bowl*. Vols. 23–24 of *The New York Edition*, New York: Scribner's.

———. 1904, 1966. *The Golden Bowl*. New York: Penguin.

———. 1904, 1983. *The Golden Bowl*. Oxford: Oxford University Press.

———. 1904, 1985. *The Golden Bowl*. Introduction by Gore Vidal. New York: Penguin.

———. 1905. *The Question of Our Speech and The Lesson of Balzac*. Boston, MA: Houghton, Mifflin and Co.

———. 1907, 1934. "Preface to Roderick Hudson." In *The Art of the Novel: Critical Prefaces*, introduction by R.P. Blackmur, 3–19. New York: Scribner's.

———. 1907, 1986. "Preface to *The American*." In *The Art of Criticism: Henry James on the Theory and Practice of Criticism*, edited by William Veeder and Susan M. Griffin, 271–85. Chicago: University of Chicago Press.

———. 1907, 1994. *The American Scene*. New York: Penguin.

———. 1908, 1945. "The Jolly Corner." *The Short Stories of Henry James*. New York: Random House.

———. 1908, 1984. "Preface," *The Awkward Age*. Oxford: Oxford University Press.

———. 1908, 1986. "Preface to *The Aspern Papers*." In *The Art of Criticism: Henry James on the Theory and Practice of Critcism*, edited by William Veeder and Susan M. Griffin, 330–45. Chicago: University of Chicago Press.

———. 1908, 1995. "Preface to Henry James's 1908 edition of *The Turn of the Screw*." In *The Turn of the Screw*, edited by Peter G. Beidler, 117–24. Boston, MA: Bedford.

———. 1908, 1996. "The Jolly Corner." In *Henry James: Complete Stories: 1898–1910*, 697–731. New York: Library of America,

———. 1909, 1972. "Crapy Cornelia." In *In the Cage and Other Stories*. New York: Vintage.

———. 1909, 1986a. "Preface to *The Golden Bowl*." In *The Art of Criticism: Henry James on the Theory and Practice of Criticism*, edited by William Veeder and Susan M. Griffin, 376–92. Chicago: University of Chicago Press.

———. 1909, 1986b. "Preface to The Wings of the Dove." In *The Art of Criticism: Henry James on the Theory and Practice of Criticism*, edited by William Veeder and Susan M. Griffin, 346–60. Chicago: University of Chicago Press.

———. 1914–15, 1968. *"Within the Rim" and Other Essays*. Freeport, NY: Books for Libraries Press.

———. 1915, 1956. "The Founding of *The Nation*: Recollections of the 'Fairies' that Attended its Birth." In *The American Essays*, edited by Leon Edel, 284–7. Princeton, NJ: Princeton University Press.

———. 1917, 1966. *The Ivory Tower*. In *Novels and Tales of Henry James*. Fairfield, NJ: Kelley.

———. 1917, 2005. *The Sense of the Past*. London: Adamant Media Corporation.

———. 1945. *The Short Stories of Henry James*, edited by Clifton Fadiman. New York: Modern Library.

———. 1975. *Henry James Letters: Volume II, 1875–1883*, edited by Leon Edel. Cambridge, MA: Harvard University Press.

———. 1983. *Henry James: Autobiography*, edited by Frederick Dupee. Princeton, NJ: Princeton University Press.

———. 1984. *Henry James: Literary Criticism French Writers; Other European Writers; The Prefaces to the New York Edition*, Vol. 2 of *Literary Criticism*, edited by Leon Edel. New York: Library of America.

———. 1986. *The Art of Criticism: Henry James on the Theory and Practice of Criticism*, edited by William Veeder and Susan M. Griffin. Chicago: University of Chicago Press.

———. 1987. *The Complete Notebooks of Henry James*, edited by Leon Edel and Lyall H. Powers. New York: Oxford University Press.

———. 2009. *Complete Letters: 1872–1876*, edited by Peter Walker and Greg Zacharias. Omaha: University of Nebraska Press.

Jameson, Fredrick. 1992. *Signatures of the Visible*. New York: Routledge.

Jay, Martin. 1994. *Downcast Eyes: The Denigration of Vision in Twentieth-Century French Thought*. Berkeley: University of California Press.

Johnson, Barbara. 1980. "Melville's Fist: The Execution of Billy Budd." In *The Critical Difference: Essays in the Contemporary Rhetoric of Reading*, 79–109. Baltimore, MD: Johns Hopkins University Press.

Johnson, Warren. 1988. "Parable, Secrecy, and the Form of Fiction: The Example of 'The Figure in the Carpet' and 'The Portrait of a Lady.'" *Journal of English and Germanic Philology*, 87 (April): 230–50.

Joyce, Simon. 2007. *The Victorians in the Rearview Mirror.* Athens: Ohio University Press.

Kenner, Hugh. 1971. *The Pound Era*. Berkeley: University of California Press.

Knapp, Lucretia. 1993. "The Queer Voice in Marnie." *Cinema Journal* 32.4 (Summer): 6–23.

Krook, Dorothea. 1968. *The Ordeal of Consciousness in Henry James*. Cambridge: Cambridge University Press.

Kucich, John. 1987. *Repression in Victorian Fiction: Charlotte Brontë, George Eliot, and Charles Dickens*. Berkeley: University of California Press.

Kucich, John and Dianne F. Sadoff, eds. 2000. *Victorian Afterlife: Postmodern Culture Rewrites the Nineteenth Century.* Minneapolis: University of Minnesota Press.

Lacan, Jacques. 1955–6, 1993. *The Seminar. Book III. The Psychoses, 1955–56*, translated by Russell Grigg. London: Routledge.

———. 1975–6, 2005. *Le sinthome, 1975–76*, edited by Jacques-Alain Miller. Paris: Éditions du Seuil.

Lebowitz, Naomi. 1963. *The Imagination of Loving: Henry James's Legacy to the Novel*. Detroit, MI: Wayne State University Press.

Lee, Benjamin and Edward LiPuma. 2002. "Cultures of Circulation: The Imaginations of Modernity." *Public Culture* 14.1: 191–213.

Lefebvre, Henri. 1995. *Introduction to Modernity*. London: Verso.

Leff, Leonard. 1987. *Hitchcock and Selznick*. Berkeley: University of California Press.

Leitch, Thomas M. 1991. *Find the Director and Other Hitchcock Games*. Athens: University of Georgia Press.

Levy, Leo. 1962. "A Reading of 'The Figure in the Carpet.'" *American Literature* 33.4: 457–65.

Lockwood, Preston. 1915. "Henry James's First Interview; Noted Critic and Novelist Breaks His Rule of Years to Tell of the Good Work of the American Ambulance Corps." *New York Times*. March 21: SM3.

Lubbock, Percy. 1957. *The Craft of Fiction*. New York: Viking Press.

Luhmann, Niklas. 1998. *Love as Passion: The Codification of Intimacy*, translated by Jeremy Gaines and Doris L. Jones. Palo Alto, CA: Stanford University Press.

Lukács, Georg. 1972. *History and Class Consciousness: Studies in Marxist Dialectics*, translated by Rodney Livingstone. Cambridge, MA: MIT Press.

Mabee, Carleton. 1969. *The American Leonardo: A Life of Samuel F.B. Morse*. New York: Octagon Books.

Malcolm, Janet. 1995. *The Silent Woman: Sylvia Plath and Ted Hughes*. New York: Vintage Books.

Manlove, Clifford. 2007. "Visual 'Drive' and Cinematic Narrative: Reading Gaze Theory in Lacan, Hitchcock, and Mulvey." *Cinema Journal* 46.3: 83–108.

Mannoni, Octave. 1969. *Clefs pour l'imaginaire ou l'Autre Scene*. Paris: Éditions du Seuil.

Martin, Michael R. 2003. "Branding Milly Theale: The Capital Case of *The Wings of the Dove*." *Henry James Review* 24: 2 (Spring): 103–32.

Mason, Michael. 1994. *The Making of Victorian Sexuality*. New York: Oxford University Press.

Matheson, Neill. 1999. "Talking Horrors: James, Euphemism, and the Specter of Wilde." *American Literature* 71.4: 709–50.

McCarron, Gary. 2008. "Undecided Stories: Alfred Hitchcock's *Blackmail* and the Problem of Moral Agency." *Canadian Journal of Communication* 33: 65–80.

McDougal, Stuart. 1998. "The Director Who Knew Too Much: Hitchcock Remakes Himself." In *Play It Again, Sam: Retakes on Remakes*, edited by Andrew Horton and Stuart Y. McDougal, 52–69. Berkeley: University of California Press.

McHale, Brian. 1987. *Postmodernist Fiction*. New York: Routledge.

McGilligan, Patrick. 2004. *Alfred Hitchcock: A Life in Darkness and Light*. New York: Harper Perennial.

McWhirter, David. 1989. *Desire and Love in Henry James: A Study of the Late Novels*. Cambridge: Cambridge University Press.

———. 1998. *Henry James's New York Edition: The Construction of Authorship* Palo Alto, CA: Stanford University Press.

Menke, Richard. 2008. *Telegraphic Realism: Victorian Fiction and Other Information Systems*. Palo Alto, CA: Stanford University Press.

Merleau-Ponty, Maurice. 1962. *The Phenomenology of Perception*, translated by Colin Smith. New York: Humanities Press.

———. 1969. *The Visible and the Invisible*, translated by Alphonso Lingis. Evanston, IL: Northwestern University Press.

Michie, Elsie. 1999. "Unveiling Maternal Desires: Hitchcock and American Domesticity." In *Hitchcock's America*, edited by Jonathan Freedman and Richard Millington. New York: Oxford University Press.

Millar, Delia. 2001. "Royal Patronage and Influence." In *The Victorian Vision: Inventing New Britain*, edited by John M. Mackenzie, 27–49. London: V&A Publications.

Miller, D.A. 1989. *The Novel and the Police*. Berkeley: University of California Press.

Miller, J. Hillis. 1980. "'The Figure in the Carpet.'" *Poetics Today* 1:3: 107–18.

———. 2005. *Literature as Conduct. Speech Acts in Henry James*. New York: Fordham University Press.

Modleski, Tania. 1989. *The Women Who Knew Too Much: Hitchcock and Feminist Theory.* New York: Routledge, Chapman and Hall, Inc.

———. 2005. *The Women Who Knew Too Much: Hitchcock and Feminist Theory.* Second edition. New York: Routledge.

Moon, Michael. 1998. *A Small Boy and Others*. Durham, NC: Duke University Press.

Moral, Tony Lee. 2005. *Hitchcock and the Making of Marnie*. Lanham, MD: Scarecrow.

"Mr. James A British Citizen." 1915. *New York Times*, July 29: 8.

Mulvey, Laura. 1975. "Visual Pleasure and Narrative Cinema." *Screen* 16.3: 6–18.

Nadel, Alan. 1995. *Containment Culture: American Narratives, Postmodernism, and the Atomic Age*. Durham, NC: Duke University Press.

———. 2002. "Ambassadors from an Imaginary 'Elsewhere': Cinematic Convention and the Jamesian Sensibility." In *Henry James Goes to the Movies*, edited by Susan M. Griffin, 193–209. Lexington: University Press of Kentucky.

Nancy, Jean-Luc. 2008. *Corpus*, translated by Richard Rand. New York: Fordham University Press.

Nardin, Jane. 1978. "The Turn of the Screw: The Victorian Background." *Mosaic* 12.1: 131–42.

Nitpickers, "Top Ten Nitpicked Movies." Accessed through http://www.nitpickers.com/movies/repository.cgi?pg=top, July 11, 2009.

Norrman, Ralf. 1977. "The Intercepted Telegraph Plot in Henry James' *In the Cage*." *Notes and Queries* 24 (October): 425.

Novick, Sheldon. 1996, 2007. *Henry James*. 2 vols. New York: Random House.

Ohi, Kevin. 2004. "Narrating the Child's Queerness in *What Maisie Knew*." In *Curiouser: On the Queerness of Children*, edited by Steven Bruhm and Natasha Hurley, 81–106. Minneapolis: University of Minnesota Press.

Otten, Thomas J. *A*. 2006. *Superficial Reading of Henry James: Preoccupations with the Material World.* Columbus: Ohio State University Press.

Parrington, Vernon. 1927. *Main Currents in American Thought*. New York: Harcourt Brace.

Paterson, Mark. 2007. *The Senses of Touch: Haptics, Affects and Technologies*. London: Berg.

Perry, Ralph Barton. 1974. *The Thought and Character of William James: As Revealed in Unpublished Correspondence and Notes, Together with his Published Writings*. Vol. 1, Westport, CT: Greenwood Press.

Peters, John Durham. 1999. *Speaking into the Air: A History of the Idea of Communication.* Chicago: University of Chicago Press.

Popova, Yanna. 2002. "The Figure in the Carpet: Discovery of Re-cognition." In *Cognitive Stylistics: Language and Cognition in Text Analysis*, edited by Elena Semino and Jonathan Culpeper, 49–72. Amsterdam: John Benjamins Publishing Co.

Porter, Carolyn. 1981. *Seeing and Being: The Plight of the Participant Observer in Emerson, James, Adams and Faulkner*. Middletown, CT: Wesleyan University Press.

Povinelli, Elizabeth, and Dilip Parameshwar Gaonkar. 2003. "Technologies of Public Forms: Circulation, Transfiguration, Recognition." *Public Culture* 15.3: 385–97.

Promotional Poster. 1974. *Caged Heat.* Accessed through http://en.wikipedia.org/wiki/Caged_Heat.

Przybylowicz, Donna. 1986. *Desire and Repression: The Dialectic of Self and Other in the Late Works of Henry James*. Tuscaloosa: University of Alabama Press.

Raubicheck, Walter. 2002–2003. "Working with Hitchcock: A Collaborators' Forum with Patricia Hitchcock, Janet Leigh, Teresa Wright, and Eva Marie Saint." *Hitchcock Annual* 11: 32–66.

Renner, Stanley. 1995. "'Red hair, very red, close-curling': Sexual Hysteria, Physiognomical Bogeymen, and the 'Ghosts' in The Turn of the Screw." In *The Turn of the Screw*, edited by Peter G. Beidler, 223–41. Boston: Bedford St. Martin's Press.

Rimmon, Shlomith. 1977. *The Concept of Ambiguity: The Example of James*. Chicago: University of Chicago Press.

Rimmon-Kenan, Shlomith. 1980–81. "Deconstructive Reflections on Deconstruction: In Reply to Hillis Miller." *Poetics Today* 2:1b: 185–8.

Rivière, Joan. 1929. "Womanliness as Masquerade." *International Journal of Psychoanalysis* 10: 303–13.

Rivkin, Julie. 1986. "The Logic of Delegation in *The Ambassadors*." *PMLA* 101.5: 819–831.

———. 1996. *False Positions: The Representational Logics of Henry James's Fiction*. Palo Alto, CA: Stanford University Press.

Rohmer, Eric and Claude Chabrol. 1979. *Hitchcock: The First Forty-Four Films*, translated by Stanley Hochman. New York: Ungar Publishing Co.

Roof, Judith. 2002. *All about Thelma and Eve: Sidekicks and Third Wheels*. Urbana: University of Illinois Press.

Rosenbladt, Bettina. 2004. "Doubles and Doubts in Hitchcock: The German Connection." In *Hitchcock: Past and Future*, edited by Richard Allen and Sam Ishii-Gonzales, 37–63. New York: Routledge.

Rothman, William. 1984. *Hitchcock's Murderous Gaze*. Cambridge, MA: Harvard University Press.

Rowe, John Carlos. 1998a. *The Other Henry James*. Durham, NC: Duke University Press.

———. 1998b. "The Use and Abuse of Uncertainty in *The Turn of the Screw*." In *The Turn of the Screw and What Maisie Knew*, edited by Neil Cornwell and Maggie Malone, 54–78. New York: St. Martin's.

———. 2002. *The New American Studies*. Minneapolis: University of Minnesota Press.

———. 2003. "Henry James and Globalization." *Henry James Review* 23.3: 205–14.

Salmon, Rachel. 1980. "A Marriage of Opposites: Henry James's 'The Figure in the Carpet' and the Problem of Ambiguity." *ELH* 47.4 (Winter): 788–803.

Salmon, Richard. 1997. *Henry James and the Culture of Publicity*. Cambridge: Cambridge University Press.

Samuels, Robert. 1998. *Hitchcock's Bi-Textuality: Lacan, Feminisms, and Queer Theory*. New York: SUNY Press.

Savoy, Eric. 1999. "Embarrassments: Figure in the Closet," *Henry James Review* 20.3 (Fall): 227–36.

———. 2001. "The Jamesian Thing." *Henry James Review* 22.3 (Fall): 268–77.

Scheiber, Andrew J. 1996. "The Doctor's Order: Eugenic Anxiety in Henry James's *Washington Square.*" *Literature and Medicine*, 15.2: 244–62.

Schneidau, Herbert N. 1977. *Sacred Discontent: The Bible and Western Tradition*. Berkeley: University of California Press.

Sedgwick, Eve Kosofsky. 2003. "Shame, Theatricality, and Queer Performativity: Henry James's *The Art of the Novel.*" In *Touching Feeling: Affect, Pedagogy, Performativity*, 67–92. Durham, NC: Duke University Press.

Seltzer, Mark. 1984. *Henry James and the Art of Power*. Ithaca, NY: Cornell University Press.

———. 1992. *Bodies and Machines*, New York: Routledge.

———. 2000. "The Postal Unconscious," *Henry James Review* 21.3 (Fall): 197–206.

Serres, Michael. 2009. *The Five Senses: A Philosophy of Mingled Bodies*, translated by Margaret Sankey and Peter Cowley. London: Continuum.

Sicker, Philip. 1980. *Love and the Quest for Identity in the Novels of Henry James*. Princeton, NJ: Princeton University Press.

Silverman, Kaja. 1983. *The Subject of Semiotics*. New York: Oxford University Press.

———. 1986. "Suture [Excerpts]." *Narrative, Apparatus, Ideology: A Film Theory Reader*, edited by Philip Rosen, 219–35. New York: Columbia University Press.

———. 1988a. *The Acoustic Mirror: The Female Voice in Psychoanalysis and Cinema.* Bloomington: Indiana University Press.

———. 1988b. "Too Early/Too Late: Subjectivity and the Primal Scene in Henry James." *Novel* 21.2–3: 147–73.

Sipière, Dominique. 1996. "*Marnie* et l'education du regard masculin." *Cycnos* 13.1: 23–33.

Smith, Allan Lloyd. 2002. "*Marnie*, the Dead Mother, and the Phantom." *Hitchcock Annual*: 164–80.

Smith, George. 2009. "The Late Phase: Henry James and the Psycho-Painterly Style." *Henry James Review* 30: 62–76.

Spigel, Lynn. 1992. *Make Room for TV: Television and the Family Ideal in Postwar America.* Chicago: University of Chicago Press.

Spoto, Donald. 1979. *The Art of Alfred Hitchcock*. Second Edition. New York: Doubleday.

———. 1983. *The Dark Side of Genius: The Life of Alfred Hitchcock.* Boston, MA: Little, Brown.

———. 2008. *Spellbound by Beauty: Alfred Hitchcock and his Leading Ladies*. New York: Crown.

Stevens, Hugh. 1998. *Henry James and Sexuality*. Cambridge: Cambridge University Press.

Strauss, Marc. 2007. "The painted jester: notes on the visual arts in Hitchcock's films." *Journal of Popular Film and Television* 35: 2 (Summer): 52–56.

Tanner, Tony. 1979. *Adultery in the Novel: Contract and Transgression*. Baltimore, MD: Johns Hopkins University Press.

Taylor, John Russell. 1978. *Hitch: The Life and Times of Alfred Hitchcock.* London: Faber and Faber.

Telotte, J.P. 2001. "The Sounds of *Blackmail*. Hitchcock and Sound Aesthetic." *Journal of Popular Film and Television* 28: 4 (Winter): 184–91.

Thurschwell, Pamela. 2001. *Literature, Technology and Magical Thinking*. Cambridge: Cambridge University Press.

Tintner, Adeline. 1982. "Hiding Behind James: Roth's Zuckerman Unbound." *Midstream* 28 (April): 121–53.

Todorov, Tzvetan. 1977. "The Verbal Age," translated by Patricia Martin Gilroy. *Critical Inquiry* 4.2 (Winter): 351–71.

Toibin, Colm. 2009. "A Bundle of Letters." *Henry James Review* 30.3 (Fall): 272–84.

Toles, George. 1999. "'If Thine Eye Offend Thee . . .': *Psycho* and the Art of Infection." In *Alfred Hitchcock: Centenary Essays*, edited by Richard Allen and S. Ishii-Gonzalès, 159–74. London: British Film Institute.

Trachtenberg, Alan. 2004. *Shades of Hiawatha: Staging Indians, Making Americans, 1880–1930*. New York: Hill & Wang.

Trask, Michael. 1997. "Getting into it with James: Substitution and Erotic Reversal in *The Awkward Age*." *American Literature* 69.1 (March): 105–38.

Truffaut, François. 1967. *Hitchcock*. London: Secker & Warburg.

Truffaut, François with Helen G. Scott. 1985. *Hitchcock*. Revised Edition. New York: Simon & Schuster.

Van Slyck, Phyllis. 2005. "Charting an Ethics of Desire in *The Wings of the Dove*." *Criticism* 47: 3 (Summer): 301–23.

Walker, Pierre, ed. 2004. *Henry James on Culture: Collected Essays on Politics and the American Social Scene*. Lincoln: University of Nebraska Press.

Weis, Elisabeth, and John Belton, eds. 1985. *Film Sound Theory and Practice*. New York: Columbia University Press.

Wells, H.G. 1915. *Boon* . . . London: T. Fisher Unwin, Ltd.

Welsh, Alexander. 1985. *George Eliot and Blackmail*. Cambridge, MA: Harvard University Press.

Westbrook, Perry. 1953. "The Supersubtle Fry." *Nineteenth-Century Fiction* 8.2 (September): 134–40.

White, Robert. 1992. "*The Figure in the Carpet* of James's Temple of Delight." *Henry James Review* 13.1 (Winter): 27–49.

Wicke, Jennifer. 1989. "Henry James's Second Wave," *Henry James Review* 10.2 (Spring): 146–51.

Williams, Linda. 1996. "When the Woman Looks." In *The Dread of Difference: Gender and the Horror Film*, edited by Barry Keith Grant, 15–34. Austin: University of Texas Press.

———. 2000. "Discipline and Fun: Psycho and Postmodern Cinema." In *Reinventing Film Studies*, edited by Christine Gledhill and Linda Williams, 351–78. London: Arnold.

Williams, M.A. 1984. "Reading '*The Figure in the Carpet*'": Henry James and Wolfgang Iser." *English Studies in Africa* 27. 2: 107–12.

Williams, Tony. 2007. "Alfred Hitchcock and John Buchan: The Art of Creative Transformation," *Senses of Cinema* 43. Accessed through http://www.sensesofcinema.com/2007/43/hitchcock-john-buchan/.

Wilson, Edmund. 1934, 1999. "The Ambiguity of Henry James." In *The Turn of the Screw*, edited by Deborah Esch and Jonathan Warren, Second Edition, 170–3. New York: Norton.

Wood, Robin. 1969. *Hitchcock's Films*. New York: Barnes and Noble.

———. 1989. *Hitchcock's Films Revisited*. New York: Columbia University Press.

———. 2002. *Hitchcock's Films Revisited*. New York: Columbia University Press.

Wyschogrod, Edith. 2003. "Towards a Postmodern Ethics: Corporeality and Alterity." In The *Ethical*, edited by Edith Wyschogrod and Gerald McKenny, 54–66. New York: Wiley-Blackwell.

Yeazell, Ruth Bernard. 1976. *Language and Knowledge in the Late Novels of Henry James*. Chicago: University of Chicago Press.

Žižek, Slavoj. 1991. *Looking Awry: An Introduction to Jacques Lacan Through Popular Culture*. Cambridge, MA: MIT Press.

———. 1992. "In His Bold Gaze My Ruin is Writ Large." In *Everything You Always Wanted to Know About Lacan But Were Afraid to Ask Hitchcock*, edited by Slavoj Žižek, 211–71. London: Verso.

———. 1999. *The Ticklish Subject: The Absent Centre of Political Ontology*. London: Verso.

———. 2006. *The Parallax View*. Cambridge, MA: MIT Press.

Zwinger, Linda, ed. 2006. "Seeing James Seeing." *Arizona Quarterly* 62:3 (Autumn).

FILMOGRAPHY

Aventure Malgache, 1944. Directed by Alfred Hitchcock, Ministry of Information.

The Birds, 1963. Directed by Alfred Hitchcock, Alfred J. Hitchcock Productions, Universal Pictures.

Blackmail, 1929. Directed by Alfred Hitchcock, British International Pictures.

Blow-Up, 1966. Directed by Michelango Antonioni, Bridge Films.

Blue Velvet, 1986. Directed by David Lynch, De Laurentiis Entertainment Group.

Bon Voyage, 1944. Directed by Alfred Hitchcock, Ministry of Information.

Caged Heat, 1974. Directed by Jonathan Demme, New World Pictures.

Dial M for Murder, 1954. Directed by Alfred Hitchcock, Warner Bros. Pictures.

Frenzy, 1972. Directed by Alfred Hitchcock, Universal Pictures.

I Confess, 1953. Directed by Alfred Hitchcock, Warner Bros. Pictures.

It's a Wonderful Life, 1946. Directed by Frank Capra, Liberty Films.

Jamaica Inn, 1939. Directed by Alfred Hitchcock, Mayflower Pictures Corporation.

The Lady Vanishes, 1938. Directed by Alfred Hitchcock, Gainsborough Pictures.

Lifeboat, 1944. Directed by Alfred Hitchcock, Twentieth Century Fox.

The Lodger: A Story of the London Fog, 1927. Directed by Alfred Hitchcock, Gainsborough Pictures.

The Man Who Knew Too Much, 1934. Directed by Alfred Hitchcock, Gaumont British Pictures.

The Man Who Knew Too Much, 1956. Directed by Alfred Hitchcock, Paramount Pictures.

Marnie, 1964. Directed by Alfred Hitchcock, Universal Pictures.

North by Northwest, 1959. Directed by Alfred Hitchcock, MGM.

Notorious, 1946. Directed by Alfred Hitchcock, RKO.

The Pleasure Garden, 1925. Directed by Alfred Hitchcock, Gainsborough Pictures.

"Promotional Trailer" for *Psycho*. 1960. Directed by Alfred Hitchcock, Universal Pictures. DVD.

Psycho, 1960. Directed by Alfred Hitchcock, Universal Pictures.

Psycho, 1998. Directed by Gus Van Sant, Universal Pictures.

Rear Window, 1954. Directed by Alfred Hitchcock, Paramount Pictures.

Rebecca, 1940. Directed by Alfred Hitchcock, Selznick International Pictures.

Rope, 1948. Directed by Alfred Hitchcock, Transatlantic Pictures.

Sabotage, 1936. Directed by Alfred Hitchcock, Gaumont British Picture Corporation.

Saboteur, 1942. Directed by Alfred Hitchcock, Frank Lloyd Productions, Universal Pictures.

Secret Agent, 1936. Directed by Alfred Hitchcock, Gaumont British Picture Corporation.

Shadow of a Doubt, 1943. Directed by Alfred Hitchcock, Skirball Productions, Universal Pictures.

"Sonata da Oz." 2003. *Oz*. HBO. Season 6, episode 3. January 19, 2003. Television.

The Sound of Music, 1965. Directed by Robert Wise, Robert Wise Productions, Twentieth Century Fox.

Spellbound, 1945. Directed by Alfred Hitchcock, Selznick International Pictures.

Stage Fright, 1950. Directed by Alfred Hitchcock, Warner Bros. Pictures.

Strangers on a Train, 1951. Directed by Alfred Hitchcock, Warner Bros. Pictures.

Suspicion, 1941. Directed by Alfred Hitchcock, RKO.

The 39 Steps, 1935. Directed by Alfred Hitchcock, Gaumont British Pictures.

To Catch a Thief, 1955. Directed by Alfred Hitchcock, Paramount Pictures.

Under Capricorn, 1949. Directed by Alfred Hitchcock, Transatlantic Pictures.

Vertigo, 1958. Directed by Alfred Hitchcock, Alfred J. Hitchcock Productions, Paramount Pictures.

The Wrong Man, 1956. Directed by Alfred Hitchcock, Warner Bros. Pictures.

Young and Innocent, a.k.a. *The Girl Was Young*, 1937. Directed by Alfred Hitchcock, Gaumont British Pictures.

CONTRIBUTORS

Brenda Austin-Smith is Associate Professor of English and Film Studies at the University of Manitoba. She is co-editor of *The Gendered Screen: Canadian Women Filmmakers* (Wilfrid Laurier UP, 2010). Her essays on James or on film have appeared in: *The Canadian Review of American Studies*, *Post-Script*, *American Studies*, *Henry James Review*, *Senses of Cinema*, *Cinephile*, and several edited books. She is currently studying women, weeping, and cinema memory.

Aviva Briefel is Associate Professor of English at Bowdoin College. She is the author of *The Deceivers: Art Forgery and Identity in the Nineteenth Century* (Cornell UP, 2006) and co-editor of *Horror after 9/11: World of Fear, Cinema of Terror* (U of Texas P, 2011). She has published essays in scholarly journals including *Camera Obscura*, *Film Quarterly*, *Narrative*, *Novel*, *Victorian Literature and Culture*, and *Victorian Studies*. Her current book project is titled *Amputations: Race and the Hand at the Fin de Siècle.*

Thomas B. Byers is Professor of English, Director of the Commonwealth Center for the Humanities and Society, and Director of the Film Studies Minor at the University of Louisville. He is the author of *What I Cannot Say: Self, Word, and World in Whitman, Stevens, and Merwin* (U of Illinois P, 1989), and essays in *Contemporary Literature*, *Modern Fiction Studies*, *Cultural Critique*, *Arizona Quarterly*, *Modern Language Quarterly*, *Science Fiction Studies*, *zeitgeschichte*, *The Year's Work in Lebowski Studies* (Indiana UP), and other venues. For ten years he has directed the U.S. Department of State Institute on Contemporary American Literature.

Brian T. Edwards is Associate Professor of English and Comparative Literary Studies at Northwestern University. He is the author of *Morocco Bound: Disorienting America's Maghreb, from Casablanca to the Marrakech Express* (Duke UP, 2005), which includes a chapter on Hitchcock's *The Man Who Knew Too Much*, and co-editor of *Globalizing American Studies* (U of Chicago P, 2010). Edwards has published essays on Edith Wharton, Paul Bowles, Frantz Fanon, the encounter of American studies and postcolonial studies, contemporary Moroccan cinema, twenty-first century Egyptian literature, and other topics. His creative non-fiction has appeared in literary journals such as *The Believer*, *McSweeney's*, *Michigan Quarterly Review*, and *A Public Space*. His new book project, *After the American Century*, examines the circulation of American culture and its forms in contemporary North Africa and the Middle East.

Jonathan Freedman, Professor of English and American Studies at the University of Michigan, is the author of *Klezmer America: Jewishness, Ethnicity, Modernity* (Columbia UP, 2008), *The Temple of Culture: Assimilation and Anti-Semitism in Making of Literary Anglo-America* (Oxford UP, 2000), and *Professions of Taste: Henry James, British Aestheticism, and Commodity Culture* (Stanford UP, 1990). He is the editor or co-editor of *Jewish in America* (U of Michigan P, 2004), *Hitchcock's America* (Oxford UP, 1999), *The Cambridge Companion to Henry James* (Cambridge UP, 1998), and *Oscar Wilde: A Collection of Critical Essays* (Prentice Hall, 1995). His essays have appeared in many journals, including *American Literary History*, *Raritan*, *Henry James Review*, and *PMLA*.

Mark Goble, Associate Professor of English at the University of California-Berkeley, is the author of *Beautiful Circuits: Modernism and the Mediated Life* (Columbia UP, 2010). His essays have appeared in *American Literature*, *ELH*, *MLQ*, *Modern Fiction Studies*, and *Postmodern Culture*.

Susan M. Griffin is Professor and Chair of the Department of English at the University of Louisville, where she is a Distinguished University Scholar. She is the editor of the *Henry James Review* (Johns Hopkins UP) and author and editor of a number of books, including *"All a Novelist Needs": Colm Toibin on Henry James* (Johns Hopkins UP, 2010), *Anti-Catholicism and Nineteenth-Century Fiction* (Cambridge UP, 2004), and *Henry James Goes to the Movies* (UP of Kentucky, 2002).

Donatella Izzo is Professor of American Literature at Università "L'Orientale," Naples (Italy). Her work on Henry James includes four books (among them *Portraying the Lady: Technologies of Gender in the Short Stories of Henry James*, U of Nebraska P, 2001) and several essays contributed to journals and volumes (most recently, in *Henry James in Context*, ed. David McWhirter [Cambridge UP, 2010]). She is the author of other books and essays on English and American writers and the editor of volumes on questions of comparative literary theory, Asian American literature, and American studies. She served as President of AISNA, the Italian Association of American Studies, for the term 2004–7, and of the Henry James Society for 2011.

Alan Nadel, William T. Bryan Chair in American Literature and Culture at the University of Kentucky, is the author of *Invisible Criticism: Ralph Ellison and the American Canon* (Iowa UP, 1988), *Containment Culture: American Narratives, Postmodernism, and the Atomic Age* (Duke UP, 1995), *Flatlining on the Field of Dreams: Cultural Narratives in the Films of President Reagan's America* (Rutgers UP, 1997), and *Television in Black-and-White America: Race and National Identity* (Kansas UP, 2005), and he has edited two collections of essays on August Wilson: *May All Your Fences Have Gates* (Iowa UP, 1993) and *August Wilson: Completing the Twentieth-Century Cycle* (Iowa UP, 2010). His essays have appeared in numerous journals, including *American Drama*, *American Literary History*, *American Quarterly*, *boundary 2*, *Centennial Review*, *Contemporary Literature*, *College Literature*, *Com-*

parative American Studies, Georgia Review, Henry James Review, Film Quarterly, Journal of Postmodern Culture, and *Theater Magazine.* He won the 1988 prize for the best essay in *Modern Fiction Studies*, and his essay on deMille's *The Ten Commandments* won the 1993 prize for the best essay in *PMLA* (1993).

Patrick O'Donnell, Professor of English at Michigan State University, is the author of *The American Novel Now: Reading Contemporary American Fiction Since 1980* (Wiley-Blackwell, 2010), *Latent Destinies: Cultural Paranoia and Contemporary U.S. Narrative* (Duke UP, 2000), *Echo Chambers: Figuring Voice in Modern Narrative* (U of Iowa P, 1992), *Passionate Doubts: Designs of Interpretation in Contemporary American Fiction* (U of Iowa P, 1986), and *John Hawkes* (G.K. Hall, 1982). He is the editor of *New Essays on The Crying of Lot 49* (Cambridge UP, 1991) and co-editor of *Approaches to Teaching Faulkner's As I Lay Dying* (MLA, 2011), *The Encyclopedia of Modern American Fiction* (Wiley-Blackwell, 2010), and *Intertextuality and Contemporary American Fiction* (Johns Hopkins UP, 1989). His work in progress includes *A Temporary Future: The Fiction of David Mitchell* (forthcoming from Continuum) and a book on Henry James and modern/contemporary cinema.

Mary Ann O'Farrell, Associate Professor of English at Texas A & M University, is the author of *Telling Complexions: The Nineteenth-Century English Novel and the Blush* (Duke UP, 1997), which received a *Choice* Outstanding Academic Book citation, and co-editor of *Virtual Gender: Fantasies of Subjectivity and Embodiment* (U of Michigan P, 1999). She is completing a book about appearances of Jane Austen in contemporary popular culture. A recent essay about blindness in Victorian literature is forthcoming from *PMLA*.

Judith Roof is the William Shakespeare Chair in English at Rice University. She is the author of *A Lure of Knowledge: Lesbian Sexuality and Theory* (Columbia UP, 1991), *Reproductions of Reproduction: Imaging Symbolic Change* (Routledge, 1996), *Come as You Are* (Columbia UP, 1996), *All about Thelma and Eve: Sidekicks and Third Wheels* (U of Illinois P, 2002), and *The Poetics of DNA* (U of Minnesota P, 2007). She is co-editor of *Who Can Speak? Authority and Critical Identity* (U of Illinois P, 1995) and editor of *Talking Drama* (Cambridge Scholars, 2009), as well as essays on topics that range from the work of Samuel Beckett, Marguerite Duras, Harold Pinter, Percival Everett, Richard Powers, and Viriginia Woolf to performance theory, Viagra, panda porn, questions of sexuality and gender, psychoanalysis, feminist theory, James Bond, and *The Big Lebowski*. She is a member of the avant-garde performance group SteinSemble.

John Carlos Rowe is USC Associates' Professor of the Humanities at the University of Southern California. He is the author of *Henry Adams and Henry James: The Emergence of a Modern Consciousness* (Cornell UP, 1976), *Through the Custom-House: Nineteenth-Century American Fiction and Modern Theory* (Johns Hopkins UP, 1982), *The Theoretical Dimensions of Henry James* (U of Wisconsin P, 1984), *At Emerson's Tomb: The Politics of Classic American Literature* (Columbia UP,

1997), *The Other Henry James* (Duke UP, 1998), *Literary Culture and U.S. Imperialism: From the Revolution to World War II* (Oxford UP, 2000), *The New American Studies* (U of Minnesota P, 2002), *The Cultural Politics of the New American* Studies (Open Humanities, 2011), and *Afterlives of Modernism: Liberalism, Transnationalism, and Political Critique* (Dartmouth UP, 2011). He is the editor of: *The Vietnam War and American Culture* (Columbia UP, 1991), *New Essays on The Education of Henry Adams* (Cambridge UP, 1996), *"Culture" and the Problem of the Disciplines* (Columbia UP, 1998), *Post-Nationalist American Studies* (U of California P, 2000), *Selections from the Writings of Ralph Waldo Emerson and Margaret Fuller* (Wadsworth, 2002), and *A Concise Companion to American Studies* (Wiley-Blackwell, 2010).

Eric Savoy is Associate Professor of Comparative Literature at Université de Montréal. He has published extensively on Henry James, queer theory, and narrative poetics, and is completing a book entitled *Conjugating the Subject: Henry James and the Hypothetical.* His most recent publications are "Literary Forensics, or the Incendiary Archive" in *boundary 2*, and "Aspern's Archive" in the *Henry James Review.*

INDEX

Italic page numbers refer to illustrations.

Printed in Great Britain
by Amazon

56663325R00164